Triumph TR5, TR250, TR6 1967-75 Autobook

By Kenneth Ball
Associate Member, Guild of Motoring Writers
and the Autopress Team of Technical Writers.

Triumph TR5 PI 1967-69
Triumph TR250 1967-69
Triumph TR6 1969-75

Autobooks

Autopress Ltd. Golden Lane Brighton BN1 2QJ England

The AUTOBOOK series of Workshop Manuals is the largest in the world and covers the majority of British and Continental motor cars, as well as all major Japanese and Australian models. For a full list see the back of this manual.

CONTENTS

Acknowledgement

Introduction

Chapter 1	The Engine	9
Chapter 2	The Fuel System	25
Chapter 3	The Ignition System	43
Chapter 4	The Cooling System	49
Chapter 5	The Clutch	53
Chapter 6	The Gearbox	57
Chapter 7	Propeller Shaft, Rear Axle and Rear Suspension	69
Chapter 8	Front Suspension and Hubs	77
Chapter 9	The Steering System	85
Chapter 10	The Braking System	93
Chapter 11	The Electrical System	105
Chapter 12	The Bodywork	121
Appendix		133

ISBN 0 85147 579 5

First Edition 1970
Second Edition, fully revised 1970
Third Edition, fully revised 1971
Fourth Edition, fully revised 1972
Fifth Edition, fully revised 1973
Sixth Edition, fully revised 1974
Reprinted 1974
Seventh Edition, fully revised 1975

© Autopress Ltd 1975

All rights reserved. No part of this publication may be reproduced, stored in a retrieval system, or transmitted in any form or by any means, electronic, mechanical, photocopying, recording or otherwise, without the prior permission of Autopress Ltd.

826

Printed and bound in Brighton England for Autopress Ltd by G Beard & Son Ltd   C

ACKNOWLEDGEMENT

My thanks are due to Standard-Triumph Motor Co. Ltd. for their unstinted co-operation and also for supplying data and illustrations.

I am also grateful to a considerable number of owners who have discussed their cars at length and many of whose suggestions have been included in this manual.

Kenneth Ball
Associate Member Guild of Motoring Writers

Ditchling Sussex England.

INTRODUCTION

This do-it-yourself Workshop Manual has been specially written for the owner who wishes to maintain his car in first class condition and to carry out his own servicing and repairs. Considerable savings on garage charges can be made, and one can drive in safety and confidence knowing the work has been done properly.

Comprehensive step-by-step instructions and illustrations are given on all dismantling, overhauling and assembling operations. Certain assemblies require the use of expensive special tools, the purchase of which would be unjustified. In these cases information is included but the reader is recommended to hand the unit to the agent for attention.

Throughout the Manual hints and tips are included which will be found invaluable, and there is an easy to follow fault diagnosis at the end of each chapter.

Whilst every care has been taken to ensure correctness of information it is obviously not possible to guarantee complete freedom from errors or to accept liability arising from such errors or omissions.

Instructions may refer to the righthand or lefthand sides of the vehicle or the components. These are the same as the righthand or lefthand of an observer standing behind the car and looking forward.

CHAPTER 1

THE ENGINE

1:1 Description
1:2 Removing engine and gearbox
1:3 Removing, replacing, cylinder head
1:4 Servicing the head and valve gear
1:5 Overhauling the valve timing gear
1:6 Removing and replacing camshaft, distributor drive spindle
1:7 Removing and replacing clutch and flywheel
1:8 The sump
1:9 The oil pump
1:10 Lubrication, oil filter and relief valve
1:11 Pistons and connecting rods
1:12 Crankshaft and main bearings
1:13 Reassembling a stripped engine
1:14 Valve rocker adjustment
1:15 The exhaust system
1:16 Fault diagnosis

1:1 Description

Although the engine and gearbox are bolted together to form a single unit, this Chapter will only deal with the engine, apart from the removal of the combined unit from the car.

The usual features of the Standard-Triumph design are again quite distinctive in the engine, though it has been redesigned from the earlier TR range of engines. The earlier four cylinder engines used wet liners and by discarding these and incorporating other improvements the power output has been increased while saving a weight of 150 lb.

FIG 1:1 shows the fixed parts of the engine, **FIG 1:2** shows the moving parts and **FIG 1:7** shows the components of the cylinder head. From these it can be seen that the engine is a six cylinder unit with overhead valves operated by pushrods from the camshaft. Details of bore and stroke are given in Technical Data at the end of this manual, together with an extensive coverage of further technical information.

The crankshaft runs in four main bearings. The main bearings and the big-end bearings use renewable steel-backed alloy shells for the crankshaft to run in. All the shells can be changed without removing the engine from the car. If the main bearings are renewed in situ, great care must be taken to change one set of shells at a time to ensure that the crankshaft is always adequately supported.

The camshaft runs in five bearings, and the end float is controlled by the thickness of the keeper plate 38. The cams move the followers (see items 12 in **FIG 1:7**) into which the pushrods seat and the motion is transferred to the rockers which operate the valves. A gear on the camshaft turns the gearing 24 which drives the oil pump, metering unit and the distributor. The tachometer drive is embodied in the distributor.

Oil is drawn from the sump, through a wiremesh filter, by the oil pump. Excess oil is bled back to the sump by a non-adjustable relief valve to limit the maximum oil pressure. The remainder of the oil is passed through a fullflow oil filter before entering an oil gallery running from the front to the back on the lefthand side of the engine. From the oil gallery the oil is distributed to the crankshaft and camshaft journal bearings. Drillings in the crankshaft lead the oil to the big-end bearings. Splash from the crankshaft lubricates the cylinder bores and small-end bearings. The timing gear and duplex timing

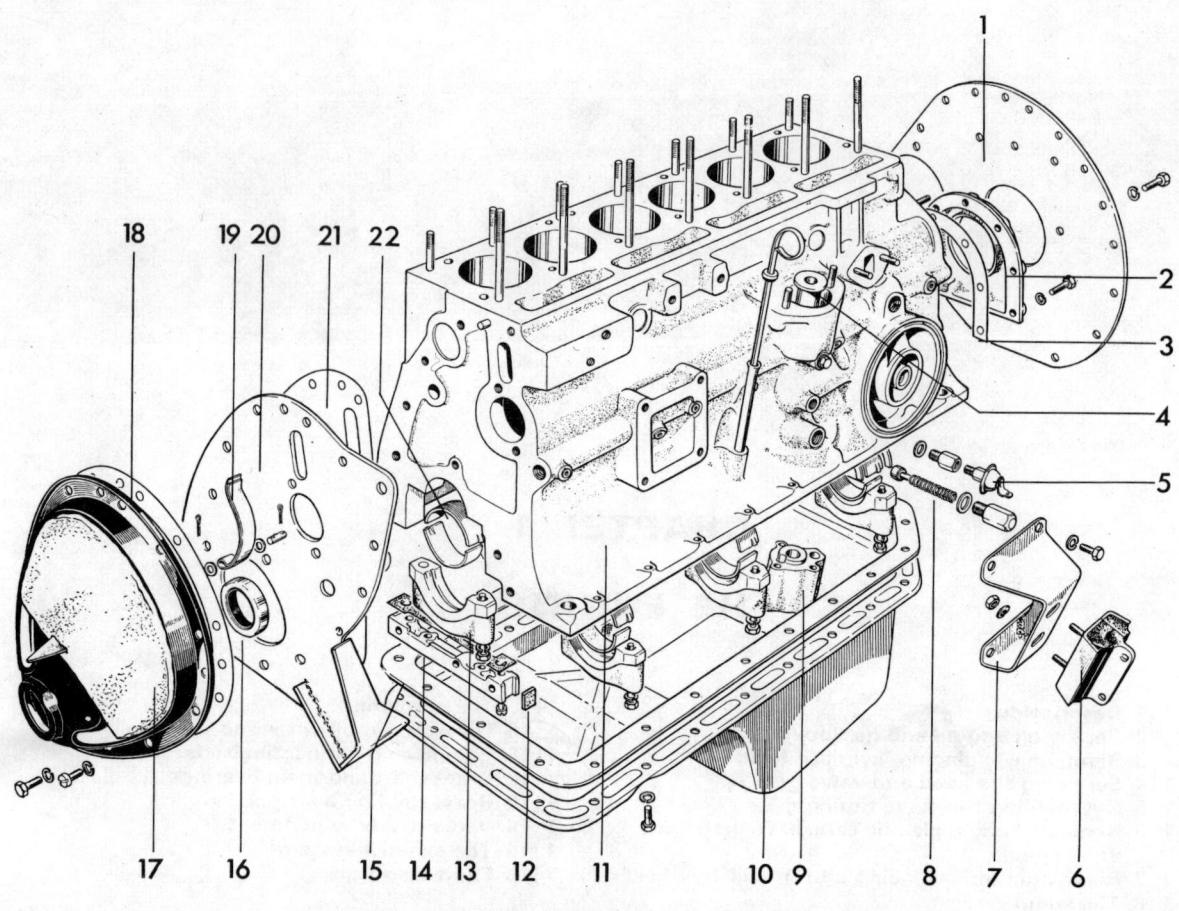

FIG 1:1 Engine details, fixed parts

Key to Figs 1:1 and 1:2 1 Engine backplate 2 Crankshaft rear oil seal housing 3 Crankshaft rear oil seal housing bracket
4 Oil pump spindle and distributor drive bush 5 Oil switch 6 Engine mounting 7 Engine mounting bracket
8 Oil pressure relief valve 9 Oil pump body 10 Sump 11 Cylinder block 12 Front sealing block packing
13 Main bearing cap 14 Front sealing block 15 Sump gasket 16 Timing cover oil seal 17 Timing cover
18 Timing cover gasket 19 Timing chain tensioner 20 Engine front plate 21 Engine front plate gasket
22 Main bearing shells 23 Camshaft 24 Distributor, oil pump and metering unit drive gears 25 Flywheel 26 Crankshaft bush
27 Crankshaft 28 Oil pump inner rotor and spindle 29 Oil pump outer rotor 30 Sprocket alignment shims
31 Crankshaft sprocket 32 Oil thrower 33 Spacer 34 Crankshaft pulley 35 Timing chain 36 Camshaft
sprocket lockplate 37 Camshaft sprocket 38 Camshaft keeper plate 39 Connecting rod bearing cap 40 Connecting
rod bearing shells 41 Connecting rod 42 Circlip 43 Gudgeon pin 44 Connecting rod bush 45 Piston
46 Piston rings

chain are lubricated by seepage from the front camshaft bearing and by the oil mist in the crankcase. A scroll and two flats on the camshaft rear journal provide a metered supply of oil to the rocker gear. This oil then runs down the pushrod tubes to lubricate the cam followers before finally returning to the sump.

A hose connects the air intake manifold to the rocker cover for crankcase ventilation. A gauze filter is fitted to the hose to prevent oil being drawn through with the fumes.

1:2 Removing the engine and gearbox

The engine and gearbox are removed and refitted from above. To gain access underneath the front of the car needs to be raised. **It must be stressed that any supports must be firmly based and not likely to collapse during the operation, or serious injury could result.**

If the operator is not a skilled automobile engineer, it is suggested that he will find much useful information in Hints on Maintenance at the end of this manual, and that he should read it before starting work. Proceed as follows:

1 Remove the bonnet, battery, radiator, air intake manifold and the tubular crossmember.
2 Remove the U-clamps securing the steering rack to the crossmember and pull the steering box forward to

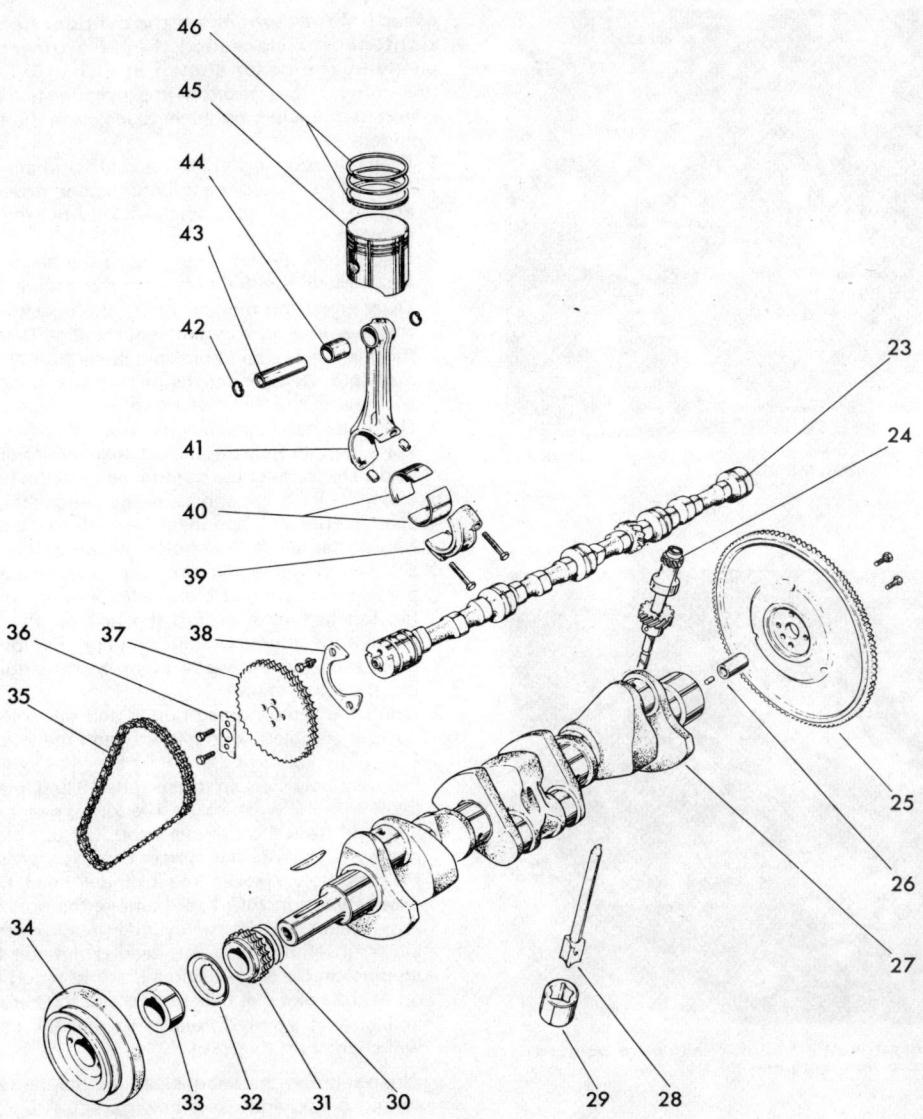

FIG 1:2 Engine details, moving parts

clear the crankshaft pulley.
3 Disconnect all the wires, cables and pipes (1 to 10 in **FIGS 1:3** and **1:4**) and the thick braided cable earthing the engine to the chassis. When undoing the fuel supply pipe 10 to the metering unit fuel will syphon out of the tank unless the level is low. Either partially drain the fuel tank or else seal the end of the fuel pipe.
4 Remove the inlet and exhaust manifolds. From underneath the car take off the starter motor.
5 From inside the car take out the seats and front carpets. Remove the console and unscrew the gearlever knob. Undo the bolts holding the gearbox tunnel. Remove the gearlever boot and take out the gearbox tunnel from the passenger side of the car.
6 Disconnect the speedometer drive from the gearbox. If they are fitted also disconnect the overdrive and reversing light cables.
7 Disconnect the gearbox from the propeller shaft at the flange shown in **FIG 1:5**. Disconnect the exhaust pipe at the gearbox mounting 12. Remove the gearbox cover 16 and cover the orifice with cardboard to prevent the entry of dirt.
8 Remove the clutch slave cylinder bracket from the bellhousing and take out the clevis pin at 13. Without straining the flexible hose carefully wire the clutch slave cylinder safely out of the way.

FIG 1:3 Righthand view of engine, showing points to disconnect before removing engine

FIG 1:4 Lefthand view of engine, showing points to disconnect before removing engine

9 Attach a sling and take the weight of the engine. Slacken the gearbox mounting at 14. Remove the front engine mounting next to the steering column and take out the two bolts from the other front mounting bracket.

10 Take the weight of the gearbox with a small jack and remove the gearbox mounting and support plate. Steady the gearbox and take away the jack. **Check to make sure there are no connections still made between the engine and the car.**

11 Lower the gearbox so that the engine tilts and manoeuvre the engine out of the car, in a 'nose up' attitude.

1:3 Removing and replacing cylinder head

This operation can be carried out either with the engine in the car or when the engine has been removed. **It is essential that whenever the cylinder head nuts are tightened or slackened they are turned progressively in the order shown in FIG 1:6.** Failure to do this correctly can result in the cylinder head becoming distorted and allowing water to leak into the bores of the cylinders.

1 Drain the cooling system and disconnect the battery earth lead. Disconnect both heater hoses from the engine, and the top radiator hose from the thermostat housing.
2 Disconnect the breather pipe to the air inlet manifold and remove the manifold from the engine.
3 Disconnect the fuel lines from the injectors, and label the lines to ensure correct replacement. Disconnect the throttle linkage and cold start cable from the induction manifold. Disconnect the pipe to the brake servo and the pipe to the fuel meter from the induction manifold.
4 Disconnect the exhaust pipe from the exhaust manifold at the flange. Remove the exhaust and induction manifolds. Disconnect the control cable to the heater valve.
5 Label the high-tension leads and remove them from the sparking plugs. Disconnect the cable to the temperature transmitter on the thermostat housing.
6 Slacken the three pivot points on the alternator and, by pressing on the end bracket holding the stay, slacken the fan belt tension. Lift the belt off the pulley and remove the alternator adjusting link. Remove the three bolts securing the water pump to the engine and lift out the water pump.
7 Undo the three domed nuts 5 and take off the rocker cover 2 complete with gasket 1 and the washers 3 and 4.
8 Progressively slacken the six nuts 29 and finally remove them with the washers 30. The rocker gear may now be lifted off from the cylinder head. Lift out the pushrods and store them in the correct order for reassembly.
9 Progressively slacken the cylinder head nuts in the order shown in **FIG 1:6**. Remove the nuts when they are all slack and lift the cylinder head squarely up the studs to remove it. If the head is difficult to free, try tapping on the sides using a block of wood to hammer on. If the head still fails to free, put the car in top gear and push it slowly forwards so that the compression will slightly lift the head.

When refitting the head, clean the mating faces of the head and block, and use a new gasket. A light smear of grease on the gasket should be sufficient sealing, otherwise use a non-setting jointing compound. Slide the head carefully down the studs onto the gasket and do up all the cylinder head nuts finger tight. Tighten them progressively in the sequence shown in **FIG 1:6** to a torque load of 65 to 70 lb ft (8.99 to 9.69 kg m). Refit the pushrods in their correct places, making sure they seat into the cam followers. Slacken the locknuts 34 and screw out the adjusters 33 to ensure there will be adequate clearance to prevent the pushrods being bent. Refit the rocker gear and progressively torque load the nuts 29 to a load of 24 to 26 lb ft (3.32 to 3.60 kg m). Adjust the valve clearance (see **Section 1:14**) and replace the remainder of the parts in the reverse order of dismantling.

After the car has been run for some time the cylinder head nuts must be retightened. Every time the torque loading of the cylinder head nuts is adjusted the valve clearances will be altered and they must be reset.

1:4 Servicing the head and valve gear

Remove the cylinder head as described in the preceding Section. To prevent dirt and chips from falling into the engine, block off the oil and water passages with clean non-fluffy rags. Scrape the carbon from the combustion spaces in the head before removing the valves, to avoid damaging the valve seats. Use a blunt tool to remove the carbon. A rotary wire brush in an electric drill is excellent for cleaning out the inlet and exhaust ports, but take great care not to damage the valve seats or the valve guides. If emery or any abrasive is used on the cylinder head wash the head in paraffin and use an air-blast to dry it. **All particles of abrasive must be removed from the cylinder head before it is reassembled and refitted.** Use a long metal straightedge, or better still a surface table and engineers blue, to check that the mating surfaces of the block and head are flat and undistorted. Regrinding is the only cure for distortion.

Before cleaning the carbon from the pistons smear a little grease around the tops of the bores. Set one pair of pistons nearly at TDC. Use a soft blunt tool (a sharpened stick of solder) to scrape the carbon from the tops of the pistons. Leave the carbon around the periphery of the piston and around the top of the bore above the piston. This carbon acts as an oil seal as well as protecting the rings from heat. **Do not use any abrasive on the pistons as particles may easily remain and work their way into the bores causing scoring and damage.** Turn the engine to bring the next pair of pistons up to TDC and repeat the process. When the final pair of pistons have been cleaned wipe away the grease from the tops of the bores. Dust and carbon chippings will stick to the grease and be removed with it.

1 Use a spring compressor to compress the valve springs. The upper collars 19 or 21 are forced down the valve stems freeing the collets 20 so they may be lifted out. Ease the spring compressor and lift off the collar 19, seat 18, springs 16 and 17 and the seat 22. The exhaust valve 14 will slide out underneath the head. The inlet valves are treated similarly except that they only have one collar 21 at the top. Mark the valves and store them with their associated parts in the correct order of assembly.

2 Valve stems must show no signs of 'picking up' or wear, nor should they be bent. If satisfactory, but the valve seats show signs of excessive pitting, have the seats reground at a garage. Do not attempt to remove excessive pitting using grinding paste as this will only remove metal from the seat in the head as well. Recut the seats in the head if they are badly worn or pitted. If the seats are then too wide they may be reduced by using a 15 deg. facing cutter. Seatings which are beyond re-cutting can be restored by having inserts fitted.

3 To grind-in valves put a light spring under the head and use medium-grade carborundum paste, unless the seats are in very good condition, when fine-grade paste may be used at once. Use a suction-cup tool and grind with a semi-rotary movement, letting the valve rise off the seat occasionally by pressure of the spring under the head. Use paste sparingly. When both seats have a smooth matt grey finish clean away every trace of grinding paste from the valve and port. If the thickness of the head above the ground seat is less than $\frac{1}{32}$ inch (.8 mm) the valve should be renewed.

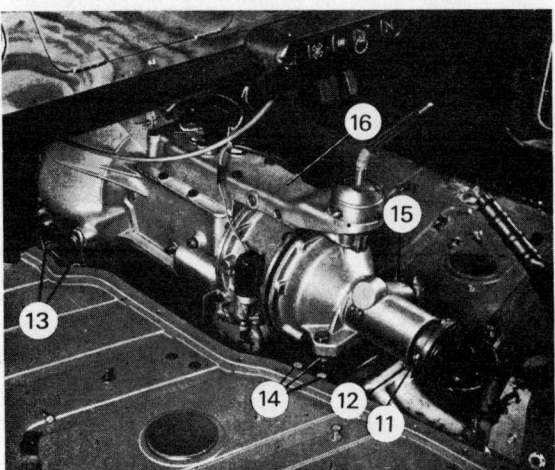

FIG 1:5 Lefthand view of gearbox, showing points to disconnect before removing engine and gearbox

4 Insert a new valve into each guide in turn. Raise the valve slightly and check the diametric movement of the valve head. If this is greater than .020 inch (.508 mm) then the guides will have to be renewed. Tool No. 60.A should be used but a snug-fitting stepped drift may be used to drive out the old guides and drive in the new ones from the top of the head. On the TR5 the guides for the exhaust valves are the longest but all guides should be driven in to protrude .63 inch (16 mm) above the top face of the cylinder head. On the TR6 the guides are 2.71 inch (68.834 mm) in length and should protrude .75 inch (19.05 mm) above the head. After fitting new guides the valve seats must be recut to ensure concentricity.

5 Remove the screw securing the rocker shaft 9 to the end pedestal 23. Pull out the splitpin 24 and remove the end plug 25. All the rockers, pedestals and springs can now be slid off the rocker shaft. Store the parts in the correct order for reassembly. Remove the other end splitpin and end plug to clean out the inside of the rocker shaft. Thoroughly clean all the parts in petrol and examine for wear. Renew the shaft if it is scored or worn. If the faces of the rockers are slightly worn they may be

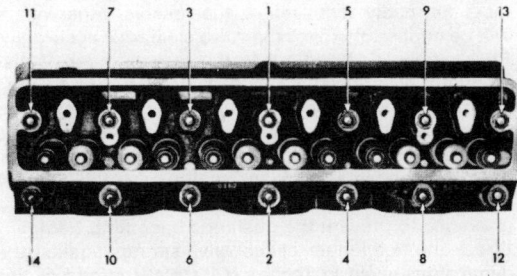

FIG 1:6 Sequence to be followed when undoing or tightening cylinder head nuts

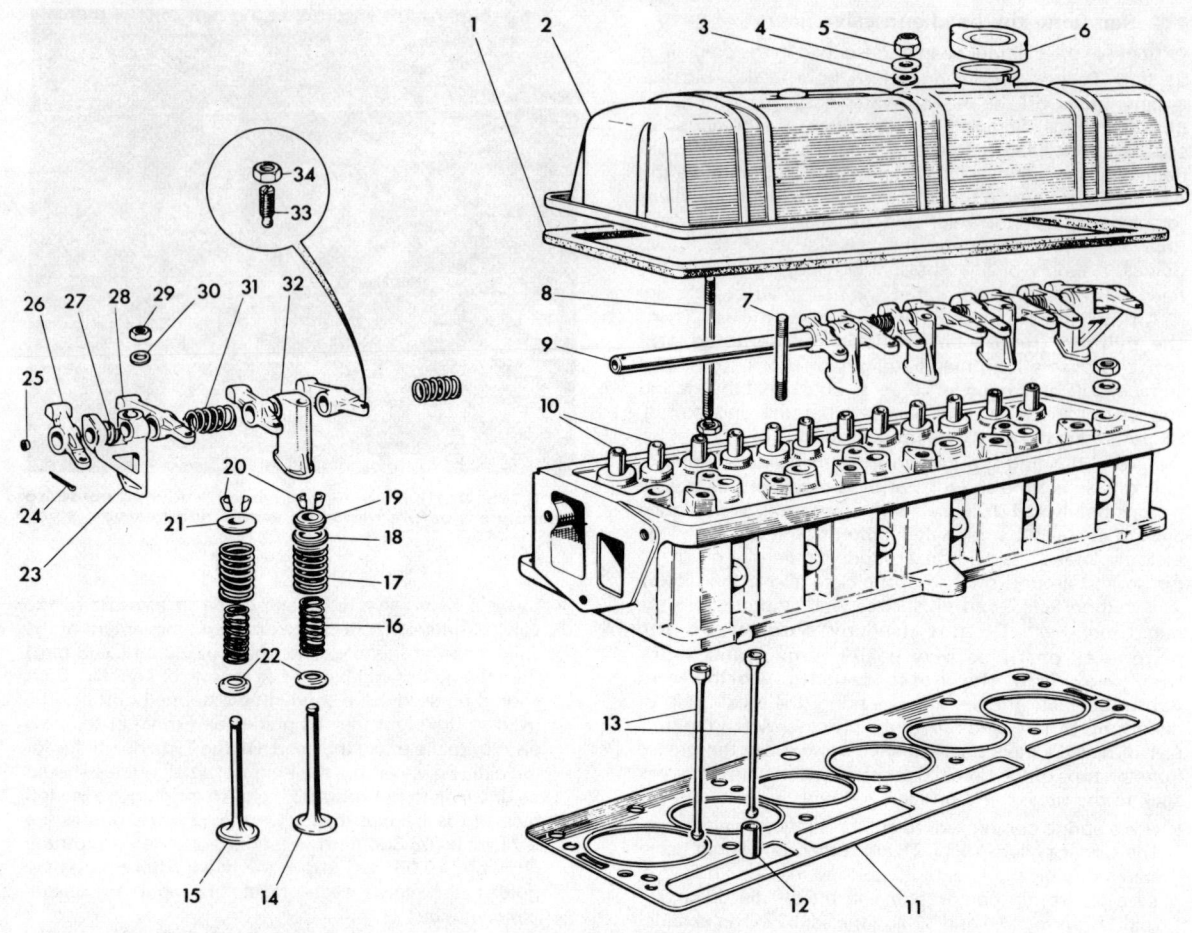

FIG 1:7 Cylinder head details

Key to Fig 1:7 1 Rocker cover gasket 2 Rocker cover 3 Fibre washer 4 Plain washer 5 Nyloc nut 6 Oil filter cap 7 Rocker pedestal stud 8 Rocker cover stud 9 Rocker shaft 10 Valve guides 11 cylinder head gasket 12 Cam follower 13 Pushrods 14 Exhaust valve 15 Inlet valve 16 Inner valve spring 17 Outer valve spring 18 Exhaust valve upper spring seal 19 Exhaust valve cap 20 Valve cotters 21 Inlet valve cap 22 Valve spring seats 23 Outer rocker pedestal 24 Cotterpin 25 Rocker shaft end plug 26 Rocker 27 End rocker pedestal double spring washer 28 Rocker 29 Nut 30 Washer 31 Rocker shaft spring 32 Intermediate rocker pedestal 33 Tappet adjuster 34 Tappet adjuster locknut

smoothed down using a fine carborundum stone. If the faces are badly worn renew the rockers, otherwise it will be impossible to set the valve clearance accurately. Reassembly is carried out in the reverse order of dismantling, ensuring that the parts are returned to their original positions, and lubricating the working surfaces liberally with clean engine oil. Before refitting the assembly check that the pushrods are straight and their ends undamaged. Slacken all twelve locknuts 34 and screw the adjustors so as to give maximum clearance to prevent the pushrods becoming bent.

6 Check the free length of the valve springs against the dimensions given in Technical Data at the end of this manual. Renew springs that are shorter than the length given, as these will have weakened with use.

Lubricate the valve stems with clean engine oil before refitting them in the reverse order of dismantling. Fit the cylinder head to the block as described in **Section 1:3**

1:5 Overhauling the valve timing gear

The components are shown in **FIGS 1:1** and **1:2**. If the engine is still in the car then drain the cooling system and remove the radiator. Disconnect the battery, slacken the alternator mountings and, by pushing the alternator towards the block, slacken the fan belt sufficiently to lift it off the pulleys. Remove the U-bolts holding the steering rack and push the rack forwards to clear it from the engine. Remove the tubular crossmember.

1 Remove the radiator fan. Undo the single bolt holding

14

the fan boss and the crankshaft pulley to the crankshaft.

2 Remove the ring of screws and bolts holding the timing cover 18 to the block and pull off the cover. Pull off the spacer 33 and the oil thrower 32 from the crankshaft.

3 Straighten the lockplate 36 and remove the two setscrews holding the camshaft sprocket 37 to the camshaft. Ease the sprocket off the camshaft and remove the duplex timing chain 35 from around sprockets 37 and 31.

4 Taking care not to damage the shims 30, use two levers to move the crankshaft sprocket off the crankshaft.

5 Wash all the parts in petrol and examine for wear. If the timing chain is noisy but not badly worn renew the chain tensioner 19. Part the blades and slip the tensioner off the pin on the timing cover, and refit a new tensioner in the same way. If the timing chain is worn renew it and both sprockets as a set. **Never renew the chain alone.**

6 Refit both timing sprockets without the chain. Press them firmly into place and lay a steel straightedge across the sides of the teeth between the sprockets. With the straightedge firmly on the camshaft sprocket measure, with feeler gauges, the gap between the straightedge and the crankshaft sprocket. This measurement is the thickness of the shims 30 required to bring the two sprockets level. Remove both sprockets and fit the correct amount of shimming 30 to the crankshaft.

7 When the timing sprockets were removed they should have been checked for timing marks. A scribed line on each will line up with the other when the timing is correct. Punch marks on the camshaft sprocket and camshaft end will identify the correct pair of fixing holes and the relation of the sprocket to the camshaft. Turn the crankshaft so it is approximately 45 deg. before TDC on Nos. 1 and 6 pistons. TDC is indicated by the key on the front of the crankshaft being vertically upwards, and the crankshaft is set before TDC to ensure that the valves do not hit the pistons when the camshaft is turned. Refit the crankshaft sprocket. Loosely refit the camshaft sprocket so the pop marks on the camshaft and sprocket are together. Turn the camshaft until the scribed lines on both sprockets line up exactly. Once a rough position is established for the camshaft, turn the crankshaft so that the key is vertically upwards and the scribed lines can then be aligned accurately. Remove the camshaft sprocket **without turning the camshaft.** Encircle the crankshaft sprocket with the timing chain **without turning the crankshaft.** Still without turning either the camshaft or crankshaft fit the camshaft sprocket into the timing chain and then back onto the camshaft. Check that the scribed lines align before locking the tabs of the lockplate 36 securing the setscrews holding the sprocket to the camshaft.

8 Lubricate the timing chain liberally with engine oil. Replace the oil thrower 32 to the crankshaft, with its concave side facing forwards. Fit a new gasket 18 to the front plate of the engine. With a finger hold back the blades of the tensioner 19 and carefully slide the timing cover back into place. Though the oil seal 16 is renewable, take great care not to damage it on the crankshaft or crankshaft key. When the timing cover is far enough on to ensure that the tensioner is properly on the idle side of the chain, release the tensioner and push the cover home. Secure it in place with the setscrews and bolts. Engage the spacer 33 onto the crankshaft, tapered end leading, and push it gently into place. Replace the fan boss and pulley, then the fan, and finally the remainder of the parts in the reverse order of dismantling.

9 If new sprockets are to be fitted, or the originals are unmarked, proceed as follows. If for any reason the cylinder head and valve gear have been removed then refit these first. With the shims 30 in place, fit the crankshaft sprocket 31 to the crankshaft. Using the marks on the flywheel turn the crankshaft so it is about 45 deg. before TDC on Nos. 1 and 6 pistons. Loosely refit the camshaft sprocket 37 to the camshaft and use it to turn the camshaft. Set the valve clearances on No. 6 cylinder (rearmost) to .040 inch (1.016 mm). Rotate the camshaft until the valves on No. 6 cylinder are at the point of balance. The rocker tip of the exhaust valve (No. 12) will be almost at the top of its travel and the rocker tip of the inlet valve (No. 11) will just be starting to move down to open the inlet valve. Use a feeler gauge and turn the camshaft until the rocker clearances on Nos. 11 and 12 valves are exactly equal. **Do not turn the camshaft at all after this.** Remove the camshaft sprocket. Turn the crankshaft until Nos.1 and 6 pistons are exactly on TDC and leave the crankshaft in this position. The two alternative pairs of fixing holes on the camshaft sprocket are offset from the teeth centres and by either using the alternate pairs or by turning the sprocket 'back to front' the sprocket can be precisely aligned to the camshaft with the chain fitted around both sprockets. Check that the valve rocker clearances are still equal on No. 6 cylinder before finally securing the camshaft sprocket in place. Reset the rocker clearances to .010 inch (.254 mm) and replace the remaining parts in the reverse order of dismantling.

1:6 Removing and replacing camshaft, and distributor drive spindle

1 Remove the cylinder head (see **Section 1:3**). Lift out the twelve cam followers (items 12 in **FIG 1:7**). As each one is removed check that it moves freely in the block and that it is not chipped, damaged or worn. Store the followers in the correct order for replacement.

2 Remove the timing cover 17, the timing chain 35 and the two sprockets 31 and 37 (see **Section 1:5**). Use a feeler gauge to check the camshaft end float as shown in **FIG 1:8**. The end float should be .004 to .008 inch (.102 to .20 mm) and if it is excessive the keeper plate 38 will have to be renewed.

3 Disconnect the tachometer cable from the distributor. Undo the two nuts, shown in **FIG 1:10**, which hold the pedestal for the distributor and fuel metering unit. The distributor, metering unit and pedestal can now be lifted off. Withdraw the driving gear 24.

4 If the engine is still fitted in the car, remove the radiator grille so that the camshaft can be taken out of the car.

5 Undo the two bolts holding the keeper plate 38 and remove the plate. Very carefully, so as to avoid damaging the camshaft bearings, withdraw the camshaft from the engine.

FIG 1:8 Measuring camshaft end float

FIG 1:9 Position of the oil pump shaft before refitting the distributor drive gear

FIG 1:10 Distributor drive gear in position with the engine at TDC with No. 1 cylinder on the firing stroke. Note that the larger offset faces rearwards

Replacing the camshaft:

This is the reversal of the removal operation. Replace the cylinder head but leave the rocker cover 2 off. When all the valve timing parts have been replaced, including the cover, then fit the driving gear 24 and pedestal assembly back as follows:

1 Undo the single bolt holding the distributor to the pedestal and remove the distributor complete with clamp. **Do not undo the clamp tightening bolt or the ignition timing will be lost.** Take out the three bolts holding the metering unit to the pedestal and separate the two. Take care not to lose the plastic drive dog. Opposite to the face for the metering unit will be found a single bolt holding in a plug. Remove both bolt and plug. Push out off the pedestal the metering unit drive pinion. If in any doubt on the instructions for removing the metering unit refer to **Chapter 2, Section 2:8**.

2 Turn the engine until the 11 deg. BTDC mark on the crankshaft pulley is in line with the pointer on the timing cover, and No. 1 cylinder is on compression (both valves shut). Use a screwdriver and turn the oil pump drive 28 until it is in the position shown in **FIG 1:9**. Insert the distributor drive gear 24 so that it meshes with the gear on the camshaft. Turn the gear slightly as it moves down to allow it to mesh properly until the dogs engage with the oil pump drive shaft. When finally fitted the gear should be set so that the larger offset is to the rear and the slot points vertically away from the engine as shown in **FIG 1:10**. Replace the distributor ensuring that the driving dogs mate.

3 If the ignition timing is lost refer to **Chapter 3** for instructions on retiming the ignition. Refer to **Chapter 2** for instructions on refitting the metering unit.

Pedestal end float:

There should be end float of .003 to .007 inch (.0762 to .1778 mm) between the driving gear 24 and the base of the distributor. This is obtained by gaskets of the right thickness below the mounting flange of the distributor pedestal. Whenever parts are renewed this clearance should be checked. As it cannot be measured directly proceed as follows:

1 Slip a flat washer on top of the bush 4 for the driving gear spindle. Mesh the driving gear 1 into the block so that the washer is between it and the bush as shown in **FIG 1:11**.

2 Replace the pedestal and measure the gap at B with feeler gauges. Remove the parts.

3 Measure the thickness of the washer A with a micrometer. Subtract the dimension B from the dimension A. A negative answer will indicate that there is preload and sufficient gaskets to make this zero will have to be added before adding gaskets to produce the correct amount of end float. If the answer is positive then the difference between the answer and .005 inch (the ideal end float) will be the thickness of gaskets required.

4 Mesh the driving gear correctly and replace the pedestal with the correct thickness of gaskets before proceeding as previously instructed.

1:7 Removing and replacing clutch and flywheel

This operation can be carried out with the engine still

in the car. First remove the gearbox as instructed in **Chapter 6, Section 6:2**.

1 Turn the engine so that Nos. 1 and 6 pistons are at TDC so that it will be easier to replace the flywheel in the correct position. Evenly slacken and remove the bolts holding the clutch cover to the flywheel. Remove the clutch assembly and driven plate.
2 Remove the four bolts holding the flywheel 25 and pull the flywheel off the dowel to release it from the crankshaft.
3 If required the engine backplate 1 can be removed by undoing the bolts securing it. If the bush in the end of the crankshaft is worn renew it.
4 Replacing the parts is the reversal of the removal operation. Use a tool to ensure that the clutch driven plate is centralized when tightening the bolts holding the clutch in place. Make sure the mating surfaces of flywheel and crankshaft are scrupulously clean. When the flywheel is fitted mount a Dial Test Indicator (DTI) on to the rear of the block and check the runout of the flywheel. The runout should not exceed .003 inch (.0762 mm). If a new flywheel is fitted set Nos. 1 and 6 pistons accurately to TDC using a DTI mounted on top of the block. Scribe a line on the flywheel so that it aligns with the mark on the engine backplate. Deepen the scribed line with a small chisel.

Fitting new starter ring gear:

Weaken a worn starter ring by drilling at the root of a tooth. **Take care not to mark the flywheel.** Use a chisel to finally split the ring and remove it from the flywheel. Clean the periphery of the flywheel very thoroughly.

Evenly heat the new ring to a maximum of 316°C (600°F). Use temperature sensitive crayon to check the temperature and make sure the ring is heated evenly all round otherwise distortion may occur. Fit the hot ring to the flywheel ensuring that the chamfered teeth face the clutch. Very lightly tap the ring all round to ensure it is fully in place and then leave it to cool.

1:8 The sump

The sump 10 can be removed or refitted while the engine is still in the car. To ensure that the oil will drain more easily from the sump take the car for a sufficiently long run to heat the oil. Slide a container large enough to take all the eight pints of oil under the sump and remove the sump plug from the front of the sump. Leave the oil to drain as long as possible then remove all the securing screws and lower the sump.

Clean the sump with petrol or paraffin and dry either with clean non-fluffy rags or with air. Renew the gasket 15 if the old one is damaged. Hold it in place either with a thin film of grease or non-setting jointing compound. Refit the sump with all the screws. The four long screws are fitted to the holes with the reinforcing plates. Change the oil filter if required and fill the engine to the correct level with clean oil.

1:9 The oil pump

The pump is continuously lubricated so it is unlikely to wear or give trouble in service. The pump is easily removed while the engine is in the car. Remove the sump

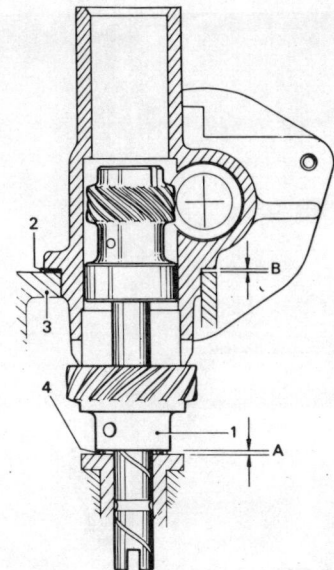

FIG 1:11 Measuring the end float for the distributor drive gear
Key to Fig 1:11   1 Distributor drive gear
2 Gaskets in place   3 Crankcase   4 Suitable washer
A Thickness of washer   **B** Gap between pedestal and crankcase

(see **Section 1:8**) and undo the three bolts holding the pump to the crankcase. Withdraw the pump. Refitting the pump is the reversal of the removal operation.

The components of the oil pump are shown in **FIG 1:12**. The filter is easily unclipped from the intake pipe and the remainder of the pump is dismantled by undoing the three setscrews holding the end plate to the body.

Wash all the parts in petrol and when dry refit the rotors back into the body. Use a feeler gauge and check that the clearance between the outer rotor and the body does not exceed .010 inch (.254 mm). Use a feeler gauge, as shown in **FIG 1:13**, to check that the clearance between the inner and outer rotor does not exceed .004 inch (.102 mm). If either of these clearances is exceeded then renew parts as required.

Lay a straightedge across the bottom of the casing and measure, with feeler gauges, the gap between the rotors and the straightedge. The end clearance should not exceed .004 inch (.102 mm) and if this is exceeded, and a serious drop in oil pressure is brought about by this, then the body should be lapped to cure excessive end clearance. If the end plate is scored this too should be lapped. Use fine carborundum paste on plate glass (not window glass) to lap on. If plate glass is not available use fine emerycloth laid on a true flat surface. Clean all the parts thoroughly to remove any abrasive particles. Reassemble the pump in the reverse order of dismantling, lubricating the parts with clean engine oil.

Refit the pump, sump and refill the sump with oil. The oil pump is self-priming so no special precautions need be taken to fill it. Start the engine and check that oil pressure builds up fairly quickly. If the oil pressure fails to build up stop the engine immediately and check the cause.

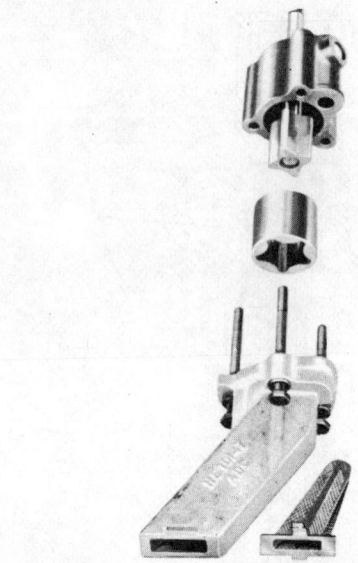

FIG 1:12 Oil pump details

FIG 1:13 Measuring the clearance between the inner and outer rotors of the oil pump

1:10 Lubrication, oil filter and relief valve

The oil circulation through the engine has already been discussed in **Section 1:1**. The parts of the relief valve are shown as 8 in **FIG 1:1**. The oil filter and the flow through it is shown in **FIG 1:14**.

The relief valve is non-adjustable, but if it is suspected that a drop in oil pressure is caused by the relief valve it should be removed and examined. Unscrew the cap and remove the parts. Wash in petrol and use a non-fluffy rag to clean the seating in the crankcase. Check the spring to ensure it is within the tolerances given in Technical Data and renew it if required, before refitting the valve.

The oil filter is fitted to the lefthand side of the engine at the rear. The filter element should be changed at regular intervals. If the element is left too long in the car it will become clogged with dirt and cease to filter the oil. A bypass valve is fitted in the filter to allow oil to reach the engine when the element is choked but it should never be allowed to reach this stage as the oil is then unfiltered and can carry dirt to the bearings and parts. Use rags or a drip tray to catch the oil split when the filter is removed. Unscrew the centre bolt 8 and remove the filter from the engine. Take out and discard the old element 3. Do not attempt to clean the element as nothing useful can be done with it. Separate the internal parts of the casing and wash out with petrol. Renew the seal 7 if required. Use a small pointed tool to remove the seal 1 from the recess in the crankcase. Fit the new seal back into the recess, taking great care to make sure that it is squarely and properly seated. Fit a new element into the casing, checking to make sure it is a correct replacement. Do not omit the washer 2 which centralizes the element. Replace the filter, making sure the casing seats properly onto the seal in the recess. Tighten the securing bolt to a torque load of 15 to 18 lb ft (2.07 to 2.49 kg m). Wipe away any oil spillage from around the filter and run the engine. Check for oil leaks as soon as the engine is started. When the oil level has settled top up with clean oil to replace that lost in the filter casing.

Check the oil level in the engine when the car has not been run for some time and is standing on level ground. Failure to do this may result in overfilling of the sump.

1:11 Piston and connecting rods

These can be removed from the engine with it still in place in the car. To change the big-end bearings only the sump need be taken off (see **Section 1:8**), but to remove the pistons and connecting rods the cylinder head must also be removed (see **Section 1:3**). For ease of access also remove the oil pump (see **Section 1:9**).

Big-end bearings:

The caps on the big-ends 39 should be marked to indicate position and order. If they are not already marked do so with light pop marks. Undo the two bolts securing the front bearing cap 39 and remove the cap. Push the connecting rod and piston up the bore of the cylinder to clear the connecting rod 41 from the crankpin and slide the shell bearings 40 out from the cap and the connecting rod. Repeat the process on the following five big-end bearings. Either loosely fit the caps back on to the connecting rods or lay them and the shell bearings out in order of removal on the bench. Ensure that the parts are returned to their original positions. Examine and measure the crankpins. They should not be tapered, oval, worn or scored. If the wear is excessive, the crankshaft will have to be removed, reground and undersized bearings fitted. Examine the shell bearings. Renew the set if any are scored, pitted or worn. New bearings are fitted as received, apart from cleaning off any protective. **The big-end caps 39 should never be filed in an attempt to take up wear on the crankpin or bearings.** Clean the parts with petrol and non-fluffy rags before reassembling in the reverse order of dismantling. Lubricate the bearings with clean engine oil.

Removing the connecting rods and pistons:

As already described, remove the cylinder head and push the connecting rod and piston assembly right up and out of the engine. When replacing the big-ends tighten the bolts securing the caps to a load of 38 to 42 lb ft (5.25 to 5.81 kg m).

When the pistons have been removed examine the bores of the cylinders for wear. If it is excessive the engine will have to be rebored and oversize pistons fitted. Pistons are available +.020 inch (+.508 mm) oversize. If the engine has already been rebored or the wear is such that oversize pistons cannot be fitted, then the bores will have to be opened up still further and dry liners pressed into them to allow standard pistons to be fitted again.

If new piston rings are to be fitted use garage equipment to remove the unworn ridge around the top of the bore. New rings will hit this ridge possibly causing the top ring to fail in a short time. Take care not to allow any metal swarf or chippings to remain in the engine after removing the ridge.

Pistons:

The piston and connecting rod assembly is shown in **FIG 1:15**, as well as in **FIG 1:2**.

Separate the piston from the connecting rod by removing the two circlips 42 and pressing out the gudgeon pin 43. All pistons will have two marks stamped on the crown. Standard pistons will have a letter F, G or H indicating the grade and oversize pistons will be marked accordingly. In addition to this there will be a triangle shown at A in **FIG 1:15** and the pistons must always be fitted to the engine so that this triangle faces forwards.

Lacquering on the side of the piston is an indication of gases blowing past the rings.

Piston rings:

Three rings are fitted to each piston; a plain compression ring at the top, tapered compression ring and then an oil control ring at the bottom. Remove the rings from the top of the piston, by sliding a thin piece of metal, such as a discarded .020 inch feeler gauge, under one end and passing it around the ring, at the same time pressing the raised part onto the land above.

Clean carbon and dirt from the ring grooves using a piece of broken ring, but do not remove metal or oil consumption will be increased.

Before fitting new rings check that the gap between the ends of the ring, when fitted, is correct. Fit the ring alone into the bore of the cylinder about an inch from the top. Use a piston to ensure that the ring is square in the bore. Measure the gap with feeler gauges and if need be carefully file the ends to adjust to the gap as given in Technical Data.

Fit the oil control ring first. This is in three parts. Slide the spacer ring (corrugated member) carefully down the piston and into the bottom groove. Take care not to score the piston and check that the ends of the spacer butt together. Fit one scraper so that it is between the lower corrugated face of the spacer and the side of the ring groove. Fit the other scraper so that it fits similarly above the spacer. Fit the stepped or tapered compression ring into the next groove so that the plain face or marking T faces the crown of the piston. The plain compression ring is fitted into the top groove. Use either a special tool for expanding the rings, or slide them into place protecting the piston with three equally spaced shims.

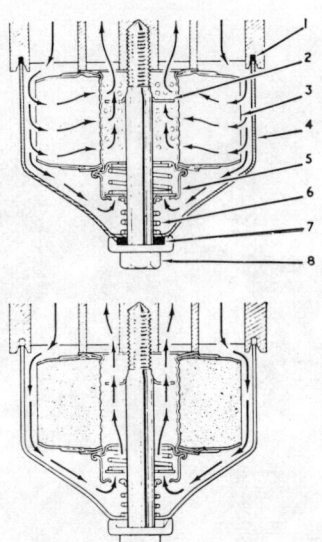

FIG 1:14 Oil filter details, also showing the oil circulation

Key to Fig 1:14   1 Rubber seal   2 Locating washer   3 Filter element   4 Container   5 Relief valve   6 Spring   7 Seal   8 Securing bolt

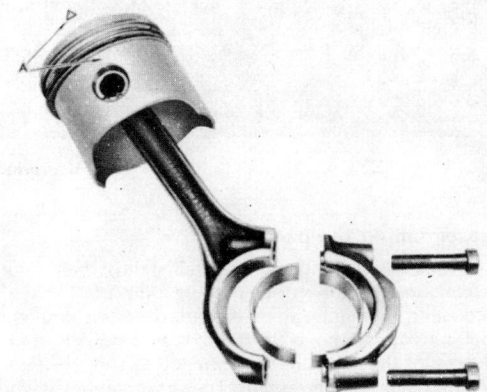

FIG 1:15 Piston and connecting rod assembly. A indicates the mark showing the front of the piston

Connecting rods:

The big-end bearings are renewable as already instructed. The gudgeon pin fits into a renewable phosphor/bronze small-end bush. The bushes must be jig-reamed to a very close tolerance after fitting to the connecting rod. The gudgeon pin should be able to be pushed through the bush by pressure of the fingers alone. If the dry gudgeon pin passes through the bush under the action of its weight alone then the bush is too slack and should be renewed. Attempts by the average owner to ream the bush would be unsatisfactory, so it is best to leave the job to a service station. Before refitting the connecting rods they should be checked for twist and bend. Accurate and specialist jigging is required so this should also be left to a suitably equipped service station.

FIG 1:16 Underside of engine with sump removed

Reassembling the parts:

Lubricate the gudgeon pin and slide it half into the piston. Line up the connecting rod so that, when the piston and connecting rod are fitted to the engine, the mark on top of the piston will face forwards and the opening of the offset in the connecting rod will face the camshaft side of the engine. The arrangement is shown in **FIG 1:16**. Press home the gudgeon pin and secure it in place with the two circlips. Ensure that the same pairs of pistons and connecting rods are assembled together as they were originally.

Turn the rings so that the gaps are evenly spaced around the piston and lightly lubricate them with clean oil. Use a piston ring clamp to compress the rings. In an emergency a large jubilee type clip can be used. With the connecting rod facing the right way, lower it down the bore of the cylinder and enter the skirt into the bore. Carry on pushing the piston gently into the bore, letting the clamp slide off the rings as they enter. **Take great care not to force or snap the rings.** Replace the shell bearings and connect the big-ends to the crankpins on the crankshaft as already instructed.

1:12 Crankshaft and main bearings

The main bearing shells can be changed while the engine is in the car, but if the crankshaft requires re-grinding then the engine must be taken out of the car.

1. Remove the engine from the car, complete with gearbox (see **Section 1:2**). Undo the ring of bolts holding the gearbox to the engine and part the gearbox from the engine. Remove the clutch and flywheel (see **Section 1:7**), and the engine backplate.
2. Remove the cylinder head (see **Section 1:3**), the valve timing gear (see **Section 1:5**) and the camshaft (see **Section 1:6**). Undo the bolts securing the engine front plate 20 and remove the plate and paper gasket 21.
3. If a stud extractor is available, remove the cylinder head studs from the top of the block, turn the engine over, and stand the engine upside down on a bench. Remove the sump (see **Section 1:8**) and remove the oil pump. Disconnect the big-ends from the crankpins, push the pistons down the cylinder bores and replace the caps and bearings loosely on their respective connecting rods.
4. Remove the seven setscrews holding the rear oil seal housing 2 to the crankcase. Remove the housing 2 and the paper gasket 3. A cross section view of the rear oil seal is shown in **FIG 1:17**. Evenly, to avoid distorting the housing, drive the oil seal out with a drift through the two holes in the housing provided for that purpose. Insert a new oil seal, with the lips facing the engine, and lay the housing to one side ready for reassembly.

5 Undo the two screws securing the front sealing block 13 and remove the block. Remove the old seals 12 from the block 13 ready for reassembly.
6 Check that the main bearing caps 13 are stamped in numerical order as shown in **FIG 1:18**. Progressively slacken the bolts holding the caps 13 in place. Remove the caps and store them in the correct order for reassembly, first taking out the shell bearings from them and laying them in the correct order.
7 Lift out the crankshaft from the block. Lift out the remaining four shell bearings from the block and lay them in order with the first four. Four renewable thrust bearings are fitted on either side of the rear main bearing as shown in **FIG 1:19** and these should also be removed.
8 Examine the journals of the crankshaft. If they are worn, scored, oval or tapered the crankshaft must be reground and suitable undersize main bearing shells fitted. Renew the complete set of shell bearings if any are worn, pitted or scored. Clean the crankshaft with paraffin, preferably under pressure, and blow through the oilways using an air-line. This is especially important when the crankshaft has been reground as otherwise particles of swarf may be left in the oilways.

Refitting the crankshaft:

1 Make sure all the parts are clean. Lay the top row of bearing shells into their correct positions in the crankcase, at the same time making sure that the tags on the bearing shells locate properly into the recesses provided. Lubricate the journals on the crankshaft with clean engine oil and lay the crankshaft back in place on the bearings. Refit the thrust bearings into the crankcase on either side of the rear main bearing so that the whitemetal surface faces the crankshaft.
2 Fit the bottom row of bearing shells into their respective caps 13, again ensuring that the tags are properly located. Fit the other pair of thrust bearings on either side of the rear main bearing cap. Replace the caps 13 in their correct order and position and secure them by replacing the bolts finger tight. Progressively tighten all the bolts to a torque load of 55 to 60 lb ft (7.60 to 8.29 kg m).
3 Mount a DTI on the crankcase as shown in **FIG 1:20**. By moving the crankshaft backwards and forwards measure the end float. The correct limits for end float are .006 to .008 inch (.1524 to .2032 mm) and if these are exceeded the thrust bearings will have to be renewed.
4 Refit the rear oil seal housing 2 complete with new oil seal and paper gasket 3. Smear the ends of the front sealing block 14 with jointing compound and lightly hold it in place with the two securing screws. Smear new packing pieces 12 with jointing compound and tap them in the slots provided as shown in **FIG 1:21**. Lay a straightedge across the front of the crankcase and align the block 13 to this. Fully tighten the securing screws and trim the ends of the packing pieces 12 off flush with the crankcase.
5 Fit a new paper gasket 21 to the front of the crankcase and replace the front engine plate 20. Reassemble the engine in the reverse order of dismantling and refit it to the car.

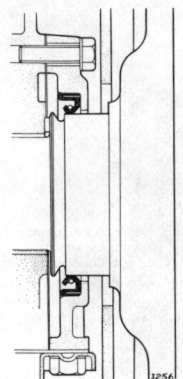

FIG 1:17 Cross-section of crankshaft rear oil seal

FIG 1:18 Position of the numbers on the main bearing caps and the crankcase

FIG 1:19 Fitting the crankshaft thrust washers to the rear main bearing

FIG 1:20 Measuring the crankshaft end float

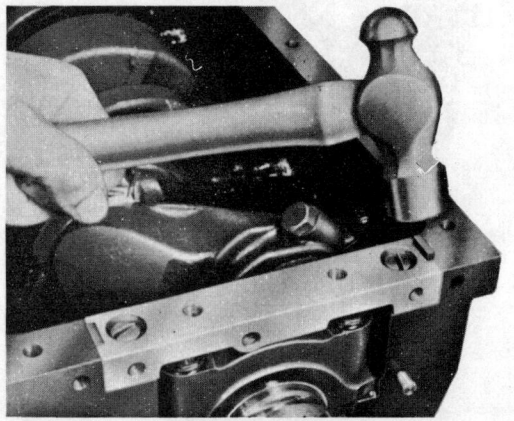

FIG 1:21 Fitting the packing pieces to the front sealing block

1:13 Reassembling a stripped engine

All dismantling and reassembling operations have been given in details in the various Sections, so that it is simply a matter of tackling the tasks in the correct sequence. Always fit new gaskets, which are available in complete sets. Lubricate all running surfaces with clean engine oil. Make sure all parts are cleaned before reassembly, using petrol or paraffin and drying it off with air or non-fluffy rags. Blow through oilways with paraffin followed by air.

Start by fitting the crankshaft, followed by the pistons, connecting rods and big-end bearings. Refit the front bearer plate followed by the camshaft. If it is possible (depending on the sprockets being marked or not) completely fit the valve timing gear. Refit the engine backplate, flywheel and clutch. The oil pump and sump can then be fitted before turning the engine the right way up and refitting the cylinder head. Leave accessories such as oil filter, distributor and metering unit, alternator and water pump to the last, as they will only be in the way and possibly get damaged if fitted earlier. Refit the engine to the car after mating it up with the gearbox. Torque wrench loads for all important fixings are given in Technical Data.

It is extremely important that all operations on the engine should be carried out in conditions of extreme cleanliness, as particles of dirt can cause damage or scoring of components before being trapped by the filter.

When all the refitting operations have been completed it is time to adjust the valve clearances as described in the following Section. Finally, not forgetting to renew the oil filter element, refill the sump with new engine oil and the cooling system with water. If the clutch slave cylinder has been disconnected the system will also require filling and bleeding.

1:14 Valve rocker adjustment

There is no starting handle provided for turning the engine so some other method will have to be found. Remove all the sparking plugs so that the engine will turn more easily. If the engine is run-in and free it may be possible to turn it over by pulling the fan belt. Otherwise engage top gear, jack up one wheel and turn the engine by rotating the road wheel.

1 All adjustments should be made with the engine cold. Undo the three Nyloc nuts holding the rocker cover in place. Remove the plain and fibre washers fitted with the nuts and carefully lift off the rocker cover with the cork gasket. Renew the gasket if it is damaged or compressed hard. A sectioned view of the valve operating details is shown in **FIG 1:22**.

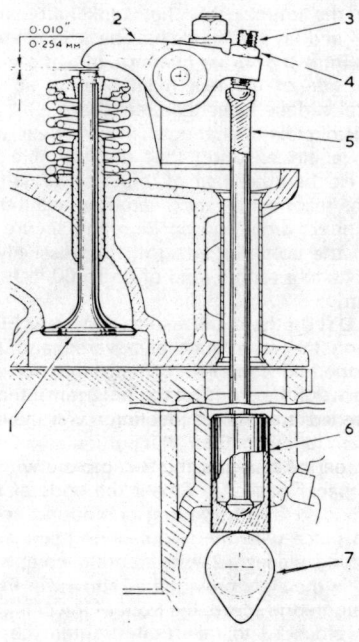

FIG 1:22 Valve gear details showing the point for setting the rocker clearance

Key to Fig 1:22   1 Valve   2 Rocker   3 Adjuster
4 Locknut   5 Pushrod   6 Cam follower   7 Camshaft

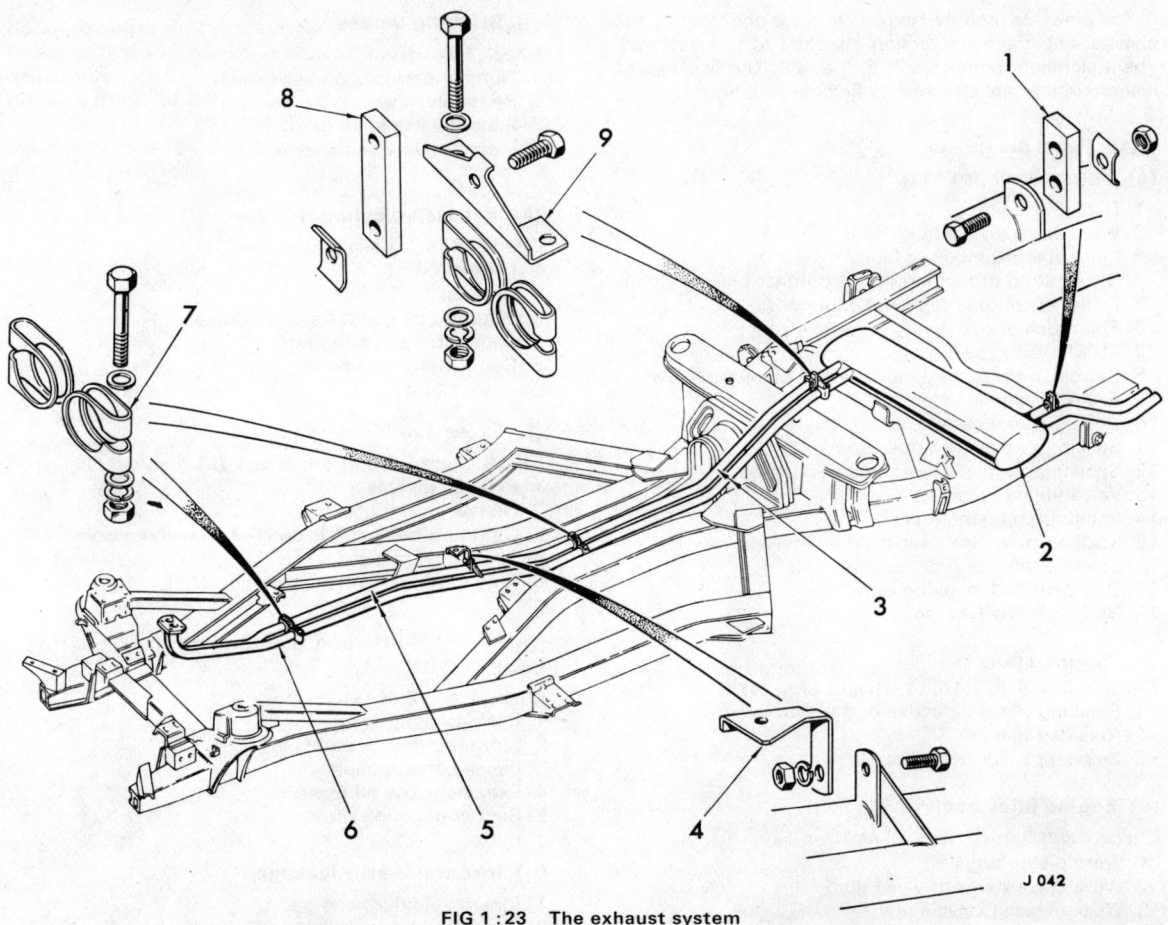

FIG 1:23 The exhaust system

Key to Fig 1:23   1 Flexible mountings   2 Silencer and tail pipe assembly   3 Rear intermediate pipes   4 Front mounting assembly   5 Front intermediate pipes   6 Front pipes and flange assembly   7 Pipe clamp assembly   8 Intermediate flexible mounting   9 Mounting bracket

2 Turn the engine over until the valves of any cylinder are at the point of balance. The rockers 2 will then be in the same position as for setting the valve timing described in **Section 1:5**. Note the number of the cylinder (counting from the front of the engine) and turn the engine one more complete revolution. This will ensure that the cam followers 6 for that particular cylinder will be resting on the bases of the two cams and that both valves are fully shut, as shown in **FIG 1:22**.

3 Insert a screwdriver into the slot on top of the adjustor 3 and with a spanner slacken the locknut 4. Press down on the screwdriver and turn it anticlockwise until a .010 inch (.25 mm) feeler gauge will pass easily between the toe of the rocker and the tip of the valve stem. Turn the screwdriver clockwise to decrease the gap until resistance is just felt on the feeler gauge when it is moved. Hold the screwdriver steady to prevent the adjustor turning, and tighten the locknut 4. Recheck the clearance after tightening the locknut, in case the adjustor has moved. Repeat the operation on the other valve of the cylinder.

4 Turn the engine through one-third of a revolution and the next cylinder in the firing order (1–5–3–6–2–4) will be in position for adjusting the valve rocker clearances. Carry on until all six cylinders have been adjusted.

5 If a new cork gasket is to be fitted to the rocker cover make sure all the remains of the old gasket are removed. Use jointing compound to stick the new cork gasket to the rocker cover before refitting the cover to the engine. After a short period of running check around the rocker cover for oil leaks.

1:15 The exhaust system

The exhaust system comprises a twin exhaust pipe and common silencer complete with twin tail pipes (see **FIG 1:23**). The system is divided into four separate sections, each of which can be renewed separately. By referring to the illustration the sections are divided up as follows:
Front pipes and flange assembly (6).
Front intermediate pipes (5).
Rear intermediate pipes (3).
Silencer and tail pipes assembly (2).

The pipes are mounted in pairs at three points along the chassis with the front section attached to the manifold. The attachment points are 4, 8, 9 and 1. The two sets of rear mountings are attached by flexible couplings.

1:16 Fault diagnosis

(a) Engine will not start

 1 Defective coil
 2 Water on sparking plug leads
 3 Ignition wires loose or faulty insulation
 4 Dirty, pitted or incorrectly set contact breaker points
 5 Faulty distributor capacitor (condenser)
 6 Too much excess fuel
 7 Insufficient excess fuel
 8 Corrosion on battery terminals or battery discharged
 9 Faulty or jammed starter
10 Defective fuel pump
11 Sticking or leaking valves
12 Sparking plug leads wrongly connected
13 Valve timing incorrect
14 Ignition timing incorrect
15 Sticking or wrongly set overfuel lever
16 Sheared drive to fuel metering unit
17 Defective fuel metering unit
18 No fuel in the fuel tank

(b) Engine stalls

Check 1, 3, 4, 5, 6, 7, 10, 11, 15 and 17 in (a)
 1 Sparking plugs defective or gaps incorrect
 2 Retarded ignition
 3 Incorrect valve clearance

(c) Engine idles badly

Check 1 and 3 in (b) as well as 15 in (a)
 1 Worn piston rings
 2 Worn valve stems or valve guides
 3 Weak exhaust valve springs
 4 Injector sticking open

(d) Engine misfires

Check 1, 2, 3, 4,5, 10, 11, 12, 13, 14 and 15 in (a) and 6 in (b)
 1 Weak or broken valve springs
 2 See **Chapter 2**

(e) Engine overheats, see Chapter 4

(f) Compression low

Check 11 in (a); 1 and 2 in (c) and 1 in (d)
 1 Worn piston ring grooves
 2 Scored or worn cylinder bores

(g) Engine lacks power

Check 4, 11, 13, 14, 15 and 17 in (a); 1, 2, and 3 in (b) and also check (e) and (f)
 1 Leaking cylinder head gasket
 2 Fouled sparking plugs
 3 Centrifugal advance not working

(h) Burnt valves or seats

Check 11 in (a); 3 in (b) and 1 in (d). Also check (e)
 1 Excessive carbon around valve seat and head

(j) Sticking valves

Check 1 in (d)
 1 Gummy deposits on valve stem
 2 Bent valve stem
 3 Scored valve stem or guide
 4 Incorrect valve clearance

(k) Excessive cylinder wear

Check 15 in (a) also check (e)
 1 Lack of oil
 2 Dirty oil
 3 Piston rings gummed up or broken
 4 Badly fitting piston rings
 5 Connecting rods bent

(l) Excessive oil consumption

Check 1 and 2 in (c) and check (k)
 1 External oil leaks
 2 Oil level too high
 3 Oil return holes in piston choken with carbon
 4 Scored cylinders
 5 Ring gaps too wide

(m) Crankshaft and connecting rod bearing failure

Check 1 and 2 in (k)
 1 Restricted oilways
 2 Worn journals or crankpins
 3 Loose bearing caps
 4 Extremely low oil pressure
 5 Bent connecting rod

(n) Internal water leakage

 1 Blown cylinder head gasket
 2 Cracked cylinder head
 3 Cracked cylinder block

(o) Low oil pressure

 1 Lack of oil in sump
 2 Oil needs changing
 3 Excessively worn engine
 4 Oil pressure gauge faulty or loose connections

(p) Poor water circulation, see Chapter 4

(q) Corrosion, see Chapter 4

Check (n)

(r) High fuel consumption, see Chapter 2

(s) Engine 'knocks'

 1 'Pinking'
 2 Worn big-end bearings
 3 Worn main bearings
 4 Excessive crankshaft end float
 5 Worn small-end bushes
 6 Piston knock (slap)
 7 Incorrectly adjusted rocker clearances

CHAPTER 2

THE FUEL SYSTEM

2:1 Description
2:2 The fuel filter
2:3 The fuel pump
2:4 Servicing precautions
2:5 The injectors
2:6 Setting the throttle butterflies
2:7 The operation of the metering unit
2:8 Removing and refitting the metering unit
2:9 Servicing the metering unit

2:10 The pressure relief valve (PRV)
2:11 Stromberg CDSE carburetters
2:12 Maintenance and adjustments
2:13 Removal and refitting
2:14 Synchronizing throttles and slow-running
2:15 Fuel pump and filter
2:16 Air cleaner
2:17 Crankcase emission control valve
2:18 Fault diagnosis

2:1 Description

The schematic layout of the fuel injection system is shown in **FIG 2:1**. The illustration shows the system for the TR5. The TR6 system differs only in that the return pipe from the pressure relief valve 3 is returned directly to the fuel tank instead of to the filter 1, and the filter 1 has no air bleed pipe leading to the return pipe.

Fuel is gravity fed to the paper element filter 1 and from there it is drawn to the electrically driven gear pump 2. Fuel under pressure from the pump is fed to the metering unit 5. The pressure is maintained between 106 to 110 lb/sq in by the pressure relief valve 3, excess fuel being fed back to the filter 1 on the TR5 and direct to the fuel tank 8 on the TR6. On the TR5 any air that is drawn into the filter is automatically bled from the filter 1 by a stack pipe from the top of the filter. This pipe is omitted on the TR6.

The metering unit precisely measures, according to engine requirements, a charge of fuel and delivers it, through the appropriate injector pipe 7, to an injector in the induction manifold at the start of that piston induction stroke. The injectors contain a poppet valve set to open at 50 lb/sq in and the charge is sprayed, in a hollow 60 deg. cone, into the induction manifold. The air and fuel mixture is then drawn into the engine and fired normally.

The metering device 5 is lubricated with fuel which is then returned by the leak-off pipe 4 to the fuel tank. An excess fuel lever is fitted to the metering unit and operating this will produce up to 300 per cent excess fuel for cold starts.

The speed of the engine is governed by the amount of air drawn in and this is controlled, from the accelerator pedal, by a butterfly valve on each cylinder.

2:2 The fuel filter

The components are shown in **FIG 2:2**, and the only routine maintenance that the whole system requires is renewal of the filter element 3 every 12,000 miles.

The filter is situated in the luggage compartment. Remove the spare wheel and place a shallow container under the filter to catch any spillage. **Clamp the inlet pipes to prevent fuel flowing when the filter is dismantled.** Unscrew the centre securing bolt and remove the lower casing, filter element 3 and lower sealing ring 2. Use a small tool to remove the upper sealing ring 2 from the upper casing and also remove the O-ring 4. Fit new seals 2 to the upper and lower casings, making sure that they are both fitted squarely and correctly. Renew the O-ring 4 and reassemble the parts in the reverse order of dismantling using a new filter element 3. Do not attempt

TR5/6

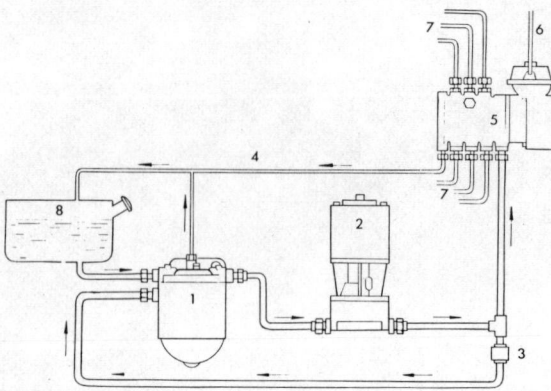

FIG 2:1 Schematic view of petrol injection circuit for the TR5. The layout of the TR6 is very similar apart from no stackpipe on the filter 1, and the return from the PRV. 3 is direct to the fuel tank 8.

Key to Fig 2:1 1 Filter   2 Motor driven pump 3 Pressure relief valve 4 Leakage fuel 5 Metering distributor control unit   6 Connection to manifold   7 To injectors 8 Fuel tank   ⟶ Direction of fuel flow

and tighten the securing bolt as soon as fuel alone leaks out. Wipe away any spillage and check for leaks. The most common cause of filters leaking is that the top sealing 2 is incorrectly seated.

2:3 The fuel pump

The pump is mounted behind the trim panel in the luggage compartment. The position of this and the fuel filter on the TR5 is shown in **FIG 2:3** while **FIG 2:4** shows the similar layout on the TR6.

Testing the fuel pump:

It should be noted that the pump is always running when the ignition is switched on and for this reason the ignition should not be left on without the engine running, unless the supply to the pump is disconnected.

If it is suspected that the pump has failed, switch on the ignition and feel the pump to check if it is running. If it is not running first check that there is an electrical supply to the pump. If supply is present connect an ammeter into the pump circuit. **The pump is polarity sensitive so take great care to ensure that the pump is correctly connected electrically.** Switch on the ignition and check the running current. Normally this is 4 amps. No or low reading indicates a defective brush assembly. A high reading indicates a tight pump, stalled motor, or a shortcircuit in the armature winding.

Disconnect the plastic pipe from the tell-tail pipe on the base of the casting. If fuel comes from the pipe then the shaft seal has probably failed. Confirm this by connecting two short pipes to the pump and dipping the ends in a container filled with paraffin. Switch on the ignition and if a continuous stream of bubbles comes from the outlet pipe then the seal has failed. The pump will have to be dismantled and thoroughly checked in case petrol has contaminated the interior.

Pump output and pressure can be checked in the same way as adjusting the Pressure Relief Valve (PRV), but timing the rate of fuel flow.

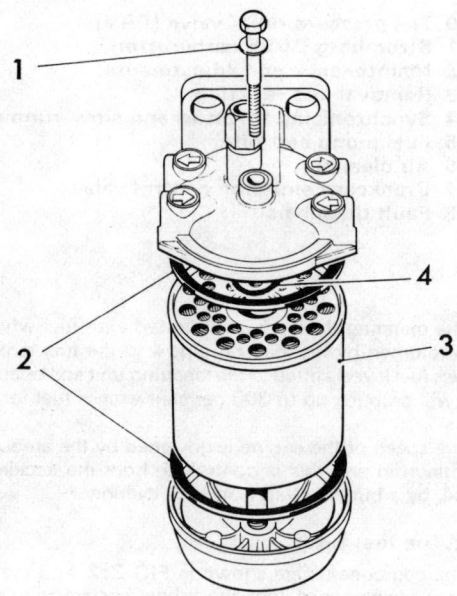

FIG 2:2   The fuel filter

Key to Fig 2:2   1 Sealing washer   2 Casing seals 3 Element   4 O-ring

to clean the old element as nothing useful can be done with it. **Make sure that the new element is marked for use with petrol,** as the element used in a diesel filter will break down under the action of petrol. On the TR6 it helps to bleed the system of air by slackening the securing bolt after the filter has been reassembled and the inlet pipes unclamped. Hold the lower casing up firmly

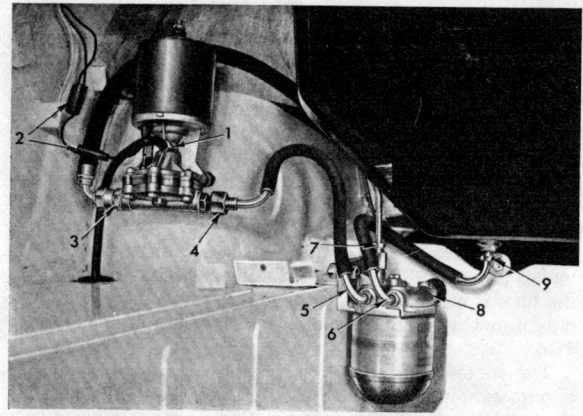

FIG 2:3   Fuel pump and fuel filter on the TR5

Key to Fig 2:3   1 Pump leak off   2 Inline electrical connectors   3 Pump outlet   4 Pump inlet   5 Filter outlet 6 Filter inlet (from tank)   7 Filter leak off   8 Filter inlet (from PRV)   9 Tank outlet

26

If after considerable serivce the pump is noisy in operation, reset the armature end float. Slacken the locknut on the top cover and, while holding the pump vertical, screw in the adjusting screw until a resistance is felt. Slacken back the adjusting screw ¼ turn and retighten the locknut.

Dismantling the fuel pump:

1 Remove the outlet connection 12 and the inlet connection 11 complete with the strainer 10. Remove the strainer from the inlet connection. The components of the pump are shown in **FIG 2:5**.

2 Progressively slacken the ring of six bolts and remove the gear pump assembly from the motor. Remove the drive coupling 15 and store it safely.

3 Remove the two long through bolts 23 holding the cover 2 in place. Carefully withdraw the cover and armature 20 a maximum of ½ inch, **not more**. The brushes will drop clear of the armature but if the cover is now removed the brushes will be damaged on the circlip or thrust washer. Push each brush back and then carefully lift off the cover and armature.

4 Pull the armature out of the cover. The resistance is due to the attraction of the permanent magnet 21 in the cover. Remove the thrust washer 18 and the circlip 19 from the armature shaft.

5 Remove the brush assembly 4, freeing the cables from the casting by carefully pushing the rubber grommet up through the hole in the casting.

6 Only if the shaft seal 16 is damaged, and a replacement is available, should the seal be forced out from its place in the casting.

Examining the parts:

Earlier pumps were fitted with a narrow top plate 9 which was matched to the motor base in production. On these the motor cannot be replaced separately and the

FIG 2:4 Fuel pump, fuel filter and PRV on TR6

Key to Fig 2:4 1 Pressure relief valve 2 Fuel filter 4 Pump inlet 5 Pump leak drain pipe 6 Fuel pump motor

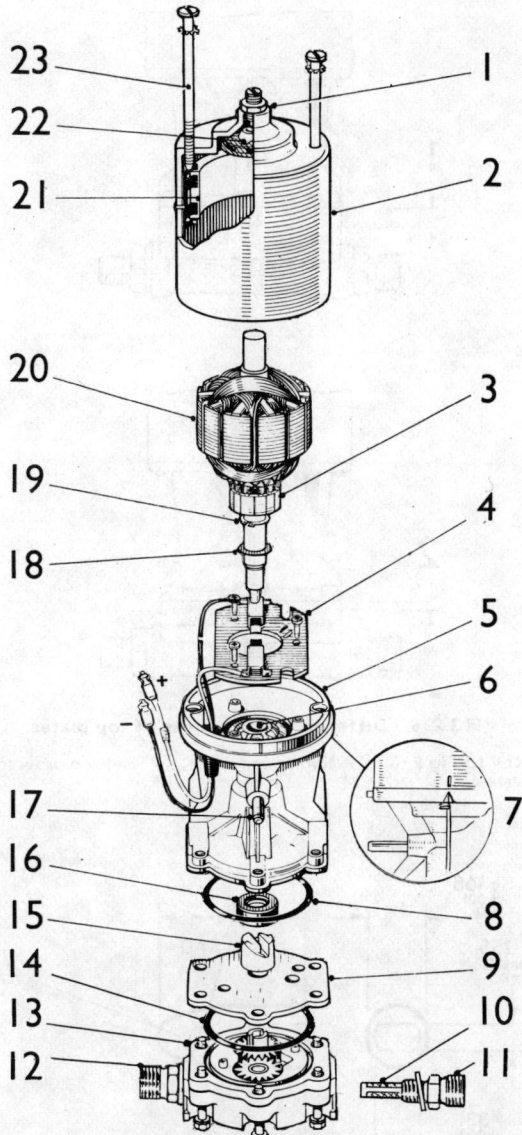

FIG 2:5 Fuel pump details

Key to Fig 2:5 1 Armature end float adjuster 2 Cover 3 Commutator 4 Brushplate assembly 5 Base casting 6 Bearing 7 Aligning marks 8 Rubber O-ring 9 Top plate 10 Strainer 11 Inlet connection 12 Outlet connection 13 Gear pump 14 Rubber O-ring 15 Drive coupling 16 Shaft seal 17 Tell-tail pipe 18 Thrust washer 19 Circlip 20 Armature 21 Permanent magnet 22 Bearing 23 Through-bolt

whole pump must be exchanged. Later pumps with a thicker top plate can have the pump or motor renewed individually. The difference in thickness of the top plate is illustrated in **FIG 2:6**.

Clean the commutator 3 with a piece of rag moistened in petrol. The surface should be smooth and free from

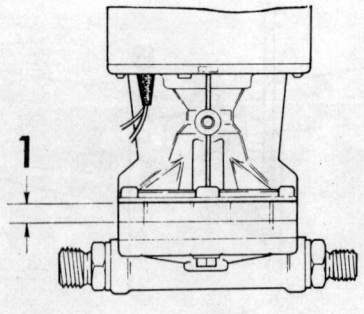

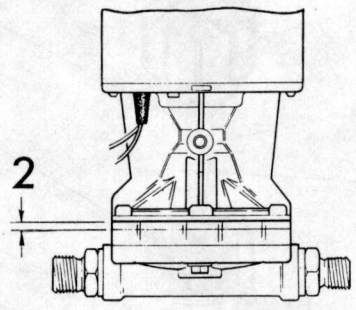

FIG 2:6 Difference in thickness of top plates

Key to Fig 2:6 1 Normal top plate 2 Earlier narrow top plate

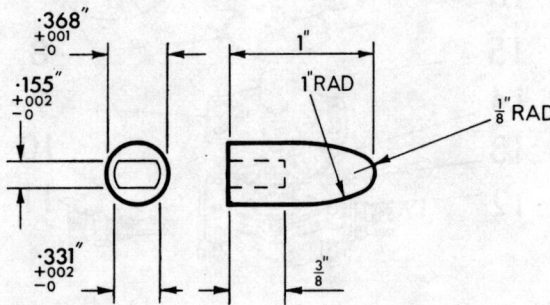

FIG 2:7 Dimensions of protective bullet for fitting pump armature

pitting. If necessary lightly polish the commutator with a piece of fine glasspaper. Renew the armature if the wear is excessive.

Clean the brushes in the assembly 4 with a piece of petrol-moistened cloth, ensuring that they move freely in their holders. Renew the brushplate 4 if the brushes are shorter than $\frac{3}{16}$ inch. Use a push-type spring scale and check that the brush springs have a tension of 5 to 7 oz when compressed to .158 inch (4 mm). Renew the plate 4 if the brush tension is low.

The performance of the gear pump should be checked with the pump assembled. 1 gallon should be delivered at a pressure of 100 lb/sq inch in $3\frac{3}{4}$ minutes with a motor terminal voltage of 13.5 volts. With the pump dismantled examine the interior for wear or damage. If parts are worn renew the complete assembly as the parts are mated and cannot be renewed individually.

The two self-aligning bearings are not replaceable.

Reassembling the pump:

The two rubber seals 8 and 10 must be renewed whenever the pump is dismantled, otherwise there will most likely be leaks.

A protective bullet, shown in **FIG 2:7**, will be required for reassembly.

1 Replace the brushplate assembly 4. Carefully work the cables and the rubber grommet through the hole in the casting. The three securing screws are offset so the brushplate assembly can only be fitted the right way round.
2 Insert the armature into the top cover 2. The permanent magnet 21 will pull the armature 20 into the cover, but make sure the journal fits into the self-aligning bearing 22. Replace the circlip 19 and the thrust washer 18.
3 If shaft seal 16 has not been removed then fit the protective bullet on the end of the armature shaft. Lightly grease the bullet and enter it into the shaft seal 16. Push back the brushes and press the armature and cover into place taking care that the brushes are not damaged and that they seat on to the commutator 3.
4 If the seal 16 is removed then replace the armature and cover without the bullet in place, again holding back the brushes until they can seat on the commutator. After securing the cover 2 in place with the screws 23, fit the bullet to the end of the armature shaft and use it as a guide to refitting a new shaft seal 16.
5 **When securing the cover 2 to the pump make sure that the marks shown at 7 align, otherwise the motor will run in reverse.**
6 Position the drive coupling 15 to the motor and reassemble the pump using new seals 8 and 14, and evenly tightening the six securing bolts.
7 Refit the strainer 10 to the inlet connection 11 and using new washers screw the adaptors back into the pump. Reset the armature end float.

2:4 Servicing precautions

Because of the high pressures and close tolerances used in a petrol injection system certain extra precautions must be taken when servicing the system.
1 If the system stands idle for long periods, such as overhaul or lack of use of the car, the petrol will evaporate leaving gummy residues which will stop the proper working of the components. To prevent this add an inhibitor to the fuel and run the engine for long enough to ensure that the inhibitor is circulated around the whole system.
2 Disconnect the battery whenever the fuel system is dismantled to avoid inadvertent operation of the fuel pump. The fuel pump is polarity sensitive so be extra careful when connecting wires.
3 If, for other tests, the ignition is required to be switched on for any length of time without the engine running, disconnect the fuel pump electrical supply.

28

4 Take great care over all unions, and make sure they are tight and secure. Whenever components are dismantled renew all rubber sealing rings as a matter of routine otherwise leaks will develop.

5 Make sure the rubber leak off pipes are not blocked or kinked. If this happens there will be a pressure build up in the metering unit which will prevent it functioning properly and cause excess fuel to be delivered, with consequent rough running, sooting of the sparking plugs and high fuel consumption.

6 After dismantling the system it will take some time for the system to be reprimed. Make sure the battery is fully charged and use the starter motor to turn the engine over until it starts on full choke.

2:5 The injectors

To check if these are working unclip the injector pipes, to prevent the pulse being reflected from one pipe to another, and start the engine. Feel the pipes in the order of firing (1–5–3–6–2–4). Distinct pulses should be felt on each pipe. No pulse or a weak one on one pipe indicates that the injector is stuck open. No pulse on two consecutive (in the order of firing) pipes indicates that the first injector of the pair is blocked.

The installation of the injectors is shown in **FIG 2:8**. To remove them hold the injector with a spanner on the hexagonal head and use another spanner to undo the

FIG 2:8 Injector in position

Key to Fig 2:8 1 Retaining bolt 2 Retaining plate 3 Injector 4 Injector pipe union

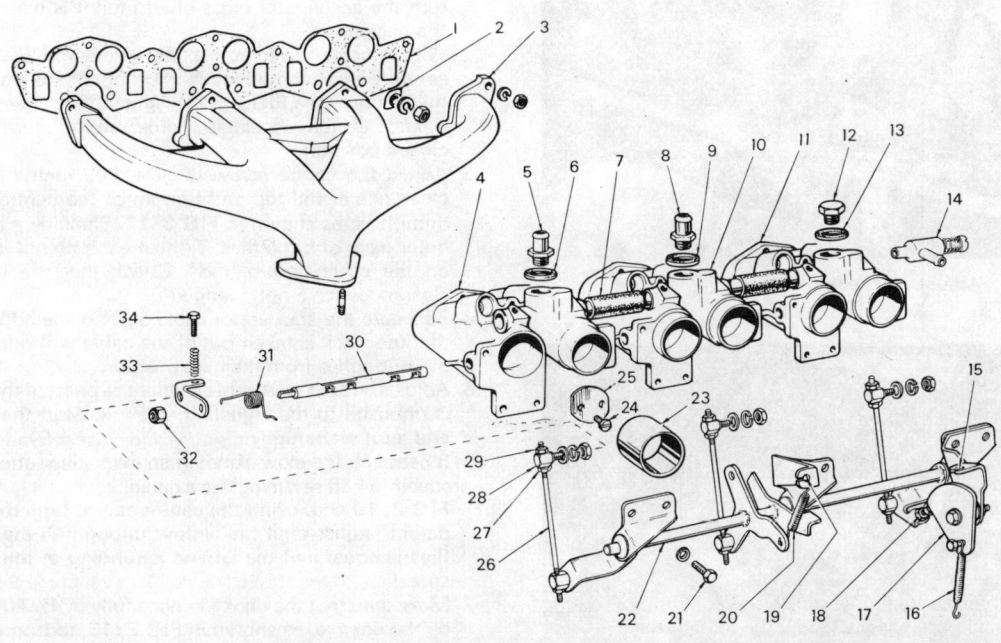

FIG 2:9 Manifolds and throttle linkage on the TR6. The TR5 does not have the air valve item 14 fitted

Key to Fig 2:9 1 Manifold gasket 2 Clamp 3 Exhaust manifold 4 Inlet manifold – rear 5 Servo adaptor 6 Sealing washer 7 Balance plug 8 Metering unit vacuum adaptor 9 Sealing washer 10 Inlet manifold – centre 11 Inlet manifold – front 12 Plug 13 Sealing washer 14 Air valve assembly 15 Cold start abutment 16 Return spring 17 Cold start cam 18 Adjusting screw 19 Accelerator abutment 20 Accelerator return spring 21 Linkage securing bolt 22 Accelerator cross rod 23 Air inlet tube 24 Butterfly securing screw 25 Butterfly valve 26 Vertical adjusting rod 27 Locknut 28 Trunnion 29 Locknut 30 Butterfly spindle 31 Return spring 32 Spindle nut 33 Adjusting screw spring 34 Adjusting screw

TR5/6

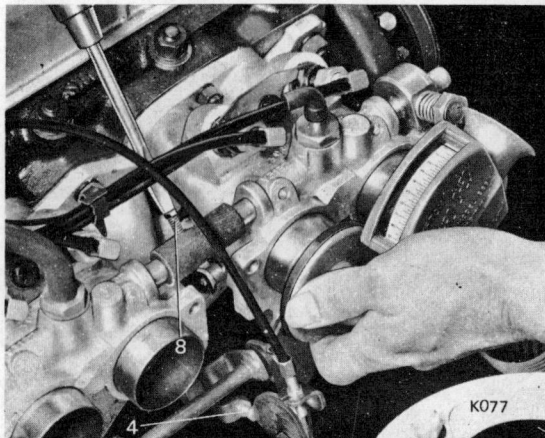

FIG 2:10 Using flow meter to measure air flow through butterflies

FIG 2:11 Adjusting the link rods

FIG 2:12 Adjusting the clearance on the TR5 throttle butterflies

union nut 4. Remove the bolt 1 and take off the retaining plate 2. The injector may now be pulled out of the manifold. If required use spanners to remove the Nylon holder and O-ring from the injector.

To clean an injector blow through it in the direction of fuel flow, using clean dry compressed air at a pressure of 80 lb/sq in (5.624 kg/sq cm). If this fails to clear a defective injector then it must be renewed as no servicing is possible on injectors.

2:6 Setting the throttle butterflies

The induction and exhaust manifolds, as well as the throttle linkage, of the TR6 are shown in **FIG 2:9**. The system for the TR5 is the same except that the air valve 14 is omitted. Because of this air valve the method of adjusting the TR6 varies slightly from that of the TR5. On the TR6 the butterflies are closed at slow-running and the air required is bled through the air valve, while on the TR5 the slow-running air passes through the throttle butterflies. Before adjusting either model remove the air intake manifold, slacken off the adjustor for the accelerator cable, and turn the screw 4 so that it is well clear of the cold start cam 7 shown in **FIG 2:13**.

TR5:

1 Slacken the slow-running screws 8, shown in **FIG 2:10**, right back. Slacken the five locknuts 5 on the adjusting rods 6, shown in **FIG 2:11**, and with the hand turn the accelerator cross-shaft until it is hard against the backstop.
2 With a screwdriver adjust the centre rod 6 until the centre pair of butterflies is wide open and parallel to the air flow (see **FIG 2:11**). Tighten the single locknut 5 and let the accelerator cross-shaft return to the closed position.
3 Adjust the centre screw to give .002 inch (.05 mm) clearance at the top and bottom of the centre pair of butterflies, as shown in **FIG 2:12**. Similarly adjust the outer pairs of butterflies. Tighten each pair of locknuts on the outer control rods. Check that the butterfly clearances have not changed.
4 Resecure the accelerator cable and set the adjustor so that the slack is taken out of the cable without pulling the butterflies from their set position
5 Adjust the cold start cable so that the point of the cam 7 is opposite to the adjusting screw 4. Start the engine and let it warm up.
6 By turning the slow-running screws adjust the engine speed to 750 rev/min. Use a balance meter as shown in **FIG 2:10** and, using the centre pair of butterflies as a datum, adjust until the airflow through all the butterflies is equal and the engine is running at the correct speed.
7 Make sure that the choke knob is fully in. Pull the cable by the linkage, as shown in **FIG 2:13**, to turn the cam 7. If the choke knob is used the excess fuel lever on the metering unit will also be operated. Adjust the screw 4 until the engine is running at 2000 rev/min. Release the cable and tighten the locknut securing the screw 4.
8 Adjust the cable on the metering unit to give full travel on the excess fuel lever, and so that the first movement of the knob takes up the free play on the lever. Replace the air intake manifold.

TR6:

1 Slacken the locknuts 5 on the three adjusting rods 6 (see **FIG 2:11**). By hand turn the accelerator shaft into the open position against the backstop. Adjust the rods 6 until all three pairs of butterflies are wide open and horizontal to the air flow. Tighten the locknuts and release the accelerator cross-shaft.

2 Reset the accelerator cable adjustor so all the free play is taken out of the cable without moving the throttle butterflies. Adjust the choke cable, with the knob fully in, so that the point of the cam 7 is opposite to the adjusting screw 4.

Turn the air valve, shown in **FIG 2:14**, fully in and then unscrew it five complete turns.

3 Start the engine and let it warm up. Place an air meter against each intake in turn. Adjust the screw 8 as shown in **FIG 2:10** until the meter shows a zero reading of air passing through the butterfly. The pull of the throttle return spring must act on the adjusting screws and not be taken up by the butterflies jamming in the bore.

4 Adjust the engine speed to 700 to 850 rev/min by turning the screw of the air valve.

5 Turn the cam 7 to its fully open position by pulling the cable as shown in **FIG 2:13**. This method prevents excess fuel being selected. Adjust the screw 4 until the engine is running at approximately 1300 to 1500 rev/min. Release the cable and tighten the locknut.

6 Adjust the cable on the fuel metering unit to give full travel of the lever, and still allowing the first movement of the control knob to take up free play in the lever. Replace the air intake manifold.

2:7 The operation of the metering unit

A sectioned view of the components is shown in **FIG 2:15**. The whole unit can, both schematically and physically, be divided into two sub-units. On the righthand side is the control unit, which is operated by vacuum from the induction manifold. The lefthand unit contains the metering shuttle and this is diagrammatically illustrated in **FIG 2:16**.

Metering shuttle:

Refer to **FIG 2:16**. Fuel is pressure fed from the pump through the inlet 9 and the rotor 6 is driven from the engine. In the top diagram A the position of the rotor 6 is such that fuel passes through the aligned ports and forces the shuttle to move from left to right. The fuel to the right of the shuttle is then passed through the ports out through 3 to No. 1 injector. A further turn of 120 deg. aligns the ports as shown in diagram B. The incoming fuel now goes to the righthand side and moves the shuttle back from right to left. The charge of fuel to the left of the shuttle is passed through the outlet 4 to No. 2 injector. Since the shuttle passes the same distance between the fixed stop 1 and the adjustable stop 5 exactly the same quantity of fuel is passed to each injector. As the rotor rotates each cylinder receives a precisely equal quantity of fuel in the order of firing.

The amount of fuel delivered at each stroke of the shuttle will be dependent on the distance between the two stops 1 and 5. The position of the fixed stop 5 is governed by the control unit.

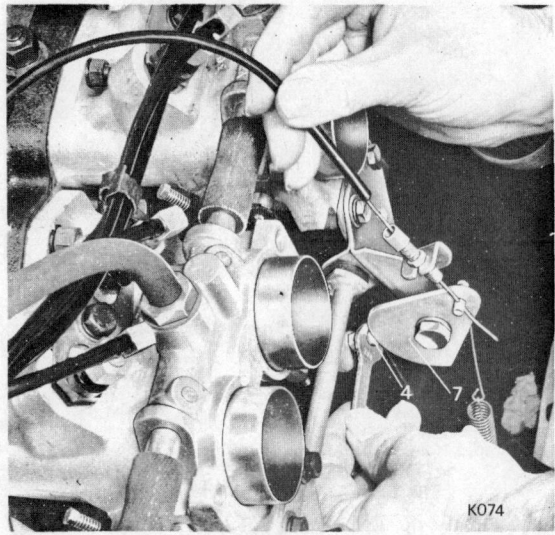

FIG 2:13 Setting the cold start cam screw

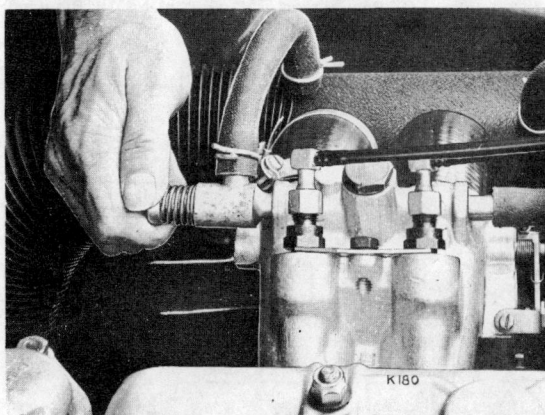

FIG 2:14 Adjusting the TR6 air valve

Control unit:

The vacuum in the induction manifold varies with the speed of the engine and the load applied, and is therefore used to operate the control unit. Referring to **FIG 2:15**, the vacuum is fed in through the inlet 6 where it pulls up the diaphragm 7 against the action of the calibration springs 3. As the diaphragm 7 moves up it pulls with it the linkage 12. The linkage 12 has a roller which as it moves up and down is pressed out sideways by the cam 11 and thus moves the adjustable stop through the follower 15. To prevent the full force of the unit acting on the stop a balance spring 2 is fitted to the follower 15 in order to relieve some of the pressure.

A full load setting screw 14 is fitted to limit the maximum output. The tension of the calibration springs is adjustable at 4 and the slope of the cam 11 can be altered by slackening the two securing screws. These three adjusting points are shown in **FIG 2:17** but they are adjusted using

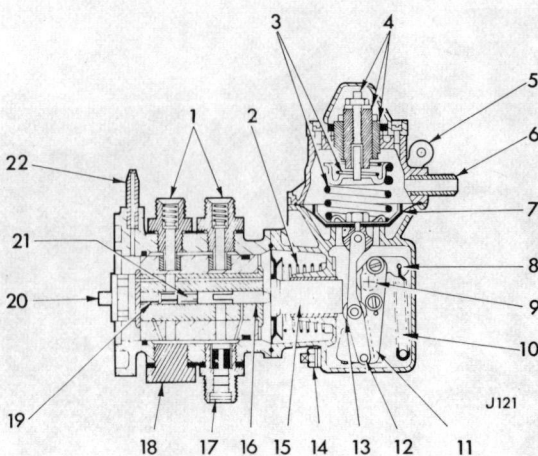

FIG 2:15 Metering unit details

Key to Fig 2:15 1 Outlet valves 2 Balance spring 3 Calibration springs 4 Calibration screws 5 Excess fuel lever 6 Connection to manifold 7 Diaphragm 8 Fuel cam carrier 9 Pivot 10 Return spring 11 Fuel cam 12 Control links 13 Rollers 14 Full load setting screw 15 Follower 16 Control stop 17 Fuel inlet 18 Blanking plug 19 Fixed stop 20 Rotor drive 21 Shuttle 22 Leakage fuel

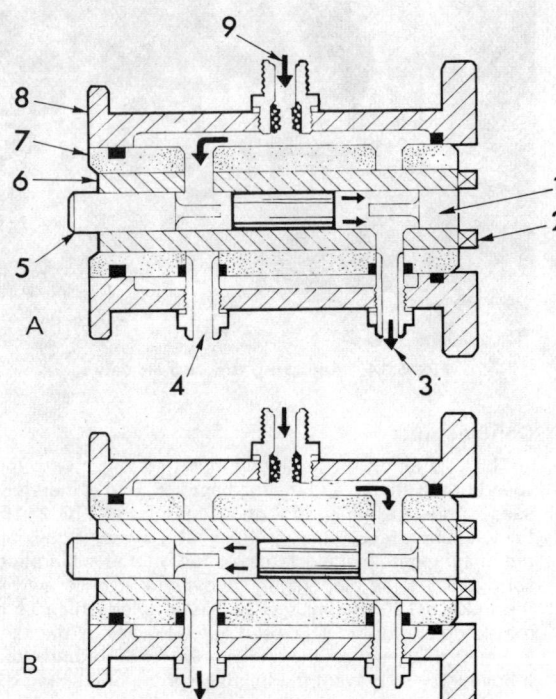

FIG 2:16 Principle of the shuttle metering system

Key to Fig 2:16 1 Fixed stop 2 Rotor drive 3 Outlet to No. 1 injector 4 Outlet to No. 2 injector 5 Adjustable control stop 6 Rotor 7 Sleeve 8 Body 9 Fuel inlet from pump

special precision equipment. **Under no circumstances may these three adjustments be altered by the owner.**

An excess fuel lever 5 is fitted so that extra fuel can be provided for cold starts. Movement of the lever is transmitted to the fuel cam 11 and its carrier, which pivot at 9 to alter the datum and provide up to 300 per cent excess fuel.

2:8 Removing and refitting the metering unit

Before removing the unit disconnect the battery leads as a safety precaution. It is possible to remove the drive pedestal, distributor and metering unit complete but they will have to be separated before reassembly. If the tank is filled above the level of the metering unit fuel will seep through the inlet pipe, unless it is clamped, when the pipe is disconnected. For ease of reassembly set the engine to TDC with No. 1 cylinder on the firing stroke.

Removing:

1 Label the injector pipes and disconnect them from the injectors. Disconnect the vacuum pipe from the metering unit. Disconnect the fuel inlet pipe and the leak-off pipe from the metering unit. **To prevent dirt entering the pipes blank them off.** Remove the cold start cable from the unit.
2 Undo the three securing bolts and lift off the unit complete with the injector pipes, taking care not to lose the plastic driving dog.
3 A sectional view of the drive pedestal is shown in **FIG 2:18**. Remove the bolt 7 and washer 6. With the fingers push out the pinion 3 and the plug 4.

The drive pedestal:

The distributor is held on to it by one bolt, and the assembly is fixed to the engine by two nuts. Refer to **FIG 2:18** for details. Two seals 8 are fitted back to back in the bore for the metering unit pinion 3. A drilling A connects to the annular gap between the two seals. If the seal nearer the metering unit fails fuel will leak from the hole A. Engine oil will appear if the other seal fails. If either seal has failed then both should be renewed as a set. The old seals are removed with a screwdriver or hook, taking care not to score the surface of the bore. Clean out the bore, remove any rust spots or burrs and make sure that the hole A is clear. Smear one seal with grease and fit it using a .9 inch (22.9 mm) punch. Fit the first seal so the lips face inwards as shown in the figure. Pack in some grease and then in a similar way refit the outer seal so that its lips face outwards. Make sure there is an annular space between the two seals and that the space connects to A.

Replacing:

Set the engine to TDC with No. 1 cylinder firing. To protect the seals 8 in the drive pedestal a bullet, shown in **FIG 2:19**, should be fitted over the end of the pinion 3 when fitting the pinion to the drive pedestal. If the bullet is unavailable and cannot be made, use a cylinder made from a sheet of thin shim steel to protect the seals.

1 Insert the pinion 3 into the drive pedestal so that when it is in position the slot in the end is vertical, as shown in **FIG 2:20**. Remove the old O-ring 5 from the plug 4 and fit a new O-ring. Push the plug 4 firmly into place

FIG 2:17 Do not alter the adjustments A, B or C

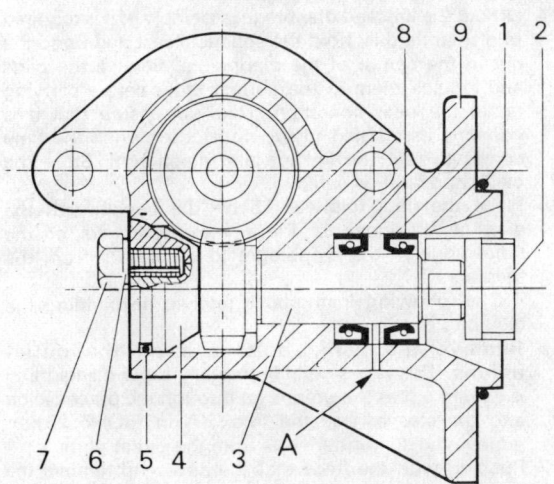

FIG 2:18 Pedestal and drive pinion arrangement

Key to Fig 2:18   1 O-ring   2 Coupling   3 Pinion
4 Plug   5 Plug O-ring   6 Washer   7 Retaining bolt
8 Lip seals   9 Pedestal

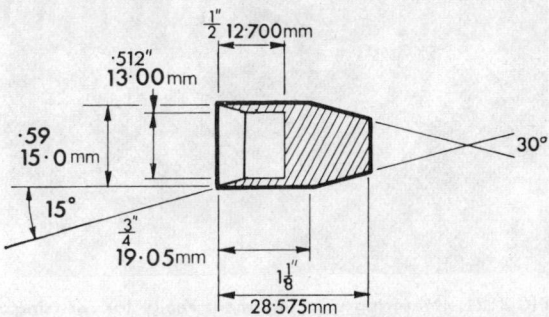

FIG 2:19 Protective cover for refitting the drive pinion

and secure it in position with the bolt 7 and the washer 6.

2 Use a little grease to hold the drive dog 2 in position on the pinion 3 in the drive pedestal. Fit a new O-ring 1 to the boss of the pedestal.

3 Turn the drive on the metering unit until the slot is horizontal, and the scribed lines are aligned as shown in FIG 2:21. The drilled hole in the drive will then be

TR5/6

33

FIG 2:20 Drive pinion correctly aligned in pedestal with engine at TDC on No. 1 cylinder firing stroke

FIG 2:21 Metering unit alignment ready for refitting. Note that the drilled hole is in the lower portion of the drive

in the lower half. If a further check is needed remove the No. 6 cylinder outlet adaptor. If the unit is correctly set the hole in the rotor will be at the start of the injection point.

4 Refit the unit to the driving pedestal with the three bolts, making sure that the driving dog is properly in place. Reconnect the pipes and excess fuel cable in the reverse order of dismantling, **not forgetting to**

remove any clamps and blanks fitted when dismantling.

5 It will take a little time to reprime the fuel lines, so turn the engine over by the starter motor, with full choke, until the engine fires. After that start the engine normally.

2:9 Servicing the metering unit

It is vital that absolute cleanliness is observed whenever the unit is dismantled; no precautions can be considered too stringent. Ideally the parts should be washed and lubricated with non-leaded fuel, but if this is unobtainable ordinary fuel will do. Whenever the unit is removed from the car for any length of time fit blanks to all the ports.

Do not alter the adjustments shown in FIG 2:17.

The special tools shown in **FIG 2:22** are required to service the unit, so either borrow these or have them made up.

Dismantling:

1 Hold the unit together against the compression of the balance spring 2 and remove the four nuts and washers holding the control unit in place. Ease the two halves apart slowly, allowing the balance spring to expand. Remove the balance spring 2 and the follower 15 with the diaphragm attached to it.

2 Hold the metering unit over a piece of thick cloth and shake out the control stop 16, the shuttle 21 and the fixed stop 19. Take great care not to damage these three parts, preferably catching them in the hand and having the cloth as a safety precaution.

The following operations deal with dismantling the control unit.

3 Refer to **FIG 2:23**. Remove the coverplate by undoing the four screws holding it in place. Remove the four screws holding the depression chamber and cable bracket in place. There is no need to undo the two screws holding the top cap in place.

4 Lift out the link and diaphragm assembly. If it is required to dismantle this, hold the spherical seat and undo the nut in the centre of the diaphragm. Service the parts and replace them in the correct order before carrying on to the next operation. This will ensure that it is correctly assembled in the right order when the time comes to refit the linkage and diaphragm. Store the calibrated springs safely.

5 Place the cam follower 15 on the bench with the diaphragm uppermost. Press, with the fingers, on the inner edge of the diaphragm to separate it from the follower.

The following instructions refer to dismantling the metering distributor.

6 **Remove the banjo bolts and all the outlet unions.** This is essential before any other dismantling is carried out as the unions go through the outer casing into the sleeve. Use the hook (A in **FIG 2:22**) to remove the six rubber seals from the outlet ports.

7 Pushing with the fingers at the drive end remove the outer sleeve and rotor. The distributor will then be as shown in **FIG 2:24**.

8 Remove the two Allen screws securing the rotor stop plate to the rotor. The rotor can now be removed from the sleeve, as shown in **FIG 2:25**.

9 Remove the fuel inlet union and take out of it the fuel strainer. **Remove all rubber seals and O-rings and discard them.**

Reassembling the unit:

The following instructions refer to reassembling the metering distributor.

1 Fit the strainer, after cleaning it in petrol and dry compressed air, to the inlet union. The end with the cone seating and longest portion of thread takes the strainer. Refit the union to the outer casing, using a new seal.
2 Wash the rotor and sleeve in clean petrol. Fit a new O-ring to the sleeve. Make sure the brass thrust plate is securely fixed to the rotor, and wet the rotor with clean petrol. Insert the rotor into the sleeve, **at the end of the sleeve fitted with the O-ring,** and very carefully ease it through into position. **Take care not to jam the rotor in the sleeve and make sure it rotates freely once in position.** Replace the stop, radiused side towards the rotor, and secure it in place with two new Allen screws. Use Locktite on the threads and tighten the screws to a torque load of 16 lb in (.184 kg m). Note that the torque is in lb in not lb ft. **Again check that the rotor rotates freely in the sleeve.**
3 Fit a new O-ring to the body and smear both this and the O-ring on the sleeve with a little clean engine oil. Fit the sleeve and rotor assembly back into the body and align so the sleeve ports line up with the threaded holes in the body.
4 Screw the alignment tool (C in **FIG 2:22**) into one of the threaded holes in the body so that it accurately locates the sleeve. Use the tool (B in **FIG 2:22**) to fit new seals to the other five outlet ports, making sure they are fully home. Check that the non-return valves in the six outlet unions are not sticking. Replace five, with new washers, into the outlet ports. Remove the alignment tool and fit a new seal, washer and the outlet union. To prevent the ingress of dirt blank off the six outlet unions.
5 Fit new O-rings to banjos and fit banjo bolts.
6 Examine the shuttle and two stops for damage, wear or scoring. **Wash them in clean fuel and replace them while wet.** The adjustable stop is the one with the axial hole.

Wrap the assembly in a clean plastic bag and store it safely ready for final reassembly.

The following instructions deal with reassembling the control unit.

7 If the nut holding the diaphragm has been removed fit it to the linkage using the first few threads only. Put one drop of Locktite in the centre of the nut and fully tighten the nut to a torque of 4 lb in (.046 kg m). Wipe away any surplus Locktite.
8 Lightly smear the link rollers with clean engine oil and refit the link arm and diaphragm assembly, making sure that the spherical seat and link arm are square to the rest of the assembly. Push the diaphragm rim into its seating in the body.
9 Fit the large calibration spring to the diaphragm, then the spring carrier and finally the small spring. Refit the suction chamber cover so that the connection to the induction manifold is on the opposite side to the

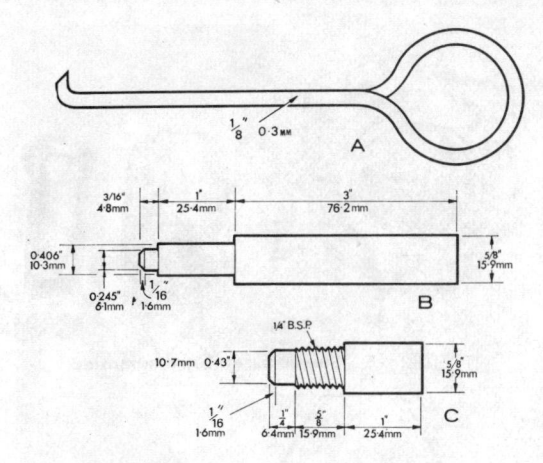

FIG 2:22 Special tools required for servicing the metering unit

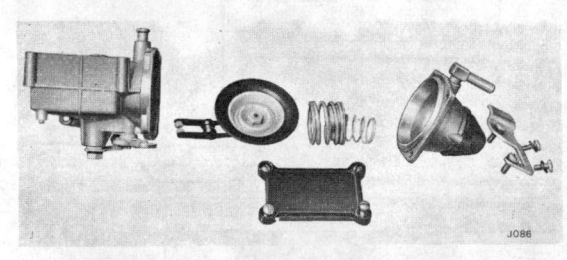

FIG 2:23 Diaphragm assembly removed

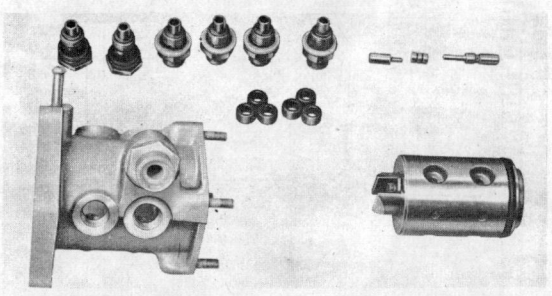

FIG 2:24 Sleeve assembly removed from the body

banjo connections. On top of this place the excess fuel lever bracket with the cranked end facing the driven end of the unit. Secure these two in place using the four screws. The longer pair of screws fit on the bracket side of the cover.

10 Hold the follower diaphragm with the three locating slots uppermost and feed the cam follower through the hole in the diaphragm. Push the diaphragm onto its seating using the fingers.
11 Fit the spring thrust plate to the follower, then the balance spring. Push the assembly gently into place on the control unit. Check that the adjustable stop and shuttle are still in place in the metering distributor and then refit the distributor to the control unit. Clamp the parts together with the hand until the four washers and nuts are tightened in place. Refit the coverplate with the four screws.

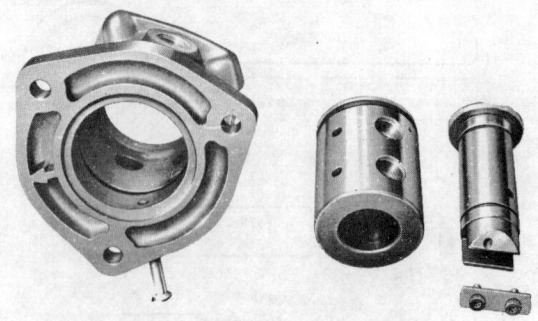

FIG 2:25 Sleeve assembly dismantled

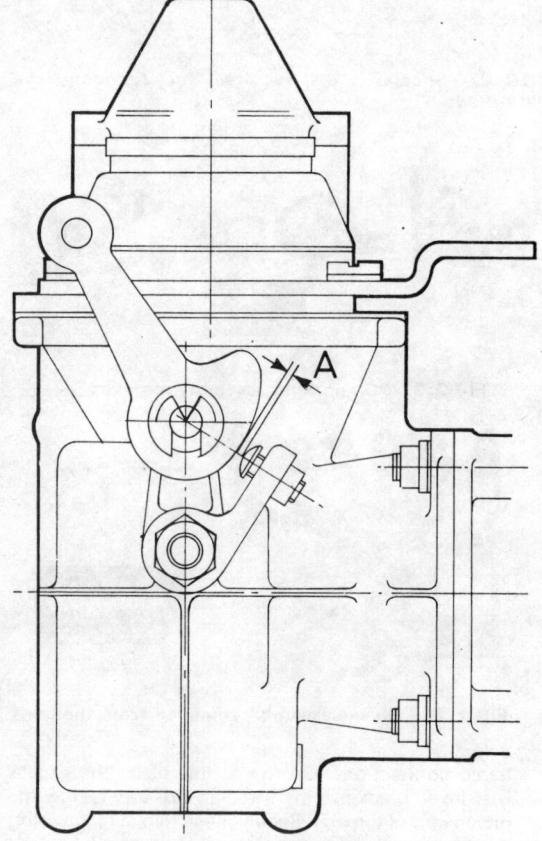

FIG 2:26 Setting excess fuel lever

FIG 2:27 Pressure relief valve fitted to TR5

Key to Fig 2:27 1 Outlet pipe 2 T-junction 3 Valve and strainer holder 4 Pressure relief valve 5 Return to filter pipe 6 Inlet pipe

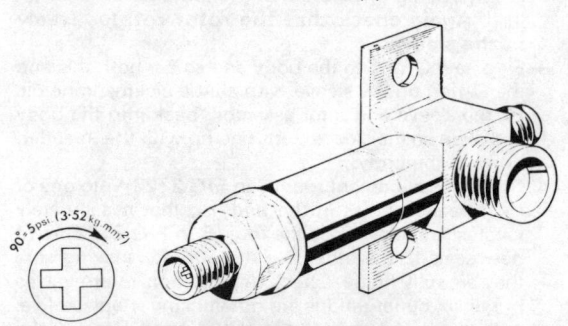

FIG 2:28 Adjusting the pressure relief valve

Excess fuel lever:

Check the clearance at A in **FIG 2:26** is .006 to .008 inch (.15 to .2 mm). Ensure also that there is free play at the cable end of the lever, approximately $\frac{1}{4}$ inch (6 mm).

2:10 The pressure relief valve (PRV)

On the TR6 the PRV is item 1 in **FIG 2:4**. On the TR5 the PRV is mounted directly to the chassis behind the rear axle as shown in **FIG 2:27**. It should be noted that the valves are similar on both models but the return from the PRV goes directly to the tank on the TR6 and to the filter on the TR5.

Removing and dismantling the PRV:

1 Remove the outlet pipe 1, inlet pipe 6 and return pipe 5 from the PRV. Either plug or clamp the pipes to prevent the ingress of dirt and fuel leaking out.
2 Remove the two bolts holding the T-junction 2 in place and lift out the valve. Mount the body in a vice and use a $\frac{5}{8}$ inch AF spanner to remove the valve and strainer.
3 Remove the strainer by hand and clean it in fuel or dry compressed air. Replace the parts in the reverse order of dismantling using new seals to ensure there will be no leaks. **Make sure all clamps and blanks are removed.**

Setting and testing the PRV:

For the correct operation of the petrol injection system it is essential that the PRV is set within the correct limits. A pressure gauge 0 to 120 lb/sq in (0 to 8500 gm/sq cm) mounted on a T-piece is required. The other two ends of the T-piece should be one female $\frac{1}{2}$ inch UNF and the other male $\frac{1}{2}$ inch UNF.

1 Disconnect the pipe between the PRV and the metering unit at some convenient point, either at 1 on the PRV or somewhere nearer the metering unit. Reconnect the

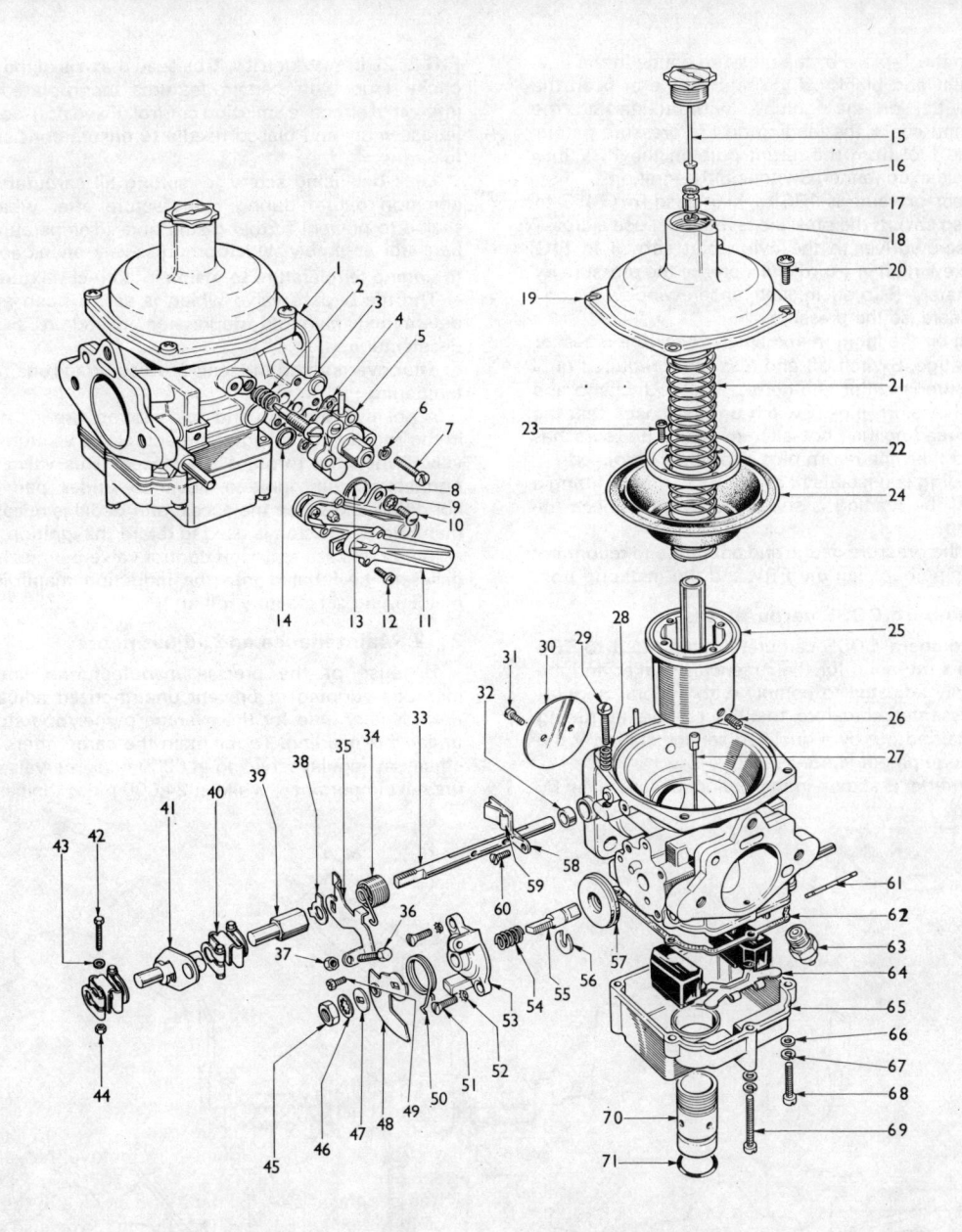

FIG 2:29 Exploded view of Stromberg CDSE carburetter

Key to Fig 2:29   1 Carburetter   2 Idle trimming screw spring   3 Idle trimming screw   4 Bypass valve gasket
5 Bypass valve   6 Lockwasher under (7)   7 Securing screw (5)   8 Temperature compensator unit   9 Lockwasher under (10)
10 Securing screw (8)   11 Temperature compensator cover   12 Securing screw (11)   13 Seal on compensator body
14 Seal inside carburetter   15 Damper rod (damper assembly)   16 Washer (damper assembly)   17 Distance sleeve (damper assembly)   18 Circlip (damper assembly)   19 Air valve cover   20 Securing screws (19)   21 Air valve return spring
22 Diaphragm attachment ring   23 Securing screw (22) (24)   24 Diaphragm   25 Air valve   26 Securing screw (27)
27 Needle assembly   28 Idle adjusting screw spring   29 Idle adjusting screw   30 Throttle disc   31 Securing screw (30)
32 Throttle spindle seal   33 Throttle spindle   34 Throttle return spring   35 Throttle lever   36 Fast-idle screw
37 Securing locknut (36)   38 Retaining lockwasher (39)   39 Throttle spindle nut   40 Throttle spindles coupling
41 Connecting lever assembly   42 Clamping bolt   43 Washer under (42)   44 Nut securing (42)   45 Nut   46 Shakeproof washer*
47 Washer*   48 Lever*   49 Cable attachment screw*   50 Return spring*   51 Screw*   52 Shakeproof washer*
53 Starter box cover*   54 Spring*   55 Spindle*   56 Retainer*   57 Valve plate*   58 Cable abutment bracket   59 Spring clip
60 Securing screw (58)   61 Float pivot pin   62 Float chamber gasket   63 Needle valve   64 Float assembly
65 Float chamber cover   66 Washer under (68/69)   67 Spring washer under (68/69)   68 Screw securing (65)
69 Screw securing (65)   70 Plug   71 Rubber O-ring for (70)
   Starter box assembly

TR5/6

37

pipe with the T-piece of the pressure gauge in the line.
2 Disconnect and blank off the return pipe at 5 on the PRV. Switch on the ignition, without starting the engine, and check the reading on the pressure gauge. Catch the fuel from the return port on the PRV in a suitable clean container. Switch off the ignition.
3 The correct pressure is 106 to 110 lb/sq in (7453 to 7734 gr/sq cm). If the pressure is incorrect use a cross-headed screwdriver to the nylon part shown in **FIG 2:28**. Screwing it in $\frac{1}{4}$ turn will increase the pressure by approximately 5 lb/sq in, and unscrewing will conversely decrease the pressure.

Switch on the ignition and again check the pressure on the gauge. Switch off and readjust if required until the pressure is within the correct limits. Unclamp and replace the return pipe. Switch on and check that the pressure reading has not altered. If the pressure has increased then the return pipe is probably blocked.
4 If the reading is unstable fit a new PRV. If after fitting a new PRV the reading is still unstable then check the fuel pump.
5 Remove the pressure gauge and adaptor and reconnect the fuel pipe between the PRV and the metering unit.

2:11 Stromberg CDSE carburetters

Twin Stromberg CDSE carburetters are fitted to TR5 and TR6 cars intended for the American market and are most carefully adjusted to comply with Federal Regulations. It is essential, therefore, that any carburetter tuning should be carried out by a qualified service station if the specialized equipment is not available.

The carburetter is shown in the exploded view given by **FIG 2:29** from which it will be seen that it is of the variable choke type with certain features incorporated in the interest of effective emission control. Fixed non-adjustable jet assembly and biased needle to ensure consistent air/fuel ratio.

Leak balancing screw for setting all carburetters to a common datum during manufacture after which it is sealed to prevent further disturbance. Temperature compensator assembly which progressively opens according to engine temperature to maintain correct mixture.

Throttle bypass valve which is set to open at a predetermined manifold depression to admit air during deceleration.

The cover is wired and sealed to discourage unauthorized tampering.

A positive idle stop and 'lost motion' are incorporated in the accelerator linkage. This actuates a vacuum control valve when the throttles are closed. This valve permits normal vacuum ignition advance under part throttle condition and when the accelerator pedal is released, full manifold depression is used to retard the ignition.

The crankcase emission control valve permits blow-by gases to be inhaled into the induction manifold while maintaining satisfactory idling.

2:12 Maintenance and adjustments

Because of the precise manufacturing limits and methods adopted to prevent unauthorized adjustments, there is very little for the average owner/operator to do under this heading. To maintain the carburetters at peak efficiency regular servicing at 6000 mile intervals is of the greatest importance, while at 24,000 miles the car should

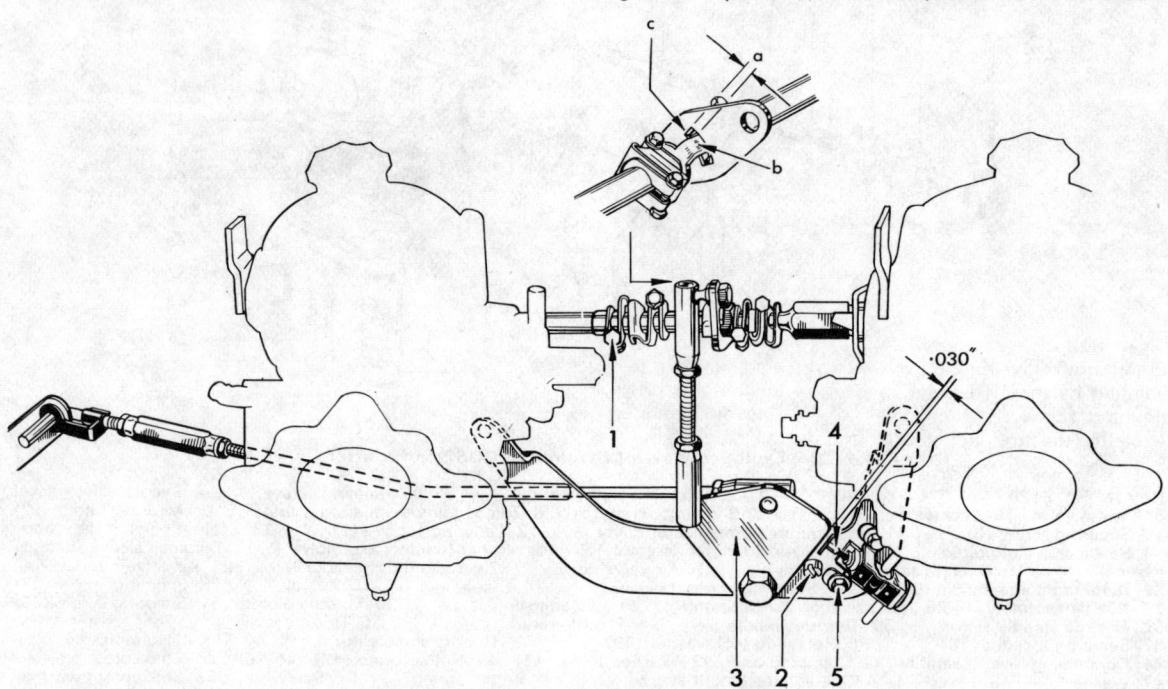

FIG 2:30 Adjusting accelerator linkage

Key to Fig 2:30   1 Spring coupling clamp bolts   2 Throttle stop   3 Relay lever   4 Vacuum valve plunger   5 Vacuum valve securing screws

38

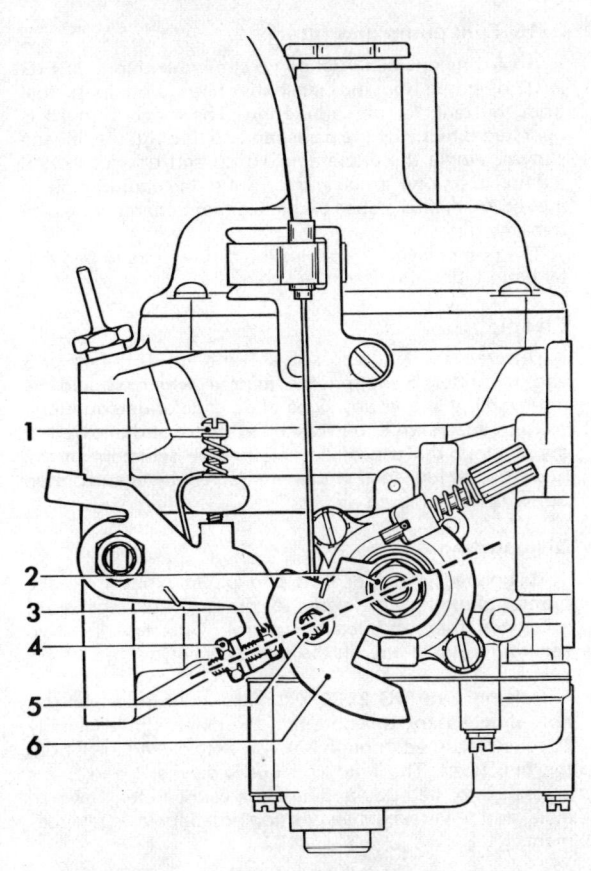

FIG 2:31 Adjusting fast-idle controls

Key to Fig 2:31   1 Idling screw   2 Starter box
3 Fast-idle screw   4 Locknut   5 Cable trunnion
6 Choke cam lever

be taken to an authorized service station for a very comprehensive check-up involving a number of new component parts. The air valve damper reservoirs should be topped up with engine oil to within $\frac{1}{4}$ inch of the top of the centre rod 15.

Check and if necessary adjust the slow-running by turning both slow-running screws 29 an equal amount to maintain balance. This may involve readjustment of the trimming screw 3 which gives a very fine adjustment regulating the introduction of air into the mixing chamber. This setting should be checked by means of a C.O. meter or an air/fuel ratio meter to the exhaust pipe. The relevant details are: Idle C.O. level with warm engine 2.5 per cent to 3.5 per cent. Air/fuel ratio at idle 13.5:1 approximately.

The fast-idling is regulated by the fast-idle screw 36.

2:13 Removal and refitting

Remove the air cleaner after detaching the emission control hose by removing the six securing bolts.

Remove the fuel feed pipes. Disconnect the choke cables.

Disconnect the vacuum valve pipes at each carburetter and both sides of the vacuum valve, also the vacuum advance pipe at the carburetter.

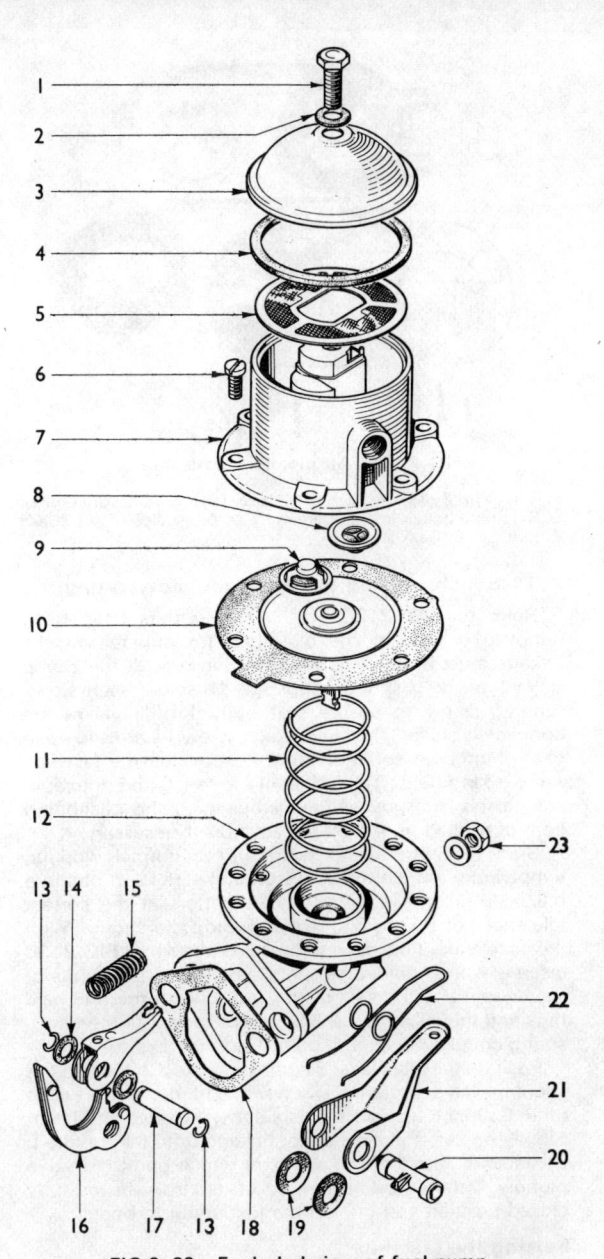

FIG 2:32 Exploded view of fuel pump

Key to Fig 2:32   1 Retaining screw   2 Washer
3 Cover   4 Joint   5 Gauze   6 Screw   7 Body
8 Inlet valve   9 Outlet valve   10 Diaphragm assembly
11 Diaphragm spring   12 Lower body   13 Circlip
14 Distance washer   15 Return spring   16 Rocker arm
17 Rocker arm pin   18 Gaskets   19 Cork seals
20 Primer lever shaft   21 Primer lever   22 Primer lever spring
23 Pump retainer nut

Disconnect the accelerator control rod at the bulkhead side of the carburetter. Remove four nuts securing each carburetter (one nut also secures the vacuum valve bracket) and lift off the two carburetters complete with linkage. Refit by reversing the above procedure and set the linkage and controls as described in **Section 2:14**.

TR5/6

39

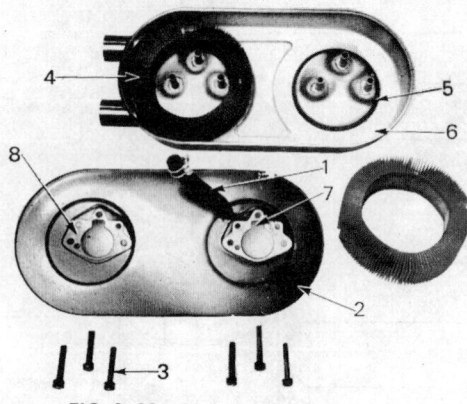

FIG 2:33 Air cleaner components

Key to Fig 2:33
1 Hose   2 Coverplate   3 Retaining bolts   4 Element   5 Gasket   6 Case   7 Slot   8 Gasket

2:14 Synchronizing throttles and slow-running

Refer to **FIG 2:30**. If the carburetters have been removed or the linkage disturbed for any reason the linkage must be reset as follows: Slacken off the clamp bolts 1 on both spring couplings. Unscrew each slow-running screw to ensure that both throttle valves are completely closed, then open each screw $1\frac{1}{2}$ turns to open each throttle an equal amount. Ensure that the fast-idle screw (3 in **FIG 2:31**) is clear of the cam 6 and both cold start levers are against their stops with the dashboard control pushed in. Adjust the controls if necessary.

Start the engine and warm up to normal working temperature. Adjust the slow-running screws to obtain a balanced air intake on both carburetters at the correct idle speed of 800 to 860 rev/min. Stop the engine. With the accelerator linkage assembled as shown in **FIG 2:30** insert a $\frac{3}{32}$ inch drill in the space a between the tongue of the lever b and the side of the slot c. With the drill held thus and the relay lever 3 against the stop 2 tighten both spring coupling clamping bolts 1 and remove the drill.

Position the relay lever 3 against the stop 2, slacken the vacuum valve securing screws 5 and move the valve until .030 inch clearance exists between valve and lever. Slowly operate the accelerator linkage until the tongue b contacts the edge of the slot c, at which point the valve plunger 4 should be at the end of its stroke in the fully closed position and the throttle just about to open.

Setting the fast-idle:

Make sure that when the choke control is pushed fully in, the choke lever 6 in **FIG 2:31** is against its stop, then pull out the control sufficiently to bring the cable trunnion 5 into alignment with the fast-idle screw 3 and the centre of the starter box 2 as shown by the dotted line. Slacken the locknuts 4 and unscrew both fast-idle screws until each is just touching the cam. Start the engine and while it is cold, turn each fast-idle screw an equal amount to give a tachometer reading of 1100 rev/min.

Tighten the locknuts and recheck the speed. **Never** attempt to set the engine or adjust the carburetters with the air cleaner removed, since this would admit air into the inlet manifold via the emission valve and upset any adjustments made at this time.

2:15 Fuel pump and filter

An AC mechanical fuel pump shown exploded in **FIG 2:32** operated from the camshaft is used to pump the fuel from the tank to the carburetters. The rocker arm 16 is operated directly by the camshaft and through the linkage shown, works the diaphragm 10 up and down to draw the fuel in on one stroke and force it to the carburetters on the return. A filter gauze 5 and sediment chamber help to trap any dirt.

The primer lever 21 enables the carburetters to be filled by hand when the engine is stationary.

Cleaning:

Unscrew the retaining screw 1 and lift off the cover 3 and the filter 5, noting the joint 4 which should be renewed if it shows any signs of damage or deterioration.

The gauze should be washed in petrol and allowed to dry without the use of any cloth. Any sediment in the body may be loosened with a small screwdriver and blown out with compressed air.

Dismantling:

Disconnect the fuel feed and outlet pipes from the pump, plugging the ends to prevent the ingress of foreign matter and leaking petrol. Unscrew the two securing nuts 23 and lift the pump away from the crankcase.

Reference to **FIG 2:32** will make any further instruction unnecessary, but note that the diaphragm assembly 10 must be turned through 90 degrees to disengage it from the link lever. The inlet and outlet valves 8 and 9 are pressed into the body and must be very carefully levered away and their respective position noted for later replacement.

Reassembly:

This is a reversal of the dismantling procedure. Make sure that the joint face is clean and use a new gasket 18, coated with jointing compound. Carefully fit the pump on the two mounting studs and press the rocker arm against the camshaft, fit the spring washers and nuts and tighten them to a torque of 12 to 14 lb ft. Reconnect the fuel pipes, prime and test for leaks.

External filter:

At intervals of 12,000 miles the in-line filter, which is fitted in the main delivery line to the pump, should be renewed as follows: Clamp the inlet hose and pull both hoses off the filter.

Fit the new filter ensuring that the side of the filter marked 'IN' faces the direction of the flow i.e. downwards.

2:16 Air cleaner

At intervals of 6000 miles (10,000 km), or more frequently if the operating conditions are very dusty, the paper elements must be taken out for cleaning.

Release the flexible hose 1 from the coverplate 2. Undo the six retaining bolts 3, take off the coverplate and lift out the elements noting the positions of the rubber ring seals.

Clean out the casing 6 and remove the dust on the paper folds by shaking and blowing with a low pressure air line.

When reassembling, make sure that the slot 7 in the coverplate and gasket 8, also the vent and bolt holes, align with those in the carburetter flanges. At 12,000 miles (20,000 km) the paper elements should be renewed.

2:17 Crankcase emission control valve

In the system employed for the TR250 the oil filler cap is sealed and ventilation air for the crankcase is drawn in through a restrictor hole on the clean air side of the air cleaner assembly. This air, together with any blow-by gases, is drawn into the combustion chambers via the emission valve which is shown in section in **FIG 2:34**. There is a small clearance between the valve pin 1 and the orifice plate 4 to allow a limited flow at engine idle, but when a vacuum is applied the plate valve 5 is sucked off its seat and a depression is formed under the diaphragm 3. If this exceeds the force of the spring 2, the valve 1 will move downwards to reduce the controlling orifice until the forces are balanced. The tension of the diaphragm spring is such that a small depression is maintained in the crankcase.

The plate valve 5 also acts as a non-return valve against back-fires from the carburetter manifold.

The emission control valve should be serviced at intervals of 12,000 miles. Remove the connecting pipes and the spring clip and coverplate. Take out the rubber diaphragm 3 noting carefully the fitted position of its top face. Remove the valve pin 1 and spring 2.

Clean the body and all components in petrol taking particular care of the diaphragm.

Check that the valve plate 5, is free to move and held correctly on its seat by the spring 6.

Any defective items should be renewed and the valve reassembled in the reverse order, ensuring that the plunger is correctly located in the centre of the guides in the orifice plate 4.

2:18 Fault diagnosis (Petrol injection system only)

(a) Engine fails to start
1 Pump motor not running
2 Blocked injectors
3 Injectors stuck open
4 Fuel pressure excessively low
5 Excessive use of excess fuel knob
6 Insufficient use of excess fuel knob
7 Excess fuel level operating incorrectly on metering unit
8 Sheared metering unit drive
   If there are regular pulses on all the fuel injection pipes then it is unlikely that the fuel system is at fault.

(b) Engine runs erratically
1 Check 3 and 7 in (a)
2 Low fuel pressure
3 Metering unit fitted 180 deg out of timing
4 Faulty metering unit

(c) Excessive fuel consumption
1 Fouled or incorrectly gapped sparking plugs

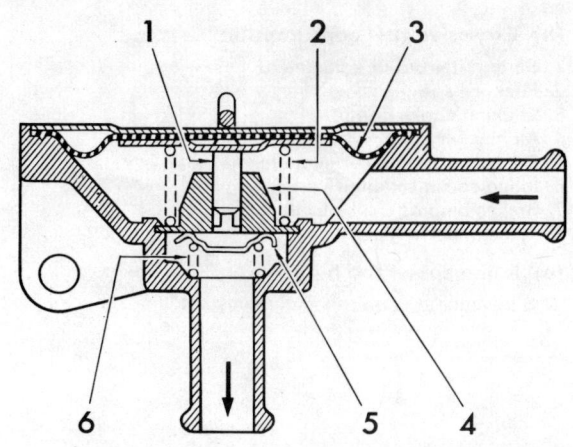

FIG 2:34 Crankcase emission control valve

Key to Fig 2:34 1 Valve pin   2 Spring   3 Diaphragm
4 Orifice plate   5 Plate valve   6 Spring

2 Dirty or incorrectly gapped contact points
3 Fuel leaks
4 Excessive engine temperature
5 Brakes binding
6 Tyres under-inflated
7 Idling speed too high
8 Car overloaded
9 Excess fuel lever operating incorrectly on metering unit
10 Incorrect PRV setting
11 Faulty metering unit
12 Blocked leak-off pipes

(d) Engine starts but does not respond to throttle
1 Faulty accelerator linkage
2 Leaking pipe connecting induction manifold to metering unit
3 Incorrect PRV setting
4 Faulty metering unit

(e) Noisy fuel pump
1 Excessive armature end float

(f) Excessive wear on control unit linkage
1 High fuel pressure

(g) Fuel or oil leaking from drive pedestal
1 Seals failed in drive pedestal

Fault diagnosis TR250

(a) Leakage or insufficient fuel delivered
1 Air vent in tank restricted
2 Fuel pipes blocked
3 Air leaks at pipe connections
4 Filter blocked
5 Pump gaskets faulty
6 Pump diaphragm defective
7 Pump valves seating badly
8 Fuel vaporizing in pipes due to heat

(b) Excessive fuel consumption

1. Carburetter out of adjustment
2. Fuel leakage
3. Sticking choke control
4. Air cleaner dirty
5. Excessive engine temperature
6. Idling speed too high
7. Brakes binding
8. Tyres under-inflated

(c) Idling speed too high

1. Slow-running controls incorrectly set
2. Rich fuel mixture
3. Carburetter controls sticking

(d) No fuel delivery

1. Float needle stuck
2. Vent in tank blocked
3. Pump diaphragm defective
4. Inlet valve in pump stuck open
5. Bad air leak on suction side of pump
6. Pipe line blocked

CHAPTER 3

THE IGNITION SYSTEM

3:1 Description
3:2 Routine maintenance
3:3 Ignition faults
3:4 Servicing the distributor

3:5 Timing the ignition
3:6 Sparking plugs
3:7 TR250
3:8 Fault diagnosis

3:1 Description

Both the TR5 and TR6 use the Lucas 22.D.6 distributor which incorporates automatic timing control by use of a centrifugal mechanism. On some later models a vacuum advance and retard unit may be fitted, but this is not used and is blanked off. A micrometer adjustment is provided to enable fine alterations to the ignition point to be made by hand. These alterations can compensate for changes in engine condition or for the use of various grades of fuel.

The centrifugally operated timing control mechanism is fitted to the distributor drive shaft immediately under the contact breaker. Two spring-loaded weights are connected by levers to the contact breaker cam. As the engine speed increases these weights are thrown outwards by centrifugal force against the action of the springs. This motion then turns the cam for the contact breaker and advances the ignition point by the amount required for the increase in engine speed.

The drive gear for the tachometer (rev counter) is incorporated in the body of the distributor.

3:2 Routine maintenance

The components of the distributor are shown in **FIG 3:3**. Release the two spring clips and lift off the distributor cap 5. Carefully pull off the rotor 1. The distributor will now appear as shown in **FIG 3:1**.

Lubrication:

Into the top of the spindle, at 1, pour a few drops of thin engine oil. There is no need to remove the screw as there is a clearance around it to provide for the passage of oil.

Put one drop only of thin engine oil onto the pivot for the moving contact point 2. Move the contact to ensure that it pivots freely and to work the oil down. Do not over-oil and wipe away any surplus.

Pour a few drops of engine oil through the gap 3 to lubricate the centrifugal timing advance mechanism.

Use the finger to smear a little Mobilgrease No. 2 or equivalent around the cam 4.

Clean the rotor on a soft piece of cloth and refit it ensuring that it is squarely seated and properly located in the slot of the spindle. Wipe out the inside of the distributor cap, and check it for cracks or other damage before refitting.

Cleaning the contact points:

Remove the distributor cap. The points assembly is shown in **FIG 3:2**. They must be free from grease or oil, and if they are burnt or blackened they should be cleaned with a fine carborundum stone or emerycloth. If the points are badly pitted they should be removed and either reground, filed or, if excessively worn, renewed.

FIG 3:1 Distributor lubrication points and contact breaker adjustment

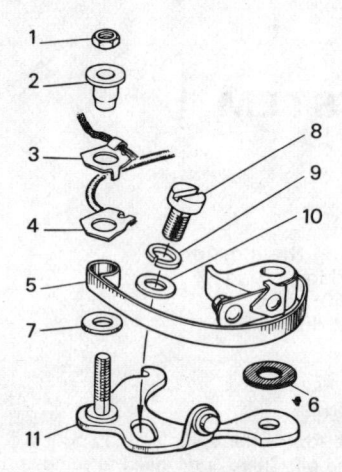

FIG 3:2 Contact points details

Key to Fig 3:2   1 Nut   2 Insulating bush
3 Low-tension wire   4 Capacitor wire   5 Moving contact
6 Large insulating washer   7 Small insulating washer
8 Lockscrew   9 Spring washer   10 Plain washer
11 Fixed contact

Take care not to remove too much material and to file the points evenly so that they meet squarely when reassembled. Check that the moving contact pivots freely. If it does not, clean the pivot with a strip of fine emerycloth and lubricate with a single drop of engine oil.

Removing and replacing contact points:

1 Remove the distributor cap and rotor arm.
2 Remove the nut 1, insulation piece 2, the low-tension terminal 3 and the capacitor terminal 4. Lift out the moving contact 5.
3 Remove the large insulating washer 6 from the pivot post and the small insulating washer 7 from the threaded post on the fixed contact.
4 Remove the screw 8, washers 9 and 10 then lift out the fixed contact 11.

5 Wipe out the interior of the distributor with a clean cloth. Clean the points. If new points are being fitted wash them in petrol to remove any preservative and wipe them dry on a clean cloth.
6 Lubricate the cam with a thin smear of grease, and the pivot post with a single drop of oil. Replace the points in the reverse order of dismantling, not forgetting the two insulating washers 6 and 7. Leave the screw 8 slightly slack and set the contact points gap as follows.

Setting the contact points gap:

Refer to **FIG 3:1**. Remove the sparking plugs and turn the engine over using the crankshaft mounted fan. If the engine is too stiff to turn by this method, jack up one rear wheel, put the car in top gear and turn the engine by rotating the rear road wheel. The points can also be adjusted with the distributor removed from the engine.

1 Slacken the securing screw 5 sufficiently to allow the fixed contact 6 to move without being free.
2 Turn the engine so that a peak of the cam is under the follower of the moving contact and the points are open.
3 Insert a screwdriver into the slot 7. By turning the screwdriver the fixed contact 6 can be adjusted. Set the points gap to .014 to .016 inch (.4 mm) using feeler gauges.
4 Tighten the securing screw 5 and check with feeler gauges that the points are still correctly set. Turn the engine over by hand and check that the points gap is still correct on the other five peaks of the cam.
5 Replace the rotor and distributor cap. Replace the sparking plugs and connect the ignition leads in their correct order.

When the points are worn and require replacement, instead of fitting the normal points, we suggest using Lucas 'Quickafit' one-piece contact sets which simplify installation. Instructions on fitting these are supplied with the kit.

3:3 Ignition faults

If the engine runs unevenly, set it to idle at a fast speed. On the TR6 this is easily done by adjusting the air valve. On the TR5 probably the best way of doing this is by pulling on the cable to the cold start cam and holding it out with a clip. **Do not use the excess fuel knob as this will also select excess fuel.**

Taking care not to touch any metal part of the sparking plug leads, pull up the insulating sleeve and short each plug in turn, using a screwdriver with an insulated handle. Connect the screwdriver blade between the plug top and the cylinder head. If shrouded cable connectors are fitted these will either have to be removed from the cable or else the same effect can be produced by pulling it off the plug while the engine is running. Shorting or cutting out a plug that is firing properly will make uneven running more pronounced. Shorting a plug in a cylinder that is not firing will make no difference.

Having located the faulty cylinder, stop the engine and remove the plug lead from the plug. Start the engine and hold the plug lead, carefully to avoid shocks, so that the metal end is about $\frac{3}{16}$ inch away from the cylinder head. A strong regular spark shows that the fault might lie with the sparking plug. Remove it and clean it according to the instructions in **Section 3:6**. Alternatively substitute a new plug. Note that a fouled plug can be caused by a fuel injector sticking open.

If the spark is weak or irregular, check that the lead is not perished or cracked. If it appears to be defective renew it and try another test. If there is no improvement, remove the distributor cap and wipe the inside clean and dry, especially in all the crannies. Clean the outside especially between the cables. Examine the cap for cracks or tracking. Tracking will show as a thin black line between the electrodes or leading to some metal part in contact with the cap. If either of these defects is present renew the cap.

Check the carbon brush (item 4 in **FIG 3:3**). It should protrude from the moulding and be free to move against the pressure of the spring. The brush is of composite construction; the ends are of soft carbon and the centre is of a resistive material to provide a measure of radio interference suppression. Renew the brush if it is defective.

Check the contact points for cleanliness and correct gap.

Testing the low-tension circuit:

Before carrying out any electrical tests, confirm that the contact breaker points are clean and correctly set. Disconnect the fuel pump from the circuit then proceed as follows:

1 Remove the distributor cap. Disconnect the thin cable from the CB terminal on the coil and connect a test lamp, or ammeter, between the cable and connector. As an alternative to this have a second operator in the car watching the ammeter on the instrument panel. Switch on the ignition and turn the engine very slowly over by hand. The lamp should light and the ammeter register a discharge when the points are closed. As the points open the light should go out and the ammeter return to zero. If the light stays off and the ammeter shows no discharge then there is a break in the circuit. The light staying on or the ammeter registering a continuous discharge indicates a shortcircuit.

2 If no current reaches the distributor check the wiring, using the Wiring Diagram in the Appendix as a guide. Either use a 0 to 20 voltmeter connected between the terminal to be checked and earth, or use a suitable 12 volt bulb similarly connected. The electrical system contains polarity sensitive parts, so make sure that all connections are properly reconnected otherwise damage to components may result.

The wiring can be checked as far as the fuse box, without any dismantling or using any instruments, as follows:

1 Turn on the headlamps. If these are bright then the battery terminal connections are sufficiently clean for power to reach the ignition circuit. Clean and remake the connections on the battery if the lights are dim, check the charge of the battery as instructed in **Chapter 11, Section 11:2**. Switch off the headlamps.

2 Switch on the ignition and use the indicator switch. If the direction indicator lights function, then the current is reaching the fuse box and the fault lies in the wiring from the fuse box or in the coil or the distributor. If the fault lies before the fuse box, check at terminals 1 and 2 on the ignition switch. If power is reaching terminal 1 but not terminal 2 with the ignition switched on, then the switch itself is faulty and will have to be renewed.

Check both terminals of the coil. If current is not passing through the coil then it is defective and will have to be renewed.

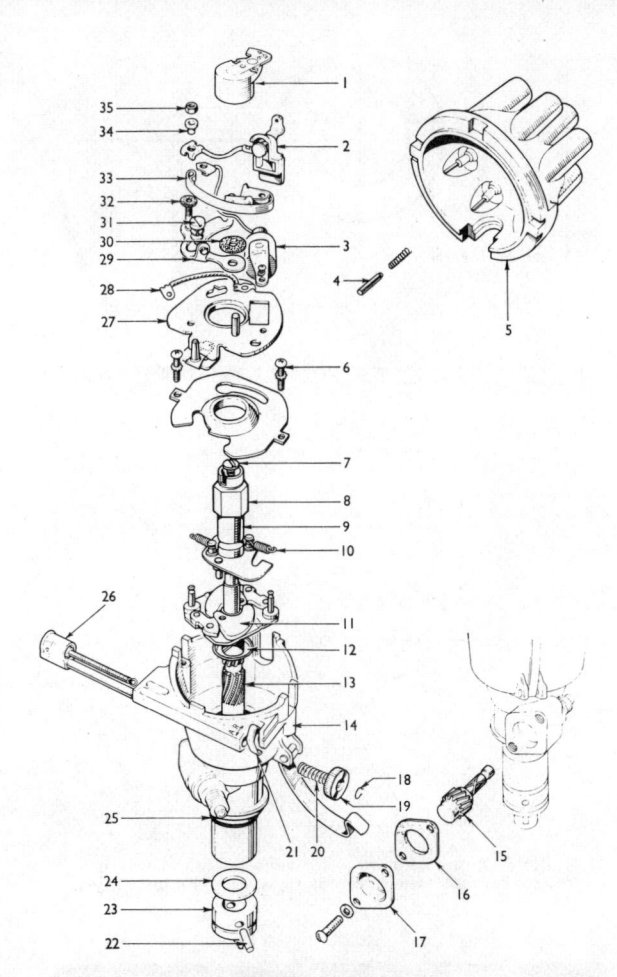

FIG 3:3 Ignition distributor details

Key to Fig 3:3 1 Rotor 2 Terminal block 3 Capacitor
4 High-tension carbon brush 5 Cover 6 Side screw
7 Cam spindle screw 8 Cam 9 Cam spindle
10 Control spring 11 Weight 12 Distance collar
13 Shaft and action plate 14 Body
15 Tachometer drive gear 16 Gasket 17 Cover
18 Circlip 19 Micrometer adjustment nut 20 Spring
21 Ratchet spring 22 Driving dog pin 23 Driving dog
24 Thrust washer 25 Rubber O-ring 26 Link carrier
27 Moving plate 28 Moving plate earth lead
29 Fixed contact 30 Large insulation washer 31 Lockscrew
32 Small insulation washer 33 Moving contact
34 Insulation piece 35 Nut

Capacitor (condenser):

Capacitor failure is most infrequent. The unit is completely sealed and utilizes metallized paper. Should the insulation break down the metal around the rupture is vaporized away by the spark and a shortcircuit is prevented. However, with the ignition switched on and voltage reaching the distributor, if no reading is shown on a voltmeter connected across the open points then the capacitor is suspect. Open circuit in the capacitor is more difficult to diagnose without special test equipment, but may be suspected when the points are either 'blued' or burned and starting is difficult. The best test available for checking

TR5/6

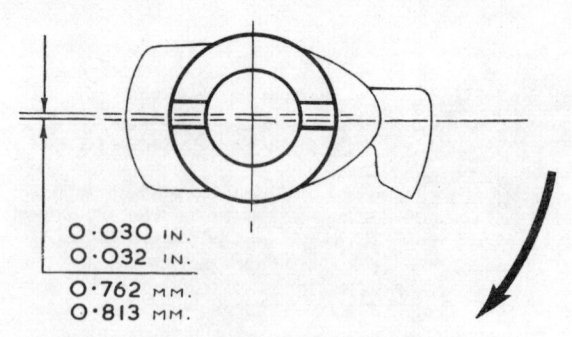

FIG 3:4 Relationship of driving dog offset tongue to rotor, view on driving dog

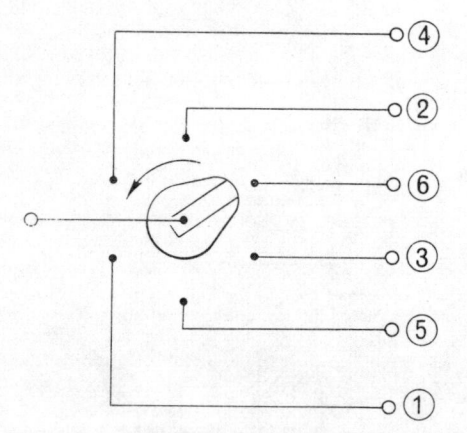

FIG 3:5 Connection of high-tension leads. Encircled numbers indicate the cylinder to which the lead goes

FIG 3:6 Setting the distributor for correct ignition timing

a faulty capacitor is by substitution with a known satisfactory one. The capacitor is held in place by one screw and the wire is fixed under the nut holding the moving contact spring.

3:4 Servicing the distributor

Removing distributor:

Remove the distributor cap. Disconnect the supply cable from the low-tension terminal. Unscrew the knurled nut holding the tachometer cable in place and withdraw the cable. Do not slacken the bolt tightening the securing clamp otherwise the ignition timing will be lost. Remove the side bolt and two washers securing the distributor clamp to the side of the drive pedestal. Withdraw the distributor upwards. A sharp upward pull may be required to free it.

Dismantling the distributor:

1 Refer to **FIG 3:3**. Remove the rotor 1. Undo the two side screws 6 and remove them, noting that the moving plate earth lead 28 is fixed under one screw. Slide out the terminal block 2. Lift off from the moving plate 27 the link from the link carrier 26. The complete contact breaker assembly can now be lifted out. The dismantling of this has been described earlier.
2 Prise off the circlip 18 and unscrew the adjustment nut 19. Pull out the link carrier 26 and remove the spring 20. The ratchet spring 21 is a push fit into the body of the distributor.
3 It is important that the tachometer drive gear is now removed before any further dismantling is carried out. Undo the two screws and pull out the cover 17, gasket 16 and the drive gear 15.
4 With a suitable punch tap out the driving dog pin 22. Remove the driving dog 23 and the thrust washer 24. Check that the shaft is undamaged and has no burrs on the end. Pull the shaft out of the body 14.
5 Remove the two control springs 10, taking great care not to stretch or distort the springs. Remove the spindle screw 7. Withdraw the cam spindle 9 and lift out the weights 11.

Reassembling the distributor:

Remove the O-ring 25 and wash all the metal parts in petrol. Examine the components and renew any that are worn. Reassemble in the reverse order of dismantling, but paying attention to the following points:
1 Lightly lubricate all bearing surfaces with clean engine oil.
2 Refit the cam spindle 9 so that the driving dog 23 offset tongue will be positioned relative to the rotor as shown in **FIG 3:4**. This is most important otherwise the timing will be 180 deg. out when the distributor is refitted.
3 Refit the shaft 13 complete with advance and retard mechanism before refitting the tachometer drive gear 15, 16 and 17.
4 Reset the contact points gap with the distributor still removed from the car as it is an easier operation than when fitted.

Refitting the distributor:

Fit a new O-ring 25 to the distributor before inserting

46

the distributor into the drive pedestal. Turn the rotor so that the offset tongue on the driving dog engages in the slot of the driving gear as the distributor is pushed home. Secure it in place with the single bolt and its two washers. Reconnect the tachometer drive cable. Fit the low-tension cable back onto the terminal on the side of the distributor. Replace the distributor cap. If the high-tension cables have been removed, replace them in the order shown in **FIG 3:5**. Provided the distributor clamp bolt has not been loosened the ignition timing will still be correct when the micrometer adjustor is reset to its original mark. If the timing has been lost refer to the next Section for details of resetting it.

3:5 Timing the ignition

1 Remove the sparking plugs and turn the engine over by hand until the 11 deg. BTDC mark on the crankshaft pulley is aligned with the pointer on the timing cover with No. 1 cylinder on the compression stroke. The engine can be turned over either by the cooling fan or by a jacked up rear wheel. As the timing mark approaches the pointer place the ball of the thumb over the plug hole on No. 1 cylinder. If no build up of pressure is felt then the piston is not on the compression stroke and the engine will have to be turned a complete revolution more.

2 The distributor and rotor should now be in approximately the positions shown in **FIG 3:6**. If they are not then check that the drive gear is correctly meshed as described in **Chapter 1, Section 1:6**, and that the distributor cam spindle has not been reassembled 180 deg. out.

3 Ensure that the contact breaker points are correctly set at .015 inch. Slacken the clamp bracket pinch bolt and turn the distributor in a clockwise direction from the position shown in **FIG 3:6** until the contact points are seen to just open. This point can be more accurately determined by connecting a low wattage 12 volt bulb in parallel with the points. One terminal of the bulb should be connected to earth and the other to the low-tension terminal on the distributor. The bulb will light as the points open, when the ignition is switched on.

4 Hold the distributor body at the point where the contact points are just opening and tighten the pinch bolt on the clamp. Replace the distributor cap, refit the sparking plugs and the ignition timing is set at the basic setting.

Manual adjustment:

Small variations on the basic setting are accomplished by turning the adjustment nut 19 (see **FIG 3:3**). A scale is marked on the link carrier 26 but the ratchet spring 21 will allow lesser adjustments to be made. Turning the nut anticlockwise, in the direction of the arrow A marked on the body, will advance the ignition. Turning the nut the other way retards the ignition point.

3:6 Sparking plugs

Inspect, clean and adjust the sparking plugs at regular intervals. The inspection of the deposits on the electrodes is particularly useful because the type and colour of the deposit gives a clue to the conditions inside the combustion chamber, and is therefore most helpful when tuning.

Remove the plugs by loosening each one a couple of turns and then blowing away loose dirt with compressed air or a tyre pump. Store the plugs in the order of removal. Examine the copper gaskets and provided they are still more than half their original thickness they may be used again.

Examine the firing end of the plug to note the type of deposit. Normally, it should be powdery and should range from brown to greyish tan in colour. There will also be slight wear of the electrodes, and the general effect is one which comes from mixed periods of high and low-speed driving. Cleaning and resetting the gap is all that is required. If the deposits are white or yellowish they indicate long periods of constant-speed driving or much low-speed city driving. Again the treatment is straightforward.

Black wet deposits are caused by oil entering the combustion chamber past worn rings, pistons or down worn valve guides. Sparking plugs which run hotter may help to alleviate the problem, but the only cure is an engine overhaul.

Dry black fluffy deposits are usually the result of running with a rich mixture. Incomplete combustion may also cause this and might be traced to defective ignition, excessive idling or a stuck open injector.

Overheated plugs have a white blistered look about the centre electrode and the side electrode may be badly eroded. This may be caused by poor cooling, wrongly set ignition or sustained high speeds with heavy loads.

Have the sparking plugs cleaned on an abrasive blasting machine and tested under pressure after attention to the electrodes. File these until they are clean, bright and parallel. Set the electrode gap to .025 inch (.635 mm). **Do not try to bend the central electrode.**

Before replacing the plugs clean the threads with a wire brush. If it is found that the plugs cannot be screwed in by hand, run a tap down the threads in the cylinder head. Failing a tap use an old sparking plug with a cross-cut down the threads. Screw the plugs in by hand finally tightening with a torque spanner to a setting of 30 lb ft. If a torque wrench is not available, tighten with a normal box spanner through half a turn.

Sparking plug leads:

New leads can be obtained already cut to length and with the correct end fixings in place. The leads should be of the resistive type which provides radio interference suppression. Check the leads for perishing or cracking and renew them when required. Use silicone grease to waterproof the ends of the cables in their fittings. They are connected in the order shown in **FIG 3:4**.

3:7 TR250

The distributor fitted to cars intended for the American market is similar to those which have been described but is provided with two single vacuum capsules, each operating in a different direction to advance or to retard the ignition. The directional control of these capsules is determined by the position of the vacuum valve which is operated by the accelerator linkage and shown in **FIG 2:30**.

Adjustment is made by turning the body of the distributor. No separate vernier adjustment is provided on these cars.

In addition to the normal lubrication requirements given in **Section 3:2** and adjustment of the contact

FIG 3:7 Timing marks

breaker points, at 12,000 miles the ignition timing at idling speed should also be checked.

Ignition timing marks:

FIG 3:7 shows how the crankshaft pulley is marked in degrees before and after TDC. A white line painted on the idling timing mark will assist in stroboscopic timing. The relevant timing details are given in the table below:

Idle speed	800 to 850 rev/min
Ignition static	10 deg. BTDC
Ignition at idle	4 deg. ATDC
C.O. at idle (warm engine)	2.5 to 3.5 per cent
Equivalent air/fuel ratio	13.5:1

Ignition timing:

The static method of timing given in **Section 3:5** does not give the degree of accuracy required for the correct functioning of the emission control system and the method employing a stroboscopic lamp must be used after the former method has been used as a preliminary to starting the engine.

Identify the idling mark (4 deg. ATDC) with white paint on the crankshaft pulley, and connect a stroboscopic timing lamp and tachometer as instructed by the instrument makers.

Run the engine up to working temperature and adjust the speed to 800/850 rev/min.

Slacken the distributor clamping plate bolt and rotate the distributor body until the idling mark appears stationary against the timing pointer in the stroboscopic beam. It may be necessary to adjust the throttle stop screws to maintain the correct idling speed.

Tighten the clamping bolt and recheck the timing.

Do not carry out this operation with the air cleaner removed.

Attention is drawn to the following CAUTION:
US Federal Standards.
Control of air pollution.

Unauthorized interference with, or adjustments to, the ignition distributor must not be made, as if made, would almost certainly result in the vehicle failing to meet the legal requirements in respect of air pollution.

3:8 Fault diagnosis

(a) Engine will not fire

1. Battery discharged
2. Distributor points dirty, pitted or maladjusted
3. Distributor cap dirty, cracked or 'tracking'
4. Carbon brush inside cap not touching rotor
5. Faulty cable or loose connections in low-tension circuit
6. Distributor rotor arm cracked, or left out when reassembling
7. Faulty coil
8. High-tension coil lead cracked or perished
9. Broken contact breaker spring
10. Contact points stuck open
11. Internal shortcircuit in capacitor

(b) Engine misfires

1. Check 2, 3, 5, 7 and 8 in (a)
2. Weak contact breaker spring
3. High-tension plug leads cracked or perished
4. Sparking plug(s) loose
5. Sparking plug insulation cracked
6. Sparking plug gap incorrectly set
7. Ignition timing too far advanced

CHAPTER 4

THE COOLING SYSTEM

4:1 Description
4:2 Routine maintenance
4:3 The radiator
4:4 Adjusting the fan belt

4:5 The thermostat
4:6 The water pump
4:7 Frost precautions
4:8 Fault diagnosis

4:1 Description

Both the TR5 and TR6 have a pressurized cooling system. The natural thermo-syphon action of the water is augmented by a centrifugal impeller-type pump, driven by a belt from the crankshaft. The impeller draws water from the bottom tank of the radiator and passes it through the cylinder block. From here it rises into the cylinder head until it reaches a thermostat valve which prevents cold water from reaching the top tank of the radiator. The water is then returned directly to the water pump by a bypass hose and recirculated through the engine until it is hot enough to open the thermostat valve, thus giving a quick warm-up. The hot water in the top tank of the radiator falls through the finned core, where it is cooled.

The radiator is cooled by the air passing over the fins. At speed this motion is caused by the movement of the car. To assist the airflow at low speeds an eight-bladed 12.5 inch diameter fan is fitted to the front of the crankshaft. A pulley at the back of this fan carries the belt which drives the water pump and alternator.

A filler cap is fitted to the top tank of the radiator. This cap incorporates two valves. A pressure valve 4 (see **FIG 4:1**) limits the internal pressure of the cooling system to 4 lb/sq in. As the system cools and the pressure drops the vacuum valve 5 will prevent the system dropping below atmospheric pressure. Any coolant passing the pressure valve 4 will pass through the outlet pipe 3 and from there into an overflow bottle (item 4 **FIG 4:2**). As the system cools the overflow will be drawn back into the radiator ensuring that there will be no loss of coolant.

The filler cap also has a safety feature in that the first movement of removing the cap only releases the internal pressure without freeing the cap. **If the cooling system boils, do not immediately remove or slacken the filler cap.** The reduction of pressure will cause the water to boil faster and the resultant steam will force scalding water out of the filler neck. Leave the car to cool down then use rags wrapped around the hand when undoing the filler cap.

4:2 Routine maintenance

At periodic intervals remove the grease plug 25 from the water pump and inject a little clean grease into the pump.

At the beginning of winter the thermostat should be

TR5/6

49

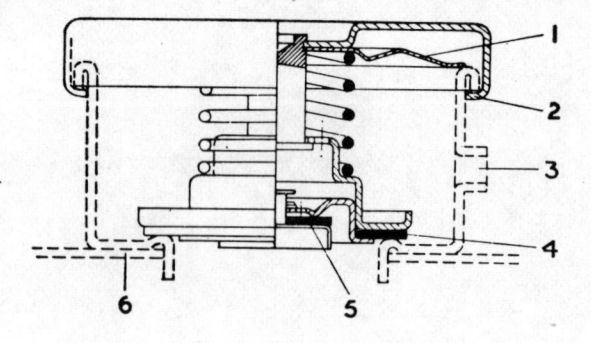

FIG 4:1 Section through radiator filler cap

Key to Fig 4:1   1 Spring friction plate   2 Retaining lugs
3 Pressure release pipe   4 Pressure valve   5 Vacuum valve
6 Header tank

changed to a winter grade, and then changed back to a summer grade at the end of winter. Antifreeze may be left in the system the whole year round, as it contains corrosion inhibitors, and may be used for up to two years. If the antifreeze is not left in the system it can be added or drained at the same time as changing the thermostat.

Periodically drain the cooling system and flush it through, either with a proprietary compound, or with clean water. Drain antifreeze and water into a clean container so that it may be reused.

Draining:

Remove the filler cap and set the heater to hot. The radiator drain tap is item 7 in **FIG 4:2**. The other drain tap is situated on the righthand side of the block at the rear, rear of the exhaust manifold pipes. Open the taps and let the water drain out.

Flushing:

If a proprietary compound is used follow the instructions on the tin. Before flushing with water drain the system as previously described and if possible remove the drain taps to give an unobstructed flow to the water. Insert a hosepipe into the filler neck on the radiator and run water through until it comes out clear from the drain holes. It helps to remove sediment if adaptors are made up to fit the hosepipe directly to the drain tap holes and water is flushed through these, letting it overflow from the filler. If the radiator is blocked, remove it, turn it upside down and let water flush through in a reverse direction.

Replace the drain taps and make sure they are closed before refilling the system.

Filling:

Make sure the drain taps are closed and set the heater to hot. Fill the system through the radiator filler with soft clean water. Refit the filler cap and run the engine till it reaches normal working temperature. Replenish the water level if required.

4:3 The radiator

The radiator assembly is shown in **FIG 4:2**. Some cars may not have the side valance sheets 2 and 13 fitted. Remove the radiator as follows:
1 Drain the cooling system. If fitted unclip the side valance sheets 2 and 13.
2 Disconnect the top and bottom hoses 3 and 8 from the radiator as well as the overflow pipe 9.
3 Undo the nuts 12 and remove the washers with them. Remove nuts 17 and bolts 16 so that the stays 11 and rubber washers 10 can be removed.
4 Undo the two bolts 15 and lift the radiator out of the car.

Replacing the radiator is the reversal of the removal procedure.

4:4 Adjusting the fan belt

Slacken the long pivot bolt and nut underneath the alternator. Slacken the pinchbolt and nut holding the alternator to the adjusting link. Pull the top of the alternator away from the block, pivoting it around the pivot bolt, until the fan belt has ¾ to 1 inch (19 to 25mm) sideways play in its longest run (between the water pump pulley and the crankshaft pulley). Hold the alternator in position and tighten the pinchbolt on the adjusting link and then the pivot bolt. Do not overtension the belt as this will cause damage to the alternator bearings.

To pull the alternator out against the fan belt, a lever may be needed. **Use only a wooden lever (such as a hammer handle) and lever only on the driving end bracket of the alternator otherwise damage may be caused to the alternator.**

To remove the fan belt slacken the two bolts as before but push the alternator firmly towards the engine block to slacken the fan belt. It may be necessary to slacken the bolt holding the inner end of the adjusting link to allow this to pivot. Lift the fan belt off the alternator pulley, then off the pump pulley and finally free it from the engine by working it over each fan blade.

4:5 The thermostat

A wax-type thermostat 6 (see **FIG 4:3**) is incorporated in the water pump body 8.

Before removing the thermostat partially drain the cooling system so that the coolant level is below the thermostat. Remove the short bolt 1 and the longer bolt 4. Raise up the cover 2, still attached to its hose, lift off the paper gasket 3 and withdraw the thermostat 6.

The thermostat can be tested by suspending it in water. Raise the temperature of the water and check, with a thermometer, the temperature at which the thermostat valve starts to open. A summer grade thermostat should start opening at 82°C. and a winter grade one at 88°C. If the valve does not start to open at the correct temperature or sticks in the open position then renew the thermostat. It is impossible to repair a defective thermostat.

Replace the thermostat in the reverse order of dismantling. Clean out all sediment and dirt from the housing and fit the thermostat before the paper gasket. Use a new paper gasket and either a little grease or non-setting jointing compound so as to prevent leaks.

50

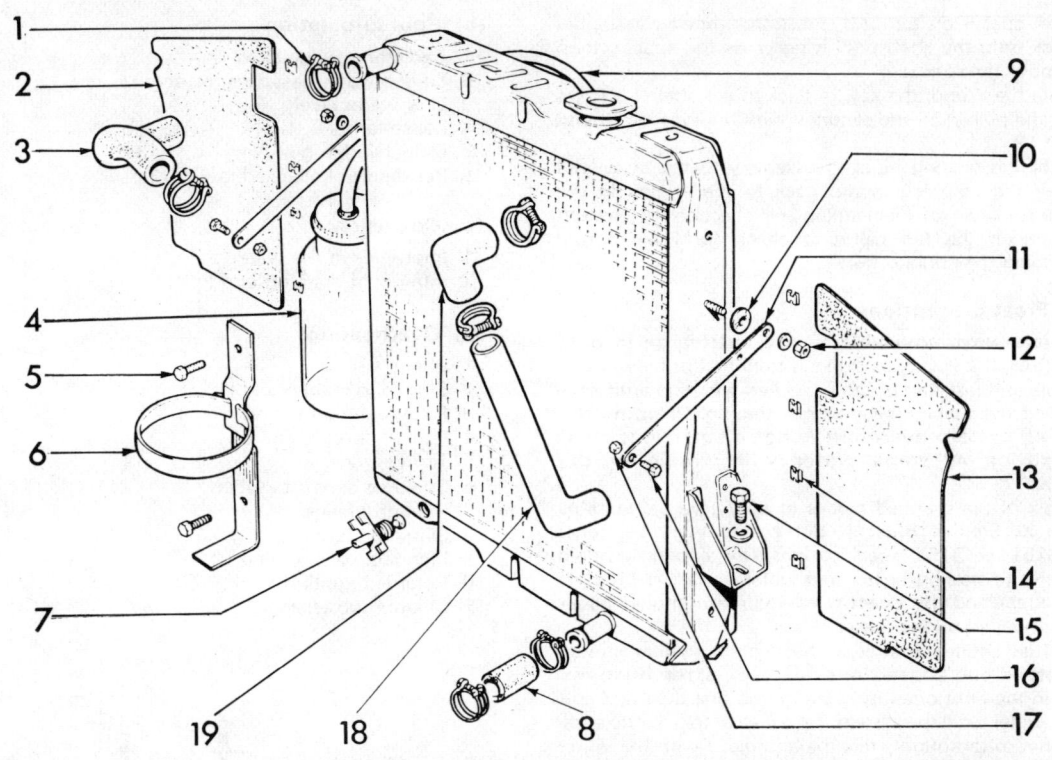

FIG 4:2 Radiator details

Key to Fig 4:2 1 Wire clip 2 Side valance sheet 3 Top hose 4 Overflow bottle 5 Setscrew 6 Bracket
7 Drain tap 8 Bottom hose 9 Overflow pipe 10 Rubber washer 11 Securing strap 12 Nut 13 Side valance sheet
14 Clip 15 Bolt 16 Bolt 17 Nut 18 Connecting pipe 19 Inlet hose

4:6 The water pump

An exploded view of the water pump and associated parts is shown in **FIG 4:3**.

Removing the water pump:

Drain the cooling system, remove the bolt 28 which secures the pump and holds the alternator adjusting stay as this will make it easier to remove the fan belt.

If the whole pump is to be removed disconnect the radiator top hose from the thermostat cover 2 and the bottom radiator hose from the pump body 8. Disconnect the connector from the temperature transmitter 5. Remove the remaining two securing bolts 26 and 27 and the pump can now be withdrawn, with the paper gasket 7, from the engine.

For servicing purposes the bearing housing assembly can be removed separately leaving the body 8 still attached to the engine. Drain the cooling system and remove the fan belt as before. Undo the three sets of nuts and washers on the studs 10 and withdraw the bearing housing assembly.

Dismantling the bearing housing assembly:

1 Unscrew the nut 19 and remove the washer 20 then pull off the pulley 21.

2 Take off the circlip 22. Mount the housing in a press and press the shaft 14 through the impeller 9 towards the pulley end of the housing. Lift out the impeller 9 and free the seal 11 from it.

3 The shaft 14 will now be free of the housing. Remove the Woodruffe key 24 then the bearings 18 and the spacer 17. Remove the washer 16, circlip 23 and finally the spinner 15.

Reassembling the bearing housing assembly:

1 Wash all the metal parts in petrol and examine them for wear. Renew any that are worn, especially the seal 11 if there has been any water leakage from the pump. The sealing face on the housing 13 can be lightly refaced if it is scored. Fit new gaskets 3, 7 and 12 if the pump has been completely dismantled, otherwise renew gaskets as required.

2 Fit the spinner 15, circlip 23 and washer 16 to the shaft 14. Pack the ballraces 8 with grease and refit them with the spacer 17 between them to the shaft 14. The bearings 18 should be fitted so that their sealing faces are outwards. Fit the shaft assembly back into the housing and secure it with the circlip 22.

3 Fit the seal 11 back into the impeller 9. Mount the bearing housing in a press and lay a .030 inch (.762

TR5/6

mm) spacer on top of it. Press the impeller assembly back onto the shaft until it just nips the spacer, then remove the spacer.
4 Refit the Woodruffe key 24 back to the shaft 14. Press on the pulley 21 and secure it with the washer 20 and nut 19.
5 Refit the bearing housing assembly to the body and then the complete pump back to the engine in the reverse order of dismantling. Fill the cooling system, retension the fan belt and check for leaks before running the engine.

4:7 Frost precautions

It is always advisable to use antifreeze in cold weather. If it is very cold the bottom half of the radiator is liable to freeze and become blocked when no antifreeze is added, even when the engine is running. **Draining the cooling system overnight is not a sufficient frost precaution as some water will remain in the heater.**

Most of the branded names of antifreeze are suitable (such as Smith's Bluecol) but ensure that they meet BSI.3151 or 3152 specification. The cooling system capacity (including heater and water bottle) is 11 pints (6.2 litres) and the quantity of antifreeze should be as recommended by the maker.

Before adding antifreeze the cooling system should be flushed out. **Close the drain taps after flushing.** Pour in the right quantity of antifreeze first then add soft clean water to fill the system. Take the car for a sufficiently long run to thoroughly mix the antifreeze with the water before letting the car stand in cold weather.

If topping up is required, use a mixture of antifreeze and water to prevent dilution of the antifreeze already in the system.

4:8 Fault diagnosis

(a) Internal water leakage

1 Cracked cylinder wall
2 Loose cylinder head nuts
3 Cracked cylinder head
4 Faulty head gasket

(b) Poor circulation

1 Radiator core blocked
2 Engine water passages restricted
3 Low water level
4 Loose fan belt
5 Defective fan belt
6 Perished or collapsed radiator hoses

(c) Corrosion

1 Impurities in the water
2 Infrequent draining and flushing

(d) Overheating

1 Check (b)
2 Sludge in crankcase
3 Faulty ignition timing
4 Low oil level in sump
5 Tight engine
6 Chocked exhaust system
7 Binding brakes
8 Slipping clutch
9 Incorrect valve timing
10 Retarded ignition
11 Mixture too weak

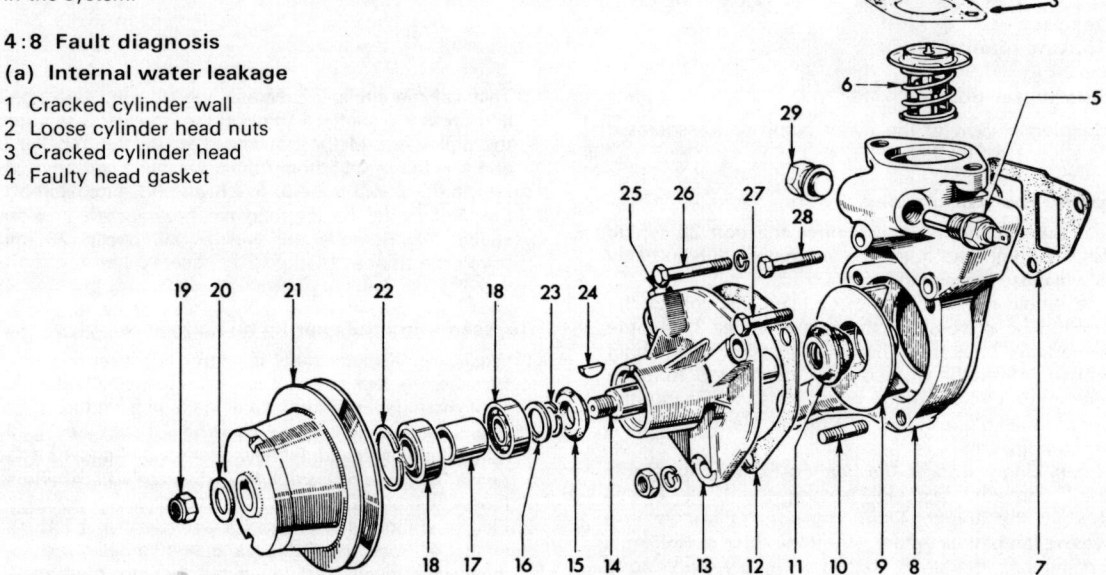

FIG 4:3 Water pump and thermostat details

Key to Fig 4:3 1 Bolt 2 Elbow 3 Gasket 4 Bolt 5 Temperature transmitter 6 Thermostat 7 Gasket
8 Body 9 Impeller 10 Stud 11 Seal 12 Gasket 13 Bearing housing 14 Spindle 15 Spinner
16 Washer 17 Spacer 18 Ballrace 19 Nut 20 Washer 21 Pulley 22 Circlip 23 Circlip
24 Woodruffe key 25 Grease plug 26 Bolt 27 Bolt 28 Bolt 29 Blanking plug

CHAPTER 5

THE CLUTCH

5:1 Description
5:2 Routine maintenance
5:3 Servicing the master cylinder
5:4 Servicing the slave cylinder

5:5 Bleeding the clutch hydraulic system
5:6 Servicing the clutch
5:7 The clutch release mechanism
5:8 Fault diagnosis

5:1 Description

The clutch has a single-plate dry disc operating on the outer face of the flywheel. An exploded view of the components is shown in **FIG 5:1**. The coverplate 7 and the driving plate 3 are securely bolted to the flywheel and rotate with it. The pressure plate 2 is free to slide axially but is rotated by the lugs fitting into the slots in the driving plate 3. When the clutch is engaged the pressure of the diaphragm spring 5 thrusts the pressure plate 2 forwards firmly gripping, by its friction surfaces, the driven plate 1 between the face of the flywheel and the face of the pressure plate. The driven plate 1 is thus made to rotate with the flywheel and so takes the drive to the gearbox through the input shaft which is splined to the centre of the driven plate.

To release the clutch a bearing presses in the centre of the fingers on the diaphragm spring 5 and by lever action draws the driving plate 2 slightly rearwards to release the drivenplate 1. The drivenplate and gearbox input shaft are then free to revolve, or come to a stop, without transmitting any drive even though the flywheel continues to turn.

The clutch release mechanism is shown in **FIG 5:2**.

Note that grease nipple 6 and fibre washer 7 are omitted from both the TR5 and TR6. The lever on the cross shaft 8 is connected to the clutch slave cylinder which is in turn hydraulically connected to the clutch pedal. As the slave cylinder extends it moves the lever so that the shaft 8 rotates. The fork 5 turns with the shaft and, by means of the pegs engaging in the annular slot of the sleeve 2, the sleeve and bearing 1 are slid forward to contact the fingers on the diaphragm spring.

5:2 Routine maintenance

1 At regular intervals check the fluid level in the clutch master cylinder reservoir. Wipe the top clean before removing the cap to ensure that no dirt falls into the reservoir. If necessary top up the level to the step inside the reservoir with Girling Brake and Clutch Fluid to SAE.70.R3 specification. Never use anything but the recommended fluid. There should be very little loss of fluid and regular topping up indicates a leak in the system which must be rectified.

2 Lubricate the single nipple (see **FIG 5:2**) with a hand grease gun. After 5000 miles 2 strokes of the gun will provide adequate lubrication. Do not overlubricate

otherwise the grease may reach the friction linings on the driven plate.

3 Every 36,000 miles completely strip the clutch hydraulic system and renew parts as required. Fit all new seals and fill the system with new hydraulic fluid.

5:3 Servicing the master cylinder

A sectioned view of the clutch master cylinder is shown in **FIG 5:3**. The clutch pedal is connected directly to the pushrod 9, so that when the pedal is pressed the pushrod moves the plunger assembly down

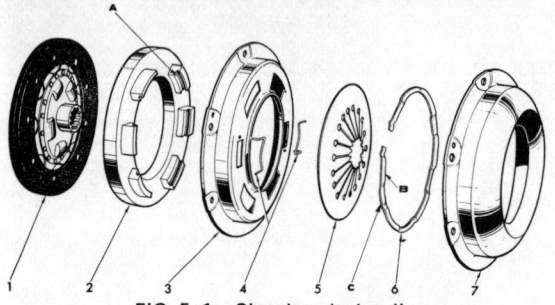

FIG 5:1 Clutch unit details

Key to Fig 5:1   1 Driven plate   2 Pressure plate
3 Driving plate   4 Spring clips   5 Diaphragm spring
6 Circlip   7 Cover pressing

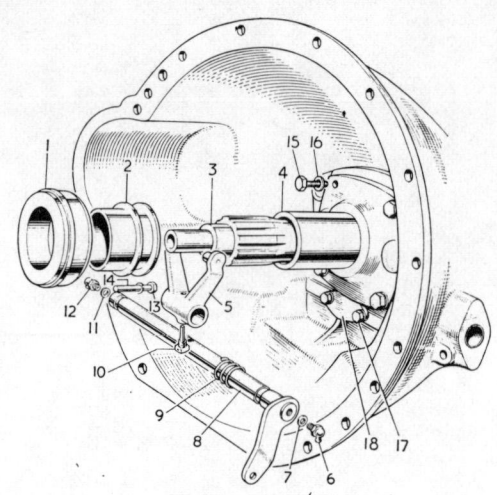

Maximum stroke available—
1·38″ (35·05 mm.).

Stroke position at maximum cut off—
0·099″ (2·5 mm.).

FIG 5:2 Clutch release mechanism

Key to Fig 5:2   1 Release bearing   2 Sleeve
3 Input shaft   4 Front cover   5 Fork   6 Grease nipple (omitted)   7 Fibre washer (omitted)   8 Cross-shaft
9 Anti-rattle spring   10 Screwed taper pin   11 Fibre washer
12 Grease nipple   13 Cross-shaft locating bolt   14 Spring washer   15 Wedglok bolts   16 Washers   17 Bolts
18 Plate

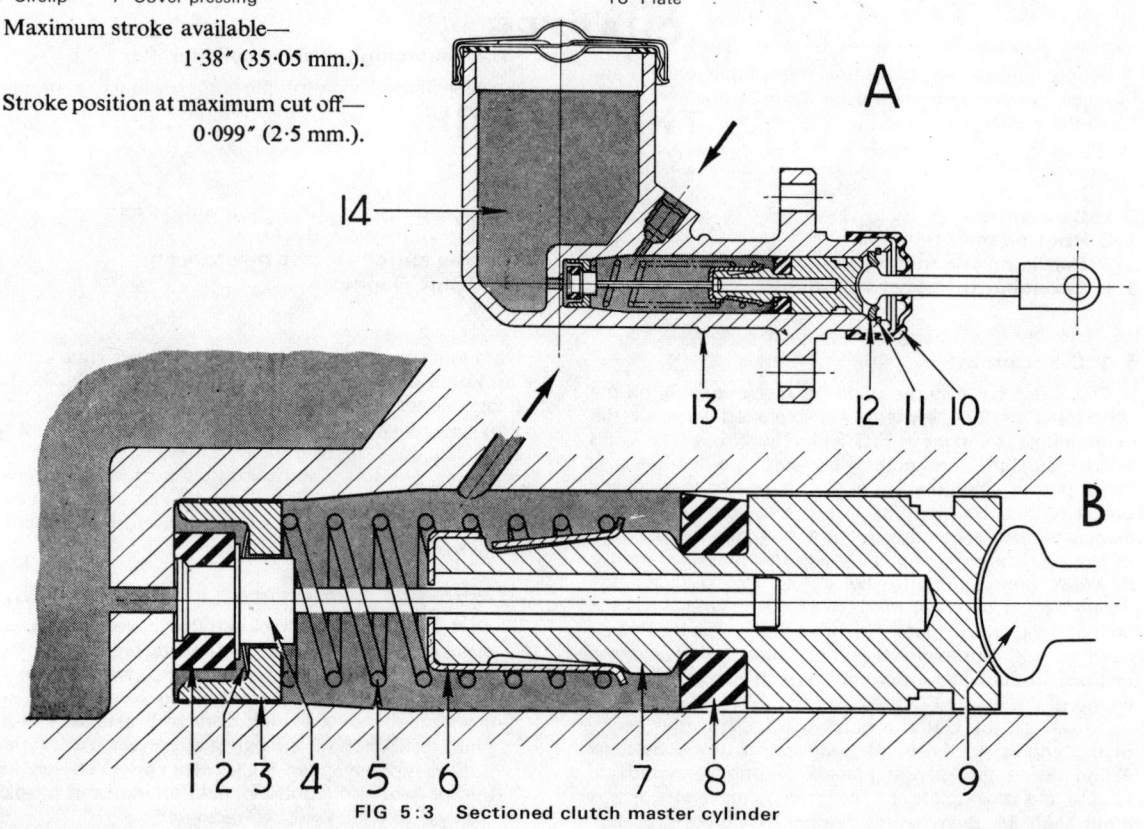

FIG 5:3 Sectioned clutch master cylinder

Key to Fig 5:3   1 Valve seal   2 Spring (valve seal)   10 Dust covers   11 Circlip   12 Pushrod stop
3 Distance piece   4 Valve shank   5 Plunger return spring   13 Identification ring   14 Fluid reservoir
6 Spring retainer   7 Plunger   8 Plunger seal   9 Pushrod

54

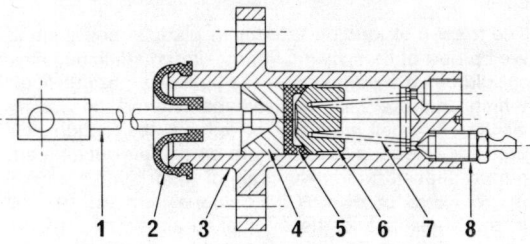

FIG 5:4 Sectioned clutch slave cylinder

Key to Fig 5:4 1 Pushrod 2 Dust cover 3 Body 4 Piston 5 Seal 6 Filler block 7 Spring 8 Bleed nipple

the bore of the cylinder. Fluid in front of the plunger will be forced out of the outlet in the side of the bore, along the pipes, and will then operate the clutch slave cylinder. Fluid leakage past the plunger 7 is prevented by the cup seal 8. When the clutch pedal is released the return spring 5 pushes the plunger 7 back out of the bore allowing the fluid from the slave cylinder to return. As the plunger reaches the end of its return stroke the head of the valve shank 4 catches in the spring retainer 6 and opens the valve 1 against the pull of the spring 2. This opens the interconnection between the reservoir and the cylinder allowing any fluid losses to be replenished. As soon as the plunger starts moving inwards this interconnection is closed and all the fluid passes to the slave cylinder.

Removing and replacing the master cylinder:

1 Working inside the car, remove the splitpin, washer and clevis pin securing the master cylinder pushrod to the clutch pedal.
2 Either drain the hydraulic system by pumping the fluid out through the bleed nipple on the slave cylinder, or use rags and blanks to prevent fluid spilling on the paintwork. Disconnect the pipe from the outlet on the master cylinder.
3 Remove the two bolts and washers holding the master cylinder to the bulkhead and withdraw the master cylinder.
4 Refitting the master cylinder is the reversal of the removal procedure. Fill the reservoir and bleed the system (see **Section 5:5**).

Dismantling the master cylinder:

1 Pull back the rubber dust cover 10. Press in the push-rod 9 to relieve the pressure of the return spring 6 on the circlip 11. With a pair of long-nosed pliers remove the circlip, and then pull out the pushrod 9 complete with circlip 11, dust cover 10 and the pushrod stop 12.
2 Shake out the internal parts, or if they are stiff to remove apply gentle air pressure to the outlet and carefully blow the parts out. Use a thin screwdriver to lift the leaf on the spring retainer 6 above the level of the shoulder on the plunger 7 and withdraw the retainer from the plunger. Use the fingers only to remove the seal 8 from the plunger 7.
3 Remove the spring retainer 6 from the valve shank 4 by passing the shank through the offset hole in the retainer. Remove the spring 5, distance piece 3 and spring 2 from the valve shank. Use the fingers only to remove the seal 1.

Reassembling the master cylinder:

1 It is advisable to discard all the rubber seals and to fit new ones, which are available in kits. Clean the metal parts, preferably with either brake fluid or methylated spirits. If any other solvent is used take great care not to allow it on the rubber seals and make sure the metal parts are completely dry before reassembling them. Examine the bore of the cylinder; it should be smooth and polished, free from corrosion or pitting. If the bore is defective then the whole assembly must be renewed.
2 Ensure absolute cleanliness. Before assembling the parts dip them in clean brake fluid and fit them wet. Use the fingers and fit seals 8 and 1 to the plunger 7 and valve shank 4. Work the seals about in their recesses so that they seat properly, and make sure they are fitted so that the lips face into the bore of the cylinder.
3 Refit the parts 2, 3 and 5 back to the valve shank 4 then insert the end of the shank through the offset hole in the spring retainer 6. Press the retainer 6 back onto the plunger 7 until the leaf seats behind the shoulder on the plunger.
4 Carefully insert the front end of the whole assembly into the bore. Taking great care, further enter the assembly into the bore so that the seal 8 enters, without damaging it or turning back the lips.
5 Use the pushrod 9 to move the plunger assembly down the bore and refit the stop 12, circlip 11 and dust cover 10. Push the plunger right down the bore and check that it is returned by the action of the return spring 5.

5:4 Servicing the slave cylinder

A sectioned view of the slave cylinder is shown in **FIG 5:4**.

Removing and replacing the slave cylinder:

1 Drain the clutch hydraulic system through the bleed nipple on the slave cylinder.
2 Remove the stay, nut and bolts holding the slave cylinder to the bracket on the bellhousing. Lift off the rubber dust cover 2 and pull the slave cylinder forward to clear it from the pushrod 1, leaving the pushrod still attached to the lever on the operating shaft.
3 Hold the hose union with a spanner and rotate the slave cylinder to unscrew it. Do not twist the hose.
4 Replace the slave cylinder in the reverse order of dismantling, without twisting the flexible hose. Refill and bleed the system.

Dismantling the slave cylinder:

Use low pressure air through the inlet port to eject the internal parts of the slave cylinder. Examine the bore of the cylinder and if it is pitted or scored the whole assembly will have to be renewed. As a precaution against leaks always renew the seal 5 after dismantling the cylinder.

Reassembling:

Lubricate the bore with clean hydraulic fluid. Insert the spring 7 into the filler block 6 and refit them into the cylinder bore. Very carefully enter the seal 5, lips first, into the bore taking great care not to damage or turn back the lips. Insert the piston 4, flat face first, into the bore and the cylinder is ready for refitting to the car. Fit it with the bleed nipple 8 uppermost.

5:5 Bleeding the clutch hydraulic system

Bleeding is always necessary after the system has

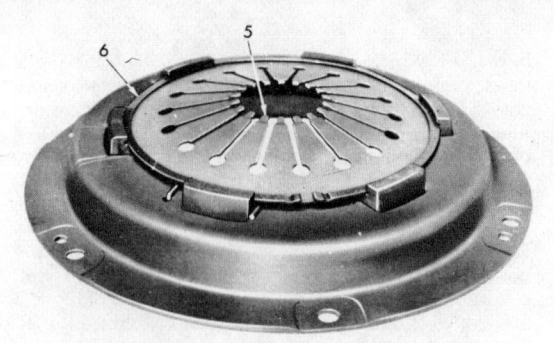

FIG 5:5 Clutch with cover removed

been dismantled or if the level in the reservoir has fallen so low as to allow air into the master cylinder. Discard fluid that has been bled from the system, unless it is very clean. If the fluid drained or bled from the system is absolutely clean let it stand in a sealed clean container for 24 hours to de-aerate before using it again.

Before bleeding fill the master cylinder reservoir right up to the top. Fluid will be used throughout the operation so keep the reservoir constantly topped up, otherwise if the level falls to low air will enter the system, necessitating a fresh start. Attach a length of plastic or rubber hose to the bleed nipple 8 in **FIG 5:4** and immerse the free end of the hose in a little clean hydraulic fluid in a clean glass container. A second operator is required to pump the clutch pedal. Undo the bleed nipple $\frac{3}{4}$ of a turn and have the clutch pedal pressed down through its full stroke. Tighten the bleed nipple and then allow the clutch pedal to return. At first air bubbles will emerge from the submerged end of the tube. When clear fluid free from air bubbles is delivered into the container close the bleed nipple on a downstroke of the clutch pedal. Remove the hose and top up the reservoir to the correct level.

5:6 Servicing the clutch

The clutch uses a diaphragm spring and is of simple construction. Normally a fault in the clutch is best rectified by fitting an exchange unit. The clutch can be removed with the engine still in the car. First remove the gearbox (see **Chapter 6, Section 6:2**). The clutch is removed by progressively slackening the ring of securing bolts. When refitting the clutch it is essential that the driven plate is centralized before fully tightening the securing bolts. Use a mandrel through the centre splines of the driven plate and in the bush of the crankshaft to locate the driven plate.

Dismantling:

1 Lay the clutch down on a flat surface. Remove the cover 7 and the clutch will then appear as shown in **FIG 5:5**. Mark the parts so that they will be reassembled in the same positions as before dismantling and ensure that the unit still remains in balance.
2 Remove the circlip 6 and lift out the diaphragm spring 5. Remove the two spring clips 4 and the driving plate 3 can be lifted off the pressure plate 2.
3 Wash all the metal parts in petrol or paraffin and examine them for wear, including the working face of the flywheel. Renew parts as required. If the flywheel is slightly scored it can be removed and skimmed down in a lathe. Do not allow any solvents onto the friction linings of the driven plate 1 and make sure all parts are dry before reassembly.

4 The friction linings on the driven plate 2 should stand well proud of their rivets. For maximum efficiency they should be light coloured with a polished glaze through which the grain of the material should be clearly visible. A small quantity of oil on the clutch will produce smearing, whilst more oil will produce a dark glazed deposit hiding the grain of the friction material. A great deal of oil will be obvious from the free oil in the housing and the oil soaked appearance of the friction linings. The source of the oil leak must be found and rectified before fitting a new clutch or refitting the old one if the oil leak is very minor. The driven plate assembly should feel solid with no loose rivets, and the cushioning springs should be free from play.

Reassembling:

Reassembly is the reversal of the dismantling process but note the following points.
1 Assemble all the parts in their correct relative positions to keep the unit balanced.
2 Apply a thin smear of zinc-base grease to the inner working surfaces of the lugs on the pressure plate 2, indicated by A in **FIG 5:1**.
3 When fitting the circlip 6 fit it so that the flat portions B are located in the lugs on the pressure plate 2, and the five undulations C bear against the diaphragm spring 5.

5:7 The clutch release mechanism

The components are mounted in the gearbox and are shown in **FIG 5:2**. Note that the grease nipple 6 and the fibre washer 7 are omitted on the TR5 and TR6. To gain access to the parts the gearbox must be removed (see **Chapter 6, Section 6:2**).

Check that the release bearing 1 rotates smoothly and is not badly worn. No provision is made for lubricating the bearing and if it is worn a new one must be fitted.

To dismantle first take out the grease nipple 12 and then the locating screw 13. Undo the tapered bolt 10 to free the fork 5. Pull out the shaft 8 from the lefthand side of the car, sliding off the fork 5 and spring 9 as they come free inside the bellhousing. The bearing 1 is a press fit on the sleeve 2.

Reassemble in the reverse order of dismantling, using a little grease to lubricate the shaft 8 in its bushes and wire locking the tapered bolt 10 in place.

5:8 Fault diagnosis

(a) Drag or spin

1 Oil or grease on driven plate linings
2 Leaking master cylinder, slave cylinder or piping
3 Driven plate hub binding on splines
4 Distorted driven plate
5 Warped or damaged pressure plate
6 Broken driven plate linings
7 Air in the clutch hydraulic system

(b) Fierceness or snatch

1 Check 1, 2, 4 and 5 in (a)
2 Worn clutch linings

(c) Slip

1 Check 1 in (a) and 2 in (b)
2 Seized piston in clutch slave cylinder

CHAPTER 6

THE GEARBOX

6:1 Description
6:2 Removing the gearbox
6:3 Dismantling the gearbox
6:4 Reassembling the gearbox

6:5 The gear selector mechanism
6:6 The overdrive
6:7 Fault diagnosis

6:1 Description

The gearbox has synchromesh engagement on all four forward gears. The gearlever is remote from the gearbox and operates the selectors in the gearbox by a system of pushrods incorporated in the gearbox top cover.

The arrangement of gears and moving parts of the gearbox is shown in **FIG 6:1** while the fixed parts are shown in **FIG 6:2**. The drive from the clutch is through the input shaft 29. By the selected gears the drive is transferred along the shaft 51 to the mainshaft 31, which is connected to the transmission. The drive is reversed by meshing in the reverse gear 56, which interposes between the gear on the countershaft 51 and the mainshaft 31 to reverse the direction of rotation. Top gear is obtained by directly connecting the mainshaft 31 to the input shaft 29 to give a direct drive.

The gearbox is filled to the correct level with oil and the parts are lubricated either by immersion or splash thrown up by the gears as they revolve. The combined filler and level plug is item 132 in **FIG 6:2**.

An overdrive may be fitted as an optional extra. It takes the place of the rear extension 96 and also requires a shorter mainshaft 31 to be fitted. The overdrive is controlled by an electric switch on the steering column, and operates in conjunction with top, third and second gears. The overdrive shares the same lubricating oil as the gearbox.

6:2 Removing the gearbox

1 **Securely raise the car on axle stands or a ramp to give access room underneath. If other supports are used make sure they are secure.**
2 Remove the front seats and carpets. Disconnect the battery leads. Remove the console and unscrew the gearlever knob. Remove the gearlever boot and disconnect the reversing light and overdrive cables if either are fitted. Unscrew the bolts holding the gearbox tunnel cover and remove the cover. Drain the gearbox into a clean container.
3 Referring to **FIG 6:3**, disconnect the propeller shaft from the gearbox flange at 11. Disconnect the exhaust bracket from the gearbox mounting at 12. Remove the clevis pin and bolts securing the clutch slave cylinder at 13. **Do not drain the hydraulic system and do not undo the flexible hose to the cylinder but wire the assembly safely out of the way.** Dis-

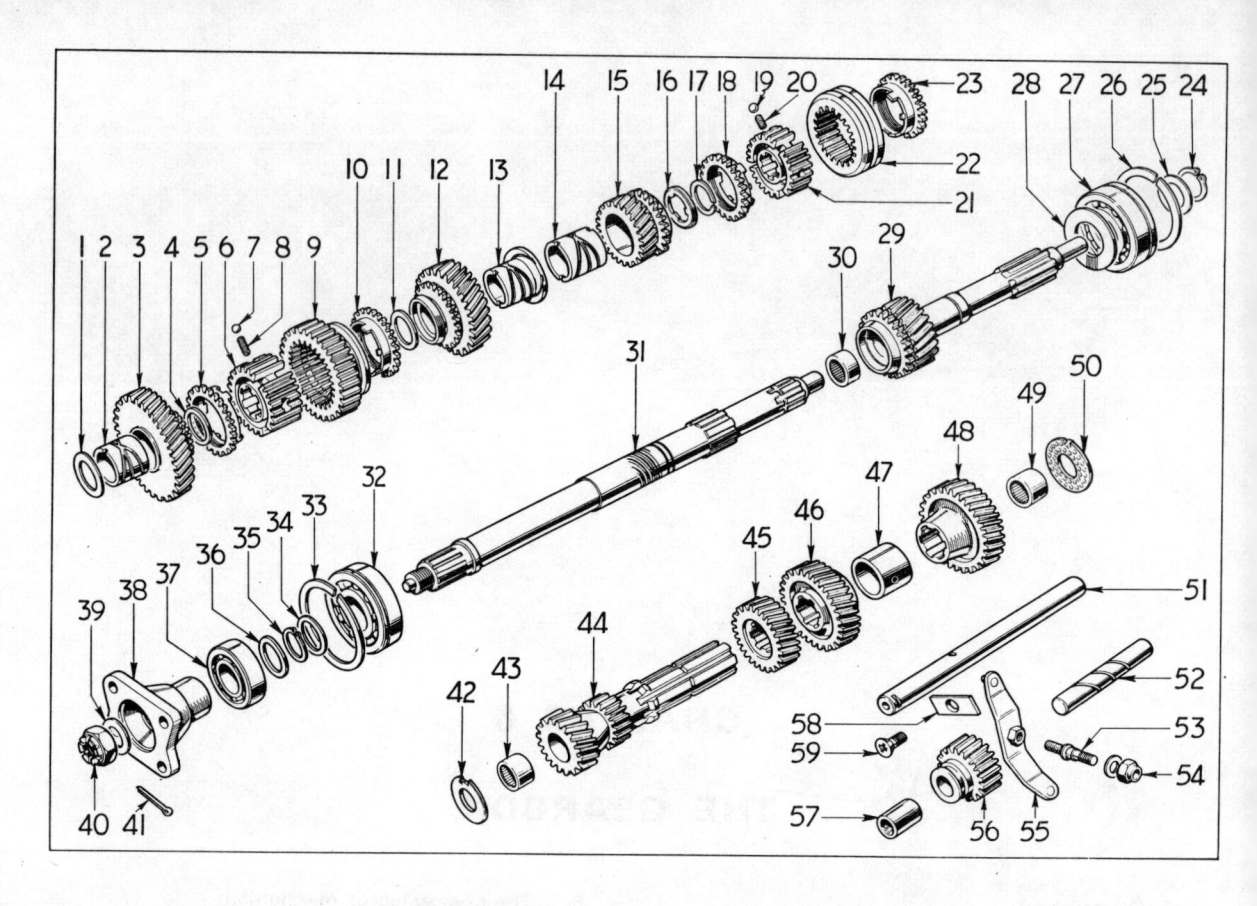

FIG 6:1 Gearbox details, moving parts

Key to Fig 6:1   1 Thrust washer   2 Bush—first-speed gear   3 First-speed gear   4 Thrust washer
5 First-speed synchro cup   6 First/Second-speed synchro hub   7 Synchro ball   8 Spring   9 Reverse mainshaft gear and synchro outer sleeve   10 Second-speed synchro cup   11 Thrust washer   12 Second-speed gear
13 Bush—second-speed gear   14 Bush—third-speed gear   15 Third speed gear   16 Thrust washer   17 Circlip
18 Third-speed synchro cup   19 Synchro ball   20 Spring   21 Third/Top synchro hub   22 Synchro sleeve
23 Top gear synchro cup   24 Circlip   25 Distance washer   26 Circlip   27 Ballrace   28 Oil deflector plate
29 Input shaft   30 Needle roller bearing (design changed, see FIG 6:4)   31 Main shaft   32 Ballrace   33 Circlip
34 Distance washer   35 Circlip   36 Distance washer   37 Rear ballrace   38 Flange (shape changed to round flange)
39 Plain washer   40 Slotted nut   41 Splitpin   42 Rear thrust washer   43 Needle roller bearing (design changed, see FIG 6:4)
44 Countershaft hub   45 Second-speed countershaft hub   46 Third-speed countershaft hub   47 Distance piece
48 Countershaft gear   49 Needle roller bearing (design changed, see FIG 6:4)   50 Front thrust washer   51 Countershaft
52 Reverse gear shaft   53 Pivot stud   54 Nyloc nut and washer   55 Reverse gear operating lever   56 Reverse gear
57 Reverse gear bush   58 Locating plate   59 Screw

connect the speedometer cable from the gearbox at 15. Undo the bolts securing the top cover 16 and remove it. Blank the orifice with cardboard to prevent the ingress of dirt.

4 Using a block of wood to protect the sump, take the weight of the engine and gearbox with a jack placed as far as possible towards the rear of the engine sump. Remove the gearbox mounting and support bolts at 14, then after slightly raising the rear end of the gearbox remove the mounting and support plate. Use another jack to support the gearbox in place of the rear mounting.

5 Remove the nuts, bolts and washers securing the bellhousing to the engine. Check that there are now no connections between the gearbox and the car or the engine. **Do not allow the weight of the gearbox to hang on the input shaft.** Draw the gearbox rearwards to clear the input shaft from the clutch and then manoeuvre it out of the car.

Replacing the gearbox is the reversal of the removal operation. Use jacks or ropes to support the weight of the gearbox and do not allow it to hang on the input shaft. Before replacing the gearbox tunnel fill the gearbox to the correct level.

58

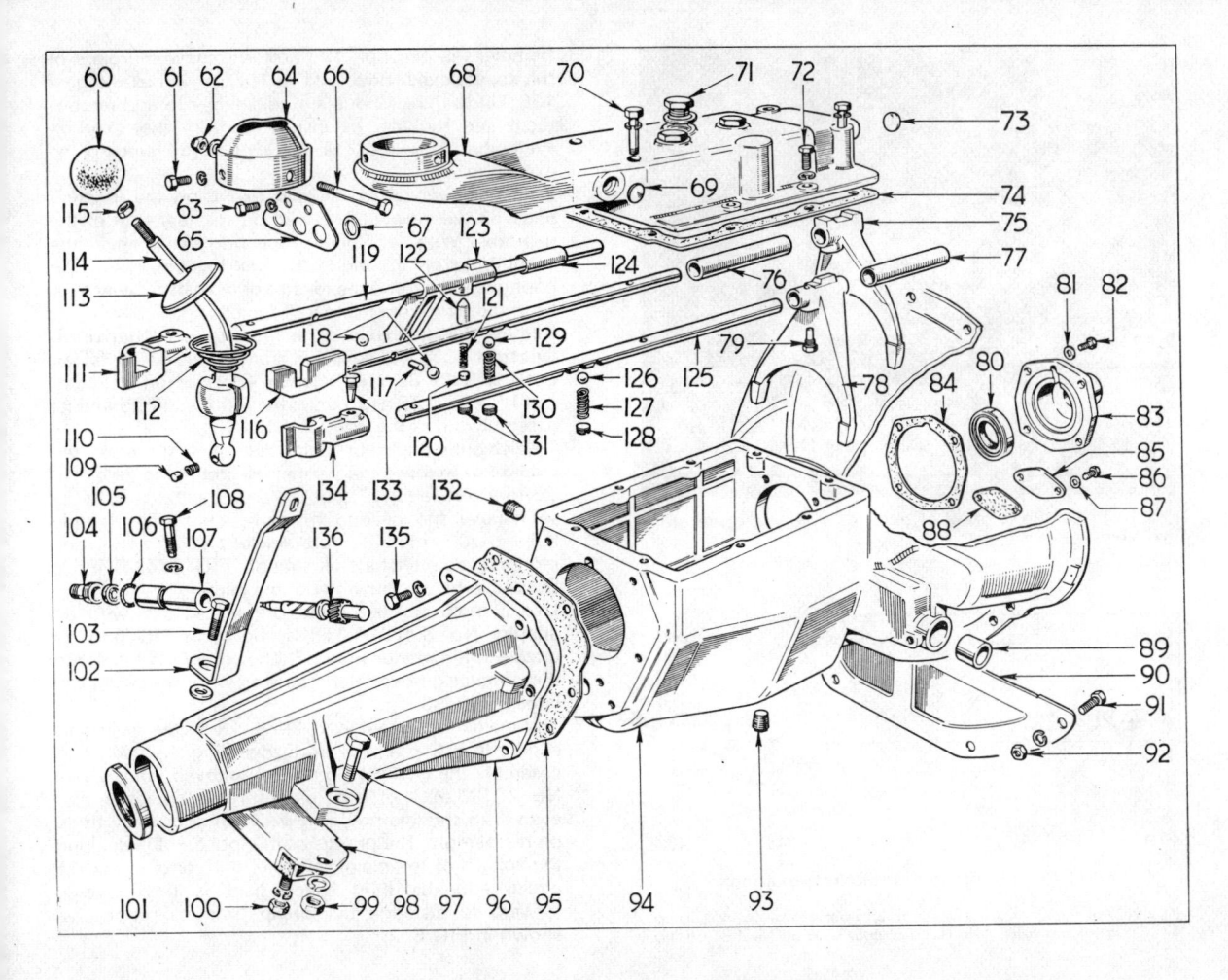

FIG 6:2 Gearbox details, fixed parts

Key to Fig 6:2				
60 Knob	61 Setscrew	62 Nyloc nut (omitted, see FIG 6:14)	63 Setscrew	64 Cap
65 End plate	66 Cross bolt (omitted, see FIG 6:14)	67 Rubber O-ring	68 Top cover	69 Welch plug	70 Bolt
71 Plug	72 Bolt	73 Welch plug	74 Gasket	75 Top/Third selector fork	76 Distance tube	77 Distance tube
78 Second/First selector fork	79 Peg bolt	80 Oil seal	81 Copper washer	82 Bolt	83 Front cover	84 Gasket
85 Countershaft end plate	86 Setscrew	87 Copper washer	88 Gasket	89 Bush	90 Cover plate	91 Setscrew
92 Nut	93 Drain plug	94 Casing	95 Gasket	96 Extension housing	97 Bolt	98 Silentbloc mounting
99 Nut	100 Nut	101 Oil seal	102 Stay	103 Bolt	104 Speedometer cable adaptor	105 Seal
106 Rubber O-ring	107 Housing	108 Peg bolt	109 Plunger—anti-rattle	110 Spring	111 Selector—reverse
112 Spring (see FIG 6:14)	113 Cap disc	114 Lever (see FIG 6:14)	115 Nut	116 Top/Third selector shaft
117 Interlock plunger	118 Balls—interlock	119 Reverse selector shaft	120 Shim	121 Spring	122 Plunger
123 Reverse actuator	124 Distance piece	125 Second/First selector shaft	126 Ball—detent	127 Spring
128 Plug	129 Plunger (similar to 122)	130 Spring (similar to 121)	131 Plug	132 Level/filler plug
133 Peg bolt	134 Selector, first/second	135 Bolt	136 Speedo drive gear

6:3 Dismantling the gearbox

Out of a total of 14 special tools the manufacturers consider 5 to be essential for working on the gearbox. If the owner has any doubt on his ability to strip and reassemble the gearbox he is advised to take it to a suitably equipped agent.

1 The top cover 68 is held in place by the bolts 70 and 72. See **Section 6:5** for instructions on dismantling the parts contained in the top cover.

2 Use a peg spanner (Tool No. 20.SM.90) to hold the flange 38 and remove the nut 40 and washer 39 after pulling out the splitpin 41. Protect the edges of the flange with wood or lead packing if a Stilson is used to hold the flange. Draw the flange 38 off from the splines on the mainshaft 31.

TR5/6

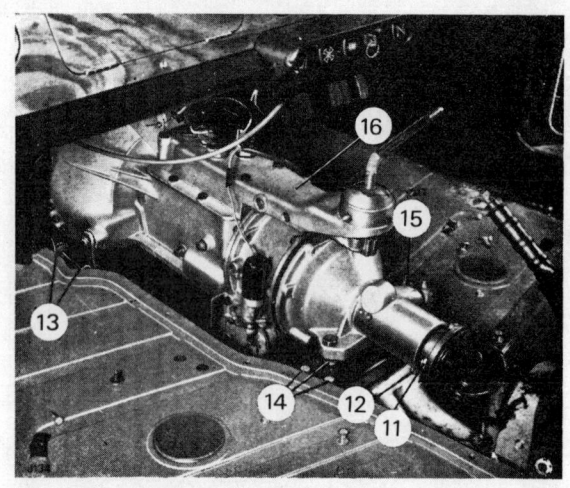

FIG 6:3 Lefthand view of gearbox and overdrive unit installed in car

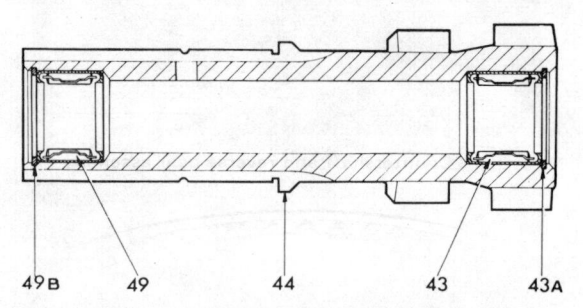

FIG 6:4 Modified countershaft bearings

Key to Fig 6:4
43 Needle roller bearing 43A Circlip
44 Countershaft hub 49 Needle roller bearing 49B Circlip

3 Remove the peg bolt 108 and withdraw the parts of the speedometer drive 104 to 107 as well as the gear 136. Undo the six bolts and washers 135 and remove them and the rear extension 96 from the gearbox Preferably use tool No. 20.S/63 to remove the extension.

4 With the removal of the rear extension the locating plate 58 will now be exposed on the rear face of the gearbox. With a Phillips screwdriver remove the securing screw 59 and lift out the locating plate. The countershaft 51 and the reverse gear shaft 52 may now be withdrawn from the rear of the casing.

5 Remove the clutch release mechanism (see **Chapter 5, Section 5:7**). Remove the front cover 83 by taking out the bolts 82 and washers 81. Use an extractor (tool No. S.4235.A) to draw the input shaft 29 and its assembly out of the front of the casing.

6 To dismantle the input shaft assembly first remove the circlip 24. Remove the washer 25 and the large circlip 26 from the bearing 27, then use an extractor (S.4221-2) to remove the bearing from the shaft. The needle bearing 30 is modified to a similar type shown in the modified countershaft illustration **FIG 6:4**. Remove the circlip before drawing out the bearing.

7 Use a multi-purpose hand press S.422A1 with an adaptor No. S.4221A-15, as shown in **FIG 6:5**, to draw out the rear bearing 32. The adaptor is fitted into the annular groove in the bearing after removing the large circlip 33.

8 The mainshaft assembly is lifted out of the casing as shown in **FIG 6:6**. Before dismantling the mainshaft assembly the circlip 17 must be removed. Ideally tool No. 20.SM.69 should be used for this operation. but even with this method a new circlip should be fitted on reassembly. The prongs of the tool are driven along the splines of the mainshaft until they pass under the circlip and the third speed gear is then levered forward to dislodge the circlip from its groove, as shown in **FIG 6:7**.

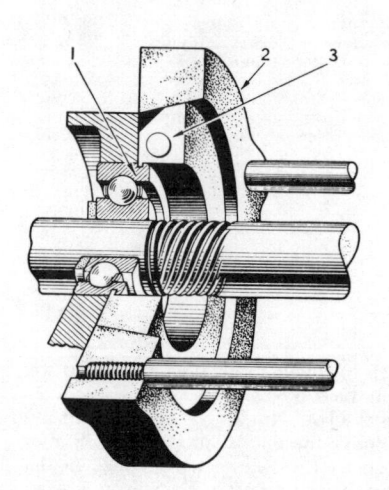

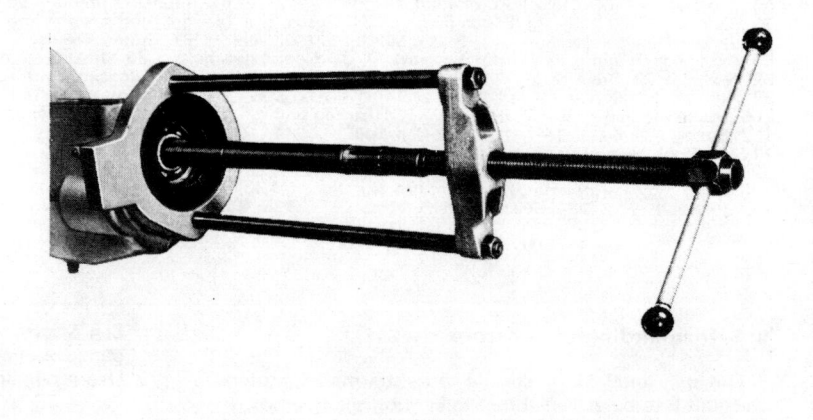

FIG 6:5 Removing mainshaft rear bearing

Key to Fig 6:5   1 Rear bearing   2 Multi-purpose hand press S.422A1   3 Adaptor No. S.4221A-15

9 When dismantling the remainder of the mainshaft assembly take care not to lose the springs 8 and 20 or the balls 7 and 19 from between the outer synchro sleeves and the inner hubs. Lay the parts out in the order in which they are removed to facilitate reassembly.

10 From inside the casing lift out the countershaft assembly and the two thrust washers 42 and 50, as well as the reverse gear 56. Slide the gears off the countershaft 51. The needle bearings are of the type shown in **FIG 6:4**, and the circlips 43A and 49B must be removed before the needle bearings 43 and 49 are removed.

6:4 Reassembling the gearbox

Thoroughly clean all the parts in petrol or paraffin and dry them before reassembly. Examine the parts for wear and renew any that are worn or damaged. Examine all the gears for chipped, worn or missing teeth. Wash the bearings separately in clean petrol and then check them for roughness or wear. Lubricate bearing surfaces with clean oil before reassembling.

1 Refit needle bearings 30, 43 and 49 if they have been removed, not forgetting the securing circlips. Replace the reverse gear 56 with the shaft 52 secured by a piece of string to prevent it sliding into the gearbox. Fit the gears 45 and 46, distance piece 47 and gear 48 to the countershaft hub 44. Secure the thrust washers 42 and 50 in place in the casing with a little grease and lower the countershaft gear cluster between them. Slide the countershaft 51 into place so that it supports the gear cluster. The assembly will now appear as shown in **FIG 6:8**.

FIG 6:7 Using tool No. 20.SM.69 to remove mainshaft circlip 17

FIG 6:8 Countershaft and reverse gear assembly

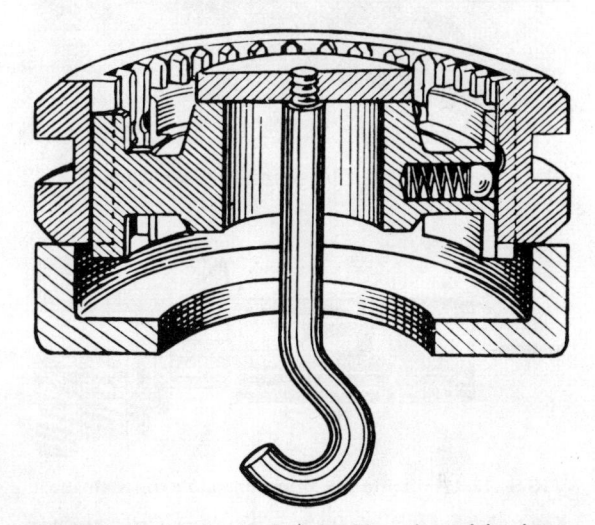

FIG 6:9 A simple rig for checking the axial release loads of the synchromesh units. Attach a spring balance to the hook and pull until the unit releases

2 Use feeler gauges to measure the end float of the gear cluster, between the thrust washer 42 and the end face of the hub 44. The correct end float is .007 to .012 inch (.18 to .3mm) and it is achieved by selective assembly of the thrust washers and the distance piece 47. When the end float is correct pull out the countershaft, allowing the gear cluster to slide to the bottom of the casing.

FIG 6:6 Removing the mainshaft assembly

TR5/6

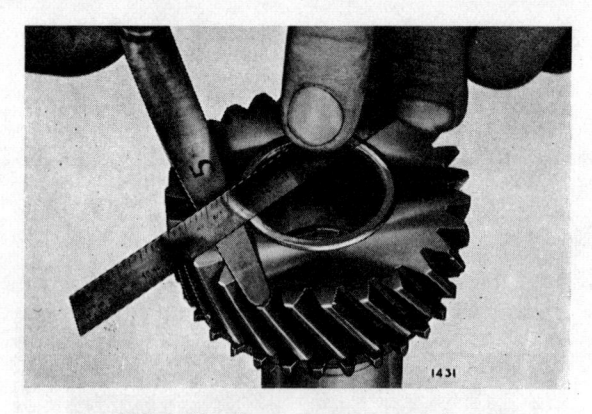

FIG 6:10 Measuring gear end float

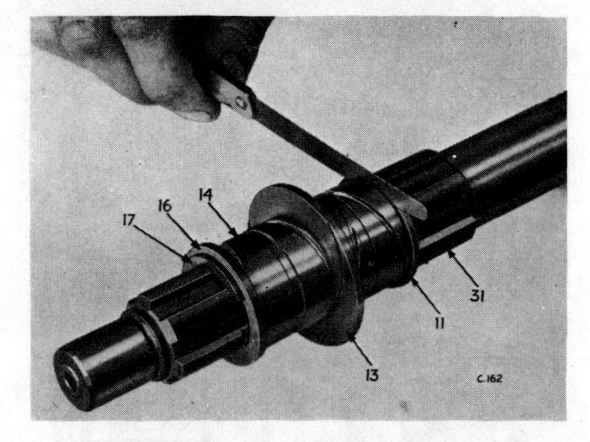

FIG 6:11 Measuring bush end float

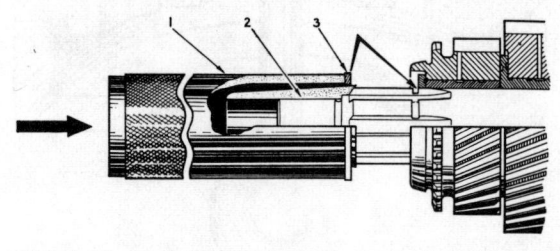

FIG 6:12 Refitting the front circlip to the mainshaft

Key to Fig 6:12   1 Driver S.145   2 Circlip expander
3 Circlip

3 Assemble the springs 20 and the balls 19 to the third/top synchro hub 21 and then fit the outer hub 22. Repeat the instructions for the second/first synchro unit. Lay each in turn in a rig as shown in **FIG 6:9** and with a spring balance on the hook test the axial release loads of each.
These should be:
   Third/top   19 to 21 lb (8.618 to 9.525 kg)
   Second/first 25 to 27 lb (11.34 to 12.247 kg)

If the release loads are incorrect adjust the number of shims under each spring. If the loads are excessive then lightly grind down the ends of the springs.

4 Measure the end float of the first, second and third speed mainshaft gears, 3, 12 and 15, on their respective bushes 2, 13 and 14, as shown in **FIG 6:10**. The end float should be .004 to .006 inch (.1 to .15mm). Fit a new bush to increase end float; decrease end float by lapping the bush on a piece of fine emerycloth spread on plate glass or a surface table. **Shortening the lengths of the bushes will increase the overall end float on the shaft when assembled.**

5 Assemble the bushes 11, 13 and 14 to the mainshaft 31 with the thrust washer 16 and half of the discarded circlip 17 to hold the parts in place. Measure the total end float with feeler gauges as shown in **FIG 6:11**. Different thicknesses of thrust washers 16 are available, see Technical Data, and these should be selectively fitted to make the end float correct at .003 to .009 inch (.08 to .23mm). Remove the parts from the mainshaft when the end float is correct.

6 Assemble the thrust washer 4, bush 2 and thrust washer 1 to the other end of the mainshaft. Drift the bearing 32 (preferably using tool No. S.314) into place and fit the washer 34 and circlip 35. Drive the bearing back against the circlip to ensure that it is firmly against the circlip. With feeler gauges measure the gap between the thrust washer 1 and the bush 2. The gap should be .003 to .009 inch (.08 to .23mm). Adjust by selective fitting of the thrust washers 1 and 4, which are obtainable in the same dimensions as the thrust washer 11. Remove all the parts from the mainshaft.

7 Assemble all the parts 1 to 23 to the mainshaft 31 in the reverse order of dismantling so that they are fitted as shown in **FIG 6:1**. Use a driver S.145 as shown in **FIG 6:12** to refit the circlip 17. Replace the mainshaft assembly through the top cover orifice. To make sure the shaft is in alignment, abutment plate No. S.134 should be fitted in place of the input shaft assembly.

8 Refit the large circlip 33 to the annular groove in the bearing 32. Use a drift (preferably tool No. S.314) to drive the bearing back into place in the casing along the rear of the mainshaft. Drive the bearing in until the large circlip 33 contacts the casing. Refit the washer 34 and the circlip 35. Hit the end of the mainshaft with a copper hammer to ensure that the bearing 32 is hard against both circlips 33 and 35.

9 Reassemble the input shaft assembly in the reverse order of dismantling. The bearing 27 is fitted so that the circlip 25 is at the front end of the bearing. Remove the abutment plate which was holding the front end of the mainshaft and drift into place the input shaft assembly.

10 Check the oil seal 80 and renew it if required. The lips of the seal should face into the gearbox. Use a new gasket 84 and carefully slide the front cover 83 into place along the input shaft. To protect the oil seal it is advisable to use a protective bullet tool No. 20.SM.47 when refitting the front cover. Secure the cover in place with the four bolts 82 and washers 81.

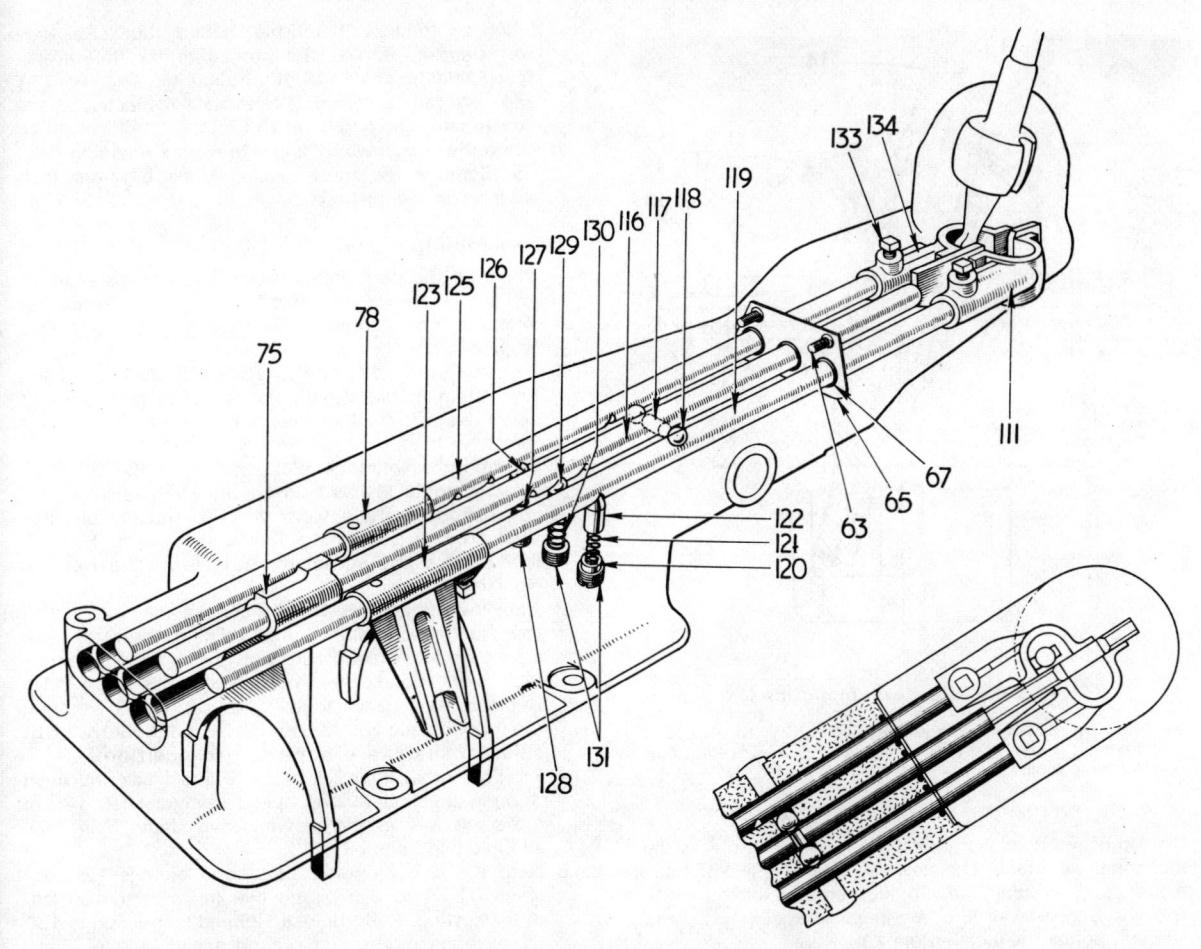

FIG 6:13 Top cover details

Key to Fig 6:13 is the same as Key to Fig 6:2

11 If not already removed, take off the countershaft end plate 85. Insert a tapered tool (20.SM.76) through the countershaft hole at the rear of the casing and use it to pick up the countershaft gear cluster. Slide the tapered tool in through the gear cluster. Follow it with the countershaft 51, with the slot at the rear, and use the countershaft to push the tapered tool out through the hole which was covered by the plate 85. Secure the countershaft and reverse shaft in place with the locating plate 58 and screw 59. Refit the cover plate 85 with a new gasket 88.

12 Place a new gasket 95 on the rear face of the gearbox and refit the rear extension 96 using the bolts 135. Fit in the distance washer 36 and drive in the bearing 37. Refit the oil seal 101 with its lips facing inwards. Replace the driving flange 38 and secure it in position with the washer 39 and nut 40. Secure the nut 40 with a new splitpin 41 after torque loading the nut to a load of 80 to 120 lb ft (11.06 to 16.59 kg/m).

13 Refit the speedometer drive parts and the clutch release mechanism in the reverse order of dismantling. Blank off the top cover orifice with cardboard to prevent the ingress of dirt before refitting the gearbox.

6:5 The gear selector mechanism

All the mechanism is contained in the top cover. **FIG 6:13** shows the details of the assembled top cover, and it should be used in conjunction with **FIG 6:2**. The top cover should be removed while the gearbox is still fitted to the engine. On the TR5 and the TR6 the gearlever assembly has been modified as shown in **FIG 6:14**. The aim is to prevent the gearlever from rattling and at the same time to damp the transference of noise from the engine.

To adjust the gearlever pins first slacken both locknuts 139. Move the gearlever over into the first/second speed gate and screw the locating pin 137 in clockwise until it just contacts the gearlever. This is best done by watching

TR5/6

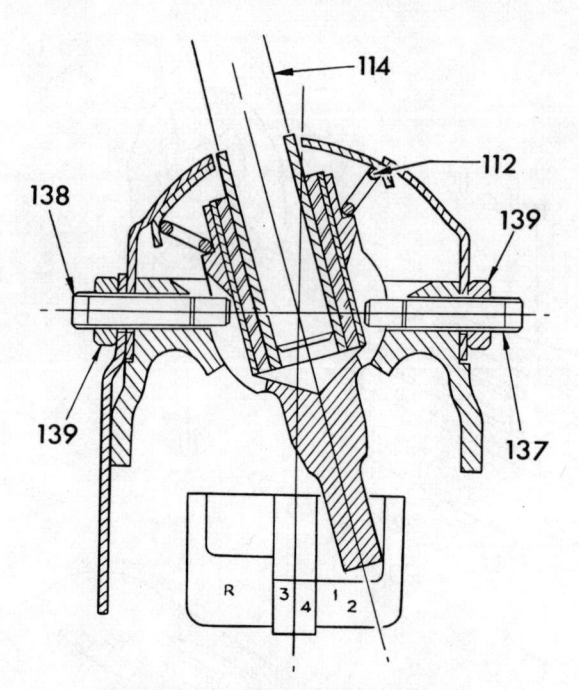

FIG 6:14 Gearlever mounting

Key to Fig 6:14 in conjunction with **Key to Fig 6:2**
112 Spring   114 Gearlever assembly   137 Locating pins
138 Locating pins   139 Locknuts

the top of the gearlever, which will move slightly as the locating pin contacts. Unscrew the locating pin 137 half-a-turn, and, holding the pin, tighten the locknut 139. Move the gearlever into the reverse speed gate and similarly adjust the locating pin 138.

Dismantling:

1 Slacken the locknuts 139 and remove the locating pins 137 and 138 shown in **FIG 6:14**. Referring to **FIG 6:2**, remove the setscrew 61, and the cap 64 complete with the gearlever assembly may be lifted out. Take care not to lose the small anti-rattle plunger 109 and spring 110 fitted to the end of the gearlever.

2 Invert the cover and unscrew one of the plugs 131. Turn the cover the right way up and catch the shims 120, spring 121 and plunger 122 as they fall out. Store them in a labelled envelope so that they will be replaced in the position from which they came. Repeat the procedure for the other plug 131. The plug 128 is fitted to the first/second speed selector but underneath it will be found a longer spring 127 and a ball 126.

3 Place the three selector rods into the neutral position and detach the three peg bolts 79. Slowly pull the third/top selector shaft 116 out of the back of the top cover, being sure to catch the two interlock balls 118 when they are released. Lift the selector fork 75 and the distance tube 76 out of the cover as they are released and remove the interlock plunger 117 from the selector shaft.

4 Pull out the first/second speed selector shaft 125,

lifting out the fork 78 and the distance tube 77 as they are released. Repeat the procedure for the reverse speed selector shaft 119. If required, the selectors 111 and 134 can be removed from their respective shafts by removing the peg bolts 133.

5 Undo the setscrews 63 and remove the retaining plate 65. Remove the three sealing rings 67 from their recesses in the casting.

Reassembling:

Clean all the parts in petrol or paraffin and examine them for wear. Renew parts as required. When re-assembling lightly lubricate all bearing surfaces with a little clean oil.

1 Fit new O-rings 67 into the recesses in the casting and hold them in place with the retaining plate 65 and setscrews 63. Replace the selectors 111 and 134 if they have been removed from their shafts.

2 Position the interlock plunger 117 in the third/top selector shaft 116 and insert the shaft into the top cover. Engage the selector fork 75 and the distance tube 76 then secure the fork with the peg bolt 79. **Make sure the selector shaft is in the neutral position.**

3 Refit the interlock ball 118 between the reverse and third/top selector shaft bores, holding it in place with a little grease. Taking care not to push out the interlock ball, replace the reverse selector shaft 119. Replace the distance tube 124 and fork 123, securing the fork in place with a peg bolt 79. **Make sure both selector shafts are in the neutral position.**

4 Refit the other interlock ball 118 into place and push through the first/second speed selector shaft 125 in the same way as the previous two shafts. Wire lock all three peg bolts 79.

5 Refit the two plungers 122, short springs 121 and shims 120 into their respective holes in the bottom of the casting. Refit the ball 129 and longer spring 130 to the hole for the first/second speed selector shaft. Screw in the two plugs 131 and the plug 128 into their respective holes until they are flush with the bottom face of the casting.

6 Use a spring balance through the selector ends of the shafts to check the axial loads required to move the shafts against the resistance of the plungers or ball. The load required for the top/third and reverse shafts should be 26 to 28 lb (11.793 to 12.701 kg) and the load for the first/second shaft should be 32 to 34 lb (14.515 to 15.422 kg). The load can be increased by fitting more shims 20 under the springs, or decreased by removing shims. If removing shims is insufficient to reduce the load then the ends of the springs may be lightly ground.

7 Refit the gearlever in the reverse order of dismantling. Use a screwdriver to hold the anti-rattle plunger 109 and spring 110 in position while refitting the gearlever.

8 Use a new gasket 74 when fitting the cover to the gearbox and ensure that all the selectors and gears are in the neutral position to make certain that they fit correctly together.

6:6 The overdrive

The components of the overdrive are shown in **FIG 6:15. Hydraulic test equipment is essential for**

FIG 6:15 Overdrive details

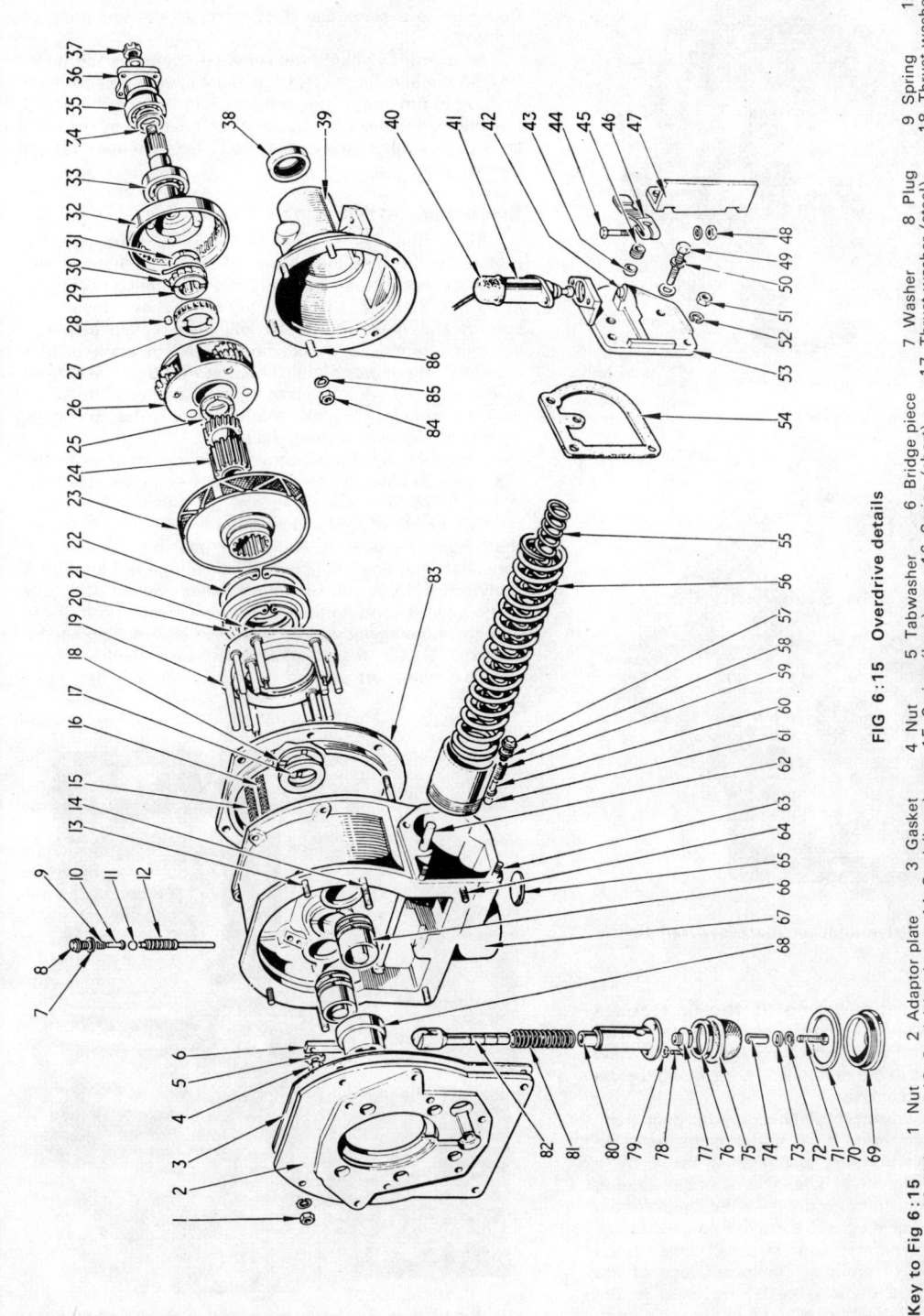

Key to Fig 6:15 1 Nut 2 Adaptor plate 3 Gasket 4 Nut 5 Tabwasher 6 Bridge piece 7 Washer 8 Plug 9 Spring 10 Plunger
11 Ball 12 Valve 13 Stud (short) 14 Stud (long) 15 Spring (long) 16 Spring (short) 17 Thrust washer (steel) 18 Thrust washer (bronze)
19 Thrust ring assembly 20 Thrust race 21 Circlip 22 Circlip 23 Clutch sliding member 24 Sun wheel 25 Thrust washer 26 Planet carrier assembly
27 Roller cage 28 Clutch roller 29 Uni-directional clutch inner member 30 Spring—inner member to cage 31 Thrust washer 32 Annulus and output shaft
33 Ballrace (front) 34 Distance washer 35 Ballrace (rear) 36 Driving flange 37 Slotted nut 38 Oil seal 39 Rear housing 40 Rubber cover
41 Solenoid 42 Rubber stop button 43 Seal 44 Pinch bolt 45 Collar 46 Operating lever 47 Dust shield 48 Nut 49 Setscrew
50 Spring washer 51 Nut 52 Spring washer 53 Ball 54 Cover plate 55 Inner accumulator spring 56 Outer accumulator spring 57 Plug
58 Sealing washer 59 Spring 60 Plunger 61 Ball 62 Operating valve cross-shaft 63 Stud 64 Stud 65 Welch plug 66 Piston 67 Body
68 Pump eccentric 69 Drain plug 70 Sealing washer 71 Setscrew 72 Spring washer 73 Plain washer 74 Distance tube 75 Brake ring
76 Seal 77 Pump end plug 78 Screw 79 Spring washer 80 Pump body 81 Pump return spring 82 Pump plunger 83 Brake ring 84 Nut
85 Spring washer 86 Stud

FIG 6:16 Overdrive thrust springs

Key to Fig 6:16   1 Long springs   2 Short springs

FIG 6:17 The overdrive adaptor plate secured to the gearbox

checking the correct function of the unit and a further fourteen special tools are also essential for dismantling and reassembling the unit. In view of this, most troubles in the unit will require taking the car to a suitably equipped agent.

The unit consists basically of an epicyclic gear train. A cam driven pump provides oil under pressure to an accumulator, excess pressure being bled away by a relief valve. Normally the whole epicyclic gearing rotates, giving a direct through drive. When the solenoid is actuated a rotary valve opens, allowing oil pressure to move two pistons which in turn move a cone clutch against the pressure of springs. The outer face of the clutch then contacts a conical brake ring fixed to the housing, bringing both the clutch and sun gear to a stop.

Drive from the planet carrier now causes the planet wheels to rotate around the stationary sun wheel and drive the outer ring at a higher speed, giving overdrive. There is more to the overdrive than given here but the foregoing gives a simplified description of the operation of the unit.

The overdrive shares the same oil supply as the gearbox, so the level in the gearbox must always be kept high enough to prevent air being drawn into the overdrive unit. For the same reason additives must never be mixed with the gearbox oil otherwise they will affect the operation of the overdrive.

Removing and replacing the overdrive:

Mount the gearbox and overdrive, vertically for preference, in the padded jaws of a vice so that the rear end is at the bottom. Progressively slacken the securing nuts and then lift the gearbox off the overdrive. The springs shown in **FIG 6:16** will then remain in place, without falling out of position. If the gearbox is dismantled the adaptor plate, shown in **FIG 6:17**, will have to be removed. When replacing the adaptor plate wirelock the securing bolts so that the wire is taut and pulls in such a way as to tighten the bolts.

When refitting the overdrive again mount it vertically in a vice and place the thrust springs into place as shown in **FIG 6:16**. There are two sets of splines in the overdrive and both of these must be in line before the mainshaft from the gearbox will fit. If possible use a spare mainshaft and ease the cone clutch bridge pieces with a screwdriver to make alignment easier. Select top gear in the gearbox and tie the reverse gear selector out of the way to prevent inadvertent selection and locking of the gearbox. Lower the gearbox onto the overdrive. The gearbox mainshaft can be turned by rotating the input

FIG 6:18 Assembling the overdrive to the gearbox

66

shaft to assist in aligning the splines. Use two screwdrivers, as shown in **FIG 6:18**, and engage the pump plunger on the cam face. One screwdriver holds back the pump plunger and the other pushes the cam into alignment as shown in the inset in **FIG 6:18**. Fit two nuts and washers on the long studs and by progressively tightening these pull the gearbox down onto the overdrive, against the pressure of the thrust springs. **Do not use undue force in mating the gearbox to the overdrive, as the splines may not be aligned and force will only cause damage.** Fit the remaining four nuts and washers.

Setting the overdrive valve:

Remove the front carpets and on the lefthand side of the tunnel will be found a small access plate. Remove this to expose the overdrive valve which is shown in **FIG 6:19**. Slacken the clamp bolt 4 and nut 5 so that the lever 3 becomes free. On the other side of the overdrive (inset in **FIG 6:19**) insert a $\frac{3}{16}$ inch diameter pin through the lever and into the hole in the casting so as to lock the valve operating shaft. Use a 12-volt battery to supply power to the solenoid and with it operating, hold the lever 3 against the head of the solenoid whilst tightening the clamp bolt 4 and nut 5. Switch off the solenoid, remove the $\frac{3}{16}$ inch diameter pin and replace the access plate and carpets.

The operating valve:

To gain access to this, remove the carpet and take out the rubber plug in the gearbox cover. A sectioned view of the valve is shown in **FIG 6:20**. To test the operation of the unit remove the plug 1 and substitute a pressure gauge and adaptor. The oil pressure should be 380 to 400 lb/sq in (26.72 to 28.12 kg/sq cm). With the plug removed the ball 4 should lift $\frac{1}{32}$ inch when the solenoid is operated. If it does not lift reset the overdrive valve as described previously. To examine the ball 4 and plunger hole 8 in the plunger is not blocked and carefully clean out any dirt. If the ball 4 fails to make proper contact in the seat, lay it in place and tap it gently with a copper drift and hammer.

6:7 Fault diagnosis

(a) Jumping out of gear

1. Broken spring behind locating ball or plunger for selector rod
2. Excessively worn locating groove in selector rod
3. Worn coupling dogs
4. Fork to selector shaft securing screw loose

(b) Noisy gearbox

1. Insufficient oil
2. Excessive end float on lay gear or mainshaft gears
3. Worn or damaged bearings
4. Worn or damaged gear teeth

(c) Difficulty in engaging gear

1. Excessively worn clutch
2. Worn synchromesh cones
3. Overdrive (if fitted) incorrectly adjusted

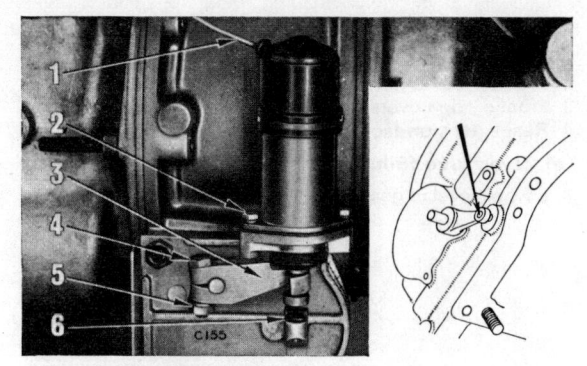

FIG 6:19 Overdrive solenoid and operating lever

Key to Fig 6:19 1 Electrical lead to solenoid 2 Securing screws 3 Operating lever 4 Clamp bolt 5 Nut and spring washer 6 Rubber stop

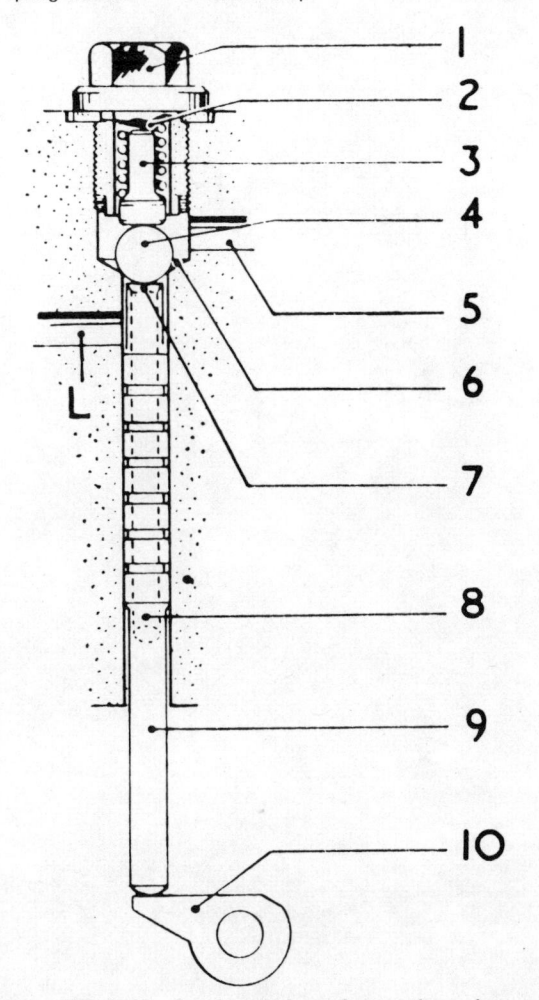

FIG 6:20 Sectioned view of operating valve

Key to Fig 6:20 1 Plug 2 Spring 3 Plunger 4 Ball 5 Passage to accumulator 6 Ball seat 7 Valve seat 8 Restrictor hole 9 Valve 10 Operating cam

(d) Oil leaks

1 Damaged joint washers or gaskets
2 Worn or damaged oil seals
3 Front or top covers loose or faces damaged
4 Rear extension face damaged

(e) Overdrive failure

1 Low oil level in gearbox
2 Overdrive valve not correctly set
3 Operating valve ball not seating properly, or restrictor orifice blocked
4 Electrical failure in the supply to the solenoid

If all four items listed for the overdrive are found to be correct then the car must be taken to a suitably equipped agent for further checks and repairs.

CHAPTER 7

PROPELLER SHAFT, REAR AXLE, REAR SUSPENSION

7:1 The propeller shaft
7:2 The rear axle
7:3 The telescopic shafts, bearings and seals

7:4 The differential
7:5 The rear suspension
7:6 Fault diagnosis

7:1 The propeller shaft

The components are shown in **FIG 7:1**. The propeller shaft transmits the drive from the gearbox to the rear axle differential. To allow for any angular misalignment a universal joint is fitted at each end of the propeller shaft. The two halves of the propeller shaft are splined together so that the propeller shaft can contract or extend slightly as the car flexes.

Routine maintenance is confined to greasing the three nipples 4 and 11 at regular intervals. Take the opportunity to check the shaft for wear. If a large amount of grease exudes from the universal joints the shaft should be dismantled and new seals fitted. Lift the shaft upwards by hand. If there is a fair amount of play the thrust faces are worn. A 'clonk' from the transmission on taking up drive could be caused by wear in the propeller shaft. Twist the shaft backwards and forwards smartly by hand. Play in this direction will indicate worn universal bearings or wear on the sliding splines.

Removing the propeller shaft:

1 Securely jack up one road wheel, both if more access room is required, but make sure that the supports are firm. This will enable the propeller shaft to be rotated by hand.
2 Turn the shaft to a convenient position for working, then stop it rotating by either applying the handbrake or engaging first gear. Remove all the nuts of the bolts holding the flange yokes 1 to the differential and gearbox.
3 Tap the four bolts out from one end and lay it on the floor, before tapping out the bolts at the other end and freeing the propeller shaft.
4 Refitting the propeller shaft is the reversal of the removal procedure.

Dismantling the propeller shaft:

1 As a universal joint rotates there are slight angular variations throughout the cycle. When correctly assembled the variations in one joint are cancelled out by the variations in the other, whilst if they are assembled out of phase the variations will augment each other. Before dismantling the shaft check the two arrows 12 on the sliding yoke 7 and the shaft 6. The arrows must be aligned, and if for some reason they are not present, mark substitute arrows indelibly so that the propeller shaft will be reassembled in the same angular plane.
2 Unscrew by hand the metal dust cover 8 and withdraw the sliding yoke 7 from the shaft 6. Remove the steel washer 9 and the cork washer 10.

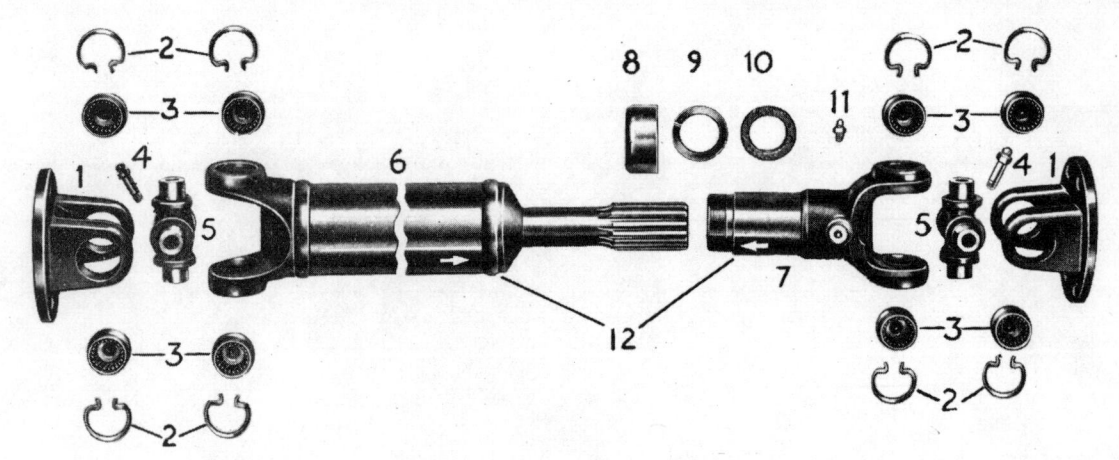

FIG 7:1 Propeller shaft details

Key to Fig 7:1   1 Flange yoke   2 Circlips   3 Cups   4 Grease nipple   5 Spider   6 Propeller shaft
7 Sliding yoke   8 Dust cap   9 Steel washer   10 Washer   11 Grease nipple

FIG 7:2 Tapping bearing cups from yoke

FIG 7:4 Removing a bearing cup from the shaft

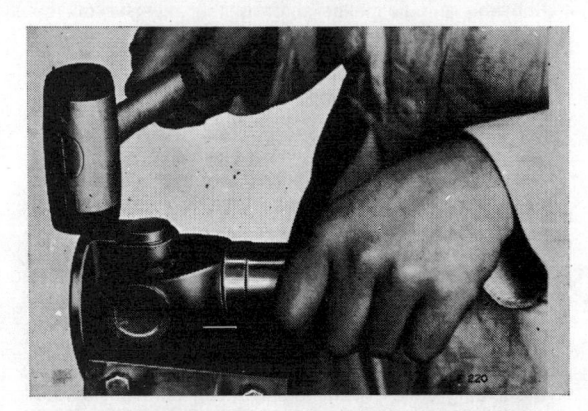

FIG 7:3 Removing a bearing cup from the flange

3 Clean enamel, dirt and rust from the recesses holding the eight snap rings 2. Remove all eight snap rings 2 by pinching together the ears with a suitable pair of pliers, prising them out with a screwdriver if necessary. If the snap rings are tight in their recesses, lightly tap the bearing caps 3 inwards to relieve the pressure on the snap ring.

4 Hold the shaft 6 in the left hand with a shaft lug uppermost, as shown in **FIG 7:2**. Tap the yoke arms with a soft-faced hammer and the bearing cup 3 should start to emerge. Keep tapping until sufficient of the cup has emerged to allow it to be gripped with the fingers, or grips, and drawn right out. If this method fails to move the cup lay the shaft lugs on two blocks of wood and tap out the bearing as shown in **FIG 7:3**. Turn the shaft right over and remove the opposite bearing in a similar manner.

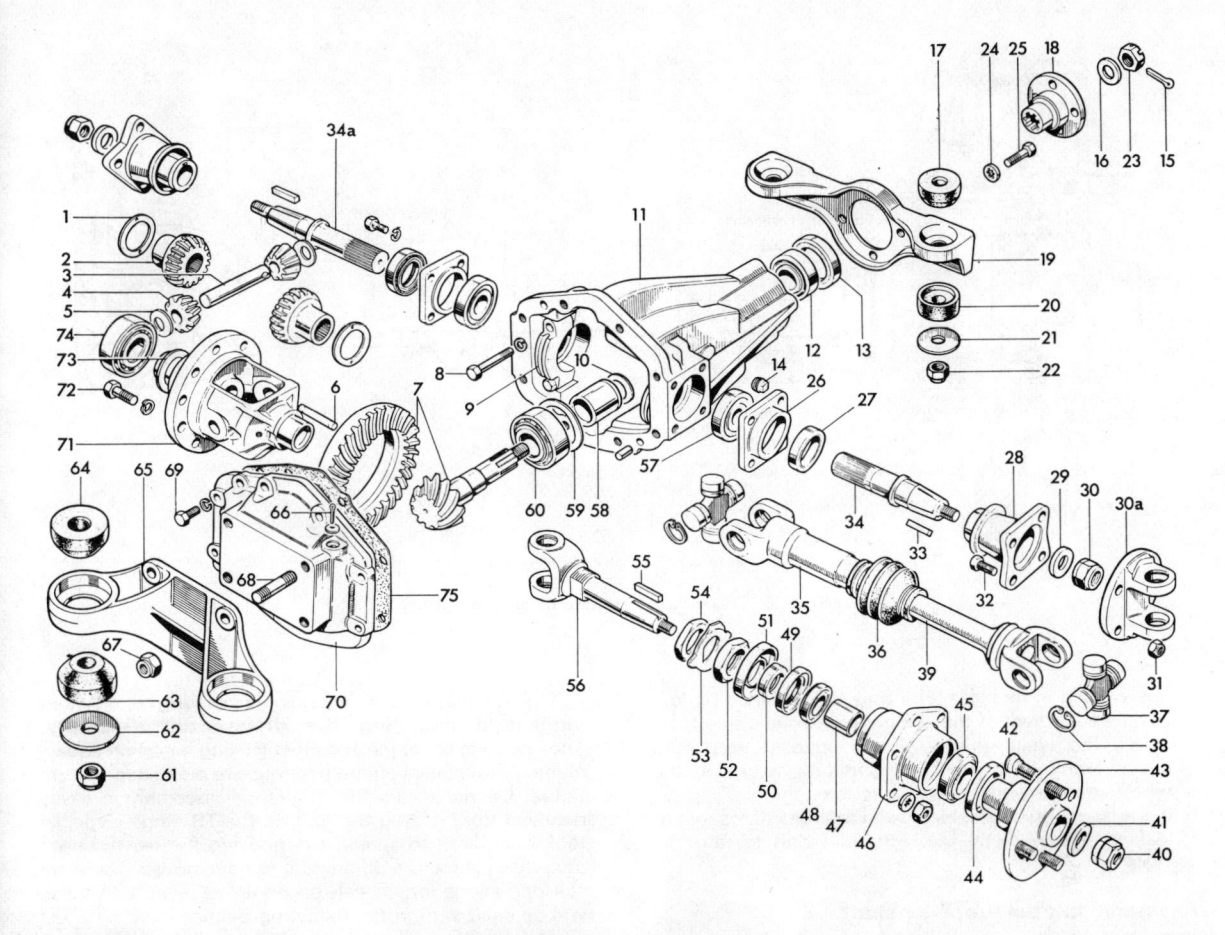

FIG 7:5 Rear axle components

Key to Fig 7:5
1 Thrust washer (sun wheel)   2 Sun wheel   3 Cross-shaft   4 Planet wheel
5 Thrust washer (planet wheel)   6 Locking pin (cross-shaft)   7 Crownwheel and pinion   8 Bolt, bearing cap
9 Bearing cap   10 Shim, pinion preloading   11 Axle casing   12 Tail bearing (pinion)   13 Oil seal, pinion
14 Filler plug (oil level)   15 Splitpin   16 Washer   17 Rubber buffer (upper)   18 Companion flange
19 Mounting (front)   20 Rubber buffer (lower)   21 Backing plate   22 Nyloc nut   23 Castellated nut
24 Lockwasher   25 Bolt   26 Bearing retainer   27 Oil seal   28 Flange   29 Washer   30 Nut
30a Yoke   31 Nut (nyloc)   32 Bolt   33 Key   34 Axle shaft, inner (short)   34a Axle shaft, inner (long)
35 Axle shaft, fixed (outer)   36 Gaiter   37 Universal spider   38 Circlip   39 Axle shaft, sliding (outer)   40 Nut
41 Washer   42 Wheel stud   43 Hub   44 Oil seal   45 Hub bearing (outer)   46 Bearing housing
47 Bearing spacer (collapsible)   48 Hub bearing (inner)   49 Oil seal   50 Bearing spacer   51 Stone guard
52 Adjusting nut   53 Tabwasher   54 Locknut   55 Key   56 Stub shaft   57 Bearing (inner axle shaft)
58 Spacer (pinion bearing)   59 Shim (pinion locating)   60 Head bearing (pinion)   61 Nyloc nut   62 Backing plate
63 Buffer (lower)   64 Buffer (upper)   65 Mounting (rear)   66 Splitpin (breather)   67 Nyloc nut   68 Stud
69 Bolt   70 Rear cover   71 Differential cage   72 Bolt   73 Shim (crownwheel preload)
74 Bearing (differential cage)   75 Gasket (rear cover)

5 Manoeuvre the shaft lugs off the spider 5. Lay the two trunnions of the spider 5 on two blocks of lead or wood and tap out the remaining two bearings as shown in **FIG 7:4**.
6 Repeat operations 4 and 5 on the universal joint of the sliding yoke 7 and dismantle it, keeping the parts separated from the front universal joint parts.

Examination of the parts:

1 Thoroughly clean all the parts in petrol or paraffin. Take care not to lose the needle rollers from the bearing cups 3.

2 The bearing races and spider trunnions are the parts most likely to show wear. Renew the parts with a complete kit. **Do not renew parts individually.**
3 It is essential that the bearing cups are a light drive fit into the holes in the yokes. After a great deal of service and inadequate lubrication it is possible that the holes in the yokes will be worn oval. The flange yokes 1 are easily renewable, but it may happen that the holes in the fixed yokes are also worn. In this case the whole propeller shaft assembly must be renewed. The propeller shaft is a balanced assembly and only in an emergency should a worn yoke be cut off and a new

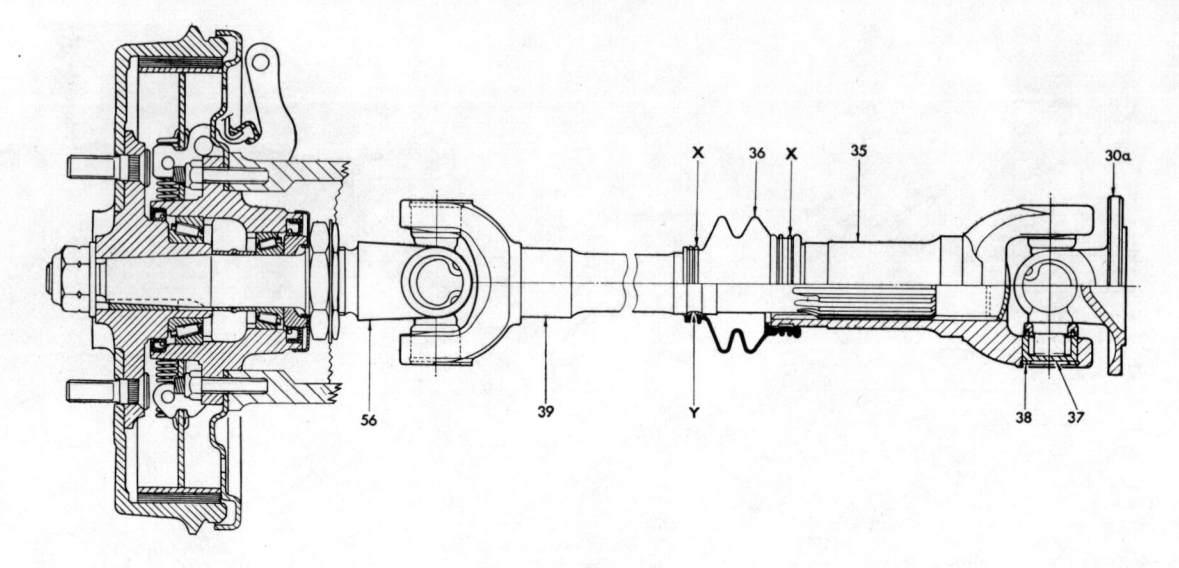

FIG 7:6 Telescopic shaft and hub assembly

one welded in its place. Not only will balance be lost but the alignment of the shaft may also be altered.
4 Check the wear on the sliding splines. Very little circumferential play is allowed and if it is excessive the whole shaft assembly must be renewed.
5 If the seals on the spider trunnions are damaged or leaking, renew them. Use a tubular drift to refit the seals.

Reassembling the propeller shaft:
1 Replace the needle bearings in the bearing cups 3, holding them in place with grease. The needles must exactly fill the cups leaving no gaps. Some universal joints do not have grease nipples fitted and these should be well packed with grease on reassembly.
2 Insert the spider 5 into the flange yoke 1. Use a soft-nosed drift just smaller than the diameter of the hole in the yoke to drive the bearings 3 into place. They must be a light drive fit. **If a bearing suddenly stops moving take it out and check that a needle roller has not become displaced,** otherwise further movement will snap the needle roller.
3 In a similar manner refit the remaining four bearings and then hold all the bearings in place with the circlips 2.
4 Slide the dust cap 8 and washers 9 and 10 into position on the shaft 6. Grease the splines on the shaft 6 and, with the arrows 12 aligned, slide the splines into the sliding yoke 7. Screw up the dust cap 8 hand tight only.

7:2 The rear axle

All the models covered by this manual have IRS (Independent Rear Suspension). The differential unit is bolted to the chassis and the drive is taken to the wheels by two axle shafts, each fitted with universal joints to allow for the movement of the suspension.

The average car owner is strongly advised against dismantling the differential assembly. The gears are set to mesh correctly using precision equipment and the bevel pinion bearings are preloaded to a set figure. On most cars the differential assembly is easily removed from its housing, but on the TR range a special tool is required to spread the housing by just the right amount to allow the differential to be removed. There are still operations which can be done however, and these will be dealt with in the following Sections.

At periodic intervals the oil in the differential unit should be changed. Take the car for a run sufficiently long to warm up the differential oil, as it will then be easier to drain out. Place a container under the differential unit and drain the oil out by removing the drain plug. **Do not flush out the unit with paraffin or petrol.** There is a danger of some solvent remaining in the housing and diluting the fresh oil. Refill, using an oil gun or adapted washing-up liquid bottle, to the level of the filler plug 14. **Do not overfill.** Check that the breather splitpin 66 is clean and not obstructed by dirt.

The components of the rear axle assembly are shown in **FIG 7:5**.

7:3 The telescopic shafts, bearings and seals

The complete assembly, including brakes and brake drum, is shown in **FIG 7:6**. The yoke 30a is bolted to the flange 28 on the differential and the bearing housing 46 is bolted to the arm of the rear suspension. The items are removed as a complete assembly, proceed as follows:
1 Securely jack up and support the appropriate rear wheel. **Do not rely on the jack supplied with the car, and make sure all supports are secure.** Remove the road wheel, take out the two countersunk screws securing the brake drum and then remove the brake drum.

FIG 7:7 Extracting a rear hub, the assembly is supported in tool No. S.318

FIG 7:8 Adjusting the bearing end float, using a DTI and wrench S.317

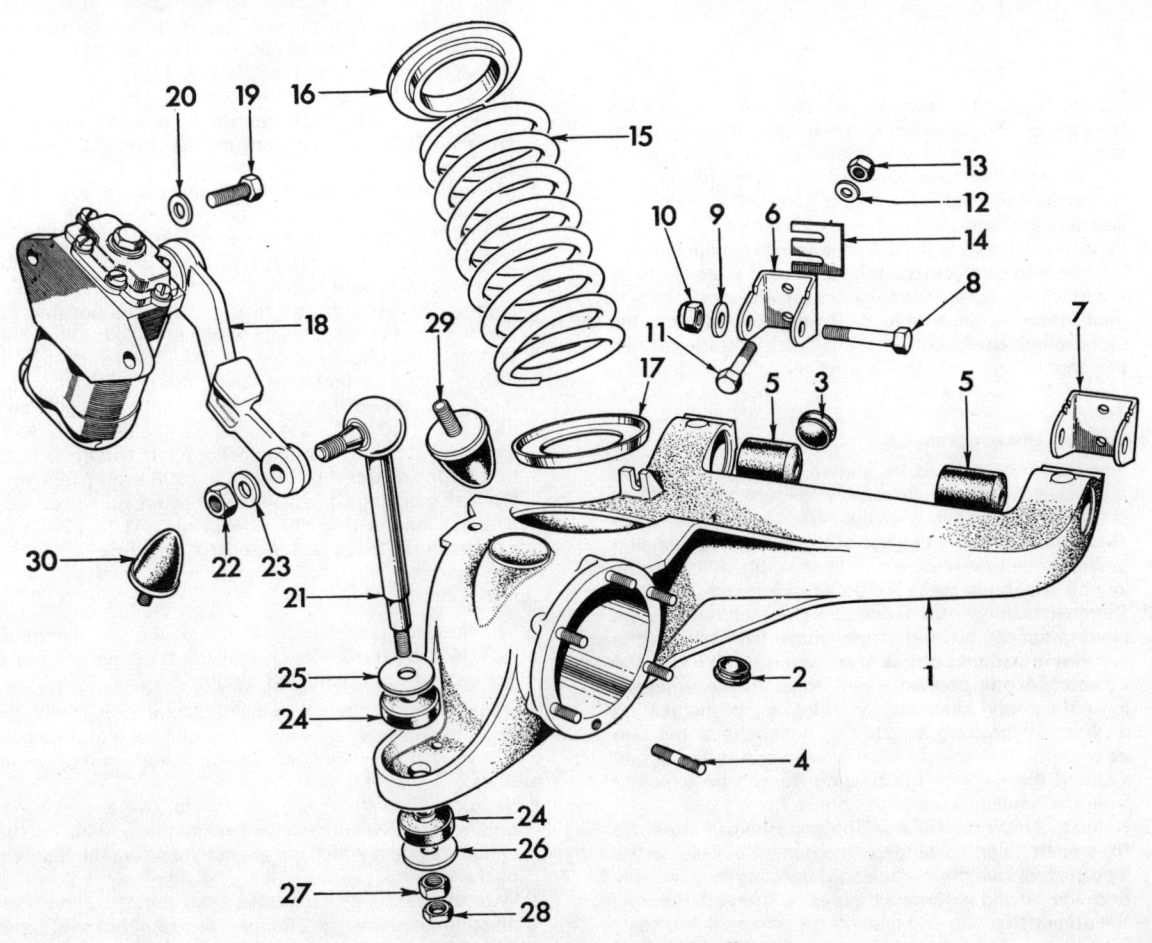

FIG 7:9 Rear suspension details

Key to Fig 7:9 1 Suspension arm   2 Rubber plug   3 Rubber plug   4 Stud   5 Metalastik bush
6 Fulcrum bracket (inner)   7 Fulcrum bracket (outer)   8 Bolt   9 Plain washer   10 Nyloc nut   11 Bolt
12 Plain washer   13 Nyloc nut.   14 Shim   15 Road spring   16 Rubber insulator   17 Rubber insulator
18 Damper arm   19 Bolt   20 Washer   21 Damper link   22 Nut   23 Washer   24 Rubber buffer
25 Backing plate   26 Backing plate   27 Nut   28 Locknut   29 Bump stop   30 Rebound rubber

TR5/6

FIG 7:10 Removing a rear road spring

2 Rotate the driving flange 43 until the two holes in it are over a pair of nuts securing the bearing housing 46 to the suspension arm. Use a socket through the holes in the driving flange to remove the nuts. Rotate the driving flange for the next pair of nuts until all six nuts and washers are removed.

3 Working underneath the car, pass a piece of wire through the two universal joints on the shaft and twist the ends together to prevent two halves of the shaft sliding apart. Remove the four nuts 31 and bolts 32 from the inboard universal joint. Without disturbing the brakes, the shaft assembly can now be slid out through the boss in the suspension arm.

Servicing the assemblies:

1 Some form of support, as shown in **FIG 7:7**, will be required to hold the assembly. Mount the shaft as shown and remove the nut 40. Use an extractor (M.86A) to remove the hub 43. The bearing housing assembly will be removed with the hub. Remove the key 55 and throw away the collapsible spacer 47.

2 Remove the inner hub bearing cone 48 followed by bearing spacer 50 and stone guard 51. Release the tabwasher 53 and screw the adjusting nut 52 with the locknut 54 one complete turn towards the universal joint. If required, drive out the outer race of the bearing 48 from the housing 46. Driving out the race will also drive out the oil seal 49. Carefully lever out the oil seal 44, and the parts of the bearing 45 can be removed from the housing 46 and the hub 43.

3 Refer to **FIG 7:6**. Release the gaiter clip X from the fixed shaft 35 and disengage the gaiter 36. Release the length of wire which was fitted on removing the assembly from the car and withdraw the sliding shaft 39. Remove the other gaiter clip and take off the gaiter 36 and sealing strips.

4 Service the universal joints as instructed in **Section 7:1**. Clean all the metal parts in petrol or paraffin and examine them for wear, especially the sliding splines. Wash the bearings separately in clean petrol. Assemble the bearings dry and rotate them between the palms while firmly pressing the two halves together. This method will make it easier to feel any roughness or wear in the bearings. Check that the rollers and races are bright, clean and free from pitting or corrosion. Renew parts as required.

5 Wrap a length of Expandite Sealer Strip around the groove in the shaft 39 and fit the smaller end of the gaiter 36 over the sealer strip. Secure the gaiter in place with a double wrap of the gaiter clip X. Liberally coat the splines with Rocal Molytone 320 or Duckhams Q5648 grease. Line up the larger master spline with its mating slot and slide the shaft 39 into the fixed shaft 35. Fit a length of Expandite Sealer Strip around the groove in the fixed shaft 35, pull the larger end of the gaiter 36 over it and secure the gaiter in place with a double wrap of the clip X. Wire-lock the shafts together to prevent them from accidentally sliding apart.

6 Reassembling the hub assembly is the reversal of the dismantling operation. The oil seals are fitted with their lips facing the bearings. Well pack the bearings with grease. When passing the stubshaft 56 through the bearing housing assembly take great care not to damage the lips of the oil seals. Refit the key 55 after the stubshaft is passed through the bearing housing assembly. **A new collapsible spacer 47 must be fitted. Tighten the adjusting nut 52 finger tight only.**

7 Mount a dial test indicator on the hub flange so that the indicator stylus contacts the bearing housing, as shown in **FIG 7:8**. With a rocking motion to settle the components, pull the bearing housing away from the indicator. When the housing is as far down as possible, set the dial test indicator to zero. Push the housing up towards the indicator, again with a rocking motion, and note the maximum reading. Tighten the adjusting nut 52 one flat at a time and check the end float as just described. When the end float lies between .004 and .002 inch (.10 and .05 mm) secure the assembly with the locknut 54 and the tabwasher 53. **If the end float has been reduced to less than .002 inch (.05 mm) then the collapsible spacer 47 must be renewed. Merely slackening the adjusting nut to give the correct end float is dangerous practice.**

8 The assembly is refitted to the car in the reverse order of removal.

7:4 The differential

As already stated it is extremely inadvisable for the average owner to attempt to dismantle the unit. However, it may be necessary to remove the unit so that it can be overhauled at a service station. Remove and replace as follows:

1 Securely raise the rear of the car to give access room underneath. Disconnect and remove any parts of the exhaust system which are going to obstruct the removal of the unit.

2 Wire the halves of each drive shaft together, and then disconnect them by undoing the four bolts 32 and nuts 31 securing each shaft to the driving flanges 28. Disconnect the propeller shaft from the companion flange 18.

3 Place a jack, preferably a trolley jack if one is available, under the differential and extend it to just support the unit. Remove the two nuts 61 and the two nuts 22 then

take off the four washers 21 and 62. The rubber buffers 20 and 63 can also be removed, but note that the front pair 20 are shaped differently from the rear pair 63.

4 Lower the jack and guide the differential off the studs. If a trolley jack is used the unit can be pulled out on this. Remove and label the upper pairs of buffers 17 and 64.

5 Replacing the differential unit is the reversal of the removal operation, making sure that the rubber buffers are replaced in their correct positions.

7:5 The rear suspension

The components of the rear suspension are shown in **FIG 7:9**. The rear wheel hubs are mounted in the bosses of the trailing suspension arms 1, which in turn pivot about the brackets 6 and 7 bolted to the chassis. The load on the wheels is taken by two coil springs 15 acting between each suspension arm and a member on the chassis. Two piston type dampers (shock absorbers) are mounted on the chassis and these are connected to the trailing arms by links 21. Metalastic bushes and rubber buffers are used throughout the rear suspension so there is no need for lubrication.

Dampers:

To remove a damper, jack up the appropriate rear wheel. Make sure the car is securely supported and then remove the road wheel. Slacken the locknut 28 and remove this as well as the nut 27. Raise the damper arm 18 to pull the link 21 out of the suspension arm 1. Collect the rubber buffers 24 and the two washers 25 and 26. Remove the two bolts 19 and washers 20 while supporting the damper, and then lift out the damper.

Mount the damper vertically in a vice, protecting it with either lead or wood. Remove the filler plug from the top of the damper, after cleaning away any dirt. Fill the unit with Armstrong Shock Absorber Fluid to the level of the bottom of the plug hole. **Do not overfill as the unit depends on the airspace above the fluid for its correct operation.** Slowly work the damper arm 18 up and down to expel any trapped air and finally top up to the correct level before replacing the filler plug.

Move the arm 18 through its full range of movement several times. There should be appreciable and constant resistance in both directions. If the resistance is so much that the arm can hardly be moved, or if it is very low or there are pockets of no resistance, then the damper must be renewed.

Once the unit has been tested and found satisfactory replace it in the reverse order of removal, keeping it vertical to keep the air at the top.

When a new damper is fitted it will be necessary to transfer the link 21. Undo the nut 22 and remove the washer 23. **Do not hammer on the threaded portion of the link.** Lay a block of metal on the side of the tapered eye in the arm 18, and whilst pulling them firmly apart, hammer on the side of the tapered eye which is opposite to the block. This will free the taper and allow the link to be removed.

Rear springs:

To remove these, raise the rear of the car and place it on stands. Remove the road wheel and then place a jack under the suspension unit. Raise the suspension. Disconnect the drive shaft at the flange of the inboard universal joint. Disconnect the damper arm 21 from the suspension arm 1. Taking care not to strain the flexible brake hose, lower the jack supporting the suspension until the top of the spring is just free from the chassis, as shown in **FIG 7:10**. Lift out the spring 15, rubber insulator 16 and 17.

Check the spring for cracks and measure the free length to ensure that the spring has not weakened with use. The dimensions of the spring are given in Technical Data.

Replace the springs in the reverse order of removal.

Suspension arms:

To remove a suspension arm proceed as follows:

1 Securely jack up the rear of the car and place it on stands. Remove the telescopic drive shafts (see **Section 7:3**). This step is not essential as the drive shafts can be removed whilst still attached to the suspension arm. Remove the road spring 15 as previously described, and then support the suspension arm on a jack.

2 Drain the brake system by pumping the fluid out through a bleed nipple, disconnect the handbrake cable from the lever on the rear brake and then remove the flexible brake hose (see **Chapter 10**).

3 Undo the nuts 10 and whilst supporting the suspension arm pull out the bolts 8 to free the arm. If required the bolts 11, washer 12 and nuts 13 can be removed to free the brackets 6 and 7 instead. Note carefully the position and quantity of the shims 14.

If the Metalastic bushes 5 are perished or distorted they should be renewed. Drift or press out the old ones, taking care not to damage the suspension arm. Press the new bushes into place using plenty of Castrol rubber grease and a bolt through the centre bush to protect the metal.

Replacing the suspension arm is the reversal of the removal process. The brackets 6 and 7 both have grooves on one side and these should be fitted uppermost. These grooves can be seen in **FIG 7:9**, note that the inner bracket 6 has only two grooves while the outer bracket 7 has four grooves. Before fully tightening the nuts 10 and bolts 8 lower the car back to the ground and place a weight of 150 lb in each seat. This ensures that the suspension bushes 5 are in their static loaded position.

If the rear suspension arms have been removed it is advisable to have the rear wheel alignment checked. It is not possible for an owner to do this satisfactorily, as specialized equipment is required for an accurate check. Take the car to a suitably equipped agent.

7:6 Fault diagnosis

(a) Noisy axle

1 Insufficient or incorrect lubricant
2 Worn bearings
3 Worn gears

(b) Excessive backlash

1 Worn gears, bearings or bearing housings
2 Worn axle shaft splines
3 Worn universal joints
4 Loose or broken wheel studs (worn hub splines when wire wheels are fitted)

(c) Oil leakage

1 Defective pinion or inner axle shaft oil seals
2 Defective hub oil seals
3 Defective seals on universal joint spiders
4 Blocked breather hole in differential case

(d) Vibration

1 Propeller shaft out of balance
2 Worn universal joint bearings
3 Propeller shaft universal joints assembled 'out of phase'

(e) Rattles

1 Rubber buffers on damper links worn through
2 Dampers loose
3 Worn Metalastic bushes in the suspension arm

(f) 'Settling'

1 Weak or broken coil spring

CHAPTER 8

FRONT SUSPENSION AND HUBS

8:1 Description
8:2 Routine maintenance
8:3 Front hubs and discs
8:4 The front dampers
8:5 The front road springs

8:6 Ball joint and upper wishbones
8:7 The lower wishbone and vertical link assembly
8:8 The anti-roll bar
8:9 Fault diagnosis

8:1 Description

All the models covered by this manual have their front wheels independently mounted using unequal length wishbones top and bottom, with a coil spring in each suspension to take the load. A telescopic damper is fitted concentrically inside each spring to provide a damping action.

The vertical link (swivel pin) swivels in a special screwed bush attached to the bottom wishbones and a ball joint attached to the top wishbones. Fixed to the vertical link is a bracket to take the front brake caliper and also a stub axle around which the hub of the wheel revolves on two tapered bearings.

The TR6 (and therefore the TR250) has a lower front suspension than the TR5, as the coil spring is shortened by half an inch, and to improve road holding further an anti-roll bar is fitted. Apart from these differences the different suspensions can all be treated in the same way.

The front view of a typical front suspension is shown in **FIG 8:1**, and an engineer's drawing of the assembly is shown in **FIG 8:2**. As an aid to description, the components of the TR4 front suspension are shown in **FIG 8:3**. Again the differences are only of a minor nature; the brackets for the inner fulcrums of the lower wishbones are shimmed and fitted as indicated by the arrows in **FIG 8:1**, and the outer pivot for the lower wishbones is a bolt and nut instead of the pin and two nuts of the TR4.

Before doing any work, including lubrication, on the front suspension, put on the handbrake or chock the rear wheels, jack up the front of the car and place it securely on stands. When undoing flexible hose unions refer to Chapter 10 for instructions.

8:2 Routine maintenance

Unless the front suspension has been 'kerbed' or otherwise damaged the only routine maintenance required is greasing.

1 Take the weight of the car off the front wheels by jacking up the chassis. Wipe the four grease nipples on each suspension clean (one on the top ball joint and three on the bottom swivel bearing). With a grease gun pump grease through until it comes out clean. Wipe away the surplus grease.

2 Remove the front wheels. Refer to **FIG 8:4**. Remove the dust cap 21 by screwing a No. 10 AF setscrew

TR5/6

77

FIG 8:1 Frontal view of suspension assembly. The arrows indicate the location of the shims behind the inner lower fulcrum brackets

through the tapped hole in the dust cap. Pack the tapered bearings with clean grease. Ideally the hub should be removed to carry out this operation. **Do not pack the dust cap with grease.**

8:3 Front hubs and discs

With the front wheels off the ground, grasp the tyre with the hands at the twelve and six o'clock positions. Rock the top of the tyre in and out. There should be very little play indeed. If, when the wheels are properly secured to the hub, there is some play, then suspect either the swivels in the vertical link or the wheel bearings to be worn. Repeat the rocking of the wheel with the hands in the three and nine o'clock positions. If the play is still present then the wheel bearings are either worn or loose. If there is now no play then the wear is in the vertical link swivels. Do not confuse movement due to the turning of the steering with that of play. Spin the road wheel, which should rotate smoothly and without grinding. If it spins

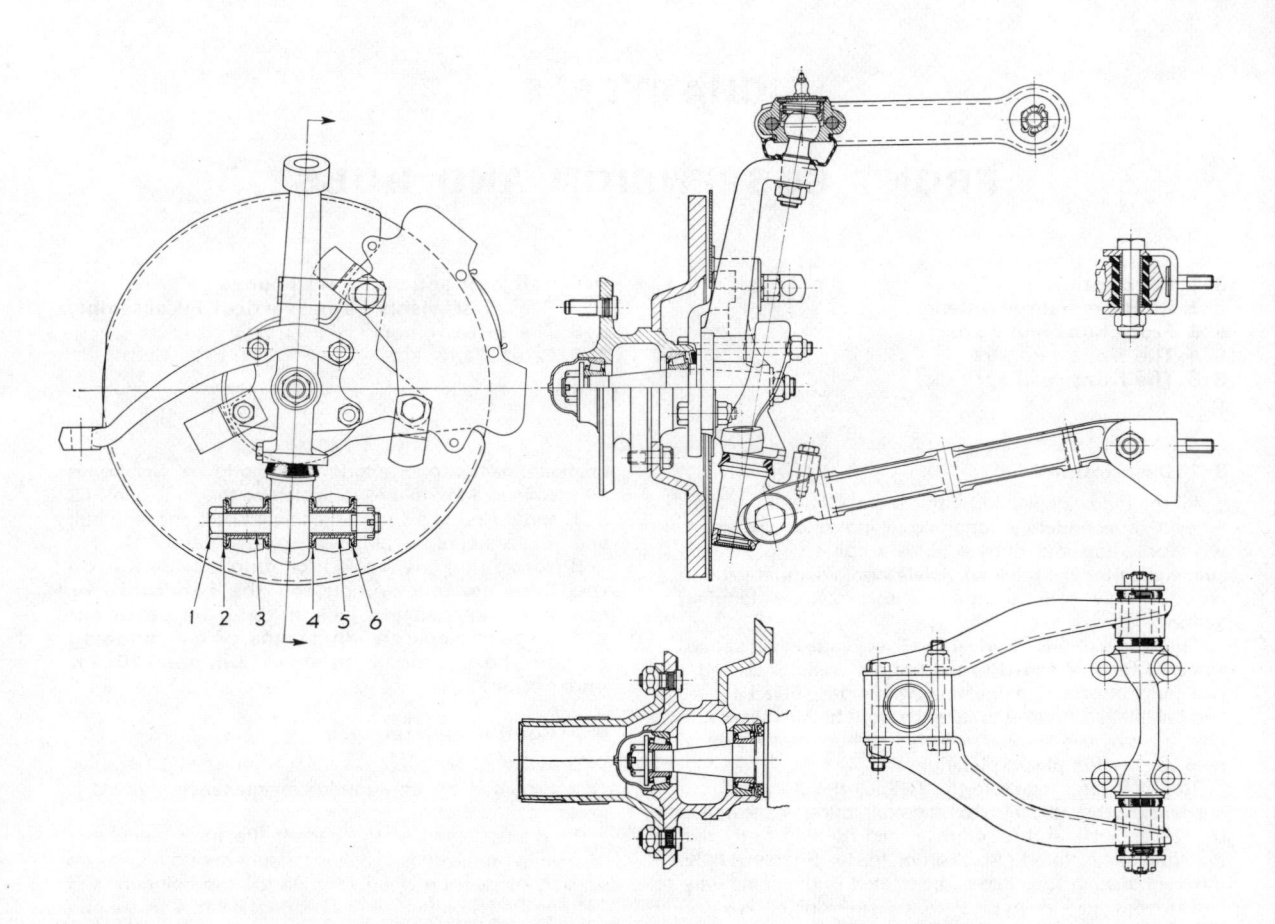

FIG 8:2 Engineers drawing of front suspension assembly. Note the design and method of attaching the inner lower fulcrum brackets and also the lower outer pivots

Key to Fig 8:2   1 Bolt   2 Thrust washers   3 Steel sleeves   4 Retainers   5 Nylon bushes   6 Dust excluders

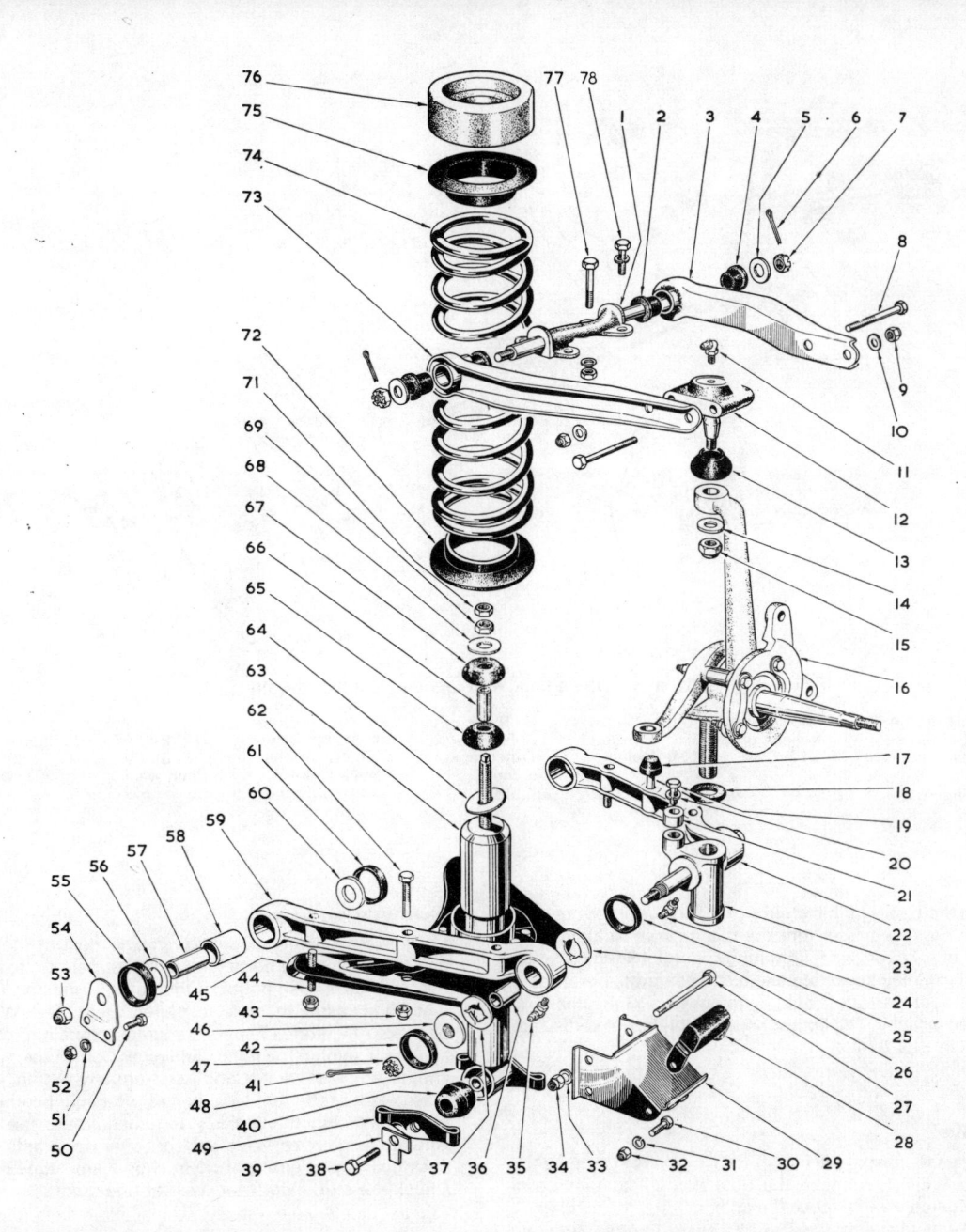

FIG 8:3 Front suspension details. Refer to FIGS 8:1 and 8:2 for the differences in design

Key to Fig 8:3   1 Upper inner fulcrum   2 Rubber bush   3 Upper wishbone arm (rear)   4 Rubber bush
5 Washer   6 Splitpin   7 Slotted nut   8 Bolt   9 Nyloc nut   10 Plain washer   11 Grease nipple
12 Upper ball joint   13 Rubber gaiter   14 Plain washer   15 Nyloc nut   16 Caliper bracket and vertical link
17 Bump rubber   18 Rubber seal   19 Bolt   20 Spring washer   21 Lockstop collar   22 Lower wishbone arm (rear)
23 Lower trunnion bracket   24 Grease nipple   25 Rubber seal   26 Thrust washer   27 Bolt   28 Rebound rubber
29 Bracket   30 Bolt   31 Spring washer   32 Nyloc nut   33 Plain washer   34 Nyloc nut   35 Grease nipple
36 Bush (nylon)   37 Thrust washer   38 Bolt   39 Tabwasher   40 Rubber bush   41 Splitpin   42 Rubber seal
43 Nyloc nut   44 Stud   45 Spring pan   46 Serrated washer   47 Slotted nut   48 Damper attachment bracket (rear)
49 Damper attachment bracket (front)   50 Bolt   51 Spring washer   52 Nut   53 Nyloc nut   54 Fulcrum bracket
55 Rubber seal   56 Thrust washer   57 Steel sleeve   58 Nylon bush   59 Lower wishbone (front)
60 Thrust washer   61 Rubber seal   62 Bolt   63 Damper   64 Washer   65 Rubber bush   66 Sleeve
67 Rubber bush   68 Washer   69 Nut   71 Locknut   72 Rubber collar   73 Upper wishbone arm (front)
74 Spring   75 Rubber collar   76 Distance piece   77 Bolt   78 Bolt

TR5/6

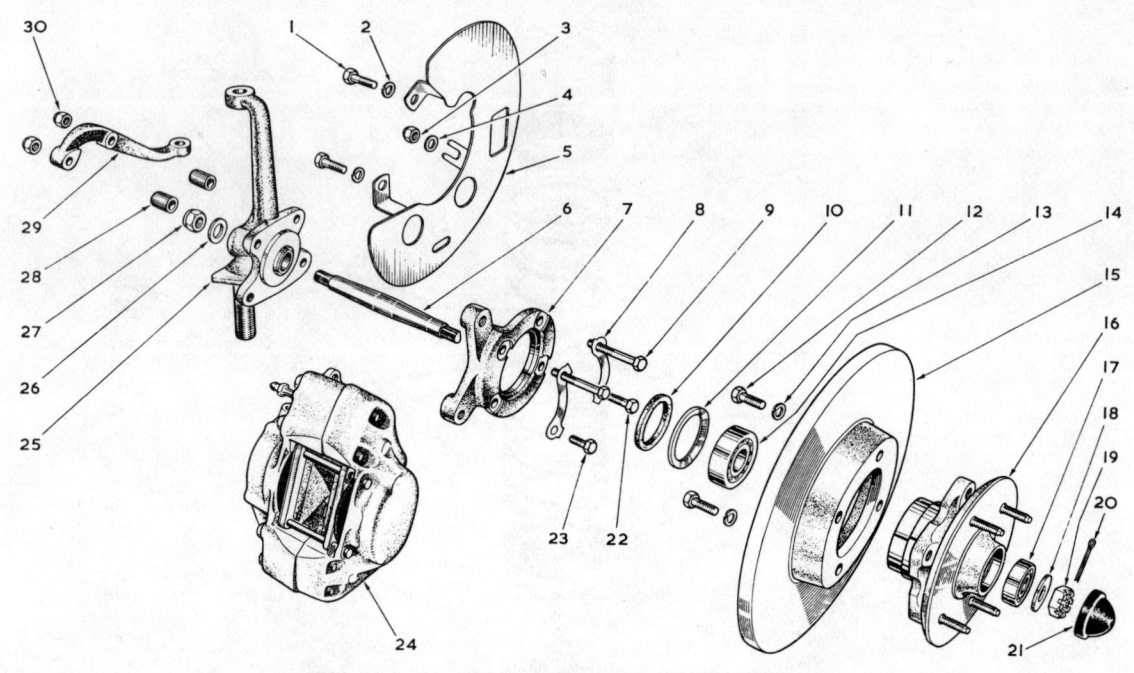

FIG 8:4 Disc brake, hub and vertical link details

Key to Fig 8:4
1 Bolt   2 Spring washer   3 Nyloc nut   4 Plain washer   5 Dust shield   6 Stub axle
7 Caliper bracket   8 Lock plate   9 Bolt   10 Felt seal   11 Seal retainer   12 Bolt   13 Spring washer
14 Inner taper race   15 Disc   16 Hub   17 Outer taper race   18 Washer   19 Slotted nut   20 Splitpin
21 Hub cap   22 Bolt   23 Bolt   24 Caliper unit   25 Vertical link   26 Plain washer   27 Nyloc nut
28 Distance pieces   29 Steering arm   30 Nyloc nut

noisily the bearings have either run dry or are worn out. Do not confuse noise from the disc brakes rotating with that of noisy bearings. Tightening the nut 19 which holds the hub on may cure the play in the bearings, but if there is any doubt the hub should be removed and the bearings checked visually. The components of the hub and disc are shown in **FIG 8:4**.

Removal:

1 Raise the front of the car off the ground and remove the road wheels. Remove the dust cap 21 as previously instructed and take out the splitpin 20.
2 Without undoing the flexible hose, remove the two bolts 1 and washers 2 securing the brake caliper 24 to the bracket 7. Remove the brake caliper and use a piece of wire to hang it safely out of the way without straining the flexible hose.
3 Wipe off surplus grease and remove the nut 19 and washer 18. Withdraw the hub 16 and brake disc 15 assembly, taking care to catch the inner race of the bearing 17 as it comes free.
4 If required, the brake disc 15 can be separated from the hub 16 by taking out the four bolts 12 and washers 13. Use a drift to remove the outer races of the bearings from the hub.

Examination of parts:

Use rags or newspaper to remove most of the grease and then wash the parts with petrol or paraffin to remove the last traces. Use petrol or trichlorethylene on the brake disc 15 to ensure that it is absolutely grease free. Wash the bearings 14 and 17 in a separate container of clean solvent. Examine the rollers and races of the bearings; they should be clean, bright and free from any pitting, wear or corrosion. Mate the two halves of each bearing and, whilst pressing them firmly together, rotate the halves. Any roughness or wear will become apparent. Renew both bearings if either of them shows any signs of wear. Check the stub axle 6 for wear or fine cracks.

Replacement:

1 If a new felt seal 10 is required, remove the old one from the seal retainer 11 and glue the new one back on with a little jointing compound. When the jointing compound is dry soak the seal in engine oil and squeeze out the surplus oil.
2 If the outer races of the bearings have been removed, refit them using a steel drift so that the larger diameter of the taper is on the outside. Refit the brake disc 15 to the hub 16 if they have been separated, making sure that the mating surfaces are scrupulously clean.

3 Pack the hub and rollers of the bearings with grease and fit the inner races to the outer races in the hub. Place the felt seal 10 and retainer 11 on the inner bearing 14 so that the felt 10 faces towards the centre of the car The complete hub assembly can now be slid back onto the stub axle 6, taking care not to push out the outer bearing 17, and then loosely held in place with the washer 18 and nut 19.
4 Use a spanner to tighten the nut 19, whilst spinning the hub. Do not overtighten the nut, just a little more than finger tight is quite sufficient. When the bearings have settled unscrew the nut 19 back to finger tight and align the slots so that a new splitpin will pass through the nut and the hole in the stub axle. The end float should be minimal without causing the bearings to bind. Secure the splitpin.
5 Replace the dust cap 21. Wipe the brake disc 15 with a petrol-soaked rag to remove any greasy finger marks and refit the brake caliper. Replace the road wheels and lower the car back to the ground.
6 When wire wheels are fitted to the car an extension hub, inset in **FIG 8:2**, is bolted to the hub. **If this extension is removed it is essential that it be refitted to the correct side of the car.** The correct side is when the knock-on hub cap tightens in the opposite direction to the direction of rotation of the road wheel. If the extension is fitted to the wrong side there is a danger that the hub cap will come loose. Check the splines on the extension hub and in the wheel.

8:4 The front dampers (shock absorbers)
Removal:

Jack up the front of the car and remove the road wheels. Refer to **FIG 8:5** (which has the same key as **FIG 8:3**). Take off the four nuts 79 and washers 80 and then remove the attachment plate 81. Undo the locknut 71 at the top of the damper. Hold the damper and remove the other nut 69. The damper can now be slid down inside the spring and removed. The rubber bush 67 and the washer 68 will remain on top of the turret while the remainder of the bushes and washers will come out with the damper. Straighten the tabwasher 39 and remove the bolt 38 to separate the parts of the lower attachment point.

Testing:

Renew the damper if it shows any signs of physical damage such as dents in the body, bent ram or leaks. If the unit appears satisfactory mount it vertically in a vice, using lead or wood to protect it. Slowly extend and compress the damper through its full range of movement ten times. There should be constant and appreciable resistance in both directions. If the resistance is so strong that the unit cannot be moved by hand then renew the damper. Similarly renew the damper if the resistance in either direction is weak or there are pockets of no resistance. The front dampers are sealed units and cannot be rectified.

Refitting:

If any of the rubber bushes are worn, distorted or perished, renew them. Fit the washer 64, rubber bush 65 and steel sleeve 66 to the top of the damper. If dismantled, reassemble the bottom attachment. Keep the damper vertical after testing and pass it, extended as far as possible, up through the spring. Replace the rubber bush 67 and steel washer 68 and then hold the damper in place with the nuts 69 and 71.

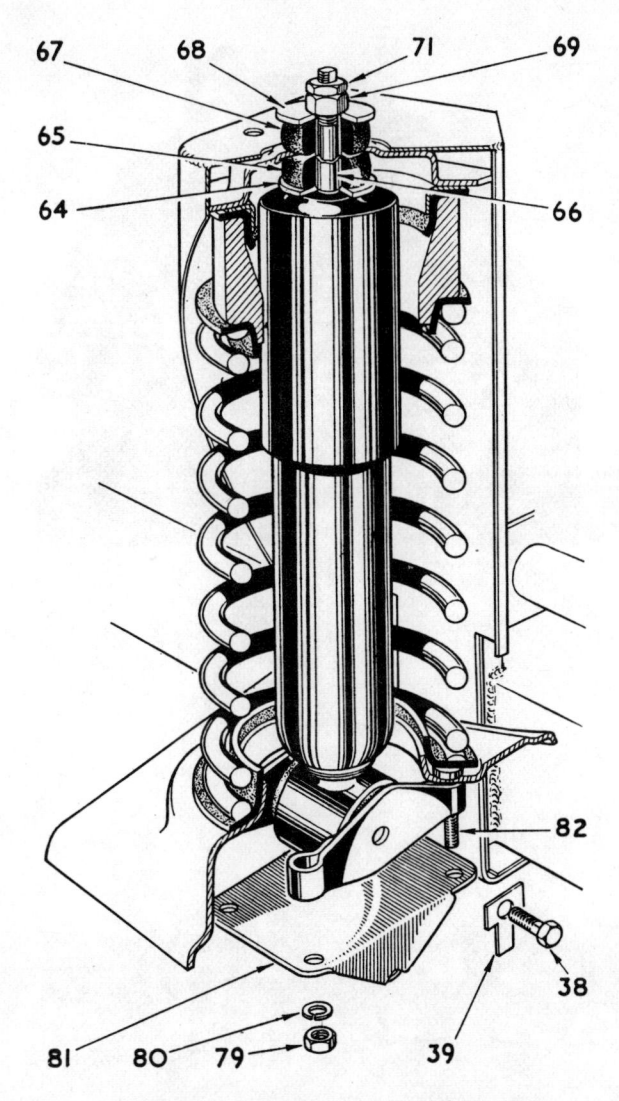

FIG 8:5 Attachment of front damper

8:5 The front road springs

The coil springs are partially compressed between the sets of wishbones and consequently exert a considerable pressure even when the front wheels are jacked clear off the ground. To remove or replace a spring some means of compressing the spring or taking the pressure must be found. The best and safest way is to use the special tool No. S.112A and adaptor S.112A.1A. Refer to **FIG 8:3** throughout this section.

FIG 8:6 Releasing the front spring

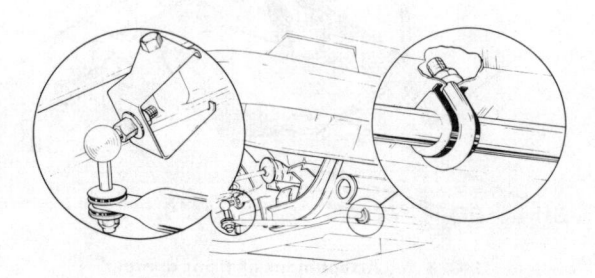

FIG 8:7 Anti-roll bar attachment details

1 Remove the damper as instructed in the previous section. Use a jack under the lower wishbone and raise the suspension until it is clear of the rebound stop 28. Detach the bracket 29 with the rebound stop 28. Lower the suspension and remove the jack.
2 Pass the special tool up through the spring pan 45, spring 74 and suspension turret. Lock the tool in position at the top. Fit the adaptor and winding nut to the thread on the tool below the spring pan 45, making sure that the bolts 82, which supported the bottom attachment of the damper, fit into the clearance holes provided in the damper.
3 Screw up the tightening nut on the special tool and compress the road spring 74 until the lower wishbone

82

assembly is horizontal. Place a block of wood between the top of the turret and the upper wishbone assembly to support the suspension.

4 Remove the bolt 62, nuts 43 and bump rubber 17 so that the spring pan 45 is free, and replace the bolt 62 and bump rubber 17 with $\frac{3}{8}$ x 6 inch (9.5 x 152 mm) guide rods as shown in **FIG 8:6**. Slowly unwind the nut on the special tool, guiding the pan 45 down the guide rods, until the spring 74 is loose. Dismantle the special tool and remove the spring pan 45, rubber collar 72, spring 74, collar 75 and distance piece 76. The four bolts 82 (see **FIG 8:5**) that hold the bottom of the damper 63 can now be removed.
5 Clean off dirt and rust from the spring and examine it for damage or cracks. Measure the spring and check that the free length conforms to the dimension given in Technical Data, to ensure that it has not weakened with use.
6 Reassembly is the reversal of the removal operation. Renew the rubber collars 72 and 75 as well as the rebound rubber 29 if any of them are perished or worn.

8:6 Ball joint and upper wishbones

On all the models covered by this manual these parts are exactly as shown in **FIG 8:3**. Wear on these parts is best checked before removing the road wheel as described in the first paragraph of **Section 8:3**.

1 Securely jack up the front of the car and, after checking for wear, remove the road wheel. Use a block of wood or a jack to support the suspension.
2 Remove the nut 15 and washer 14 from the ball joint 12. Use an extractor S.166 to separate the ball joint 12 from the vertical link 16. If no extractor is available pull the two apart and hammer on one side of the tapered eye, using a block of metal on the other side to prevent distortion. The ball joint 12 is held between the upper wishbones 3 and 73 by two sets of bolts 8, washers 10 and nuts 9.
3 Some play may be caused by the failure of the rubber bushes 2 and 4. Extract the two splitpins 6, and remove the two nuts 7 and washers 5. The front wishbone 73 has the greater amount of offset, but if there is any doubt label both wishbones before removing them and the rubber bushes from the inner fulcrum 1. Check that the pins of the fulcrum 1 are clean and free from score marks.
4 Reassembly is the reversal of the dismantling operation. Statically load the car, with 150 lb in each seat, before finally tightening and splitpinning the two nuts 7.

8:7 The lower wishbone and vertical link assembly

Check the wear as described earlier with the car jacked up and the wheels in place. Unless otherwise stated, refer to **FIG 8:3** throughout this section.

1 Remove the front hubs and discs (see **Section 8:3**), remove the dampers (see **Section 8:4**), remove the road springs (see **Section 8:5**). Disconnect the ball joint 12 from the vertical link as described in operation 2 in **Section 8:6**.
2 Vertical play between the lower trunnion bracket 23 and the vertical link will be a further confirmation of wear.
3 Remove the Nyloc nut and disconnect the outer tie rod ball joint from the steering arm part 29 in **FIG 8:4**.

4 Remove the Nyloc nuts and carefully tap out the bolts securing the inner ends of the lower wishbones 22 and 59 to the chassis mounted brackets. Hold the wishbones while performing this operation as they will come free from the car when the two bolts are removed. The brackets are held on by nuts behind the chassis, but it should be noted that they are shimmed to adjust the steering and suspension geometry.
5 Refer to **FIG 8:2**. Remove the splitpin, unscrew the nut and withdraw the bolt 1 to free the wishbones from the lower trunnion bearing.
6 Unscrew the bolt 19 and remove the washer 20 and the eccentric lock stop collar 21. The lower trunnion bracket 23 can now be unscrewed from the vertical link.
7 If either the vertical link or the trunnion bracket are worn they must both be renewed as a set. Referring to **FIG 8:4** dismantle the vertical link as follows. Straighten the ears of the lock plates 8, and holding the bolts 9 remove the two nuts 30. Lift off the steering arm 29 and the two distance pieces 28. Remove the two bolts 23 and slide the caliper bracket 7 off along the stub axle 6. Remove the Nyloc nut 27 and the washer 26. Press out the stub axle 6 from the vertical link 25.

Reassembling the front suspension:

1 Wash all the metal parts in petrol or paraffin and examine them for wear, distortion or damage, especially all pivots. Check all rubber bushes for wear, distortion or perishing and renew them if they appear at all doubtful. Reassembly is the reversal of the dismantling operation but the following points should be noted.
2 When securing the lower trunnion bearing back onto the vertical link ensure that there is full and free movement from lock to lock. When fitting the wishbones to the lower trunnion bracket, after assembling the pivots as shown in **FIG 8:2**, tighten the nut and bolt 1 sufficiently to settle the parts. Slacken back the nut and tap back the bolt so that there is an equal end clearance of .004 to .012 inch (.1 to .3 mm) at either end. Splitpin the nut in place.
3 The securing nuts on the inner wishbone pivots should not be fully tightened until the suspension is completely assembled and the car lowered back to the ground with a load of 150 lb in each front seat. This will ensure that all the rubber bushes are in their statically laden position.
4 The suspension geometry is controlled by the shims fitted between the lower inner fulcrum brackets and the chassis. **It is strongly advised that the car be taken to a suitably equipped service station for the geometry to be checked after reassembling the suspension.** Very accurate and specialized equipment is required for these checks, and without such equipment the task is beyond the capabilities of any owner.

5 The steering lock will have to be adjusted to the figures given in **Technical Data**. The eccentric lockstop collar on the vertical link controls the amount of lock on the steering. When all operations are finished jack up the front of the car and check that the steering moves freely from lock to lock without the wheels hitting the body or chassis. **Freedom of movement should be checked at regular intervals as parts are reassembled.**

8:8 The anti-roll bar

This is only fitted to the TR6 and TR250. The attachment details are shown in **FIG 8:7**. It functions as an interconnection between the front wheels so that as one wheel is pressed up by cornering forces the load is partially transferred through the anti-roll bar to the other front wheel. When both suspensions are level the anti-roll bar is torsion free.

8:9 Fault diagnosis

(a) Wheel wobble
1 Unbalanced front wheels
2 Worn hub bearings
3 Weak front springs
4 Loose wheel fixings
5 Worn suspension linkage
6 Uneven tyre wear

(b) 'Bottoming' of suspension
1 Check 3 in (a)
2 Rebound rubbers worn or missing
3 Dampers not working

(c) Heavy steering
1 Neglected ball joint and trunnion bracket lubrication
2 Incorrect suspension geometry

(d) Excessive tyre wear
1 Check 5 in (a); 3 in (b) and 2 in (c)

(e) Rattles
1 Rubber bushes worn in pivots
2 Damper mountings loose or worn rubber buffers and bushes
3 Anti-roll bar mountings loose, bearings worn or bar broken*

(f) Excessive rolling
1 Check 3 in (a); 3 in (b)
2 Check 3 in (e)*
*TR6 and TR250 only

NOTES

CHAPTER 9

THE STEERING SYSTEM

9:1 Description
9:2 Routine maintenance
9:3 Removing and replacing the steering unit
9:4 Servicing the steering unit

9:5 Track (front wheel alignment)
9:6 The steering column
9:7 Fault diagnosis

9:1 Description

The steering operates from the steering wheel through a system of shafts and universal joints to a rack and pinion steering box. At either end of the steering unit is a tie rod which is connected by a ball joint to the steering arm on each vertical link. The vertical link is free to swivel allowing the front wheels to provide the steering action.

The steering column is designed, with an impact clamp, so as to telescope together if it is forced against the driver in an accident. The steering column head contains the horn press button, the indicator switch and, if fitted, the overdrive switch. The cables for these pass out through a hole in the head and are then led away by a cable trough so there is no stator tube running the length of the column.

The steering wheel on the TR5 is integral with the hub, while on the TR6 and TR250 the steering wheel is a separate item bolted to the hub. Apart from this all three models are the same.

9:2 Routine maintenance

When greasing the suspension units also grease the two nipples 38 (see **FIG 9:1**) on the outer tie rods. At periodic intervals remove the sealing plug 10 on the steering unit and replace it with a grease nipple. Pump in a maximum of five strokes using a hand grease gun, then replace the nipple with the sealing plug 10. Do not overgrease the unit as the surplus will only be fed into the bellows 15 and 29, pressurizing them and possibly causing them to fail.

At regular intervals check the security of the steering unit mounting and also check the bellows and seals for damage. Dirt in the unit will cause excessive wear and it will enter if the bellows are damaged.

9:3 Removing and replacing the steering unit

The attachments are shown in **FIG 9:2**.

Removing:

Raise the front of the car on to stands. Remove the front road wheels. Take out the pinch bolt securing the bottom universal joint of the steering column to the rack pinion. Remove the engine cooling fan. Detach the outer tie rod ball joints from the steering arms on the suspension. If possible use an extractor, otherwise follow the instructions in **Chapter 8, Section 8:6**.

Remove the nuts 17, washers 18 and locating plates 16. From above lift out the U-bolts 7. Pull the rack forward to clear it from the column universal joint and manoeuvre the unit out of the car.

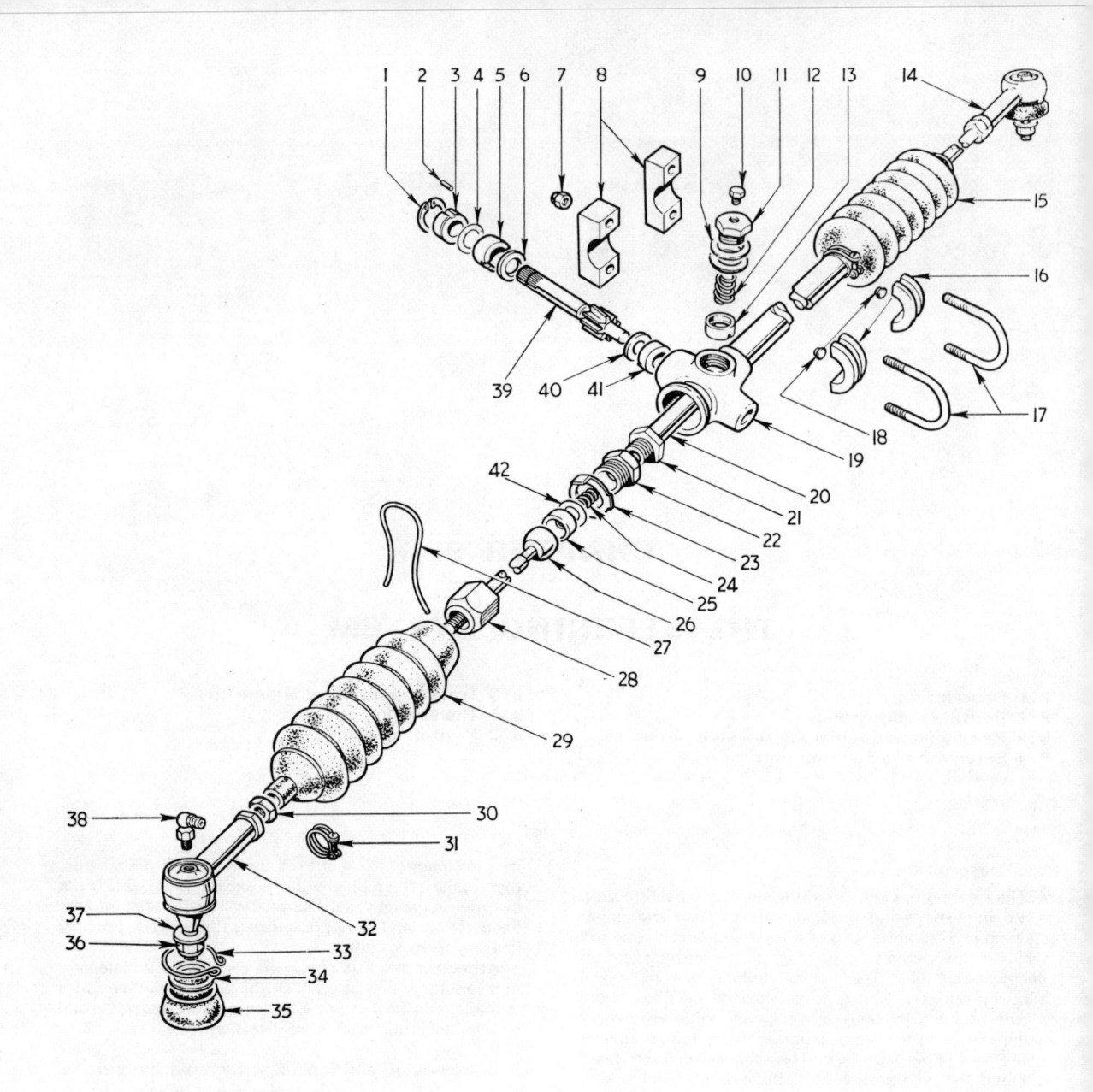

FIG 9:1 Steering unit details

Key to Fig 9:1   1 Circlip   2 Peg   3 Retainer   4 Shim   5 Bush   6 Thrust washer   7 Nyloc nut
8 Packing pieces (rear)   9 Shim   10 Plug   11 Cap   12 Spring   13 Thrust button   14 Tie rod ends
15 Rubber gaiter   16 Packing pieces (front)   17 U-bolts   18 Dowels   19 Rack tube   20 Rack
21 Locknut   22 Sleeve nut   23 Lock plate   24 Spring   25 Cup   26 Outer tie rod   27 Locking wire
28 Cup nut   29 Rubber gaiter   30 Locknut   31 Wire clip   32 Outer tie rod end   33 Clip   34 Washer
35 Rubber gaiter   36 Nyloc nut   37 Washer   38 Grease nipple   39 Pinion   40 Thrust washer
41 Bush   42 Shim

Replacing:

1 To obtain the correct clearances the rubber bushes 8 require to be partially compressed. A type of tool shown in **FIG 9:3** will be required for this operation. Note that one rod is threaded with a lefthand thread and the other with a righthand thread so that when they are turned the outer pieces move apart or together.

2 Fit new rubber bushes 8 to the rack and then manoeuvre it back into place in the car. Replace the locating plates 16 and the U-bolts 7. Secure the parts loosely in place with the washers 18 and the nuts 17.

3 Push one U-bolt to the outer end of the elongated holes in the chassis crossmember bracket, and slide that side locating plate 16 inwards until the flanged end of the plate is in full contact with the crossmember at **B**. If necessary elongate the holes in the plate 16. Tighten the two nuts 17 to a load of 12 to 14 lb ft (1.659 to 1.936 kg m).

4 Fit the expander tool and compress the rubber bushes 8 until there is a clearance of $\frac{1}{8}$ inch (3.175 mm) between the flange plates on the rack and the retainers on the U-bolts, shown at **A**. Torque load the remaining two nuts 17 to hold the U-bolt in place.

5 Replace the engine cooling fan. Reconnect the outer tie rod ball joints to the steering arms. Replace the road wheels and set them in the straight-ahead position. Turn the steering wheel until that too is in the straight-ahead position, and then reconnect the steering column universal joint to the rack pinion. Check for full and free movement from lock to lock before lowering the car back to the ground.

6 After replacing the steering unit it is advisable to check the track on the front wheels (see **Section 9:5**).

9:4 Servicing the steering unit

Dismantling:

1 Undo the clips 31 securing the bellows 15 and 29 and slide the bellows outwards towards the tie rod ends. Slacken the locknuts 21 and by undoing the sleeve nuts 22, remove the outer tie rod assemblies. Withdraw both springs 24 from the ends of the rack.

2 Release the tabwashers 23. Unscrew the sleeve nuts 22 from the nuts 28 and remove the thrust pads 25, shims 42 and tabwashers 23. Slacken the locknuts 30 and unscrew the tie rod ends 14 and 32.

3 Remove the locknuts 21 from the ends of the rack. Remove the plug 11 and withdraw the shims 9, spring 12 and thrust button 13.

4 With a pair of circlip pliers remove the circlip 1 and withdraw the pinion assembly, taking care not to lose the dowel 2. From the pinion 39 remove parts 3 to 6. Remove the O-ring from the annular groove inside the retainer 3.

5 Withdraw the rack 20 from the housing 19. Extract the thrust washer 40 and the bush 41 from the housing. If required drift out the bush in the end of the rack tube and press in a new bush.

6 Wash all the parts, except the bellows, in petrol and examine them for wear. Wipe out the bellows with rag and examine them for splits. Renew all worn parts.

Adjusting pinion end float:

1 Insert the bush 41 and thrust washer 40 into the

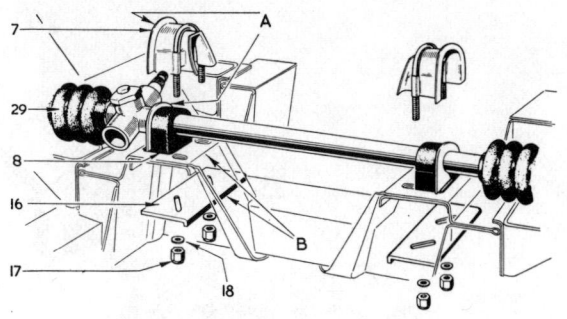

FIG 9:2 Steering unit attachments

Key to Fig 9:2   **A** Distance between flanges must be $\frac{1}{8}$ inch (3.17 mm)   **B** Flange of item 16 must contact innermost flange of frame   7 U-bolt   8 Rubber bush   16 Locating plate   17 Nyloc nut   18 Plain washer   29 Rubber washer

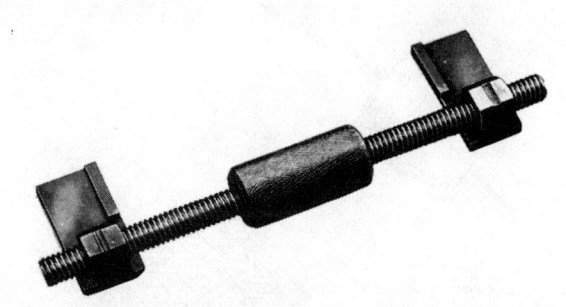

FIG 9:3 Expander tool for use when fitting steering rack

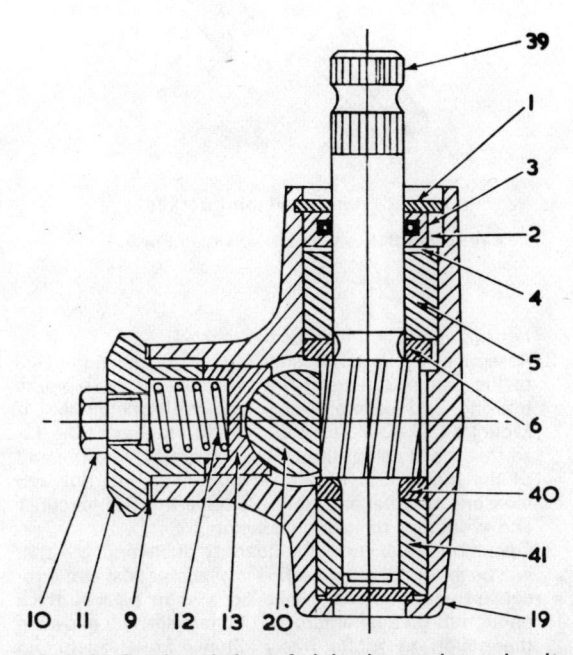

FIG 9:4 Sectioned view of pinion in steering rack unit

Key to Fig 9:4 is the same as key to **Fig 9:1**

TR5/6

87

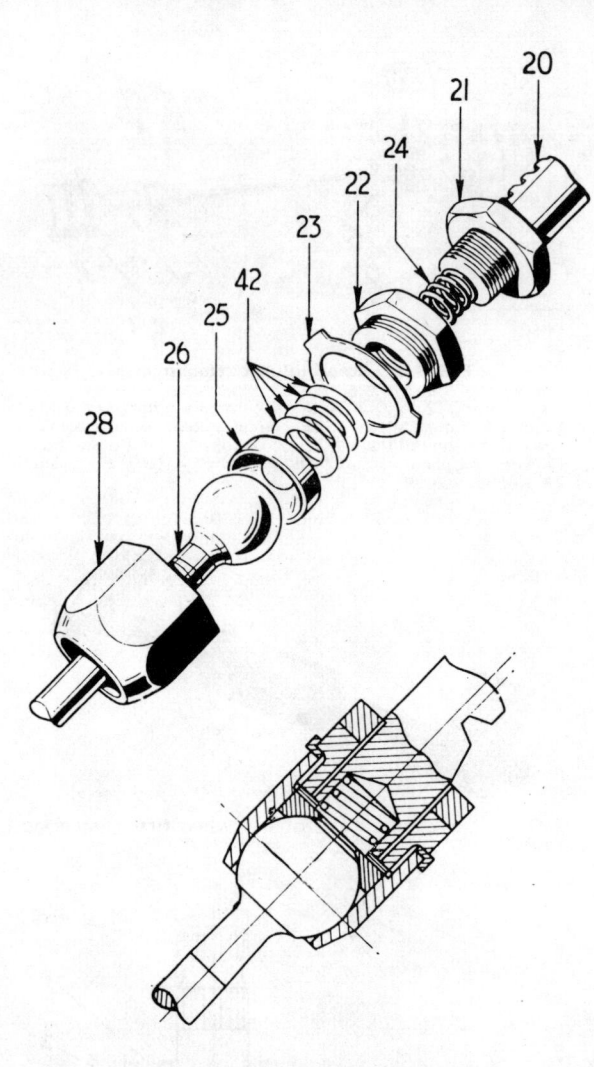

FIG 9:5 Inner ball joint details

Key to **Fig 9:5** is the same as key to **Fig 9:1**

housing, and then replace the rack 20.
2 Assemble the thrust washer 6, bush 5 and retainer 3 to the pinion 39. Insert the assembly into the pinion housing and secure it in place with the circlip 1. Mount a DTI (Dial Test Indicator) on the rack tube 19, so that the stylus of the DTI rests vertically on the end of the pinion 39. Move the pinion in and out and measure the total end float. Remove the DTI, circlip 1 and withdraw the pinion assembly.
3 Operation 2 will show the quantity of shimming 4 that will be required, but if no DTI is available trial and error can be used instead. Make up a shim pack 4 thick enough to give minimum end float while still allowing the pinion to rotate freely. Shims are available in .004 and .010 inch thicknesses.
4 Remove the retainer 3 from the pinion assembly.

Fit a new O-ring into the recess in the retainer 3. Fit the previously made up shim pack 4 to the pinion assembly and then the retainer 3. Replace the assembly into the pinion housing and secure it in place with the circlip 1, not forgetting to fit the locating dowel 2. To show the relation of the various parts a sectioned view of the pinion assembly and thrust button is shown in **FIG 9:4**.

Adjusting the pinion pressure pad:

1 Insert the thrust button 13 into the housing 19 so that it fits over the rack 20 as shown in **FIG 9:4**. Leave out the spring 12 and shims 9, screw in the cap 11 tight enough to eliminate all end float, without over-tightening. With feeler gauges measure the gap between the inner face of the cap 11 and the outer face of the housing where the shims 9 will fit. Remove the cap 11 and thrust button 13. Make up a shim pack 9 equal in thickness to the clearance just measured plus .004 inch allowance for end float.
2 Pack the steering unit with grease. Refit the thrust button 13, spring 12 and shim pack 9, and secure them to the housing with the cap 11.
3 Drill a hole in a piece of wood about a foot long, so that the hole will fit tightly over the pinion. Measure a distance of eight inches from the hole centre and cut a notch in the wood. Using a piece of wire, suspend a two pound weight from the wood at the notch. The pinion should just rotate when the wooden bar is horizontal. Adjust by removing or adding shims 9 under the cap 11 until the pinion rotates at the required torque.

Inner ball joints:

A more detailed drawing of the inner ball joints is shown in **FIG 9:5**, which uses the same key as **FIG 9:1**.
1 Slide the nut 28 onto the tie rod 26. Insert the thrust cup 25 into the nut 28 over the end of the ball on the tie rod. Fit the lockwasher 23 to the sleeve nut 22 and screw the pair fully home in the nut 28. Hold the cup nut in a vice, protected with lead or wood, and pull and push on the tie rod to estimate the amount of end float. Make up a shim pack 42 just slightly thicker than the estimated end float.
2 Dismantle the joint and then reassemble it with the shim pack 42 in place between the thrust cup 25 and the nut 22. Add or remove shims until the end float is .002 inch with the nut screwed firmly into the cup nut. **The joint should move quite freely and if there is tightness at any angle, increase the shim thickness until the tightness is just cured.**
3 Pack the ball joint with grease and finally assemble it, locking the nuts together by bending the ears of the tabwasher 23. Fit a locknut 21 to each end of the rack 20, and into each end of the rack insert a spring 24. Screw the ball joints to the ends of the rack but do not tighten the locknuts 21. Slide the bellows 29 and 15 into place on the outer tie rods 26.

Outer tie rod ends:

These items are sealed units and if they are damaged or seized they must be renewed. Examine the rubber gaiters 35 and renew these separately if they are split. If it is suspected that dirt has entered the assembly,

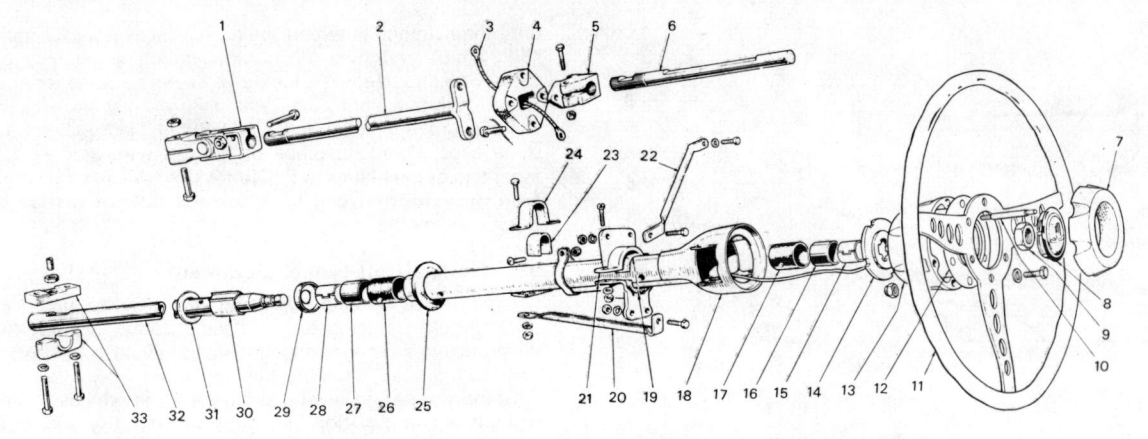

FIG 9:6 TR6 and TR250 steering column details

Key to Fig 9:6 1 Lower steering coupling   2 Lower steering column   3 Earth cable   4 Rubber coupling
5 Adaptor   6 Intermediate steering column   7 Padded bezel   8 Horn push   9 Column nut   10 Horn connection brush
11 Steering wheel   12 Horn push retaining plate   13 Steering wheel support boss   14 Slip ring   15 Nylon bush
16 Steel bush   17 Rubber bush   18 Upper steering column (outer)   19 Felt pads   20 Lower stay bracket
21 Upper clamp bracket   22 Upper stay bracket   23 Felt pad   24 Clamp   25 Rubber grommet
26 Rubber bush   27 Steel bush   28 Nylon bush   29 Cap   30 Trafficator canceller   31 Washer
32 Upper steering column (inner)   33 Impact clamp

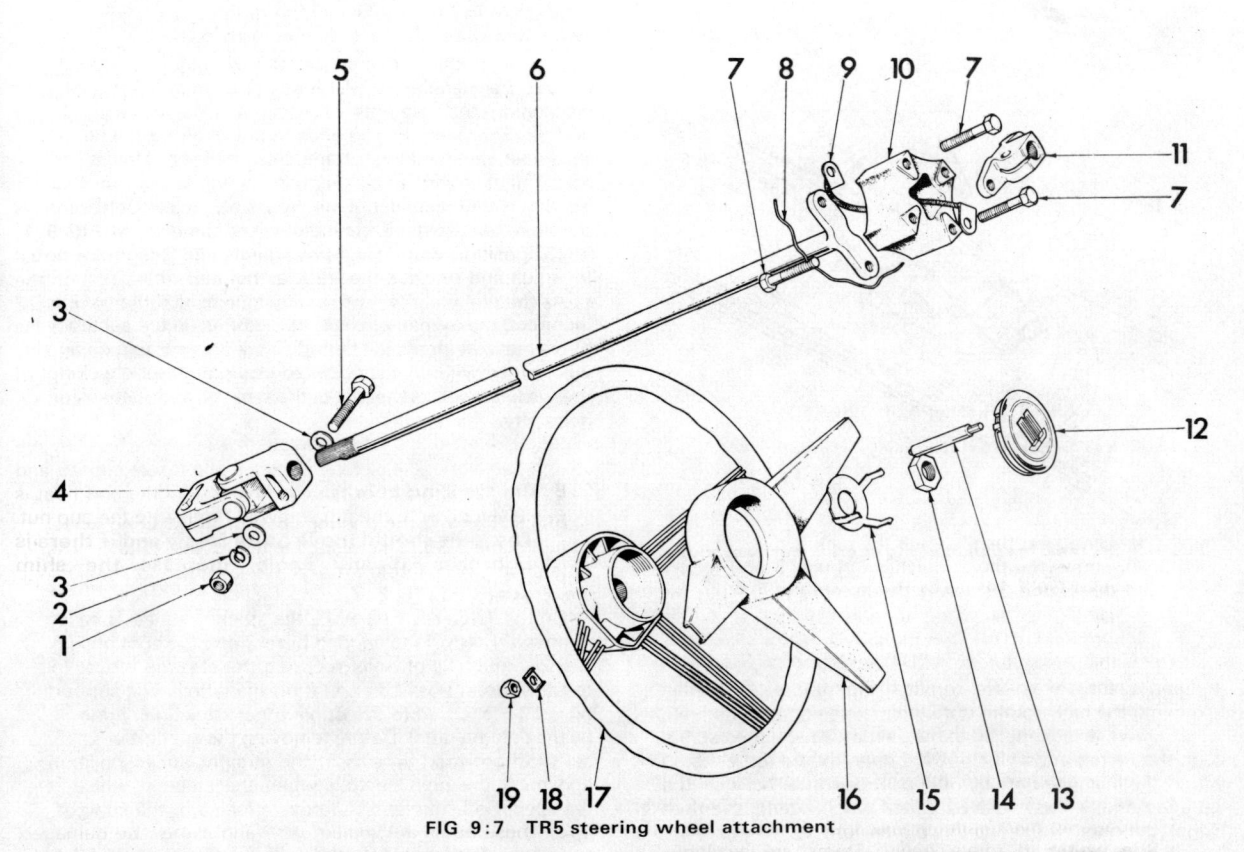

FIG 9:7 TR5 steering wheel attachment

Key to Fig 9:7 1 Nut   2 Spring washer   3 Plain washer   4 Universal coupling   5 Pinch bolt
6 Lower steering column   7 Bolt   8 Locking wire   9 Earthing cable   10 Rubber coupling   11 Adaptor
12 Horn push   13 Horn brush   14 Nut   15 Clip   16 Wheel trim   17 Steering wheel   18 Clamp   19 'Dotloc' acorn unit

TR5/6

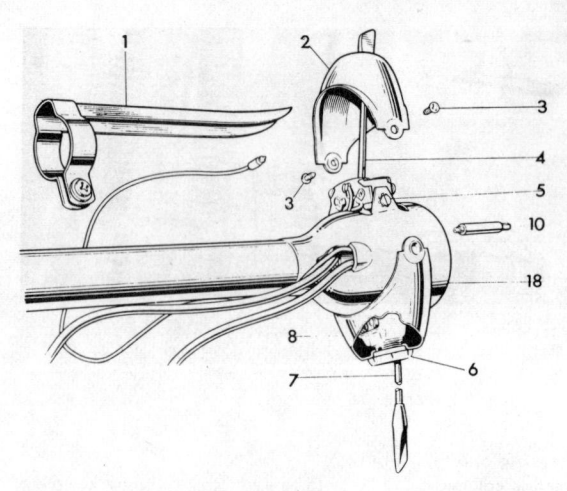

FIG 9:8 Direction indicator and overdrive switches

Key to Fig 9:8   1 Cable trough   2 Direction indicator switch cover   3 Direction indicator cover securing screws   4 Direction indicator switch   5 Direction indicator switch securing screws   6 Overdrive cover securing nut   7 Overdrive switch   8 Overdrive switch cover   10 Horn brush   18 Upper outer column

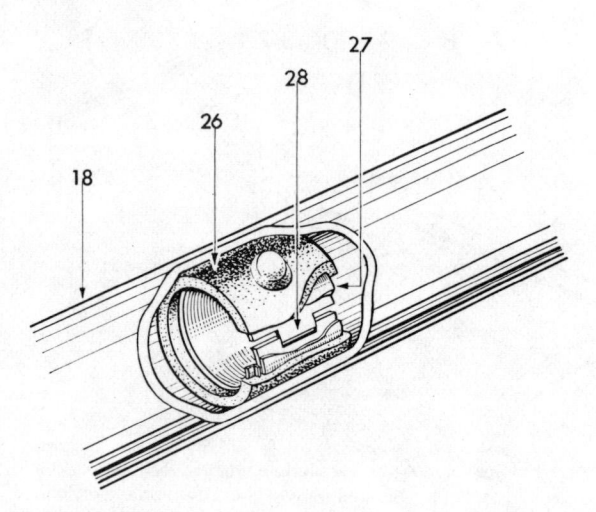

FIG 9:9 Section through steering column bush assembly

Key to Fig 9:9 is the same as key to Fig 9:6

pump plenty of grease through the nipple 38, whilst moving the ball around, until the grease comes out clean.

Screw the locknuts 30 to the tie rods 26 and then screw on the tie rod ends 15 and 32. Adjust the tie rod ends so that the distance between the centres of the balls on the tie rod and tie rod end is 8.42 inch (213.8 mm), and then lock the nuts 30 to keep this dimension.

Turn the pinion and count the number of turns from lock to lock, then centralize the unit by turning the pinion back half that number of turns. Turn the locknuts 21 until the distance between their inner faces is 23.94 inch (60.81 cm) and they are equidistant on either side of the centre line. Hold the locknuts 21 with a spanner and tighten the ball joint nuts 22 and 28 onto the locknuts.

Resecure the bellows 15 and 29 in place using the three clips 31 and a piece of locking wire around the inner end of the bellows 29. **Check the unit for full and free movement from lock to lock before refitting it to the car.**

9:5 Track (front wheel alignment)

After removing and replacing the steering unit the track should be checked. If, after a period of running, the front tyres are wearing unevenly, giving a feathered edge to the tread, then the tracking is probably out.

Stand the car on level ground with the wheels in the straight-ahead position. Without turning the steering, push the car forward a few yards to settle the wheels and bearings. Measure, as accurately as possible, the distance between the front wheel rims at the front of the wheel and at wheel centre height. Mark the wheels with chalk as a guide, and push the car forwards so that the wheels turn exactly half a revolution. This is to ensure that any innaccuracies in the wheel rims are accounted for. Measure, again as accurately as possible, the distance between the wheel rims at wheel centre height but at the rear of the front wheels. The difference between the two dimensions will be the amount of 'toe-in'.

On all models covered by this manual the 'toe-in' should be parallel to $\frac{1}{16}$ inch (1.6 mm). Adjust by slackening the locknuts securing the tie rod ends 15 and 32. Screw the tie rod ends in or out along the tie rod to adjust the tracking of the front wheels. Unless the adjustment is very small it is best to adjust both tie rods equally, otherwise if one tie rod only is adjusted it is possible that the steering wheel will not be in the straight-ahead position when the front wheels are. Retighten the locknuts and recheck the track as before.

As the tyre wear will be greatly increased if the track is incorrect, the owner who has any doubts on the accuracy of his measurements is advised to take his car to a garage where they will have specialized equipment for checking the track, as well as the rest of the steering and suspension geometry.

9:6 The steering column

FIG 9:6 shows the steering column and steering wheel fitted to the TR6. This also applies to the TR250. The differences in the column and wheel fitted to the TR5 are illustrated in **FIG 9:7**.

On the TR6 (see **FIG 9:6**) the steering wheel is easily removed. Take off the padded bezel 7 and the horn push 8. Remove the ring of bolts securing the steering wheel 11 to the support boss 13 and lift off the wheel. The support boss 13 is secured to the upper inner steering column 32 by the column nut 9. Before removing the support boss 13, set the front road wheels in the straight-ahead position and mark the boss so that when the steering wheel is replaced, both this and the boss are also in the straight-ahead position.

On the TR5 (see **FIG 9:7**) the steering wheel 17 is fixed directly to the inner column. Prise out the horn push 12 and withdraw the horn brush 13. Remove the nut 14 and the acorn nuts 19 with the clamps 18. The clip 15 and the wheel trim 16 can now be removed. Mark the steering wheel hub so that it will be replaced in the correct angular relationship with the column. Use an extractor to withdraw the steering wheel from the column.

Both types of steering wheels are refitted by the reversal of the removal operation. Put a drop of Locktite on the threads of the hub nut to prevent it working loose in service.

Removal of the steering column:

1 Disconnect the battery. Disconnect the horn, direction indicator and, if overdrive is fitted, the leads from the overdrive switch at the snap connectors nearest the steering. If the colours have faded on the cables, label them to ensure that they will be reconnected correctly.
2 Remove the bolt securing the lower all-metal steering coupling 1 to the pinion on the steering rack unit. Undo the bolts and remove the two parts of the impact clamp 33. The threaded portion is removed complete with the Allen screw and its locknut. Push the intermediate column 6 upwards inside the inner column 32 to disengage the lower coupling 1 from the pinion on the steering rack unit. Swing the coupling to one side and withdraw the intermediate shaft 6, complete with both steering couplings and the lower column 2 from inside the upper inner steering column 32. Remove the nylon washer 31.
3 It is not necessary to dismantle the steering couplings unless they are damaged or the rubber coupling 4 has cracked or become perished. The bottom all-metal coupling 1 can be washed out in a tin of petrol and the pivots lightly lubricated with oil. If the upper coupling is dismantled make sure that the earth cable 3 is reconnected to the securing bolts and that the bolts are wire locked on reassembly.
4 Working inside the car, release the nuts and bolts holding the clamp 24 and felt 23. Remove the stay 22 and the upper clamp half 21 with its felt 19. Pull the steering column assembly, complete with the steering wheel, out through the grommet 25 and the aperture in the facia.

Dismantling the steering column:

1 Refer to **FIG 9:8**. Undo the screws 3 and remove the covers 2. Remove the Phillips screw and take off the cable trough 1. If an overdrive is fitted remove the cover 8 by unscrewing the nut 6 from the switch. Both switches are held in place by screws. Take these out and carefully remove the direction indicator switch 4 and, if fitted, the overdrive switch 7 feeding the cables out after them through the hole.
2 Remove the steering wheel and boss as described earlier.
3 Remove the end cap 29. A section through the lower bush assembly is shown in **FIG 9:9**, and the top bush assembly is of a similar construction. Press in the protrusions on the rubber bush 26 and use a long shaft to press out the bush assembly from the upper column 18. Remove the nylon bush 28 and the steel bush 27 from the flexible end of the rubber bush 26. Repeat the procedure for the top bush assembly, parts 15, 16 and 17.

FIG 9:10 Aligning the direction indicator cancelling lugs with the steering wheel and switch

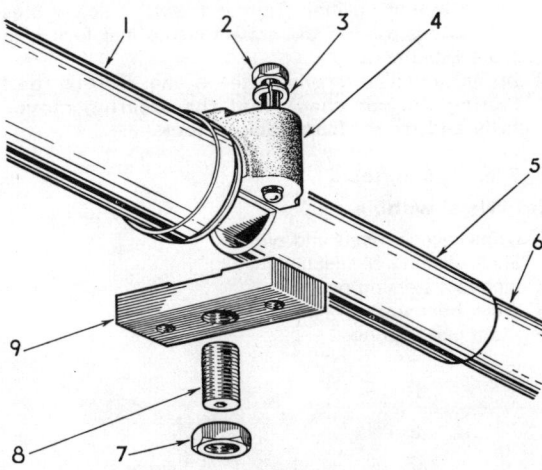

FIG 9:11 Impact clamp details

Key to Fig 9:11 1 Upper outer column 2 Bolt
3 Washer 4 Impact column 5 Upper inner column
6 Lower column 7 Locknut 8 Allen screw
9 Impact clamp plate

Reassembling the steering column:

Wash all the metal parts in petrol or paraffin. Use rags to wipe dirt off the larger parts which do not require washing in solvent. Check all the parts for wear, especially the felt pieces in the clamps and the components of the upper and lower bushes. If these parts are worn or damaged the steering column will be loose and cause rattles. Reassemble the steering column in the reverse order of dismantling, paying particular attention to the bushes and ensuring that the metal reinforcing rings on the rubber bushes 17 and 26 are towards the bottom of the column.

The steering wheel, direction indicator switch and cancelling lugs 30 should be aligned as shown in **FIG 9:10** when refitting the steering wheel.

Refitting the steering column:

1 Refitting is the reversal of the removal operation. Slide the top column assembly back into place, making sure that it passes through the rubber grommet 25. Secure it

loosely in place with the clamps and stays, leaving the assembly free to slide in the clamps.
2 To refit the impact clamp refer to **FIG 9:11**. Slacken the locknut 7 and unscrew the Allen screw 8 two complete turns. Turn the shaft 6 to align the machined flat with the slot in the upper inner steering column 5. Fit the two halves of the clamp 4 and 9 and secure them in place with the pair of bolts 2 and washers 3. Do not tighten the Allen screw. Push the column 6 up inside the column 5 and fit the lower steering coupling 1 back onto the pinion of the steering unit, so that both the steering wheel and front road wheels are in the straight-ahead position. Refit the pinch bolt to the steering coupling and secure it with the nut.
3 Pull or push the steering column to the desired height and finally tighten the upper and lower clamps to hold the column in position. Tighten the Allen screw 8 as hard as possible on the impact clamp and lock it in place with the nut 7.
4 Do not forget to reconnect the wiring. **Before road testing the car check that the steering moves fully and freely from lock to lock.**

9:7 Fault diagnosis
(a) Wheel wobble
1 Unbalanced wheels and tyres
2 Slack steering connections
3 Incorrect steering geometry
4 Weak front springs
5 Worn hub bearings

(b) Wander
1 Check 2 and 3 in (a)
2 Front suspension and rear axle mounting points out of line
3 Uneven tyre pressures
4 Uneven tyre wear
5 Weak dampers or springs

(c) Heavy steering
1 Check 3 in (a)
2 Very low tyre pressures
3 Neglected lubrication
4 Wheels out of track
5 Steering rack unit maladjusted
6 Steering column bent or misaligned
7 Steering column bushes tight
8 Seized tie rod ends

(d) Lost motion
1 Loose steering wheel
2 Worn splines
3 Worn steering couplings
4 Worn ball joints
5 Worn steering rack unit
6 Worn suspension system and vertical link

CHAPTER 10

THE BRAKING SYSTEM

10:1 Description
10:2 Maintenance
10:3 The front disc brakes
10:4 The rear brakes
10:5 The master cylinder
10:6 The Pressure Differential Warning Actuator (PDWA)

10:7 Bleeding the brakes
10:8 Removing a flexible hose
10:9 The handbrake
10:10 The vacuum servo unit
10:11 Fault diagnosis

10:1 Description

Disc brakes are fitted to the front wheels and drum brakes to the rear wheels. All four are hydraulically operated from the brake pedal, and the handbrake operates the rear brakes only.

The handbrake is of the fly-off type. The button on the end of the handbrake lever is pressed in to hold the handbrake on. To release it the handbrake lever is pulled on further to free the ratchet, after which it can be let go off and the lever will be pulled to the off position by the action of springs. The linkage to the rear wheels is mechanical and normally requires no separate adjustment. Adjusting the rear brakes automatically adjusts the free travel of the handbrake lever.

All the models covered by this manual have a tandem system of braking and use a servo to augment the thrust of the brake pedal. The master cylinder is internally split into two portions and by the action of the brake pedal, and servo unit, pressure is generated in each of these portions. One portion feeds the rear brakes and the other portion feeds the front brakes. The system is so designed that if there is a failure in one half of the braking system the other half will still function correctly and at its full efficiency. The total efficiency of the system will be reduced when one half fails but the foot brake will still be effective.

A PDWA (Pressure Differential Warning Actuator) is fitted to the TR250 and other lefthand drive models to warn the driver when one half of the braking system has failed. The difference in pressure between the two systems moves a shuttle which then operates an electric switch. This switch controls a warning light but the two are interconnected with the oil pressure warning light and switch. When the engine is switched on both lights should glow faintly. As soon as the engine has started and built up oil pressure both lights should go out. If, with the engine running, both lights continue to glow then the engine oil pressure is low. On the other hand, if the oil pressure warning light stays out but the brake warning light glows brightly then one half of the braking system has failed.

The brake pedal is connected directly to the servo unit, but again the system is so designed that any failure in the servo unit allows the pressure from the brake pedal to be transmitted through the servo unit directly to the master cylinder. The brake system will lose efficiency because of

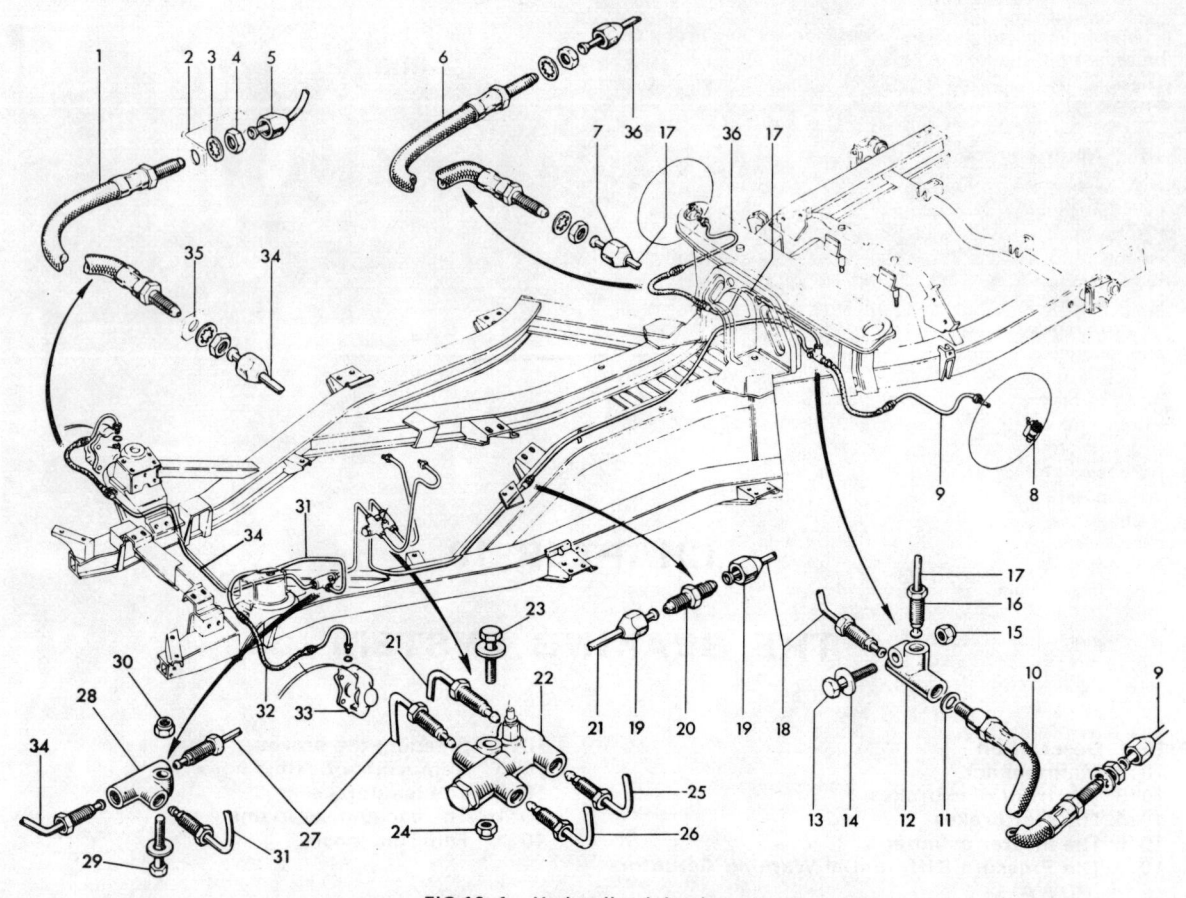

FIG 10:1 Hydraulic piping layout

Key to Fig 10:1   1 Flexible hose—righthand front   2 Support bracket—hose to caliper   3 Shakeproof washer   4 Nut
5 Tube nut—female   6 Flexible hose—righthand rear   7 Tube nut—female   8 Wheel cylinder   9 Pipe—hose to rear cylinder   10 Flexible hose—lefthand rear   11 Copper washer   12 Three-way union   13 Bolt   14 Washer   15 Nut
16 Tube nut—male   17 Pipe—three-way to righthand rear hose   18 Pipe—connector to three-way   19 Tube nut—female
20 Pipe connector   21 Pipe—PDWA to connector (lefthand drive vehicles only)   22 Pressure differential warning actuator (lefthand drive vehicles only)   23 Bolt (lefthand drive vehicles only)   24 Nyloc nut (lefthand drive vehicles only)   25 Pipe—PDWA to master cylinder (lefthand drive vehicles only)   26 Pipe—PDWA to master cylinder (lefthand drive vehicles only)
27 Pipe—PDWA front three-way (lefthand drive vehicles only)   28 Three-way connector—front   29 Bolt   30 Nyloc nut
31 Pipe—three-way to lefthand front hose   32 Flexible hose—lefthand front   33 Disc brake caliper—lefthand front   34 Pipe—three-way to righthand front hose   35 Bracket—flexible hose support   36 Pipe—hose to righthand rear cylinder

the loss of the servo unit, but the brake pedal will still be effective. The servo unit uses the vacuum from the inlet manifold to move a diaphragm which assists the action of the brake pedal onto the master cylinder.

The front brakes are of the rotating disc and rigidly mounted caliper type. Each caliper consists of two friction assemblies between which the disc rotates. Each friction pad is pressed out against the disc by a piston moved by hydraulic pressure from the master cylinder. They are automatically retracted when the pressure is released. Both pistons operate simultaneously to exert equal pressure on the friction pads. Wear is taken up automatically and no provision is made for adjustment.

The rear brakes are of the internally expanding shoe type with one leading and one trailing shoe to each brake.

Both brake shoes pivot about an adjuster assembly while the other ends of the shoes abut against the piston, for one shoe, and the base of the wheel cylinder for the other shoe. Pressure from the master cylinder forces the piston out of the cylinder and thus presses the corresponding shoe against the brake drum. The wheel cylinder is free to slide in a slot in the backplate, and the reaction of the shoe against the drum slides the cylinder in its slot forcing the other shoe into contact with the drum. Return springs pull the shoes out of contact with the brake drum when the pressure is released. The assembly is illustrated in **FIG 10:6**. As the brake drum revolves one shoe is wedged into tighter contact, and is thus given some assistance. With the drum rotating in a forward direction this is the leading shoe.

Metal pipes and flexible hoses convey the hydraulic pressure from the master cylinder to the wheel cylinders. These, and more important, their unions are shown in **FIG 10:1**.

10:2 Maintenance

At weekly intervals check the fluid level in the master cylinder reservoir. The reservoir is translucent so the level can be checked without removing the filler cap. A slow steady drop in fluid is normal since the brake calipers require more fluid to fill them as the front friction pads wear. A sudden drop in the level or an increase in the rate of dropping must be investigated and the fault immediately rectified.

Before removing the reservoir filler cap, wipe the top clean to prevent any dirt falling into the reservoir. **Never allow the reservoir level to fall below the danger line of the seam between the top and bottom halves of the reservoir.**

Adjust the rear brakes when the pedal travel becomes excessive. The adjuster is arrowed in **FIG 10:2**. Jack up each rear wheel in turn off the ground, and screw in the adjuster in a clockwise direction until solid resistance is felt. Slacken back the adjuster one notch. This should allow the brake drum to rotate without binding. If the drum still binds slacken the adjuster one more notch. Adjusting the rear brakes also automatically adjusts the free movement on the handbrake lever.

Preventative maintenance:

Never use anything but the recommended fluid, which is Castrol Girling Clutch and Brake Fluid to specification SAE.70R3. Do not leave the fluid in unsealed containers as it will absorb moisture from the air, causing the boiling point to be lowered and making the fluid dangerous to use. **It is best to discard fluid which has been bled or drained from the system.** Only if the fluid is perfectly clean should it be stored for re-use, and even then it should be allowed to stand for at least 24 hours to allow it to de-aerate before using again.

Observe absolute cleanliness when working on any part of the hydraulic system

Regularly examine friction pads, rear brake linings and all pipes, unions and hoses. If one friction pad is worn more than the other, change them over.

Every 36,000 miles or 3 years the system should be completely dismantled. Brake fluid should be discarded and all seals renewed. Examine the working surfaces of all cylinders and pistons. If any surfaces are worn, scored or corroded the affected assemblies should be renewed.

The air filter on the servo unit should be renewed at the same time as rear brake linings of front friction pads are renewed.

10:3 The front disc brakes

The disc brake caliper assembly details are shown in **FIG 10:3**.

Renewing friction pads:

These must be renewed if they are worn down to $\frac{1}{8}$ inch thickness. If they are allowed to wear thinner than this excessive heat may be transferred

FIG 10:2 Rear brake adjuster shown arrowed

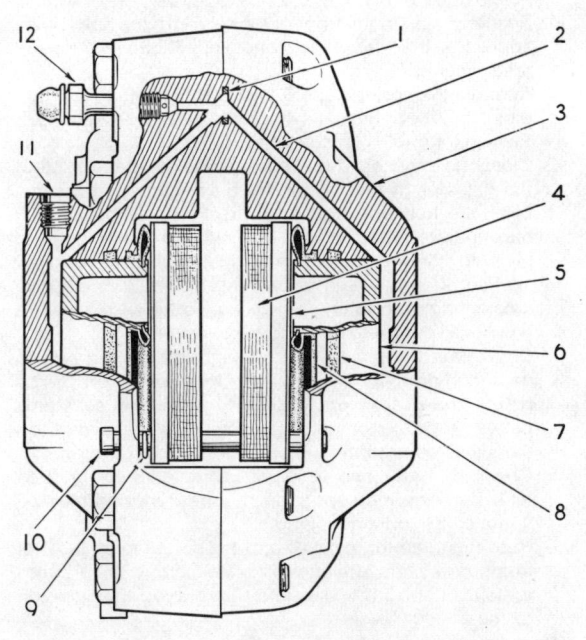

FIG 10:3 Disc brake caliper details

Key to Fig 10:3 1 Rubber O-ring 2 Fluid transfer channels 3 Caliper body 4 Brake pad 5 Anti-squeal plate 6 Piston 7 Piston sealing ring 8 Dust cover 9 Retaining clip 10 Retaining pin 11 Flexible hose connection 12 Bleed nipple

FIG 10:4 Renewing disc brake friction pads. Note the arrow on the anti-squeal shim pointing in the direction of forward rotation

through them from the friction disc, causing damage to the caliper assembly.

1 Securely jack up the front of the car, with the handbrake applied or the rear wheels chocked. Remove the front road wheels.
2 Remove the spring clips 9 and withdraw the retaining pins 10. Lift out the pads 4 and the anti-squeal shims 5. This operation is illustrated in **FIG 10:4**.
3 Clean the exposed face of the pistons 6 and ensure that the recesses in the caliper, for the friction pad assemblies, are free from rust and dirt. Press each piston 6 back into its cylinder. This will lead to a rise in the fluid level in the master cylinder reservoir. If necessary syphon off some fluid to prevent it overflowing. Have rags handy to mop up any spillage, otherwise the fluid will quickly soften and remove paintwork.
4 Check that the pistons are correctly positioned and fit new friction pad assemblies. **Do not attempt to reline the old assemblies.** Fit the anti-squeal shims between the pistons and pads so that the arrows on the shims point in the direction of forward rotation.
5 Check that the pad assemblies move freely in their recesses. Any high spots on the pressure pad may be removed by judicious filing.
6 Refit the retaining pins 10 and the spring clips 9. After fitting new pads, operate the brake pedal several times to adjust the front brakes and then top up the reservoir to the correct level.

Removing and replacing a disc brake caliper:

1 Chock the rear wheels, jack up the front of the car and firmly support it under the chassis. Remove the front road wheels. Remove the friction pads as described earlier.
2 Referring to **FIG 10:1** disconnect the flexible hose to the brake caliper, as described in **Section 10:8**. Use a small driptray to catch the hydraulic fluid spillage. Remove the two bolts securing the caliper and shims to the bracket on the vertical link of the suspension. Slide the caliper off the brake disc.
3 Refit the caliper in the reverse order of dismantling, not forgetting to replace the shims between the caliper and the bracket.
   Reconnect the flexible hose and refill the master cylinder reservoir. As the front and rear brake systems are isolated from each other only the front brakes need to be bled when a caliper has been removed.

Servicing a disc brake caliper:

1 Remove the caliper from the car as previously instructed. Withdraw the pistons 6 from the body. If they cannot be drawn out by hand, reconnect the flexible hose and hold the caliper so that the hose is not strained. Apply a clamp to hold one piston in place and apply gentle pressure on the brake pedal. The other piston will then be forced out, so be prepared for a spray of fluid if it comes free suddenly. Service the side from which the piston is removed first, then replace the piston and clamp it to remove the other piston.
2 Use the fingers to remove the dust cover 8 and the piston sealing ring 7 from the bore of the caliper. Though the two halves of the caliper are bolted together they should not be separated.
3 **To clean the internal parts of the caliper use only methylated spirits or the correct grade of hydraulic fluid. Use only hydraulic fluid on the rubber seals. All parts must be spotlessly clean and free from pitting or corrosion.**
4 Renew all the rubber seals, which are available in kits. Never re-use old seals if there has been the slightest sign of leakage. Wet the seals 7 with Castrol Girling Clutch and Brake Fluid and fit them into the recesses in the brake caliper. Use only the fingers and ensure that the seals are properly and squarely seated. Again using only the fingers, refit the projecting lips of the dust covers 8 into the outermost recesses in the calipers.
5 Coat the working faces of the pistons 6 with brake fluid and insert them, closed ends leading, squarely into the bores of the calipers. Take great care not to tilt the piston and so damage either the face of the bore or the seals. Push the pistons fully home and fit the outer lips of the dust covers 8 into the recesses in the pistons. Refit the caliper to the car as previously described.

Removing and refitting a brake disc:

Remove the brake caliper as previously instructed. If the caliper is not to be dismantled the flexible hose need not be disconnected. Support the caliper on a piece of wire so that the flexible hose is not strained. Remove the front hub and then separate the brake disc from the hub as instructed in **Chapter 8, Section 8:3**.

When the disc is refitted to the car use a Dial Test Indicator to check the runout of the disc. The runout should not exceed .002 inch (.0508mm). If the runout limit is exceeded check that there is no dirt between the mating surfaces of the hub and disc as well as turning the disc in relation to the hub. If the discs are scored it is permissible to machine them down. The minimum thickness allowed for the discs is .440 inch (11.18mm) and if the scoring is too deep the discs will have to be renewed. After machining the discs must have a high standard of finish (measured in microns).

10:4 The rear brakes

An exploded view of a rear brake is shown in **FIG 10:5** and the lefthand assembly is shown in **FIG 10:6**.

Removing rear brake shoes:

1 Chock the front wheels, jack up the rear of the car and place it securely on stands. Remove the rear road wheels and make sure the handbrake is off. Clean off road dirt from around the brake assembly.
2 Slacken back the adjuster 3 so that the brake shoes are clear of the brake drum. Remove the two setscrews 1 and withdraw the brake drum 2. Use a screwdriver or similar implement to compress the spring clip 24 and, with a pair of pliers, turn the steady pin 12 through 90 deg. The steady pin 12 may now be pulled out from behind the backplate.
3 Lever or pull the upper brake shoe up against the pull of the return springs 8 and 18 and lift the end of the shoe out of the slot in the expanding adjuster. This will slacken the tension on the return springs. Free the return springs from the brake shoes, if need be pulling the other brake shoe out of its slot in the adjuster. With the return springs freed both shoes can be lifted out of the brake assembly.
4 Do not press the brake pedal when the brake shoes are removed otherwise the piston 7 will be ejected from the wheel cylinder 21. To prevent this happening accidentally, wrap a length of wire around the piston and cylinder assembly. Use an airline or brush to remove all dust and dirt from inside the brake and brake drum. Check the wheel cylinder for leaks and that the adjuster assembly moves freely.

Relining rear brake shoes:

If the linings are worn down to the rivets, renewal is essential. It is not recommended that owners reline brake shoes themselves. It is important that the linings should be perfectly bedded down on the brake shoes and then ground to perfect concentricity with the brake drums. For this reason it is best to obtain

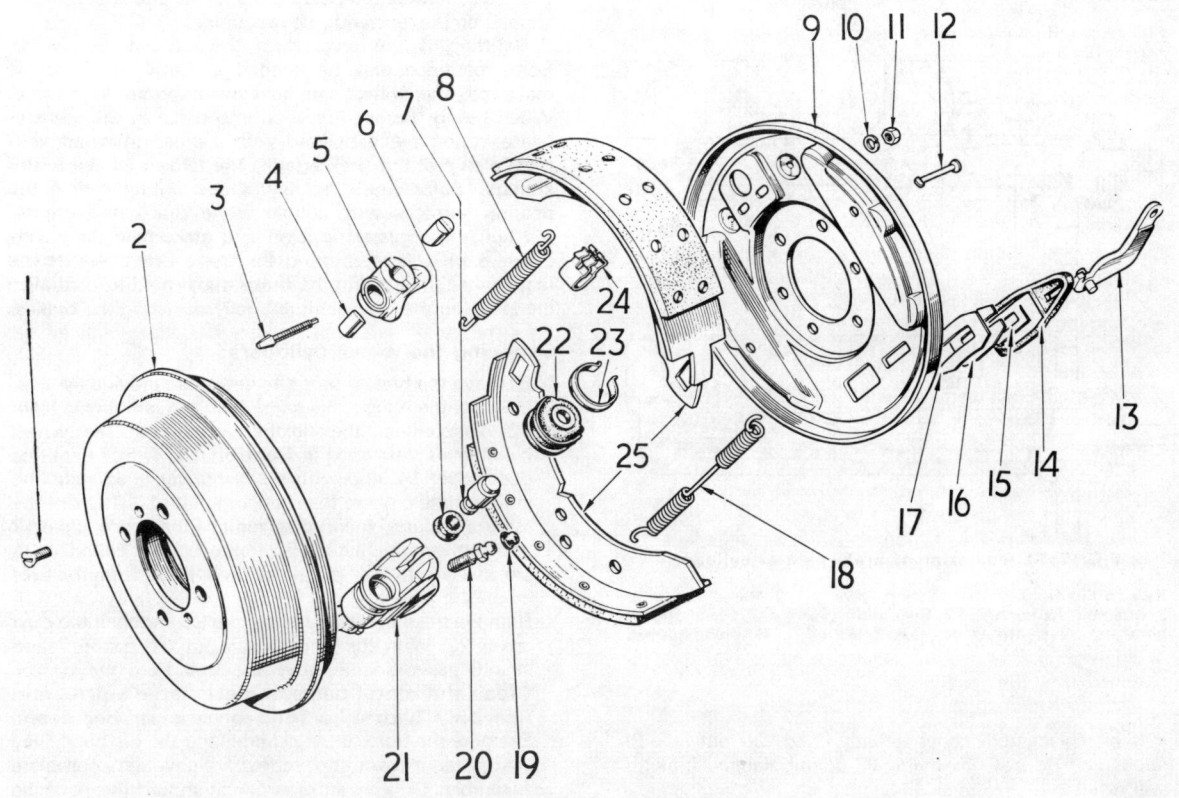

FIG 10:5 Rear brake details

Key to Fig 10:5 1 Screw   2 Brake drum   3 Tappet   4 Expander-adjuster   5 Adjuster housing   6 Piston seal
7 Piston   8 Spring   9 Backplate   10 Spring washer   11 Nut   12 Steady pin   13 Handbrake lever   14 Dust excluder
15 Abutment plate   16 Spring plate—retaining   17 Spring plate   18 Spring   19 Dust cap   20 Bleed nipple
21 Hydraulic cylinder   22 Dust excluders   23 Clip   24 Spring clip—steady pin   25 Brake shoes

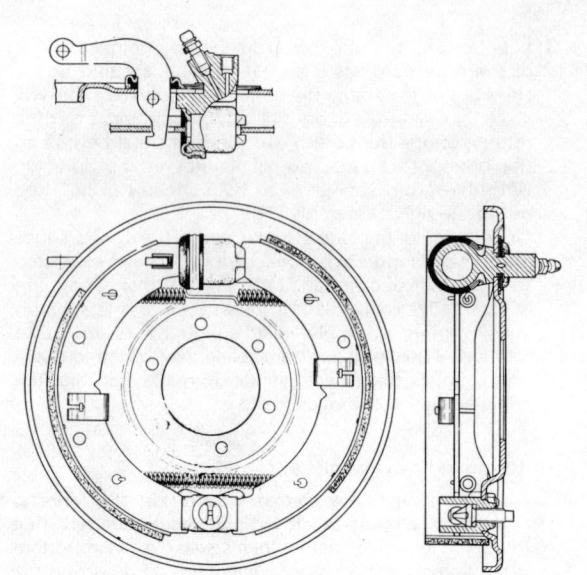

FIG 10:6 Lefthand rear brake assembly

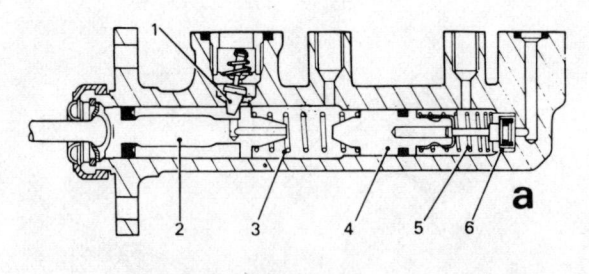

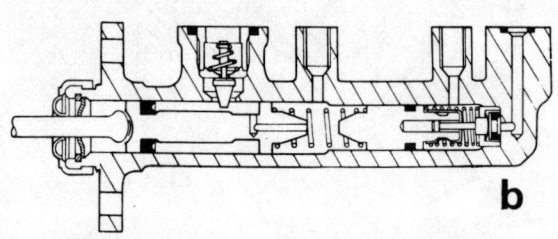

FIG 10:7 Operation of brake master cylinder

Key to Fig 10:7 1 Tipping valve 2 Primary plunger 3 Intermediate spring 4 Secondary plunger 5 Secondary plunger 6 Centre valve A Brake off B Brake applied

Do not allow grease, oil or paint to contact the friction linings. If the original linings are contaminated with grease or oil do not attempt to clean them with solvents or by baking as nothing useful can be done and new linings must be fitted.

Brake drums:

If the linings have worn down to the rivets then the hard surface of the rivets may have scored the working face of the drum. Slight scoring may be skimmed off in a lathe. Do not mount the drum in a four-jawed chuck as the pressure will slightly distort the drum preventing it being skimmed perfectly circular. Use an arbor or mandrel instead. If the drum is deeply scored it will have to be renewed otherwise poor braking will result.

Check that the drum is not cracked. A simple way of checking is to suspend the drum, through the large centre hole, on the wooden handle of a hammer. Tap the drum with a small spanner. A cracked drum will ring flat while a satisfactory drum will ring true.

Refitting rear brake shoes:

The end of the brake shoe with the greatest length of metal exposed is called the 'toe'. The toe of the leading shoe is installed against the piston of the wheel cylinder. **FIG 10:6** shows the positioning of the shoes and return springs on the lefthand side rear brake.

Refitting is the reversal of the removal procedure. Some patience may be needed as, until the knack is mastered, the shoes can be very stubborn to replace. When lifting the second shoe into place in the adjuster use a strong piece of cord with a piece of wood as a handle to pull the shoe against the tension of the return springs. Before refitting the shoes lightly smear the bearing surfaces with a little white zinc-based grease. Slacken the adjuster right off and make sure the handbrake is off before refitting the brake drum. Adjust the rear brakes then pump the brake pedal hard to centralize the shoes in the drum before finally adjusting the brakes.

Servicing the wheel cylinders:

1 Remove the brake linings as described previously. Disconnect the handbrake cable from the handbrake lever 13. Disconnect the flexible hose from the wheel cylinder as described in **Section 10:8**. Pull back the dust cover 14, and with a screwdriver prise apart the spring plate 17 and the retaining plate 16. Tap out the retaining plate 16 and then remove the spring plate 17 and abutment plate 15. Remove the cylinder 21 complete with the handbrake lever 13 through the hole in the backplate.

2 Remove from the cylinder the clip 23 and then the dust cover 22. With the fingers pull out the piston 7 and seal 6 assembly. Remove the seal from the piston. **Clean the metal parts in methylated spirits and use only hydraulic fluid on the rubber seals.** Examine the bore of the cylinder and the piston. If they are pitted, worn or scored renew the complete assembly. Only in an emergency should the parts be cleaned with fine emery and then they must be cleaned out thoroughly to remove any abrasive particles. If they have been cleaned out in this manner they should be renewed at the next possible opportunity.

sets of replacement shoes already lined. Do not fit odd shoes and do not mix materials or unbalanced braking will result.

When fitting new linings, if not already done, it is advisable to chamfer the ends of the linings to provide a smooth flow in for the brake drum. This helps to prevent brake squeal. A small $\frac{1}{8}$ to $\frac{1}{4}$ inch chamfer is quite sufficient.

3 Dip a new seal 6 in clean new brake fluid and, with the fingers only, replace it on the piston 7. Work the seal around to make sure it is properly seated. Very carefully, so as not to damage the seal, slide the piston back into the cylinder. Replace the dust cover 22 and the retaining clip 23.
4 Refitting is the reversal of the removal operation. Before refitting the road wheels bleed and adjust the rear brakes.

10:5 The master cylinder

A diagrammatic view of the master cylinder is shown in **FIG 10:7**. The pushrod on the left is connected, through the servo unit, to the brake pedal. When the brake pedal is depressed the pushrod moves into the cylinder. The initial movement allows the tip valve 1 to close and the fluid in front of the primary plunger 2 is then pressurized. This pressure is fed from the outlet, via the pipe runs, to the wheel cylinders. At the same time the pressure moves the secondary plunger 4 down the bore of the cylinder causing the fluid in the chamber surrounding spring 5 to become pressurized, and this pressure is fed to the rear wheels.

When the brake pedal is released both plungers move back up the bore under the action of the springs 3 and 5. As the secondary plunger 4 reaches the end of its travel the valve 6 is opened, allowing the chamber to connect with the reservoir and replenish any losses in the rear brake circuit. This valve is closed by the initial inward movement of the plunger 4. The primary plunger 2 opens the tip valve 1 at the end of its stroke, allowing the chamber to be connected to the reservoir.

If the rear brake circuit fails or leaks, then the plunger 4 is forced down the bore until the spring 5 is fully compressed and the plunger 4 can move no further. The pressure then builds up normally in the front circuit chamber and the brakes are applied. Failure in the front circuit allows the primary plunger 2 to move forward and contact the secondary plunger 4 thus making a direct link to actuate the rear wheel chamber.

The mounting for the servo unit, master cylinders and pedals is shown in **FIG 10:8**.

Removing and replacing brake master cylinder:

1 Drain the brake system either by pumping the fluid out through a bleed nipple on one front brake and one rear brake, or by syphoning the fluid out of the master cylinder reservoir. Have rags handy to catch any spillage when the pipes are disconnected.
2 Disconnect the metal pipes (shown in **FIG 10:1**) from the side of the master cylinder. Undo the two sets of nuts and washers securing the master cylinder to the servo unit 2 and lift out the master cylinder.
3 Replacing the master cylinder is the reversal of the removal procedure. Both brake systems must be bled after a master cylinder has been replaced.

Servicing the master cylinder:

1 Remove the master cylinder as previously described. The details of the master cylinder are shown in **FIG 10:9**. Undo the four screws 9 and remove the reservoir 4.
2 Use an Allen key to remove the tipping valve securing nut 5, then lift out the tipping valve 6 and

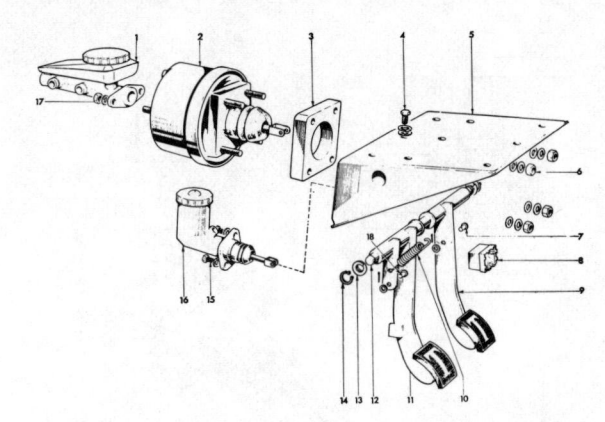

FIG 10:8 Master cylinder and servo unit mountings

Key to Fig 10:8   1 Brake master cylinder   2 Servo unit   3 Spacer   4 Bolt   5 Pedal box   6 Nut   7 Clevis pin—brake   8 Stoplight switch   9 Brake pedal   10 Clutch pedal pull-off spring   11 Clutch pedal   12 Pedal fulcrum shaft   13 Spring washer   14 Circlip   15 Bolt   16 Clutch master cylinder   17 Nut   18 Clevis pin—clutch

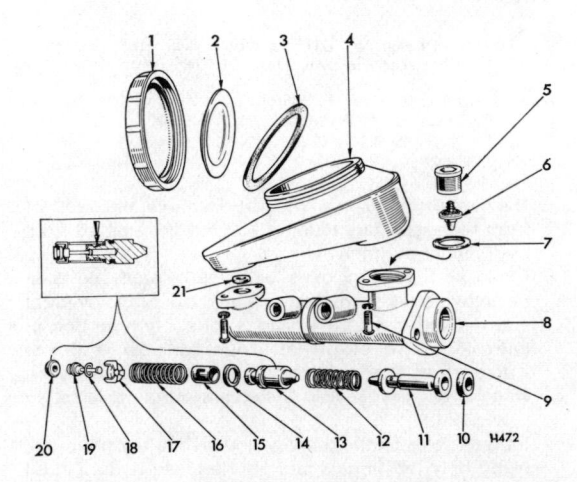

FIG 10:9 Master cylinder details

Key to Fig 10:9   1 Cap   2 Baffle plate   3 Seal   4 Reservoir   5 Tipping valve securing nut   6 Tipping valve   7 Seal—reservoir to body   8 Body   9 Screw—reservoir to body   10 Seal   11 Primary plunger   12 Intermediate spring   13 Secondary plunger   14 Seal   15 Spring retainer   16 Secondary spring   17 Valve spacer   18 Spring washer   19 Valve   20 Seal   21 Seal—reservoir to body

the seal 7. Remove the seal 21 from the master cylinder. Depress the pushrod to free the tipping valve 6.
3 Lift off the dust cover and, pressing in the pushrod, remove the circlip holding the pushrod and retaining plate in place. Blow gently through the outlets to remove the internal parts of the master cylinder.
4 Lift the leaf spring of the spring retainer 15 (see inset in **FIG 10:9**) and remove the spring 16 and the centre valve subassembly from the secondary plunger 13.

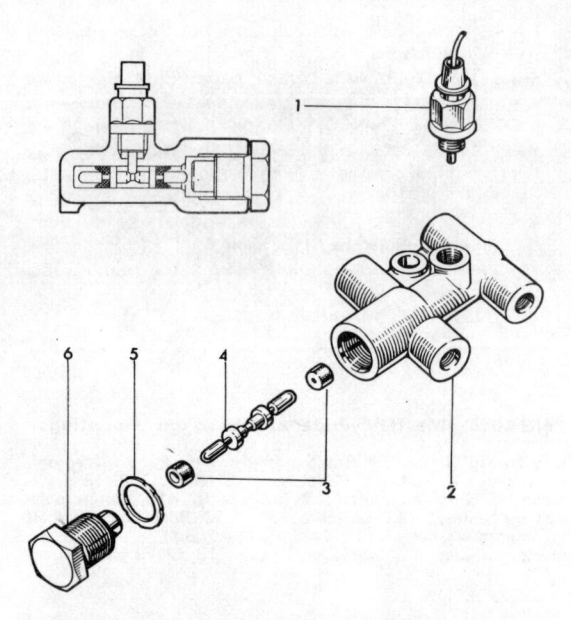

FIG 10:10 Pressure Differential Warning Actuator (PDWA). This item is only fitted to lefthand drive cars

Key to Fig 10:10 1 Switch 2 Body 3 Seal
4 Shuttle valve 5 Washer 6 End plug

5 Dismantle the parts 15 to 20. Remove the seal 14 from the secondary plunger 13, and the seal 10 from the primary plunger 11.
6 Clean all the metal parts with methylated spirits or clean hydraulic fluid. Examine the bore of the cylinder and the surfaces of the pistons for scoring, pitting or corrosion. **The slightest imperfection will require that the whole assembly be renewed.** Renew all the seals. These are obtainable as a service kit.
7 Fit new seals to the primary and secondary plungers, using only the fingers and a little clean hydraulic oil as lubrication. The lips of both these seals will face into the bore of the cylinder. In a similar manner, refit the seal 20 to the valve stem 19 with the smaller diameter of the seal leading.
8 Place the spring washer 18 on the valve stem 19, so that it 'flares' away from the valve stem shoulder, then replace the valve spacer 17, legs first, onto the valve stem. Onto this assembly fit the spring 16 followed by the spring retainer 15, keyhole end first.
9 Position the assembly on the secondary plunger 13. Use clean paper on the jaws of a vice, to prevent any dirt coming onto the assembly, and squeeze the assembly together until the spring 16 is almost coil bound. Use a small screwdriver, inserted between the coils of the spring, to press the spring retainer 15 right home on the secondary plunger 13. Squeeze the leaf spring on the spring retainer 15 into place behind the shoulder of the secondary plunger 13, using a long-nosed pair of pliers and ensuring that the leaf spring is squarely and firmly in place.

10 Dip the secondary plunger assembly in clean hydraulic fluid. Place into position the intermediate spring 12 and primary plunger assembly. Very carefully refit the parts back into the bore of the cylinder, using clean hydraulic fluid as a lubricant. **Take great care when inserting the seals into the bore as the lips can easily be bent back or damaged.** Replace the pushrod assembly, holding it in place with the circlip, and refit the dust cover. Press in the pushrod and check that the inner assemblies return under the action of the springs.
11 Hold in the pushrod and refit the seal 7 and tipping valve 6. Hold them in place with the retaining nut 5 tightened to a torque of 35 to 40 lb ft (4.84 to 5.53 kg m). Replace the seal 21 and then the reservoir 4, securing them in place with the four screws 9.
The ratio of volume between the front and rear chambers varies in different tandem master cylinders so it is absolutely essential that the correct new parts are ordered and fitted.

10:6 Pressure Differential Warning Actuator (PDWA)

This is fitted to lefthand drive cars only and the components are shown in **FIG 10:10**. The mounting point and pipe runs are shown in **FIG 10:1**.

To dismantle the unit, unscrew the switch 1 and then the end plug 6. Shake out the shuttle valve 4 and carefully, so as not to damage the shuttle, remove the two seals 3.

Check the nylon-bodied switch 1 by pressing the plunger against an earthed metal part of the car.

Reassembly is the reverse of the dismantling operation. Fit a new copper gasket 5 and tighten the end cap 6 to a torque of 16 to 17 lb ft (2.21 to 2.35 kg m). Take great care not to cross the threads when fitting the switch 1 and tighten this to a torque of 15 lb ft (2.07 kg m). Use methylated spirits or clean hydraulic fluid to clean the parts and use hydraulic fluid as a lubricant when reassembling.

10:7 Bleeding the brakes

This is not routine maintenance and is only necessary if air has entered the system because parts have been dismantled, or if the fluid level in the reservoir has dropped so low that air has been drawn into the system. As the front and rear brakes are hydraulically isolated it is necessary to bleed only that half of the system which has been dismantled, unless air has been drawn in through the master cylinder, in which case both halves must be bled.

Hydraulic fluid is pumped out of the system when the brakes are bled and, unless this is replaced, the level in the master cylinder will drop until air is again drawn into the system. Before starting to bleed the brakes fill the reservoir up to the top and keep it constantly topped up while bleeding is being carried out.

Start with the brake farthest from the master cylinder in one pair. If both halves of the system have to be bled, bleed the rear brakes first. Clean the bleed nipples.
1 Attach a length of $\frac{1}{4}$ inch bore plastic or rubber hose to the bleed nipple and immerse the free end in a little clean brake fluid contained in a clean glass jar.
2 Slacken the bleed nipple approximately half a turn and

have a second operator depress the brake pedal. On cars fitted with a PDWA the pedal pressure must be light and the pedal must not be pushed all the way down, otherwise the differential pressure will move the shuttle in the PDWA. For the same reason the pedal pressure or movement must not be 'tried' before bleeding is completed.

3 Allow the pedal to return slowly after a pause, and again depress the pedal. On the first strokes air bubbles will be ejected with the fluid. Continue pumping until only clean fluid flows from the bleed tube. Tighten the bleed nipple when the brake pedal is depressed. Repeat the operation on the other brake.

Recentring the PDWA shuttle:

1 Fit a rubber tube to a bleed nipple on the half of the system opposite to the failure. If the shuttle moved during bleeding operations then finish bleeding those brakes and fit the bleed tube to the other half of the system. Open the bleed nipple half a turn.
2 Switch on the ignition but **do not start the engine.**

The brake warning light will glow but the oil pressure light will remain off.

3 Press steadily on the brake pedal until the brake warning light dims and the oil pressure warning light glows. At the same time as the lights change there should be a click in the pedal. **Do not press any further.** The shuttle will have moved to the centre position and any further pressure will move it over to the other side, requiring the procedure to be repeated on the other half of the brake system.
4 Tighten the bleed nipple and remove the rubber tube.

10:8 Removing a flexible hose

The unions to all flexible hoses are shown in **FIG 10:1.** Never try to release a flexible hose by turning the ends with a spanner. The correct procedure is as follows:

Unscrew the metal pipeline union nut from its connection with the hose. Hold the adjacent hexagon on the hose with a spanner and release the locknut which secures the hose to its bracket. The hose can now be

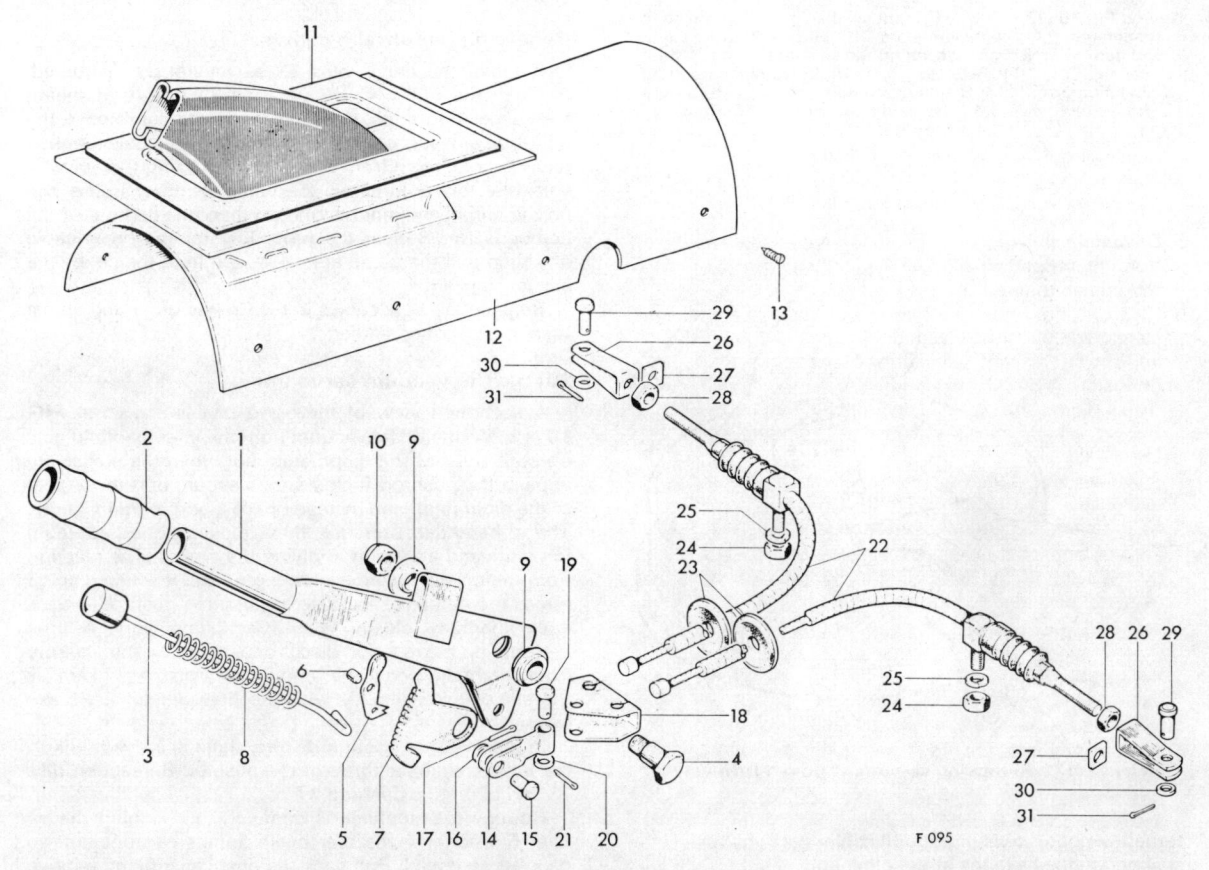

FIG 10:11 Handbrake details

Key to Fig 10:11 1 Handlever 2 Rubber grip 3 Operating rod, pawl 4 Fulcrum pin, handlever 5 Pawl 6 Pivot pin, pawl 7 Ratchet 8 Spring 9 Nylon washer 10 Nyloc nut 11 Carpet trim 12 Cardboard cover 13 Screw 14 Link 15 Clevis pin 16 Washer 17 Splitpin 18 Compensator 19 Clevis pin 20 Washer 21 Splitpin 22 Cable assembly 23 Rubber grommet 24 Nut 25 Lockwasher 26 Fork end 27 Nut 28 Locknut 29 Clevis pin 30 Washer 31 Splitpin

TR5/6

101

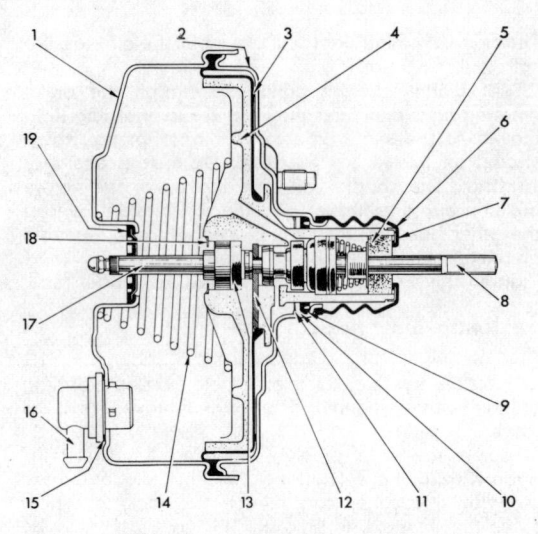

FIG 10:12 Vacuum servo unit details

Key to Fig 10:12 1 Front shell 2 Rear shell
3 Diaphragm 4 Diaphragm plate 5 Filter 6 Dust cover
7 End cap 8 Valve operating rod assembly 9 Seal
10 Bearing 11 Retainer 12 Valve retaining plate
13 Reaction disc 14 Diaphragm return spring 15 O-ring
16 Non-return valve 17 Hydraulic pushrod 18 Retainer/sprag washer 19 Seal and plate assembly

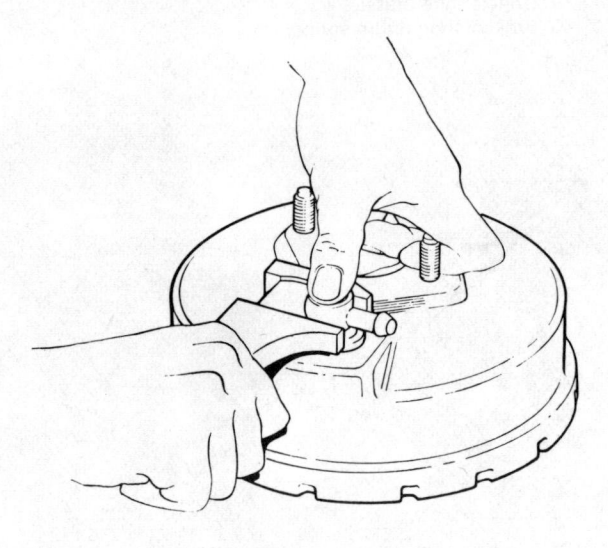

FIG 10:13 Renewing servo unit non-return valve

turned without twisting the flexible part, by using a spanner on the hexagon at the other end.

10:9 The handbrake

Normally, adjusting the rear brakes will take up excessive handbrake travel. If there is too much travel after adjusting the rear brakes, first check that the rear linings are not excessively worn. Only when everything else has been checked and adjusted should the handbrake cables be adjusted. The assembly is shown in **FIG 10:11**.

Adjusting the handbrake cables:

1 Chock the front road wheels and jack up the rear of the car. Place the rear end securely on stands, and remove the rear road wheels.
2 Slacken both locknuts 28, and with the handbrake off remove the two splitpins 31 and washer 30, allowing the clevis pins 29 to be withdrawn.
3 Screw each fork 26 along the cable until, with the clevis pins loosely refitted, the compensator 18 is level and the handbrake is tight on the fifth notch of the ratchet. Lightly press in the button on the end of the handbrake lever and count the number of clicks as the handbrake is applied.
4 When the cables are correctly adjusted, secure the clevis pins with the washers 30 and new splitpins 31. Refit the road wheels and lower the car back to the ground.

Renewing handbrake cables:

Remove the clevis pins 29 as previously instructed. Remove the nuts 24 and washers 25 from underneath the suspension arms. Working inside the car remove the handbrake lever covers. Pull the outer cable slightly rearwards to free it from the tunnel mounting then pivot it vertically forwards about the compensator 18. The ball on the end of the inner cable can then be lifted out of the compensator. Repeat the procedure for the other cable and then pull the complete cables out from the car by the suspension arms.

Replace the new cables in the reverse order and adjust them as described earlier.

10:10 The vacuum servo unit

A sectioned view of the servo unit is shown in **FIG 10:12**. Normally the vacuum from the inlet manifold acts on both sides of the diaphragm, but when the brakes are applied the pushrod 8 closes the vacuum port to the rear of the diaphragm and instead opens a port to atmosphere. The differential pressure then moves the diaphragm forwards and assists in applying the brakes. The reaction from the master cylinder pressing on the reaction disc 13 forces the centre of the disc to push the pushrod 8 back again partially closing the atmosphere port. As the pressure on the reaction disc is dependent on the pressure from the brake pedal the amount of assistance given by the servo unit will vary with the pressure on the brake pedal.

In the event of vacuum failure, there is a direct link to the master cylinder through the pushrod 8, reaction disc 13 and hydraulic pushrod 17.

Routine maintenance is confined to changing the air filter 5 whenever the rear brake linings or front friction pads are renewed. Pull back the dust cover 6 and remove the old filter from the diaphragm plate neck. Replace it with a new filter and pull the dust cover back into position. To facilitate assembly cut the new filter diagonally from the outer edge to the centre hole. Examine the dust cover and if it is damaged renew it.

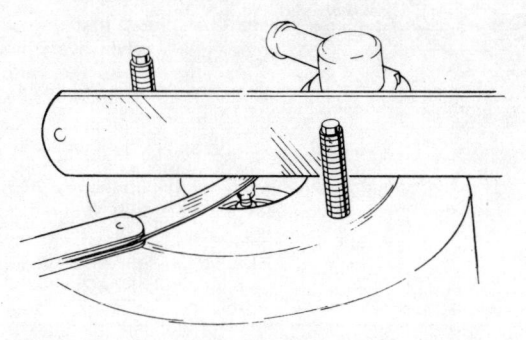

FIG 10:14 Measuring the clearance between the servo unit casing and the pushrod

If the air valve 16 has failed it may be renewed. Note the angle the old valve makes with the body of the servo unit. Press it down and turn it anticlockwise one third of a turn and lift the valve out. Fit a new O-ring to the valve and fit the assembly back to the servo unit as shown in **FIG 10:13**.

The only other part of the servo that can be renewed is the seal and end plate assembly 19. A service kit is available containing a new filter, dust cover, non-return valve, seal and plate assembly as well as grease for the seal and plate assembly. The old seal and plate assembly is removed by gripping the centre rib with a pair of long-nosed pliers. Lubricate the new assembly with the grease provided before fitting it in place.

Place a straightedge across the front shell recess and check, with feeler gauges (see **FIG 10:14**), the gap between the straightedge and the end of the pushrod. If this gap varies beyond .011 to .016 inch (.28 to .41 mm) then the whole servo unit must be renewed. Similarly any other faults beyond those mentioned will require renewal of the complete unit.

10:11 Fault diagnosis

(a) 'Spongy' pedal
1 Leak in either system
2 Worn master cylinder
3 Leaking wheel cylinders
4 Air in either system
5 Gaps between the rear shoes and underside of linings

(b) Excessive pedal movement
1 Check 1 and 4 in (a)
2 Excessive lining wear
3 Very low fluid level in master cylinder reservoir
4 Excessive wear in the servo unit

(c) Brakes grab or pull to one side
1 Rear brake backplate loose
2 Scored, cracked or distorted rear brake drum
3 High spots on rear brake drum
4 Cracked or distorted front brake disc
5 Wet or oily friction linings (or friction pads)
6 Front suspension or rear suspension anchorages loose or worn
7 Worn steering connections
8 Mixed linings of different grades
9 Uneven tyre pressures
10 Broken shoe return springs
11 Seized handbrake cable
12 Seized wheel cylinder

NOTES

CHAPTER 11

THE ELECTRICAL SYSTEM

11:1 Description
11:2 The battery
11:3 The alternator
11:4 The starter motor
11:5 The windscreen wipers
11:6 The horns
11:7 Fuses

11:8 Hazard warning system
11:9 Flasher unit
11:10 Fuel and temperature gauges
11:11 The headlamps
11:12 Lighting circuits
11:13 Fault diagnosis

11:1 Description

All the models covered by this manual have the negative terminal of the battery earthed to the chassis. They are fitted with alternators, instead of generators, so the charging circuit contains items which are polarity sensitive. Some other items fitted to the electrical system are also either polarity sensitive or will operate in the wrong direction if the polarity is reversed. All these items may be irreparably damaged if incorrectly connected.

It is advisable not to make or break any connections in the charging circuit while the engine is running, and this includes the battery connections, otherwise components may be damaged.

Excessive voltages will damage the diodes in the charging circuit, so withdraw the multi-pin plugs from the alternator and control box before boost charging the battery or performing any arc welding on the car.

There are wiring diagrams in Technical Data at the end of this manual to enable those with electrical experience to trace and correct wiring faults.

To test the continuity of a circuit cheap instruments are adequate, but when making performance checks, or adjusting components, first class instruments are essential. Cheap or unreliable instruments will not measure to the accuracy required, and by using them more faults will be introduced than have been cured.

Detailed instructions for servicing the electrical equipment will be found in this chapter, but it must be pointed out that it is not sensible to try to repair items which are seriously defective, electrically or mechanically. Such equipment should be replaced by new or reconditioned units, which can be obtained on an exchange basis.

11:2 The battery

This is of the 12-volt lead/acid type and has to meet heavy demands for current, particularly in winter when it also loses efficiency because of the low temperature. To maintain the performance of the battery at its maximum it is essential to carry out the following operations.

Keep the top of the battery and surrounding parts clean and dry, as dampness can cause leakage between the securing strap and the positive terminal. Clean off

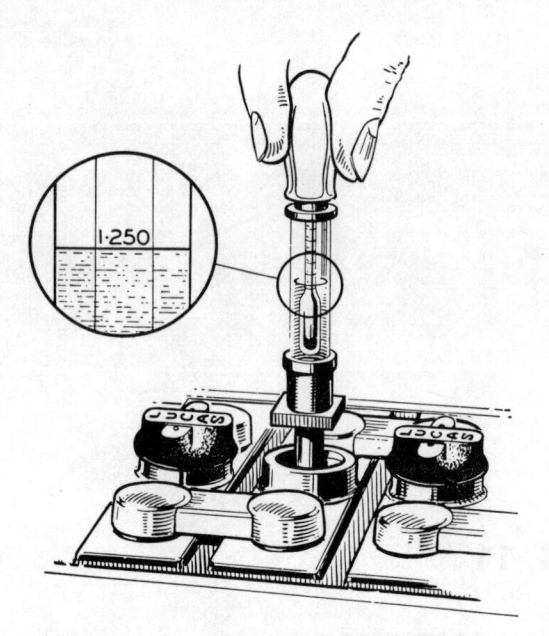

FIG 11:1 Testing the battery with a hydrometer

FIG 11:2 Unsoldering the stator wires from the diodes

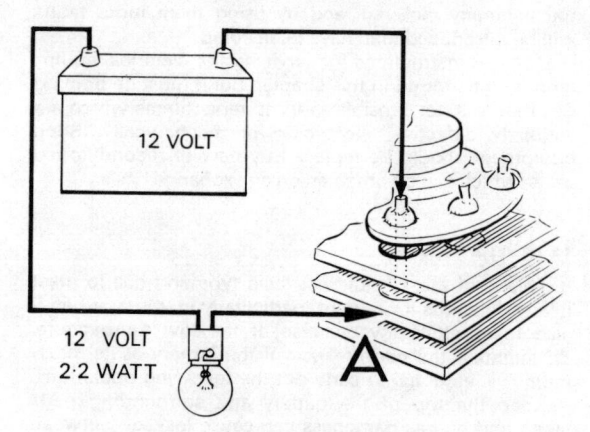

FIG 11:3 Checking the diodes

corrosion from the metal parts of the battery mounting with diluted ammonia and then paint them with antisulphuric paint. If the terminal posts are corroded, remove the connectors and clean them all with diluted ammonia. Smear the posts and connectors with petroleum jelly before remaking the connections and fit the terminal screws securely. High electrical resistance at the terminal posts is often responsible for lack of sufficient current to operate the starter motor. If acid is accidentally spilt, neutralize it immediately with either diluted ammonia or, better still, baking powder mixed with warm water. The baking powder will fizz in contact with acid and thus will indicate when the acid is neutralized by the absence of fizzing. Wash the area with plenty of clean water.

At regular intervals top up the electrolyte level, with distilled water only, to just above the tops of the separators. **Never add neat acid.** If it is necessary to make new electrolyte to replace any lost by spillage or leakage, add acid to distilled water. **It is highly dangerous to add water to concentrated acid.** Allow the electrolyte to cool before adding it to the battery.

If acid or electrolyte is accidentally splashed in the eyes, irrigate them copiously with clean water and obtain medical assistance.

To test the condition of the cells use an hydrometer to check the specific gravity of the liquid. The method is shown in **FIG 11:1** and the indications from the readings are as follows:

For climates below 32°C (90°F):

Cell fully charged — Specific gravity 1.270 to 1.290
Cell half discharged — Specific gravity 1.190 to 1.210
Cell discharged — Specific gravity 1.110 to 1.130

For climates above 32°C (90°F):

Cell fully charged — Specific gravity 1.210 to 1.230
Cell half discharged — Specific gravity 1.130 to 1.150
Cell discharged — Specific gravity 1.050 to 1.070
Use electrolyte of 1.210 specific gravity to replace spillage.

These figures are given assuming an electrolyte temperature of 16°C (60°F). Add .002 to the specific gravity reading for each 3°C (5°F) rise in temperature of the electrolyte, and subtract it for each equivalent fall in temperature.

All six cells should give approximately the same reading, and if one differs radically from the rest it may be due to an internal fault. Examine the electrolyte drawn up into the hydrometer. If it appears full of small particles or cloudy it is possible that the cell is in bad condition.

The cells may also be tested using a heavy discharge tester. Never use this test on a semi-discharged battery. A good cell should maintain a voltage reading steadily between 1.2 and 1.7 volts for 5 or 6 seconds. A rapid drop in the voltage reading indicates a faulty cell.

11:3 The alternator

This replaces the generator in the conventional charging circuit. Two of the main advantages of the alternator are that it will produce a charging current at lower rev/min and yet can be run up safely to higher speeds than a generator. The alternator produces AC current which is rectified to charge the battery. A control

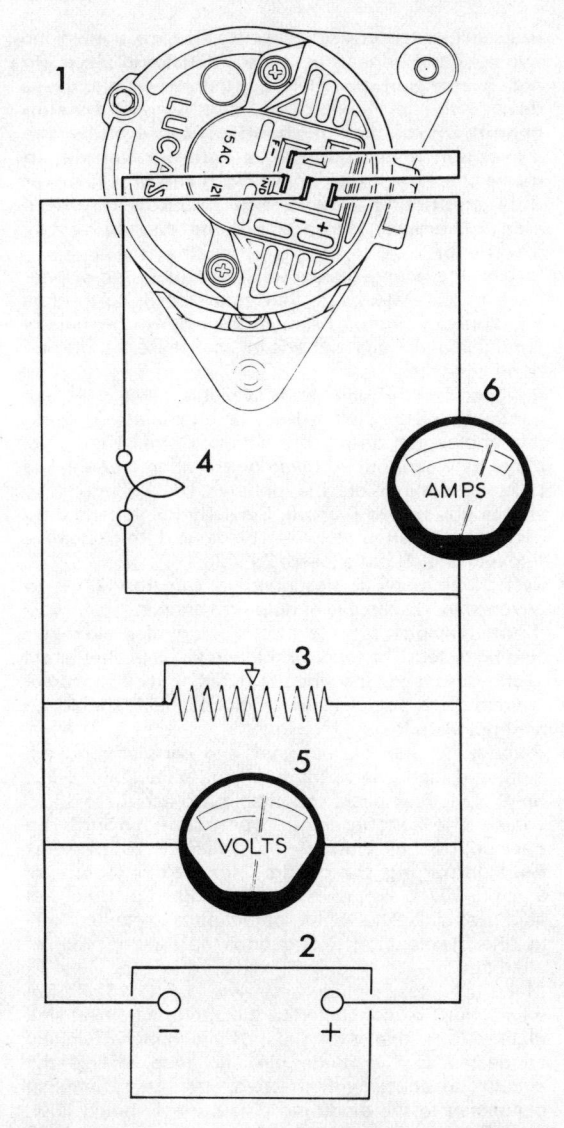

FIG 11:4 Circuit for testing the alternator fitted to the TR5

Key to Fig 11:4   1 Alternator   2 Battery (12-volt)
3 Variable resistor (0-15 ohm—35 amp)   4 Light (12-volt
—2.2 watt)   5 Voltmeter (0-20 volt)   6 Ammeter
(0-40 amp)

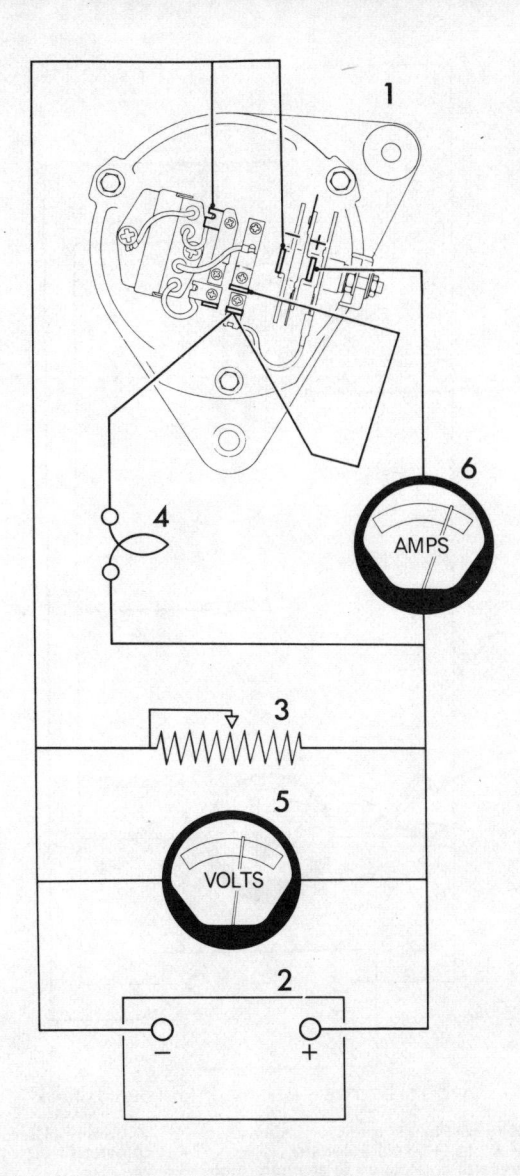

FIG 11:5 Circuit for testing only the alternator fitted to the TR6 (and TR250), control unit inoperative

Key to Fig 11:5   1 Alternator   2 Battery (12-volt)
3 Variable resistor (0-15 ohm—35 amp)   4 Light (12-volt—
2.2 watt)   5 Voltmeter (0-20 volt)   6 Ammeter (0-40 amp)

unit then varies the current to meet the demands of the battery. On the TR5 the control unit is a separate item mounted on the bulkhead, but by employing microcircuit techniques the control unit is embodied in the alternator fitted to the TR6 and TR250. The main current is produced in the windings and control is exercised by varying the current in the lighter revolving field coils. Current to and from the field coils is by brushes and slip rings. The design, method of construction and basic principles employed ensure that the alternator will be more reliable than a generator of equal capacity.

A tapping from the field coil circuit is connected to a warning light. When the alternator is charging, the terminal voltage for the indicator approximates to that of the battery and the light goes out. The warning light remaining on when the alternator should be producing current indicates a fault in the system.

Diodes are used to rectify the AC current and as these will not tolerate high reverse voltages it is essential that the correct polarity is observed whenever connections are made in the charging circuit.

Routine maintenance on both types of alternators is

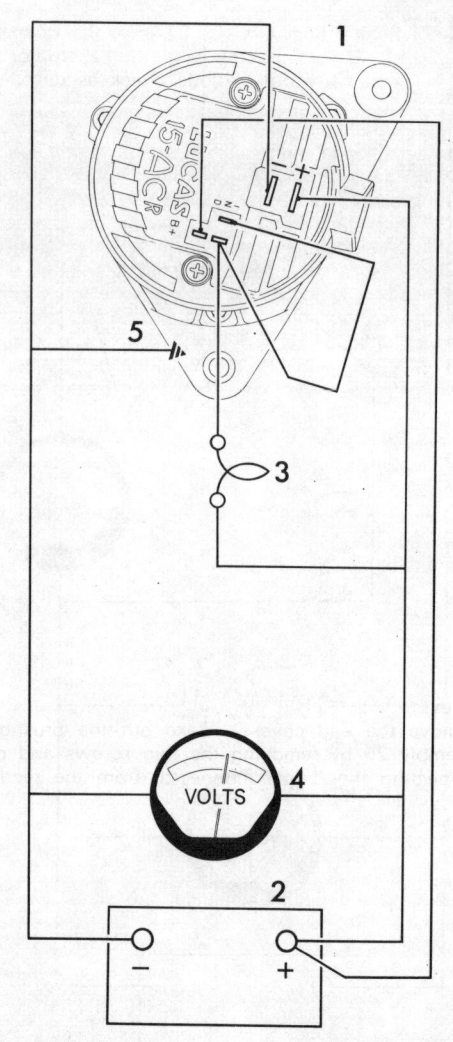

FIG 11:6 TR6 control unit functional check

Key to Fig 11:6   1 Alternator   2 Battery (12-volt)
3 Light (12-volt–2.2 watt)   4 Voltmeter (0-20 volt)
5 Earth connection to alternator body

confined to ensuring that the air cooling vents are clear and that the fan belt is maintained at the correct tension. No routine lubrication is required.

Testing when the alternator is not charging:

It must be stressed that when voltage or current readings are required it is essential to use high-grade instruments. Before checking the alternator carry out the following checks:
1 Check that belt slip is not the cause of the trouble. With moderate hand pressure the belt should deflect a maximum of 1 inch total at the centre of the longest run. If the belt is slack, loosen the nut and bolt to the adjusting link as well as the bottom pivot bolt and nut. Pull the alternator away from the block until the belt has reached the correct tension and then tighten the two nuts and bolts to hold the alternator in place. Do not overtension the belt as this will only cause damage to the alternator bearings. **If belt tension cannot be reached by hand pressure alone use a wooden lever, such as a hammer handle, to move the alternator away from the block. Lever only against the drive end bracket, nowhere else, otherwise damage will be caused to the alternator.**
2 Inspect the wiring system for faulty insulation or poor connections. Make sure that multi-socket connectors are correctly fitted. Examine especially the battery terminals and leads and ensure that these are making good connection.
3 If a good quality voltmeter is available use it to test the continuity of the circuit. Run the engine at 2870 rev/min and switch on the headlamps. Connect the voltmeter between the '+' blade on the alternator and the positive terminal on the battery. The voltage drop should not exceed 0.5 volt. Similarly the voltage drop between the alternator '—' blade and the negative terminal should not exceed .25 volt.
4 Test the battery as described in **Section 11:2** to ensure that it is capable of holding a charge.

If the previous tests are satisfactory the alternator should be tested. The tests for the two types of alternators will be described individually later, but if accurate instruments are not available a diode check should be carried out as follows:
1 Remove the rear plastic cover and parts as required. Note and mark the positions of the three stator wires on the rectifier pack and then unsolder these three wires. **The unsoldering operation should be carried out as quickly as possible to prevent heat damaging the diode.** Grip the diode pin with a pair of pliers, as shown in **FIG 11:2**, so that they act as a heat sink. This whole operation is described fully in the dismantling instructions for each type of alternator.
2 Make up a test circuit as shown in **FIG 11:3**. The wire A must be connected to the appropriate heat sink plate. Check first with the positive battery terminal connected to the diode pin and then reverse the circuit and check with the negative battery terminal connected to the diode pin. The current should flow, and the bulb light, in one direction only. The bulb failing to light or lighting in both directions indicates a faulty diode.
3 Test each of the nine diodes in turn. The failure of any diode to pass this test will mean that the complete rectifier pack will have to be renewed.

Testing the type of alternator fitted to the TR5:
1 Run the engine for a sufficient time to allow the alternator to reach its normal working temperature. The stated output may be slightly exceeded when the alternator is cold, giving misleading results.
2 Switch off the engine and disconnect the multi-socket connector. Make up and fit a circuit as shown in **FIG 11:4**, ensuring that correct polarity is observed. Leave the variable resistor 3 disconnected until the checks are to be made as it will otherwise drain the battery.

3 Start the engine and gradually increase the speed. The warning light 4 should go out at an engine speed of 720 rev/min. Increase the engine speed until it reaches 2870 rev/min and then hold it steady. Adjust the variable resistor 3 until the voltmeter 5 reads 14 volts. The ammeter 6 should give a reading of approximately 28 amps, and if this reading is not reached the alternator is suspect. Before dismantling and overhauling the alternator carry out a diode check as described previously. If the alternator and the rest of the checks are satisfactory renew the control unit.

4 A further check on the control unit is to connect an accurate voltmeter across the battery terminals. If no other instrument is available use the ammeter fitted to the car dashboard, but it is preferable either to substitute this with, or connect it in series with an accurate ammeter. Start the engine and run it at a speed of 2400 rev/min. Run at this speed for at least a minute to allow the system to stabilize. Switch accessories and lights on or off until the ammeter indicates a charging current of 5 amps. The voltmeter should read 14.3 to 14.7 volts. It is essential that when this test is carried out the battery is fully charged and in good condition. An inability to decrease the charging current to 5 amps indicates that the battery is only partially charged.

Testing the type of alternator fitted to the TR6 and TR250:

1 Run the engine for a sufficient time to allow the alternator to reach its normal working temperature. Switch off the engine and remove the multi-socket connector. Remove the plastic end cover.

2 To test the alternator alone, connect up a circuit as shown in **FIG 11 : 5**, ensuring that the correct polarity is observed. Do not connect the variable resistor 3 into the circuit until the tests are to be made, otherwise it will drain the battery.

3 Start the engine and gradually increase the speed. The warning light 4 should go out at an engine speed of 720 rev/min. Raise the engine speed to 2870 rev/min and hold it steady. Adjust the variable resistor 3 to give a voltage reading of 14 volts on the voltmeter 5.

If the ammeter 6 does not read 28 amps the alternator is suspect. Before overhauling the alternator, if it is suspect, carry out a diode check as described previously.

4 To test the control unit, connect up a circuit as shown in **FIG 11 : 6**. Start the engine and gradually increase the speed. The warning light 3 should extinguish at 720 rev/min. Hold the engine speed steady at 2870 rev/min. The voltmeter 4 reading should be steady between 14.0 and 14.4 volts. If the alternator alone has passed its checks and the voltmeter reading is not steady between the limits given, then the control unit is at fault and it should be renewed.

Dismantling the type of alternator fitted to the TR5:

The details of the alternator are shown in **FIG 11 : 7**. Some earlier types of alternator were fitted with a larger type of rectifier pack 24 which is screw mounted to both the slip ring end bracket 3 and the brushbox assembly 25. Provided this fact is born in mind the following instructions apply to both types of alternator fitted to the TR5.

1 Remove the alternator from the car. Disconnect the multi-socket connector, remove the top and bottom nuts and bolts while supporting the alternator and then lift it out from the car, freeing the fan belt from the pulley.

2 Remove the end cover 1. Take out the brushgear assembly 25 by removing the two screws and disconnecting the 'Lucar' connector from the rectifier pack 24. Servicing of the brushgear will be dealt with separately later.

3 Note and mark the position of the three stator wires on the rectifier pack 24. Rapidly, so as to avoid heat damage to the diodes, unsolder the stator wires as shown in **FIG 11 : 2**, using a pair of pliers as an additional heat sink and taking care not to bend the diode pins. Slacken the nut 23 and remove the rectifier pack 24. The testing of this has already been dealt with. Remove the three through-bolts. Place an

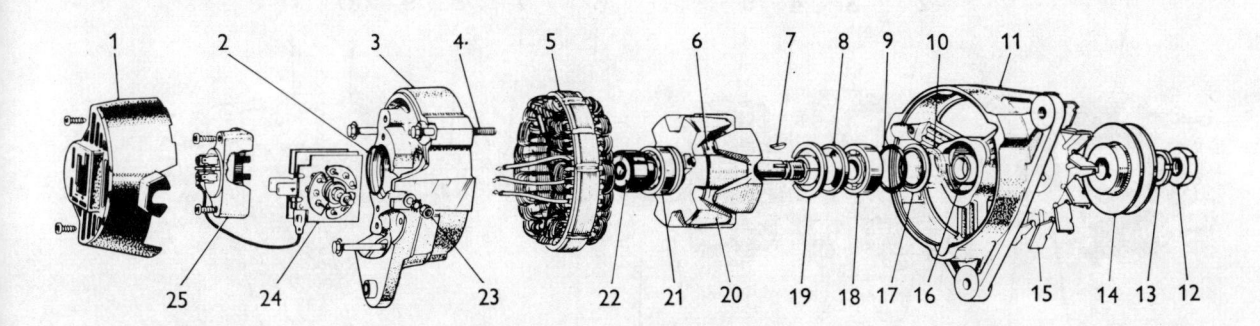

FIG 11 : 7 TR5 alternator details

Key to Fig 11 : 7 1 Moulded cover 2 Rubber O-ring 3 Slip ring end bracket 4 Through bolt 5 Stator windings 6 Field winding 7 Key 8 Bearing retaining plate 9 Pressure ring 10 Felt ring 11 Drive end bracket 12 Nut 13 Spring washer 14 Pulley 15 Fan 16 Spacer 17 Pressure ring and felt ring retaining plate 18 Drive end bearing 19 Circlip 20 Rotor 21 Slip ring end bearing 22 Slip ring moulding 23 Nut 24 Rectifier pack 25 Brushbox assembly

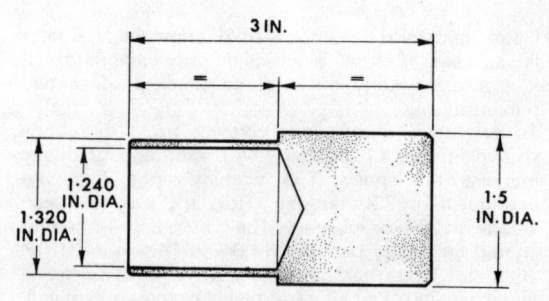

FIG 11:8 Extractor tool details

extractor tool, as shown in **FIG 11:8**, on the outer journal of the slip ring end bearing 21. It may be necessary to carefully file away any surplus solder from the two field winding connections so as to allow the extractor tool to pass over the slip ring moulding 22.
4 Have a second operator holding the slip ring end bracket 23 in his hands and carefully tap on the extractor tool to drive the bearing out of the end bracket. The bearing 21 is sealed for life and need not be dismantled. If it is worn renewal procedure is dealt with separately and later. The rubber O-ring 2 need not be removed from the end bracket 3 unless it is to be renewed.
5 Lift out the stator windings 5 from the drive end bracket 11, marking both so that they will be replaced in the correct angular relationship. Wrap a length of old fan belt around the pulley 14 and, holding this in a vice, remove the nut 12 and washer 13. Withdraw the pulley from the shaft of the rotor 20 and remove the key 7 and fan 15. Use a press to remove the rotor from the drive end bracket. Renewal of the bearing will be dealt with separately.

Reassembly of the alternator is the reversal of the dismantling process, but note the following points:
1 When refitting the rotor 20 to the drive end bracket 11 make sure that the spacer 16 is in position and press the bracket into place using a tube against the inner journal of the bearing 18. Never press on the drive end bracket.
2 Solder the three stator wires to the rectifier pack 24 as quickly as possible, using pliers as an additional heat sink and 'M' grade 45 to 55 tin lead solder. **Never use an acid-type flux.**
3 When refitting the nut 12, wrap a length of old fan belt around the pulley 14 to protect it from the jaws of a vice, and tighten the nut to a torque load of 25 to 30 lb ft.

Dismantling the type of alternator fitted to the TR6 and TR250:

The details of this alternator are shown in **FIG 11:9**. The components are exactly the same, and bear the same key numbers, as the alternator fitted to the TR5 (see **FIG 11:7**), except the control unit 26 which is mounted on the brushbox assembly. Dismantling and reassembly operations are the same, with the addition of the control unit. When this is removed from the brushbox assembly 25 note and mark the position of the three wire eyelets to ensure that they will be correctly connected on reassembly.

Servicing the brushgear and slip rings:

These operations are common to all three types of alternator.
1 Dismantle the alternator sufficiently to remove the brushbox assembly 25, and if required remove the slip ring end bracket 3 to gain better access to the slip ring moulding 22.
2 Clean the brushes with a petrol-moistened rag. Check that the brushes move freely in their holders, if necessary lightly cleaning the sides of the brushes with a smooth file. At least .2 inch of brush should protrude from the holder when the brushes are free. If the brushes are worn shorter than this dimension renew the brushbox assembly. Use a push-type spring scale and check that the spring pressure is between 7 and 10 oz when the brushes are in flush with the face of the brushbox. Low spring pressure will also require renewal of the brushbox assembly.

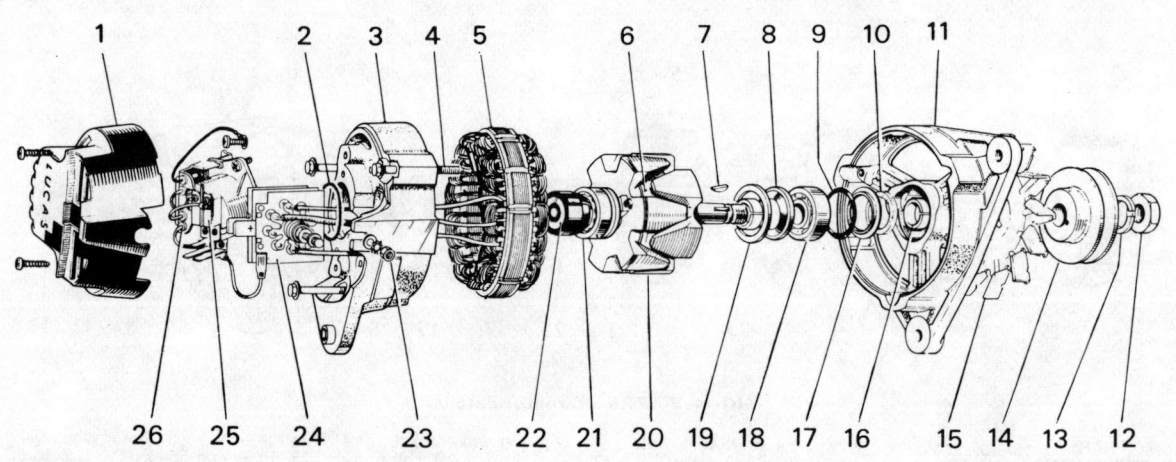

FIG 11:9 TR6 (and TR250) alternator details. Key to Fig 11:9 is the same as the Key to Fig 11:7 except for the control unit 26

110

3 Clean the slip rings and face of the slip ring moulding 22 with a piece of petrol-soaked rag. Burn marks or light pitting may be removed using very fine glasspaper. **Never use emerycloth or some such similar abrasive. Do not skim the face in a lathe** as this may upset the high-speed performance of the alternator.

The alternator bearings:

These are packed with grease in manufacture and normally should last the life of the alternator, without attention or lubrication. The alternator must be dismantled in order to examine or renew the bearings. The slip ring end bearing is shown in **FIG 11:10** and the drive end bearing is shown in **FIG 11:11**.

1 Referring to **FIG 11:10**, unsolder the field coil connections on the slip ring moulding 6 and pull it off the shaft. Using a suitable extractor draw the bearing 1 off the shaft. Remove the O-ring 2 from the bracket 3. Pack a new bearing 1 with Shell Alvania RA grease (or equivalent) and drive it back onto the shaft. The shielded face of the bearing must face the slip ring moulding. Use a suitable tube as a drift, applying the pressure onto the inner journal of the bearing only, and drive it as far as possible towards the rotor. Fit a new O-ring 2 into the bracket 3. Replace the slip ring moulding 6, either way round, and resolder the connections using Fry's HT3 solder. **Never use an acid-type flux.**

2 Referring to **FIG 11:11,** insert a large screwdriver into the extractor notch and prize out the circlip 8. Remove the bearing retaining plate 7 and push out the bearing and its associated components. Reassemble the bearing in the reverse order of dismantling, using new parts as required and ensuring that the bearing 1 is packed with Shell Alvania RA grease. Reassemble the alternator.

11:4 The starter motor

A sectioned view of the Lucas M418G starter motor is shown in **FIG 11:12**, the type 2M100 which is now fitted is similar in all respects, but has a face type commutator. From this it will be seen that the starter solenoid is mounted directly onto the starter motor. The initial movement of the solenoid moves the pinion 22 into contact with the flywheel ring gear. Further movement of the solenoid then makes the contacts 6 and the current flows through the starter motor. The solenoid contains a heavy duty coil which does the initial movement but is shorted out when the contacts 6 close. The hold-in coil, which also assists in the initial movement, is left energized until the starter button is released. The springs 5 and 12 return the solenoid plunger 9 when the solenoid is de-energized, opening the contacts before the pinion 22 is disengaged. The spring 13 takes up the lost motion, though a certain amount of lost motion is designed into the system. If the teeth on the pinion are not aligned with the teeth on the ring gear then they will abut. The springs 10 and 11 compress, allowing the plunger to continue moving and make the contacts 6. Initial rotation of the armature turns the teeth into line and they are engaged both by the pressure of the engaging springs 10 and 11, and by the action of the helix on the drive sleeve 25. The terminal connections on the solenoid and a schematic wiring diagram of the starter motor is shown in **FIG 11:13**.

A clutch assembly is fitted to the starter motor to prevent the armature from overspeeding when the engine starts.

Tests for a starter which does not operate:

Check the condition of the battery. Pay particular

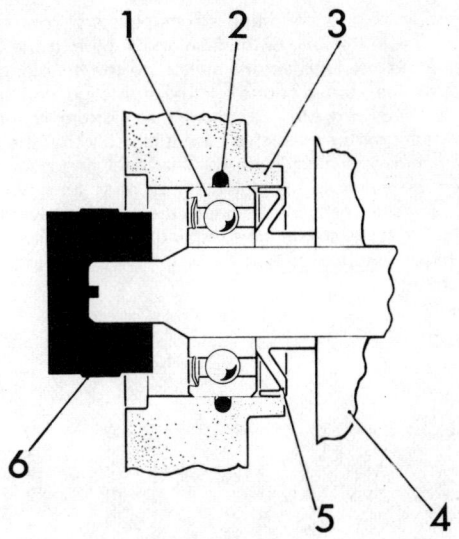

FIG 11:10 Slip ring end bearing

Key to Fig 11:10   1 Bearing   2 Rubber O-ring
3 Slip ring end bracket   4 Rotor   5 Grease retainer
6 Slip ring moulding

FIG 11:11 Drive end bearing

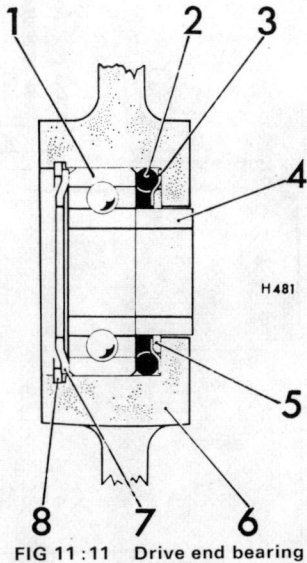

Key to Fig 11:11   1 Bearing   2 Pressure ring
3 Pressure ring and felt ring retaining plate   4 Spacer
5 Felt ring   6 Drive end bracket   7 Bearing retaining plate
8 Circlip

attention to the condition of the battery connections, making sure they are both clean and secure. If the battery is charged and satisfactory, switch on the headlamps and operate the starter control. If the lights go dim but the starter does not turn, it shows that current is reaching the starter motor. In such a case it is likely that the pinion has jammed in mesh with the flywheel ring gear. It can often be released by selecting a gear and, with the ignition switched off, rocking the car backwards and forwards. If the starter jams regularly or proves impossible to free, then the motor must be removed for further examination.

If the lights do not go dim, first check the solenoid. Use a test lamp or voltmeter to check that current is reaching the unmarked terminal 1, shown in **FIG 11:13**, when the starter switch is operated. If no current is reaching the solenoid trace back through the wiring until the fault is found. If current reaches the solenoid but the starter motor does not operate, short across the terminals 5 and 6 with a thick piece of metal, such as an old pair of pliers. If the starter motor now operates then the solenoid is at fault. If the starter motor still fails to operate, remove it for further checks and possible dismantling.

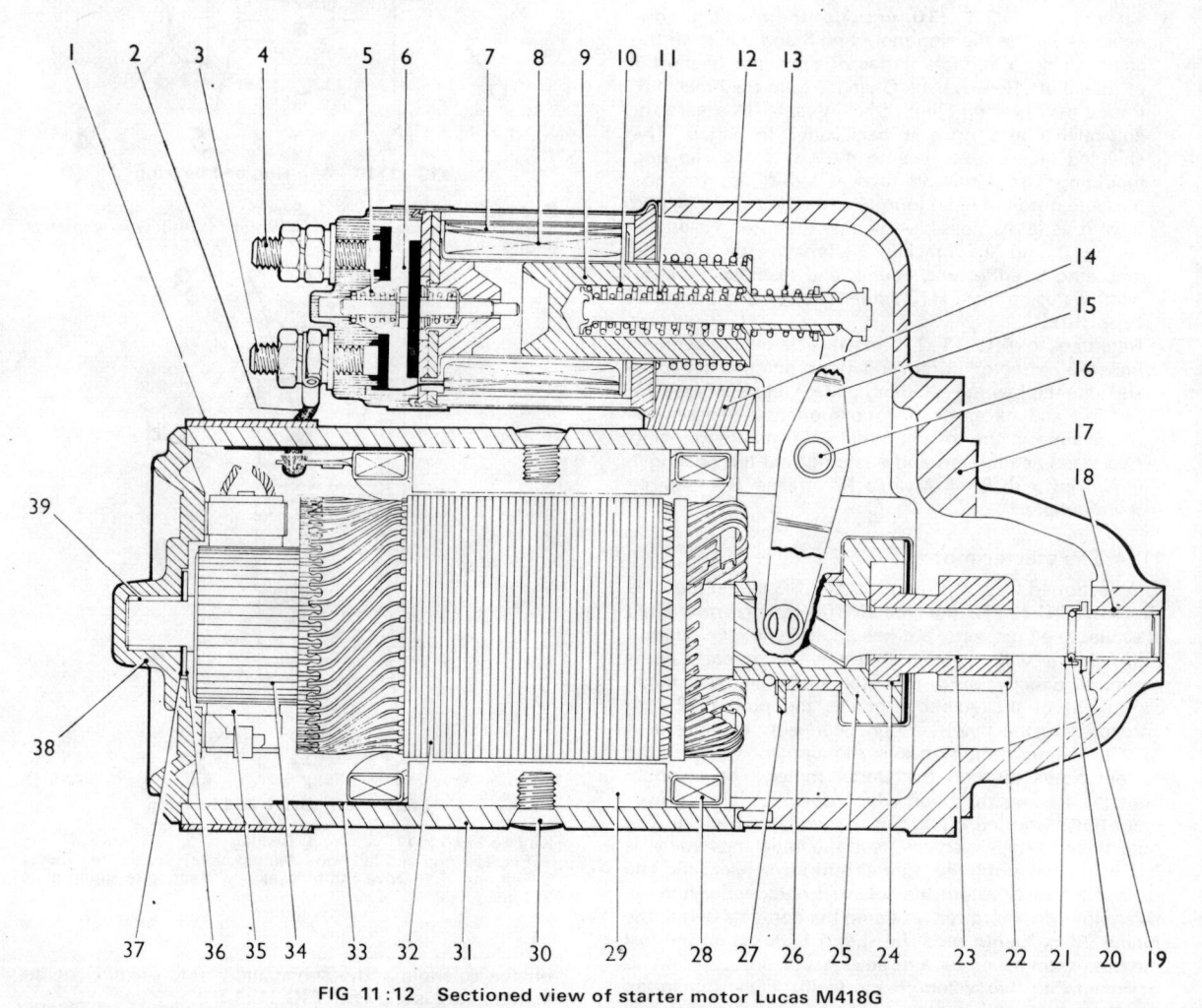

FIG 11:12 Sectioned view of starter motor Lucas M418G

Key to Fig 11:12 1 Cover band   2 Motor lead   3 'STA' terminal   4 Solenoid battery terminal   5 Contact assembly spring   6 Contact assembly   7 Hold in winding   8 Pull in winding   9 Plunger   10 Outer engaging spring   11 Inner engaging spring   12 Return spring   13 Lost motion spring   14 Rubber moulding   15 Engaging lever   16 Eccentric pin   17 Fixing bracket   18 Fixing bracket bearing bush   19 Thrust washer   20 Jump ring   21 Thrust collar   **Starter drive—**   22 Pinion   23 Pinion bearing   24 Roller clutch action   25 Drive sleeve   26 Distance piece   27 Drive operating plate   28 Field winding   29 Pole shoe   30 Pole shoe screw   31 Yoke   32 Armature   33 Insulation strip   34 Commutator   35 Brush   36 Steel thrust washer   37 Fabric thrust washer   38 Commutator end bracket   39 Commutator end bracket bearing bush

112

Removing the starter motor:

Disconnect the battery leads. Disconnect the heavy cable from the terminal 5 and the light cable from the unmarked terminal 1 on the solenoid. Remove the two bolts securing the motor and manoeuvre it out of the car.

The starter solenoid:

Refer to **FIG 11:12**. Remove the outer nut and washer from the 'STA' terminal 3 to free the motor lead 2. Undo the two nuts (not shown) on the fixing bracket 17 which secure the solenoid assembly. Withdraw the solenoid assembly from the starter motor leaving the plunger 9 still attached to the engaging lever 15. The solenoid contacts can be dismantled, though it is not recommended. Remove the adhesive tape from around the body and unscrew the remaining nut from the 'STA' terminal 3. Apply a hot soldering iron to the unmarked terminal 'WR' and, having removed the two cross-headed screws, when the solder melts free the wire from the terminal. With the solder still molten, carefully draw out the contact assembly. The terminal 3 will remain in place in the body. Take care not to lose the spring 5. Clean the copper contacts 6 and reassemble the contact assembly in the reverse order of dismantling. Clean the bore of the solenoid and the surface of the plunger 9 before replacing the solenoid.

Examining the commutator and brush gear:

Remove the cover band 1. A view of the brush gear is shown in **FIG 11:14**. Hold back each of the brush springs in turn and pull gently on the flexible connection to the brush. If the brush does not move freely, remove it from its holder and polish the sides on a fine file. Clean the inside of the holder with a piece of rag moistened in petrol. If the brushes are worn shorter than $\frac{5}{16}$ inch they will have to be renewed. This will entail dismantling the starter motor.

If the commutator 34 is blackened, clean it with a piece of petrol-moistened cloth. One in good condition should have a darkened polished surface free from pitting or burn marks. If the commutator is in poor condition the motor will have to be dismantled and the commutator either cleaned and polished with fine glass-paper or, if the damage is deeper, skimmed off at high speed in a lathe, using a sharp tool. **Never use emery-cloth to clean the commutator, and do not undercut the insulation between the copper segments.** Do not machine the commutator below $1\frac{17}{32}$ inch diameter.

Dismantling the starter motor:

1 Remove the solenoid and take out the return spring 12. Free the plunger 9 from the engaging lever 15. Slacken the locknut, unscrew and withdraw the eccentric pin 16 (see also **FIG 11:15**).
2 Remove the cover band 1 and, holding back the brush springs, remove all four brushes 35 from their holders. Remove the through bolts. Carefully tap on the mounting lugs to remove the fixing bracket 17 from the yoke 31. Take out the rubber moulding 14.
3 Remove the commutator end bracket 38 and, if required, take out from it the steel thrust washer 36 and the fabric thrust washer 37. Withdraw the armature and drive assembly from the yoke. Remove the engaging lever 15 and for safety remove the thrust washer 19 from the end of the shaft.
4 Use a $\frac{5}{8}$ inch diameter tube to force the thrust collar 21 off the jump ring 20 towards the armature 32. Prize off the jump ring 20 and remove the thrust collar 24 followed by the starter drive.

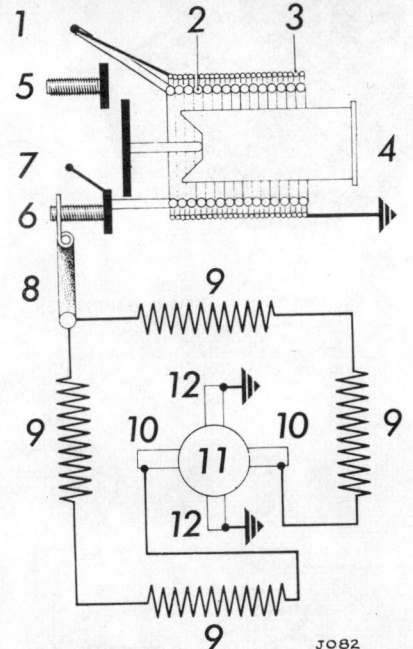

FIG 11:13 Terminals, connectors and wiring diagram of starter motor

Key to Fig 11:13 1 Unmarked 'WR wire' connector
2 Pull in winding 3 Hold in winding 4 Plunger
5 Solenoid battery terminal 6 'STA' terminal 7 'IGN' connector (not used. Full system voltage is available at the connector when the solenoid is energised) 8 Motor lead
9 Field windings 10 Field winding brushes 11 Commutator
12 Earth brushes

FIG 11:14 Brush assembly

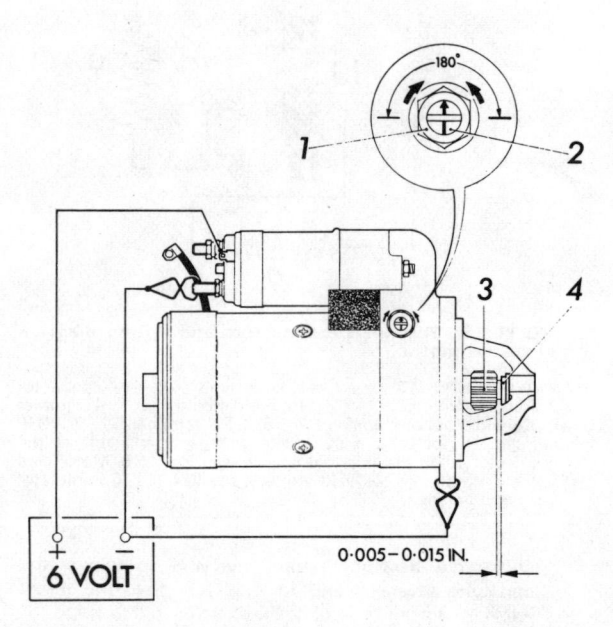

FIG 11:15 Adjusting the pinion movement

Key to Fig 11:15   1 Locknut   2 Eccentric pin
3 Pinion   4 Thrust collar

Reassembly is the reversal of the dismantling procedure, but pay attention to the following points:
1 Lightly grease the eccentric pin 16 bearing surface and screw it back into place only far enough to keep it in position. Make sure it passes through the engaging lever 15.
2 Lubricate the drive sleeve 25 splines and pinion bearing 23 with Shell Retinax A grease, or equivalent. When the jump ring 20 has been refitted to the shaft, drive the thrust collar 21 firmly over the jump ring.
3 Adjust the pinion movement as described next.

Adjusting pinion movement:

1 Disconnect the motor lead from the 'STA' terminal. Connect up a circuit as shown in **FIG 11:15. Note that a 6-volt supply is required.** This can be obtained by using only three of the cells of the battery fitted to the car, tapping off from the connector joining the centre pair of cells.
2 Slacken the locknut 1 and screw the eccentric pin 2 fully home. The range of adjustment is through 180 deg., so after adjustment the arrow on the eccentric pin must point to the top 180 deg. arc indicated by the two arrows on the body.
3 Energize the pull-in windings so that the pinion moves to its engage position. Press the pinion 3 back towards the motor to take up any slack and measure, with feeler gauges, the gap between the pinion 3 and the thrust collar 4. Turn the eccentric pin 2 until the gap is .005 to .015 inch and tighten the locknut 1.
   Check that the gap has not altered and that the arrow is pointing to the correct arc of adjustment.
4 Disconnect the circuit and reconnect the motor lead to the 'STA' terminal on the solenoid.

Renewing the brushes:

If the brushes have worn to less than $\frac{5}{16}$ inch they must be renewed. With the commutator end bracket removed from the motor carefully unsolder and open up the clips holding the flexible connections. Solder the new brushes into place taking care not to allow the solder to creep up the flexible connection. The new brushes are preformed and do not require bedding in. Renew the brush springs if their tension is less than 36 oz.

Checking the armature:

When the starter motor has been dismantled the armature should be checked to ensure that it is straight. Do not attempt to straighten or machine a bent armature. Special equipment is required to check the electrical circuits in the armature so the best test for a doubtful armature is to substitute it with one known to be satisfactory. Score marks on the laminations will indicate either a bent armature or a loose pole shoe.

Renewing the bearings:

With the starter motor dismantled remove the bushes from the end brackets. Screw a $\frac{9}{16}$ inch tap squarely into the old bushes and withdraw them with the tap. New bushes must be soaked in engine oil for 24 hours, or the period can be reduced to 2 hours by heating the oil to 100°C. Press the new bearings into place using a stepped mandrel. The portion that fits into the bush should be the length of the bush and must be highly polished with a diameter of .4729±.0005 inch diameter for the fixing bracket bearing, and .5000±.0005 inch diameter for the commutator end bracket bearing. The mandrel will leave the bush ready to accept the armature shaft and no further reaming or scraping should be carried out.

Field coils:

Connect a test lamp and battery across the terminals 10, shown in **FIG 11:13**. If the lamp fails to light the circuit is broken. Check that the insulation has not broken down by holding one wire from the lamp on a terminal 10 and the other wire on a clean part of the yoke. If the lamp lights the insulation has broken down. Renewal of the field coils is an operation best left to a service station.

Roller clutch assembly:

This is a prelubricated sealed unit and should be renewed if faulty. Do not wash the starter drive in petrol or paraffin as this will remove the lubricant from the sealed roller clutch.

11:5 The windscreen wipers

The TR5 has a single speed motor fitted while the TR6 (and TR250) has a two-speed motor which is completely different in construction. Routine maintenance on all models is confined to changing the wiper blades when they have deteriorated and occasionally lubricating the rubber grommets around the arm drive spindle with a few drops of glycerine. The motor gearboxes and operating cable racks are packed with grease during manufacture and should need no further attention.

Both types of motor are fitted with internal self-parking switches. When the main switch is turned off, the motor continues to run until the wiper arms reach the parked position, when the internal switch turns off the current and stops the motor. The park position on the TR5 can be altered by rotating the domed cover on the motor gearbox, but on the two-speed motor the park position is non-adjustable. On all models the wiper arms

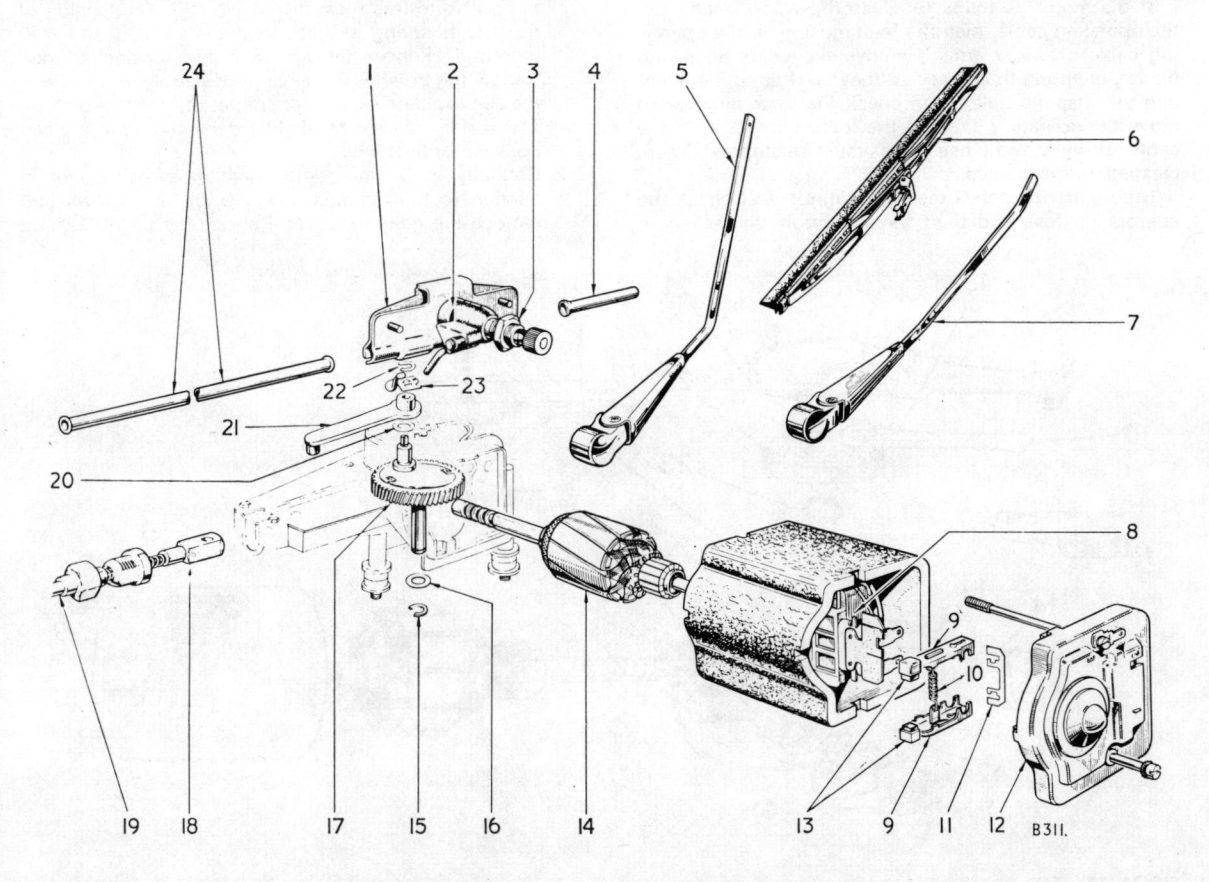

FIG 11:16 Single-speed windscreen wiper motor details

Key to Fig 11:16 1 Wheel box 2 Jet and bush assembly 3 Nut 4 Rigid tubing—righthand side 5 Wiper arm 6 Blade 7 Wiper arm 8 Field coil assembly 9 Brush gear 10 Tension spring and retainers 11 Brush gear retainer 12 End cover 13 Brushes 14 Armature 15 Circlip 16 Washer 17 Final drive wheel 18 Cable rack 19 Rigid tubing—lefthand side 20 Spacer 21 Connecting rod 22 Circlip 23 Parking switch contact 24 Rigid tubing—centre section are fitted to the wheel box spindles by splines so they can be repositioned to alter the arc of sweep, though not the length of the arc.

Wiper motor fails to operate, or operates poorly:

Remove the gearbox cover and disconnect the operating cable rack, as described in the appropriate dismantling section. Connect an accurate ammeter in series with the wiper motor circuit. On the two-speed motor the two circuits will have to be checked individually. Switch on the wiper motor and allow it to run for one minute before noting the current consumption. The single speed motor should take between 2.7 and 3.4 amps. The two-speed motor should take 1.5 amps at normal speed and 2.0 amps at high speed.

Count the revolutions of the final gear (number of strokes the wiper motor makes). The single-speed motor should operate between 44 and 48 cycles per minute. The two-speed motor should run at 46 to 52 cycles per minute at normal speed and 60 to 70 cycles per minute at high speed.

If the motor performs satisfactorily when freed from the operating cable, then the fault must lie in the operating cable or wiper arms. Remove the wiper arms and blades, or spring them back so they are free of the glass, and use a spring balance to check the force required to move the operating cable. If the force exceeds 6 lb the cable assembly and wheel boxes must be stripped down, cleaned and examined.

If no current reaches the wiper motor, first check the appropriate fuse and then trace through the wiring to discover the fault. Low current consumption can be caused by faulty field coils, faulty armature or faulty brushgear. An abnormally high current can be caused by the same faults as cause low current consumption, or by excessive friction in the motor.

Servicing the single-speed motor:

The motor is mounted on a bracket which is secured to the car by three bolts; two are reached from inside the car under the facia and the third is accessible under the bonnet. Remove and replace the motor complete with the bracket. The details of the motor are shown in **FIG 11:16**. When removing the motor either take off the gearbox cover, remove the connecting rod 21 and lift out the cable rack 18, or else remove the windscreen wiper arms 5 and 7 from the wheel box spindles and draw out the cable rack with the motor.

1 The brushgear 9 can be examined without removing the motor. Remove the end cover 12. Check that the brushes 13 bear firmly on the commutator. The brush levers should move freely on their pivots, so work them to and fro to free them if they are stiff. The tension of the brush spring should be between 125 and 140 grammes. Renew the spring if the tension is low. Renew the brushes if they are excessively worn. Clean the commutator with a piece of petrol-moistened cloth. The surface should be slightly darkened, with a clean polished appearance.

2 Carefully mark the domed parking switch cover in relation to the gearbox cover. Undo the screws and remove the gearbox cover. Release the circlip 22 and

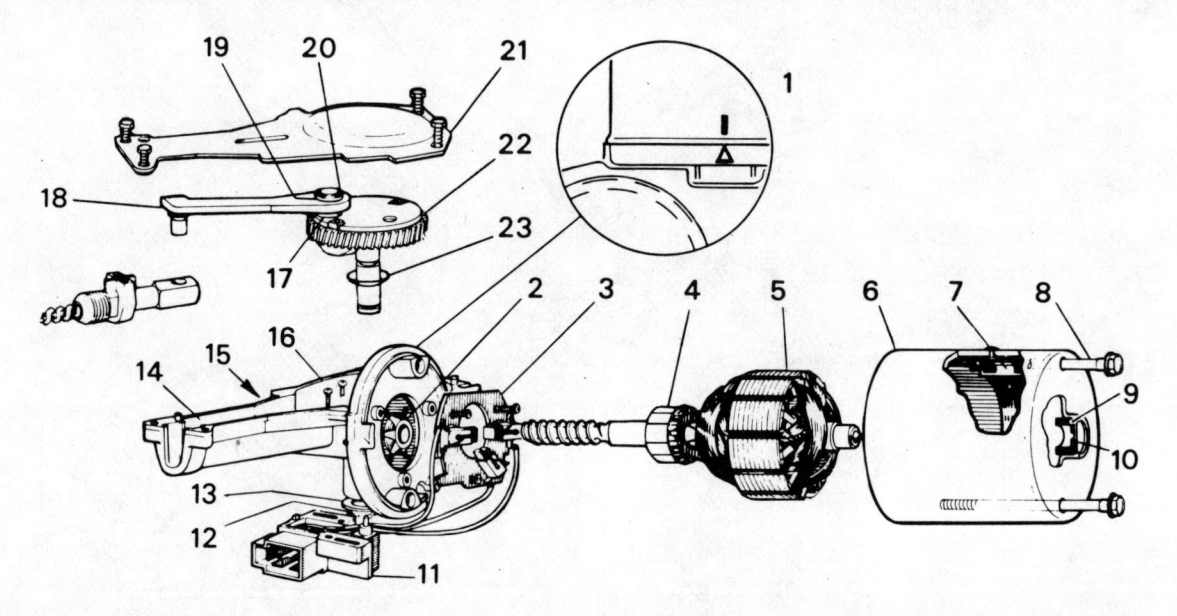

FIG 11:17 Two-speed windscreen wiper motor details. If aligning marks are not aligned on reassembly the motor will run in reverse

Key to Fig 11:17   1 Aligning marks   2 Self aligning bearing   3 Brush assembly   4 Commutator   5 Armature   6 Cover   7 Permanent magnet   8 Through-bolt   9 Cover bearing   10 Felt washer   11 Limit switch unit   12 Final gear shaft spring clip (adjustable)   13 Washer   14 Crosshead guide channel   15 Thrust screw (non-adjustable) or thrust screw and locknut   16 Gearbox   17 Washer   18 Connecting rod   19 Washer   20 Crankpin spring clip   21 Gearbox cover   22 Final gear   23 Dished washer remove the parking switch contact 23. Lift out the connecting rod 21 and the spacer 20 to free the cable rack 18. If required the final drive gear 17 can be taken out by freeing the circlip 15 and washer 16. Remove any burrs from the end of the final drive shaft before withdrawing it.

3 To completely dismantle the motor, remove the brush-gear retainer 11 and extract the brush gear assembly. The earth cable is long enough to allow the yoke to be freed from the armature.

4 The field coils 8 are held in by screws. Their resistance should be 8 to 9.5 ohms ($1\frac{1}{2}$ to $1\frac{1}{4}$ amps when connected across a 12-volt supply). The only available test for a suspected faulty armature is to check with a known satisfactory armature fitted in its place.

5 Reassemble the parts in the reverse order of dismantling. Set and lock the adjusting screw to give an armature end float of .008 to .012 inch. If the gearbox has been washed clean, repack it with 25 to 35 cc of Ragosine Listate grease. Use engine oil on the bearings. Check the wiring and insulation for signs of charring or overheating.

Servicing the two-speed motor:

The details of the motor are shown in **FIG 11:17**, and a simplified wiring diagram is shown in **FIG 11:18**. For normal operation the two brushes 2 and 6 are used but for high-speed operation the positive supply is transferred from brush 2 to brush 3. When the current supply is cut off at the main switch the motor continues running, using the supply through the limit switch 8. The cam 7 on the final gear opens the contacts 8 when the blades approach the parked position. The inertia of the motor turns the cam until the high point closes the switch 8 lower contacts, making a continuous circuit through the motor and providing regenerative braking to hold the blades in place at park.

The motor gearbox is dismantled and serviced in exactly the same manner as the gearbox fitted to the single-speed motor, but noting that the crankpin mounting plate should not be removed from the moulded gear wheel, assembly 22.

To gain access to the brush gear, first remove the two through-bolts 8. Withdraw the cover 6 and magnet 7 assembly about $\frac{3}{16}$ inch. The armature 5 will follow the magnet 7. Allow the brushes on the assembly 3 to drop clear of the commutator 4 and withdraw the cover and armature, taking care that the brushes are not contaminated with grease. Pull the armature assembly out of the cover 6 against the pull of the magnet 7. Clean the commutator 4 with a piece of rag moistened in petrol. If the commutator is lightly burnt or scored remove the

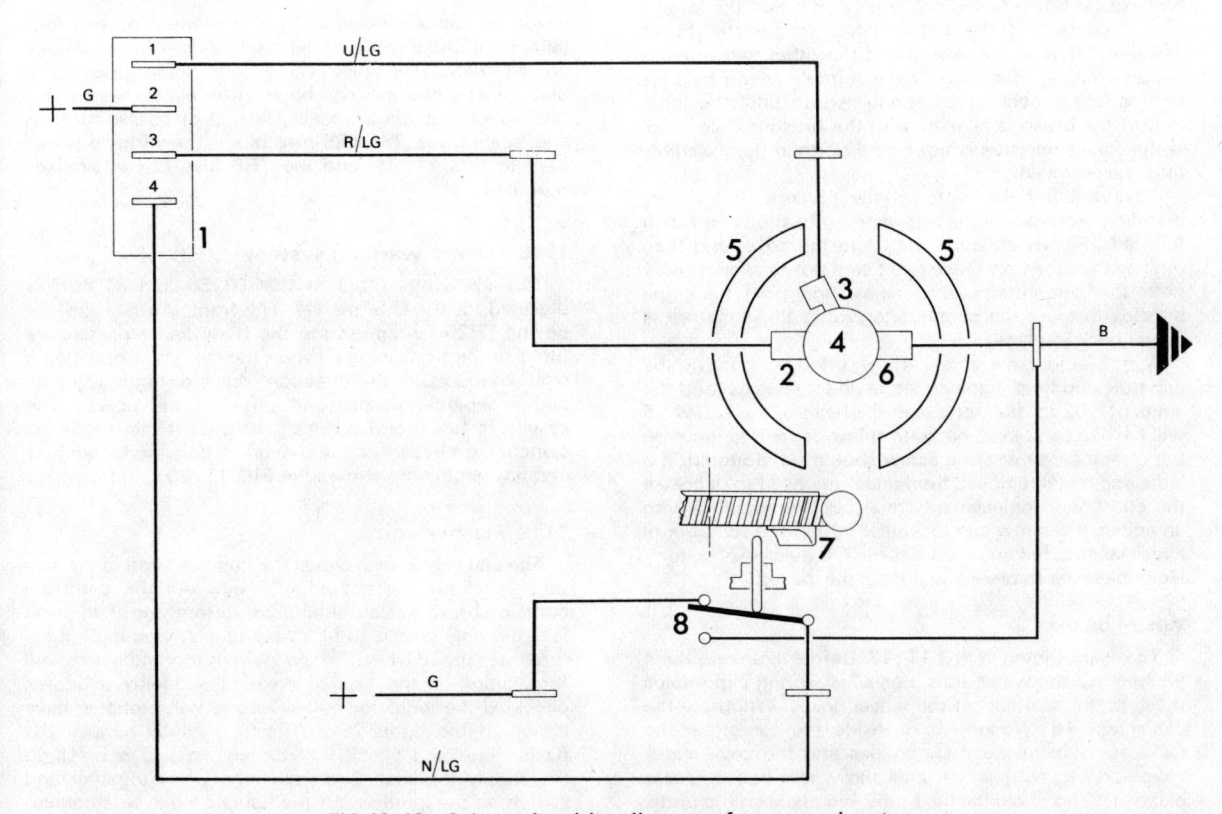

FIG 11:18 Schematic wiring diagram of two-speed motor

Key to Fig 11:18   + Supply   1 Facia switch: OFF—3 connected to 4; NORMAL—2 connected to 3; HIGH—2 connected to 1
2 Normal speed brush   3 High speed brush   4 Commutator   5 Permanent magnet   6 Earth brush   7 Final gear cam
8 Limit switch unit

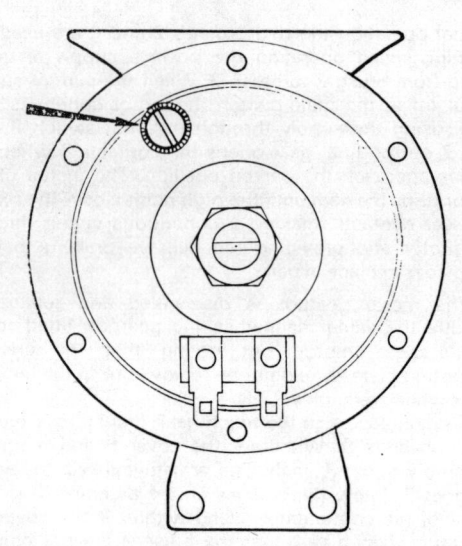

FIG 11:19 Arrow points to horn adjusting screw

damage with fine glasspaper. Examine the brushes. If the high-speed brush has worn so far down that the step is nearly contacting the commutator, renew the brush assembly. Renew the assembly if the other two brushes are less than $\frac{3}{16}$ inch long. Use a suitable spring balance and compress each brush spring in turn until the inner end of the brush is aligned with the brushbox slot end. If the spring pressure is not 5 to 7 oz then the assembly must be renewed.

Reassembling the motor is the reversal of the dismantling process. Oil the self-aligning bearings and their felt pads. Fit the armature back into the cover and then replace the assembly. Take great care not to allow grease onto the commutator or brushes, and hold back the brushes to clear the commutator when the armature is nearly back in place.

A non-adjustable screw 15 is fitted to control the armature end float. If the armature end float is beyond the limits of .002 to .008 inch then the head of the screw 15 will have to be packed out with shims under it to increase the clearance, or else the screw should be mounted in a lathe and metal removed from under the head to decrease the end float. Replacement armatures are supplied with an adjustable screw and locknut. Tighten the screw until a resistance is felt and then slacken it a quarter-of-a-turn. Hold the screw in place and tighten the locknut.

Wheel boxes:

These are shown in **FIG 11:16**. Before removing them first remove the wiper arms 5 and 7. A spring clip retains these to the spindles on the wheel boxes. Withdraw the cable rack 18. Working from inside the car under the facia, remove the demister nozzles and the coverplates (two screws each) which hide the wheel boxes. Use a piece of wire to hold the rigid tube 4 in place on the body. Outside the car undo the nuts 3 and back inside the car withdraw the jet and bush assembly about two inches. Disconnect the plastic water pipes for the screen washers and remove the wheel box backplate. Grip the wheel box with a pair of long-nosed pliers and draw it out of the aperture.

Clean the parts and check the teeth for wear. Replace them in the reverse order of removal. Make sure that the wheel box is aligned so that the cable rack will pass smoothly through the rigid tubes and wheel boxes, without chafing or binding. Seal the coverplates back in place before using the two securing screws.

11:6 The horns

The horn adjusting screw is shown in **FIG 11:19**. **Under no circumstances should the central screw and locknut be turned.** If the horns fail to operate first check the appropriate fuse and then the wiring. Check the contacts in the horn push button as after long service they may become burnt and have a high resistance. If the wiring is satisfactory the fault will lie in the horn and this should be replaced with a new unit.

The horn is adjusted by inserting an ammeter into the circuit and turning the adjusting screw until the best performance with the minimum current consumption is obtained. If an ammeter is not available unscrew the adjusting screw until the horn just ceases to sound and then screw the adjuster back in by quarter of a turn.

11:7 Fuses

All the models covered by this manual have a fuse carrier mounted on the lefthand side of the engine compartment. The fuse carrier has three operational stations and one that can be used for accessories, but is not in use on standard models. The pull-off lid also contains two spare fuses. The TR5 fuse box is the lefthand centre item in **FIG 11:20**, and the TR6 fuse box is similarly mounted.

11:8 Hazard warning system

This system is fitted to the TR250 and all models destined for the U.S. market. The front and rear flashers on the TR250 wrap around the body and repeaters are fitted to the front wings. When the system is operated a relay connects all the direction indicator lights together and a separate flasher unit provides the power. The system is fused and so designed that it can safely be switched on even if the bodywork is damaged. The relay and flasher unit are arrowed in **FIG 11:20**.

11:9 Flasher unit

The unit is held by a clip at the bulkhead end of the side trim panel on the passenger's side. All the parts are contained in a sealed aluminium casing and if the unit fails the only cure is to fit a new unit. A warning light is fitted to the dash to show when the indicators are functioning. If the rate of flashing suddenly increases check all the indicator bulbs, as one will probably have blown. If the lights fail to flash, carefully remove the flasher unit and check that battery voltage is reaching the supply terminal. Short all three wires together and switch on the ignition. All the lights on one side coming on, when the direction switch is operated, show that the flasher unit has failed. Handle the flasher unit with care, and replace or remove it only when the circuit is switched off. Mis-handling will cause the unit to fail.

11:10 Fuel and temperature gauges

A voltage stabilizer unit is fitted to the rear of the speedometer. This contains a bi-metallic spring and heating element. Over a period of time the bi-metallic spring heats up, bends and opens the contacts. The current stops flowing and the bi-metal spring cools and closes the contacts. The unit is so designed that over a period of time the average voltage is 10 volts and this is fed to the fuel and temperature gauge circuits. The temperature transmitter in the cooling system contains a temperature sensitive element that varies its resistance with temperature. The current from the transmitter is fed to the temperature gauge where another bi-metal strip heats and bends in proportion to the current, moving the gauge pointer. The fuel gauge works on similar principles, but the rise and fall of a float in the fuel tank sweeps a wiper across a potentiometer varying the current in proportion to the fuel level.

If the systems fail check through the wiring and supply. Do not connect full battery voltage across gauges or indicators. Test faulty parts by substitution with known satisfactory parts. A normal voltmeter will not measure the average voltage in the system.

11:11 The headlamps

Remove the front chrome trim rim and the rubber dust excluder under this. The headlamp assembly is mounted by the rim, on three adjusting screws. Do not turn these screws or the beam alignment will be upset. Turn the headlamp assembly anticlockwise so the screws can pass through the larger keyholes in the rim. Disconnect the wires from the headlamp assembly. Some units will have all sealed reflectors and bulbs, where the reflector and front lens are part of the bulb, whilst others will have pre-focus bulbs fitted into the reflector. Replace the parts in the reverse order of dismantling, still without turning the adjusting screws.

Beam setting:

Accurate setting is best left to a service station having the necessary equipment. The beams must be set to conform with local regulations, but usually they are set so that the main beams are parallel with the road surface. The top adjusting screw sets the angle to the road surface and the other two screws set the angle in relation to the centre line of the road.

11:12 Lighting circuits

Lamps give insufficient light:

Test the charge of the battery as described in **Section 11:12** and recharge it if necessary from an independent supply. If the bulbs or reflectors have darkened with age, fit new ones. Have the settings of the headlamps checked.

Bulbs burn out frequently:

If this is accompanied by a need for frequent topping up of the battery and high hydrometer readings, check the charging rate when the car is running. A regular high reading over 5 amps indicates a fault in the system.

Lamps light when switched on but gradually fade:

Check the battery as it is incapable of supplying current for any length of time.

FIG 11:20 Hazard relay and flasher unit indicated by arrows. Fuse box and alternator control in the centre

Lamp brilliance varies with the speed of the car:

Check the condition of the battery. Examine the battery connections, making sure that they are clean, tight and secure.

11:13 Fault diagnosis

(a) Battery discharged

1. Terminals loose or dirty
2. Short circuit in the system
3. Alternator not charging
4. Control unit not working properly
5. Battery internally defective

(b) Insufficient charging current

1. Loose or corroded battery terminals
2. Alternator driving belt slipping

(c) Battery will not hold charge

1. Low electrolyte level
2. Battery plates sulphated
3. Electrolyte leakage from cracked casing or top sealing compound
4. Plate separators ineffective

(d) Alternator output low or nil

1. Belt broken or slipping
2. Control unit failed
3. Diodes failed in rectifier pack
4. Brushes excessively worn or slip rings dirty

(e) Starter motor lacks power or will not operate

1. Battery discharged, loose cable connections
2. Starter pinion jammed in mesh with flywheel gear
3. Starter switch faulty
4. Starter solenoid faulty
5. Brushes worn or sticking, leads detached or shorting
6. Commutator worn or dirty
7. Engine abnormally stiff
8. Armature or field coils faulty

(f) Starter motor runs but does not turn engine
1 Pinion engaging mechanism failed
2 Engagement spring broken
3 Broken teeth on pinion or flywheel gears
4 Failed roller clutch assembly

(g) Noisy starter pinion when engine is running
1 Failed or weak return springs

(h) Starter motor rough or noisy
1 Mounting bolts loose
2 Damaged pinion or flywheel gear teeth
3 Weak or broken return spring

(j) Lamps inoperative or erratic
1 Battery low, bulbs burned out
2 Faulty earthing of lamps or battery
3 Lighting switch faulty, loose or broken connections

(k) Wiper motor sluggish, taking high current
1 Faulty armature
2 Commutator dirty or short circuited
3 Wheel box spindle binding, cable rack tight in housing

(l) Wiper motor operates but does not drive arms
1 Wheel box and spindle worn
2 Cable rack faulty
3 Gearbox components badly worn

(m) Fuel gauge does not register
1 No battery supply to voltage stabilizer
2 Faulty voltage stabilizer
3 Cable between gauge and tank unit broken

(n) Fuel gauge registers full
1 Cable between gauge and tank unit earthed
2 Faulty voltage stabilizer

(o) Fuel gauge intermittent
1 Faulty voltage stabilizer
2 Faulty tank unit
3 Loose connections or broken wires
4 Poor insulation on cables

CHAPTER 12

THE BODYWORK

12:1 Bodywork finish
12:2 Seat belts
12:3 The doors
12:4 The door fittings
12:5 The bonnet

12:6 Luggage locker lid
12:7 The windscreen assembly
12:8 The facia and instruments
12:9 The heater

12:1 Bodywork finish

Large-scale repairs to body panels are best left to expert panel beaters. Even small dents can be tricky, as too much hammering will stretch the metal and makes things worse instead of better. Filling minor dents and scratches is probably the best method of restoring the surface. The touching-up of paintwork is well within the powers of most owners, particularly as self-spraying cans of the correct colours are now readily available. It must be remembered, however, that paint changes colour with age and that it is better to spray a whole wing or panel rather than to try touching-up a small area.

Cellulose paint can never be sprayed over an original synthetic finish. The synthetic paint will lift off in blisters. It is possible to spray synthetic over cellulose, but if cellulose is then later applied the synthetic paint will still blister. If there is any doubt try a spot of new paint in an area where it will not show.

Before spraying it is essential to remove all traces of wax polish with white spirits. More drastic treatment is required if silicone polishes have been applied as the wet paint will not stick to silicone but will leave little craters down to the original surface.

Lightly scuff the area to be sprayed. Mask off surrounding areas with newspaper and masking tape to prevent spray dust settling on them. Use a primer surfacer or paste stopper according to the amount of filling required. Keep the paste as level and smooth as possible as this will save effort and time in rubbing it down later. When it is dry, rub it down with 400 grade 'Wet or Dry' paper, using plenty of water until the surface is smooth and flush with the surrounding areas. If required use two, or even more, coats of stopper or filler to achieve a perfect surface. Spend plenty of time in getting the best finish as this will control the final effect. Small blemishes which are hardly noticeable on the matt surface will stand out startlingly on the final polished finish.

Apply the retouching paint, heavier in the centre and lighter around the edges. It is better to apply two thinner coats of paint, rubbing down lightly between coats, than one thick one which may run.

After several hours, when the paint is dry and hard, use a cutting compound to lightly polish the surface and remove any spray dust. Leave the paint to dry for at least a couple of days before applying wax polish.

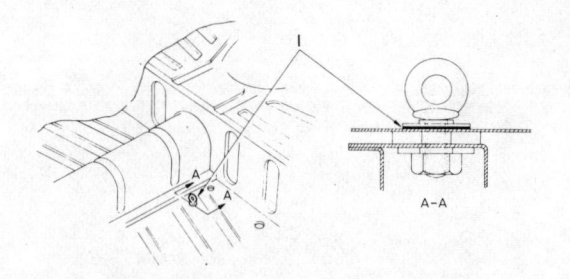

FIG 12:1 Floor safety harness bolts, TR6

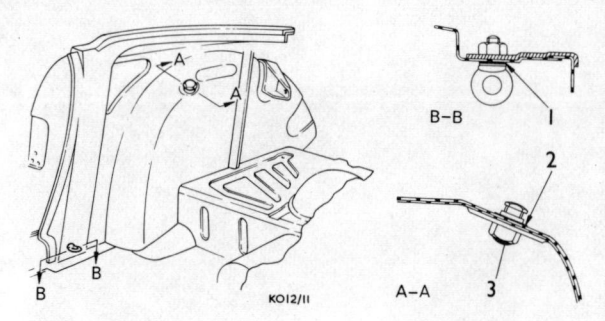

FIG 12:2 Pillar and wheel arch safety harness bolts, TR6

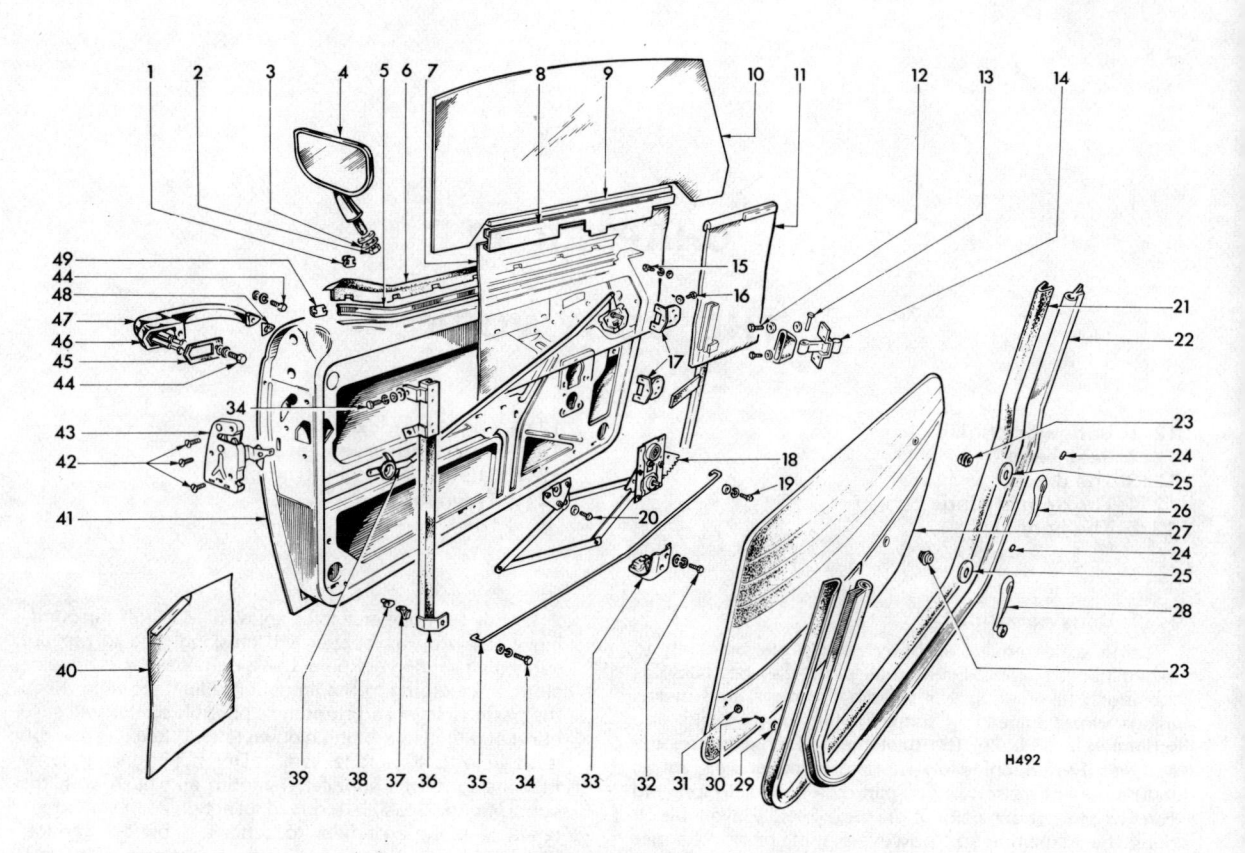

FIG 12:3 Door details

Key to Figs 12:3, 12:4, 12:6 and 12:7 1 Trim clip 2 Nut (Door mirror attachment) 3 Washer (Door mirror attachment) 4 Exterior door mirror 5 Inner weatherstrip 6 Outer weatherstrip 7 Water deflector curtain 8 Glass channel 9 Glazing strip 10 Glass 11 Water deflector curtain 12 Screw—check arm 13 Pin—check arm 14 Check arm 15 Bolt—hinge to 'A' post 16 Bolt—hinge to door 17 Door hinge 18 Window regulator mechanism 19 Setscrew (Window regulator attachment) 20 Setscrew (Window regulator attachment) 21 Sealing rubber 22 Draught excluder 23 Spring 24 Retaining pin 25 Escutcheon plate 26 Remote control handle 27 Trim panel 28 Window regulator handle 29 Cover button (Door pocket attachment) 30 Screw (Door pocket attachment) 31 Retaining washer (Door pocket attachment) 32 Screw—stop bracket 33 Glass—stop bracket 34 Setscrew—glass run channel 35 Tie rod 36 Glass run channel 37 Clip 38 Snap-sac 39 Remote control unit 40 Water deflector curtain 41 Door 42 Screw—lock attachment 43 Anti-burst lock 44 Setscrew—door handle attachment 45 Seating washer 46 Outside door handle 47 Push button—door handle 48 Seating washer 49 Trim-clip 50 Locknut 51 Adjustment screw 52 Lock contactor 53 Anti-burst strap 54 Screw—striker plate 55 Striker plate 56 Waved washer 57 Spring clip 58 Lever 59 Spring 60 Setscrew—remote control unit 61 Lock operating lever 62 Locking lever 63 Operating fork 64 Spring collar

122

FIG 12:4 Door component attachments

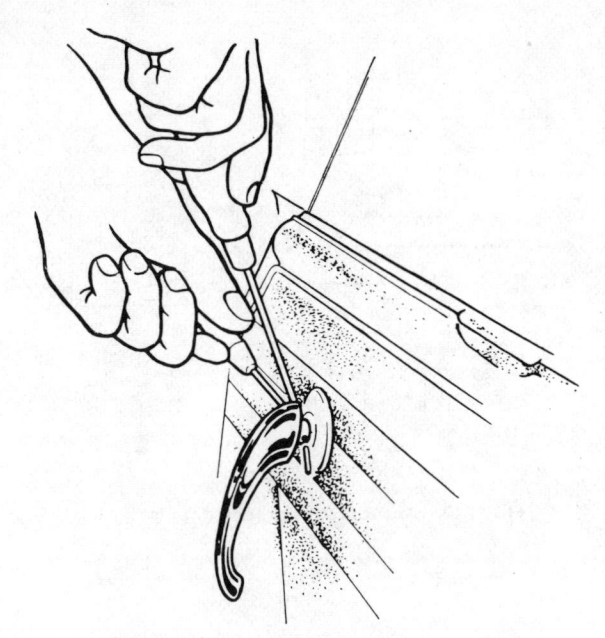

FIG 12:5 Removing interior door handles

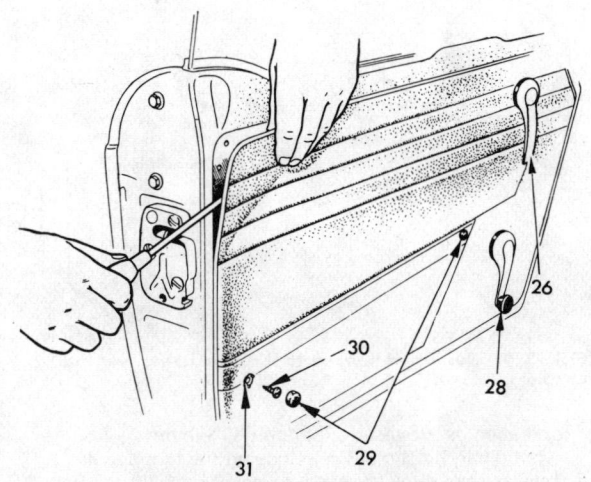

FIG 12:6 Removing door trim panel

12:2 Seat belts

The seat belt securing points for the TR6 are shown in **FIG 12:1** and **FIG 12:2**. The strong points on the TR5 are similarly situated. **It is extremely dangerous if the seat belts are not properly fitted. If an owner has any doubts on his ability to make a correct and safe installation he is strongly advised to take the car to an authorized dealer.** On later models, of course, the fitting of front seat belts is compulsory and will be fitted before the car leaves the service agent.

Not all seat belts are suitable for fitting to sports cars, so make sure that any belts purchased are of the right type for the car, also check that they meet the approved standards and any local regulations.

12:3 The doors

Details of the door assembly and interior parts are shown in **FIG 12:3** and the door with the trim panel removed is shown in **FIG 12:4**. It should be noted that the doors on the TR5 are identical with the doors on the TR6. Door interior handles are easily removed by pushing out the retaining pins 24 as shown in **FIG 12:5**. When the handles 26 and 28 have been removed take out the two cover buttons 29, screws 30 and washers 31 to free the door pocket. The trim clips can then be freed using a screwdriver as shown in **FIG 12:6**.

To remove the door first undo the four screws securing the dash side carpet to the A post. Remove the small spring clip and withdraw the pin 13 from the check arm 14. Support the door and use a socket spanner and extension to remove the six bolts 15 securing the door to the A frame post. Lift out the door.

Refitting the door is the reversal of the removal operation. Vertical adjustment of the door is by the six bolts 15 securing the hinges to the A frame, so tighten these only sufficiently to grip the door yet allowing it to be moved up and down. When the height is correct fully tighten the six bolts. In and out adjustment of the leading edge of the door is similarly carried out by slackening the bolts securing the hinges to the door.

12:4 The door fittings

The doors are fitted with anti-burst locks which are designed to prevent the doors flying open in the event of serious distortion in a crash.

When reassembling the door fittings make sure that all moving parts are adequately greased. Once a month put a few drops of thin oil into the key slot on the outside lock and onto the latch inside the lock case.

Door locks:

The components of the lock are shown in **FIG 12:7**. Remove the lock as follows:
1 Remove the door trim panel as described earlier. Remove the spring clip 57 and the waved washer 56 and release the link arm 39 from the anti-burst lock. This

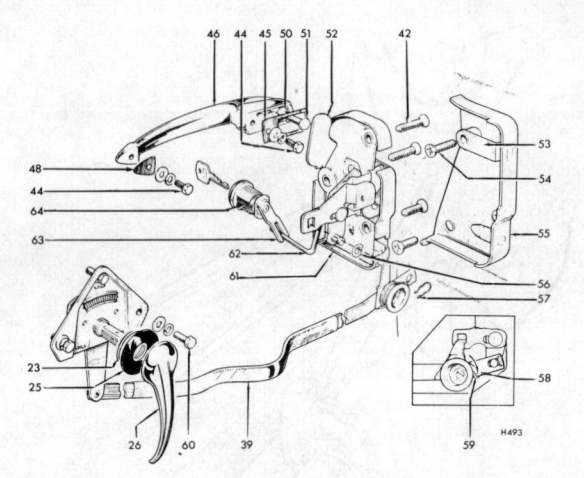

FIG 12:7 Anti-burst door lock details

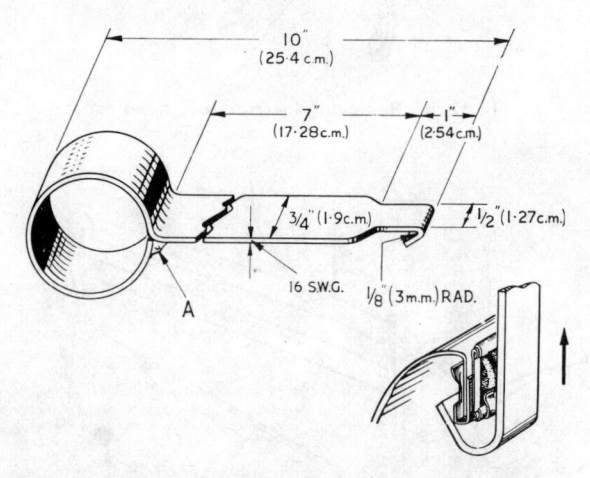

FIG 12:8 Details of hooked tool for refitting weatherstrip

operation is easiest to perform if window glass is wound fully closed before removing the trim panel.
2 Take out the three countersunk screws 42, lift the lock operating lever 61 sufficiently to allow the lock assembly to be withdrawn from the door and withdraw the lock.
3 The remote control assembly 39 can be removed from the door by undoing the three bolts and washers 60.
Replacing the locks is the reversal of the removal procedure. The anti-burst lock requires no adjustment but the remote control mechanism must be set correctly. Refit the anti-burst lock securely and the remote control mechanism with the three bolts 60 just gripping it. Manually move the latch-claw to the fully locked position, when two distinct clicks will be heard. Slide the remote control along the elongated securing holes until the spring-loaded lever 58 just contacts the spring 59 as shown in the inset in **FIG 12:7**. Tighten the three bolts 60 to hold the remote control in place. Grease the moving parts and replace the door trim and handles.

Exterior handle and security lock:

The exterior handle is held in place by the two bolts 44. The trim panel must be removed to gain access to these bolts, as well as to the twin-legged spring collar 65 which holds the security lock in place. A tool must be used to compress the legs of the spring collar 64 to allow the security lock to be withdrawn. The security lock is refitted, with the spring collar in place, by pressing it firmly into place with its operating fork inclined to the shut face.

The push button on the exterior door handle is adjusted by slackening the locknut 50 and turning the bolt 51 until the correct movement is obtained. Retighten the locknut to secure the adjusting bolt in place.

Window regulator mechanism:

1 Remove the interior door handles and trim panel. Leave the window glass in the half-open position.
2 Remove the three screws and washers 20 and the four screws and washers 19 holding the window regulator mechanism in place.
3 Use the large door aperture to work through. Slide the complete regulator mechanism to free the lifting studs from the glass lifting channel and withdraw the regulator assembly out of the door.
4 The regulator is replaced in the reverse order of dismantling.

Door glass:

1 Remove the interior door handles and trim panel, leaving the door glass in the fully down and open position.
2 Remove all the screws securing the window regulator mechanism and free the lifting studs from the glass lifting channel.
3 Remove the upper weatherstrip 5 by pushing its lower edge upwards with a screwdriver from inside the door.
4 Taking care not to damage the deflector 40, which is attached to the glass by the lower channel, lift the glass out of the door.

The door glass is replaced in the reverse order of removal. Fold the deflector 40 flat against the inner side of the glass when lowering them back into position. The deflector can then be replaced correctly. Use a tool, as shown in **FIG 12:8**, to hold the seven clips 49 in place and to refit the weatherstrip 5.

Striker plate:

The striker plate 55 is held to the rear door post by three countersunk screws 55, and though adjustment is provided it should not normally be required. If the striker plate does require adjustment slacken the screws and move the plate slightly. Do not slam the door when the striker plate is out of adjustment. Adjust until the door shuts satisfactorily. Make sure the striker plate is parallel to the line of the door shutting and firmly tighten the three securing screws.

12:5 The bonnet

The bonnet on the TR6, though different, is of similar construction and is removed and replaced in the same way as the TR5 bonnet. As they are so similar only the bonnet on the TR5 is illustrated, in **FIG 12:9**.

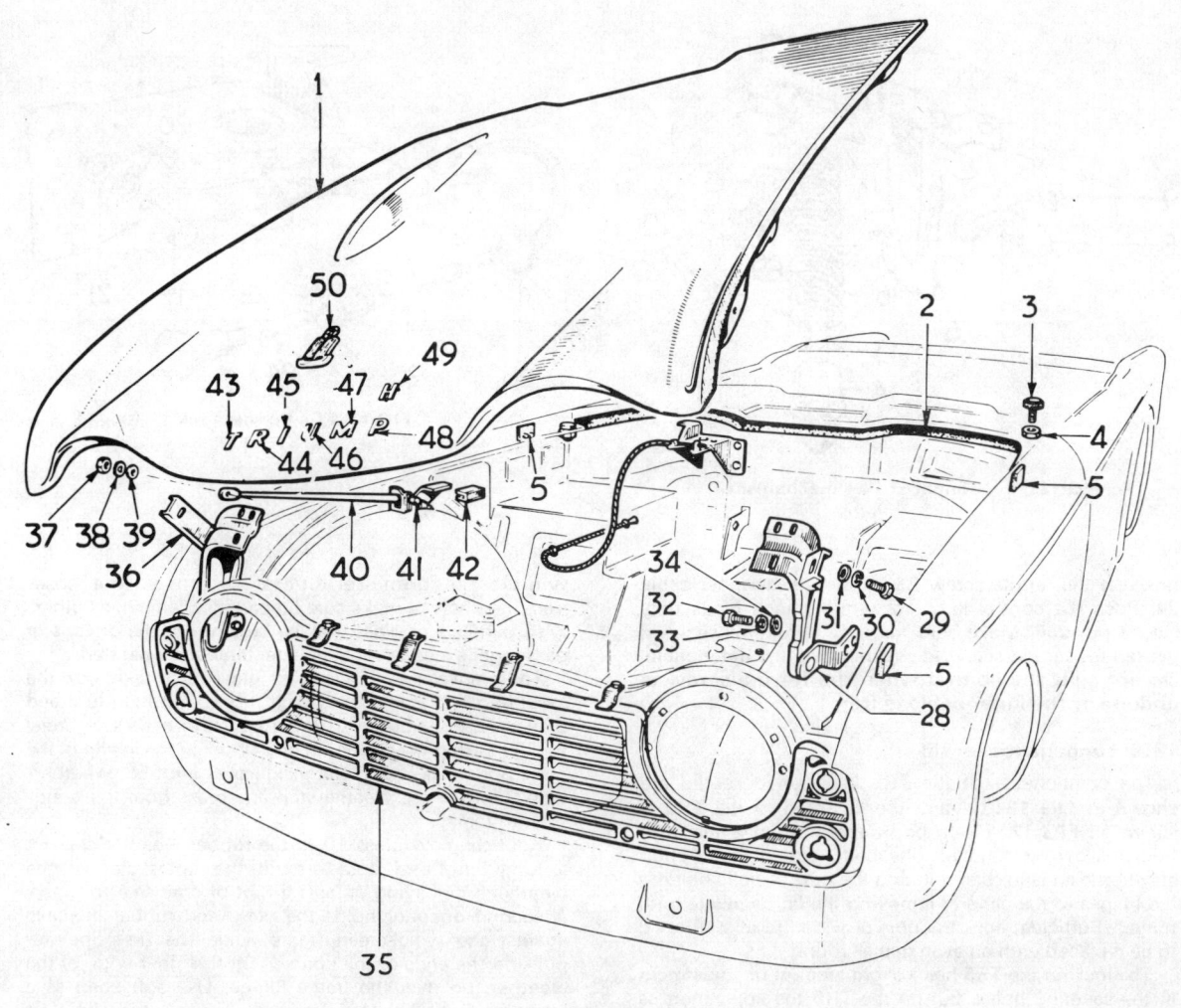

FIG 12:9 Bonnet details, TR5

Key to Figs 12:9, 12:10 and 12:11 1 Bonnet 2 Sealing rubber 3 Bonnet stop 4 Locknut 5 Rubber buffer
6 Bonnet catch (early models only) 7 Bolt 8 Washer 9 Washer 10 Bonnet fastener assembly 11 Bolt 12 Washer
13 Washer 14 Spring retaining cup 15 Striker pin 16 Spring 17 Nut 18 Bracket 19 Bolt 20 Washer 21 Washer
22 Lever 23 Screw 24 Inner cable 25 Outer cable 26 Grommet 27 Cable clip 28 Bonnet hinge 29 Bolt
30 Washer 31 Washer 32 Bolt 33 Washer 34 Washer 35 Grille 36 Bonnet hinge 37 Nut 38 Washer
39 Washer 40 Bonnet support stay 41 Bonnet stay bracket 42 Rubber buffer 43 'T' 44 'R' 45 'I' 46 'U'
47 'M' 48 'P' 49 'H' 50 Medallion

To remove the bonnet, prop it open and disconnect the support stay 40 from the bonnet. Remove the two bolts securing each hinge to the wing valance and lift the bonnet away. Each hinge is secured to the bonnet by four bolts, the long bolt in the outer position.

When replacing the bonnet leave the securing bolts only just tight enough to prevent the bonnet from moving under its own weight. Close the bonnet, and adjust it so that there is an even gap all round. Fully tighten the bolts when the bonnet fits satisfactorily. The rubber buffers 3 are adjustable for height to prevent excess vertical movement of the rear of the bonnet.

Striker mechanism:

This is illustrated in **FIG 12:10**. If the bonnet is difficult to close, or is loose when closed, first check the rubber buffers 3. If these are correct then adjust the striker mechanism. Slacken the locknut 17 and screw the striker pin 15 up to tighten the bonnet when closed, or down to make it easier to shut the bonnet. When the bonnet shuts satisfactorily tighten the locknut to secure the striker pin. Lightly oil the sliding parts and pivots.

Bonnet lock:

The lock is illustrated in **FIG 12:11**. To adjust the lock,

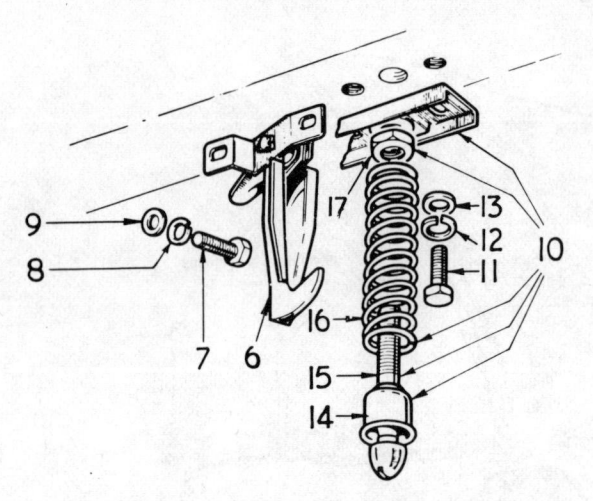

FIG 12:10 Bonnet striker mechanism

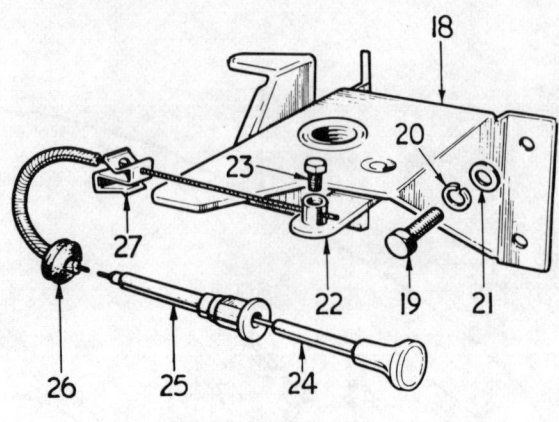

FIG 12:11 Bonnet lock

unscrew the ferrule screw 23 to release the inner cable 24. Push the control knob to within $\frac{1}{8}$ inch of its fully closed position. Make sure the lock is fully closed and tighten the ferrule screw to securely grip the inner cable. **Do not shut the bonnet when the ferrule screw is undone or the inner cable is free.**

12:6 Luggage locker lid

The components of the TR5 luggage locker lid are shown in **FIG 12:12**, and the lid fitted to the TR6 is shown in **FIG 12:13**. In both cases the lid is removed from the car by removing the bolt holding the support stay to the lid, and then undoing the nuts or bolts holding the hinges to the car and removing the lid complete with hinges. Sufficient adjustment is provided to allow the lid to be replaced with an even gap all round.

The lock on the TR5 has a slight amount of adjustment in the securing holes, but on the TR6 the adjustment is carried out on the striker assembly 10. Elongated holes are provided so that the whole assembly can be moved around on the boot lid, to ensure correct alignment relative to the lock. The striker pin is screwed into a weldnut on the base plate and locked in position by a locknut. By slackening the locknut the striker pin can be screwed in or out to achieve positive locking.

12:7 The windscreen assembly

The details of this are shown in **FIG 12:14**. The complete assembly may be removed from the car by slackening the bolts 16 and 17, and removing the nuts 24 from underneath the facia in the car. Remove the three sets of chrome-headed bolts 22 and plates 21 from on top of the dashboard. Use two operators to lift the assembly squarely out of the car. When replacing the assembly, preferably use a new seal 23 and secure it in place with sealant. Elongated securing holes provide a limited degree of adjustment to allow the windscreen frame to be lined up with the door glass.

If a windscreen glass 10 has broken make sure that all particles of glass are removed, **especially from the windscreen demister ducts**. Disconnect the hoses from the ducts to make sure no particles remain, as otherwise particles of glass may be blown into the driver's or passenger's face when the heater blower is operated.

To remove the windscreen glass first take out the moulding 1. A screwdriver with its end ground blunt and then polished smooth using emerycloth makes an ideal tool for easing the moulding out. Press on the inside of the glass and work round the inside of the rubber weatherstrip 9 to free the weatherstrip and glass from the windscreen frame.

Refit the new glass 10 to the rubber weatherstrip. Fit a long length of cord around the outer slot of the weatherstrip leaving at least a foot of cord free to grasp. A second operator holds the glass and rubber in place against the windscreen frame while the first operator pulls on the ends of the cords to lift the inner edge of the weatherstrip over the frame flange. Use soft soap as a lubricant. Refit the moulding strip.

12:8 The facia and instruments

The facia details are shown in **FIG 12:15**. The loom connections to the back of the instrument panel are shown in the wiring diagrams in the appendix. Before doing any work on either the instruments or the facia panel disconnect the battery. The facia is the same on both the TR5 and the TR6. The TR250 is as shown and it should be noted that there is an extra warning light for the brake failure circuit.

Removing veneered facia panel:

Remove the five cross-headed screws 5 and washers 4 and the two screws 41 securing the check link 40 to the glove box lid. Disconnect the speedometer and tachometer cables from the back of the instruments and remove the instruments. Unscrew the oil pressure pipe from the oil pressure gauge, taking care not to lose the leather sealing washer. Disconnect the loom from all the switches and instruments. Lift the veneered facia panel complete with instruments from the facia. Replace the

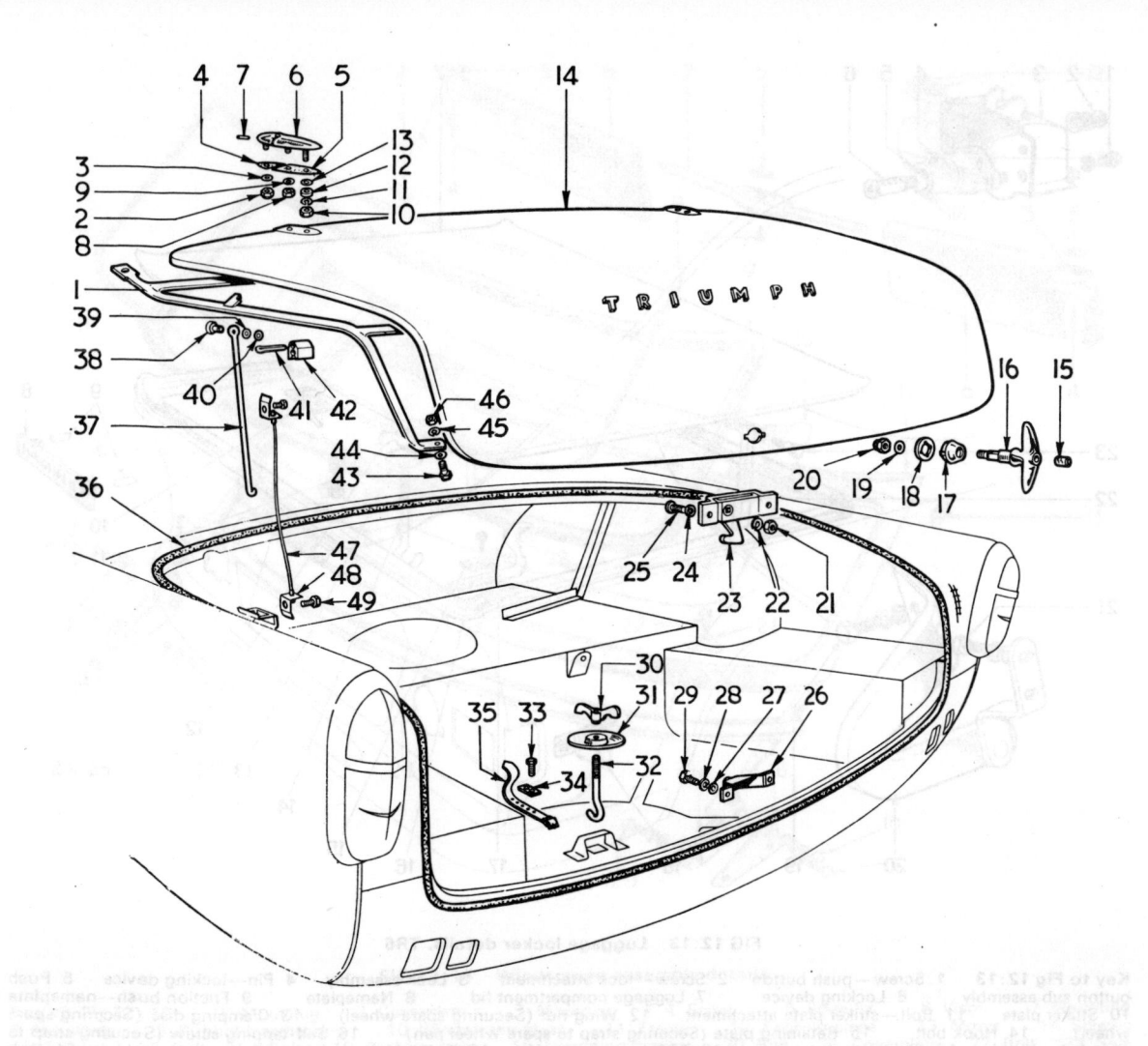

FIG 12:12 Luggage locker details, TR5

Key to Fig 12:12   1 Lid reinforcement tube   2 Nut   3 Washer   4 Fibre washer   5 Fibre washer   6 Hinge   7 Hinge pin   8 Nut   9 Washer   10 Nut   11 Washer   12 Washer   13 Washer   14 Locker lid assembly   15 Lock cylinder   16 Handle   17 Escutcheon   18 Washer   19 Washer   20 Nut   21 Nut   22 Washer   23 Lock   24 Washer   25 Screw   26 Striker   27 Washer   28 Washer   29 Screw   30 Wing nut   31 Disc plate   32 Hook bolt   33 Screw   34 Plate   35 Strap   36 Sealing rubber   37 Lid support   38 Pivot pin   39 Washer   40 Clip   41 Splitpin   42 Retainer   43 Screw   44 Washer   45 Washer   46 Nut   47 Restrainer   48 Bracket   49 Screw

panel in the reverse order of removal, using the wiring diagram to check that the wires are connected correctly.

Facia assembly:

1 Remove the four bolts 46 and two bolts 54 and remove the facia support bracket 47, and the gearbox side trim (one screw),
2 Refer to **FIG 12:16**. Disconnect the facia ventilation hoses 27 from the heater box and free the clips that hold the hoses. Free the support channel 32 by removing the bolts 38 and associated washers 36 and 37. Slacken the bolt 35 and swing the support outwards out of the way.
3 Remove the steering column cowl. Unscrew the six screws 16 securing the glove box 18 to the facia. Disconnect the drive cables to the tachometer and speedometer and remove these two instruments. Disconnect the wiring loom from the instruments and switches. Disconnect the heater control cables from the heater box and water control valve. Disconnect the oil pipe from the oil pressure gauge. Disconnect the cold start cable from the metering unit and the throttle

TR5/6

127

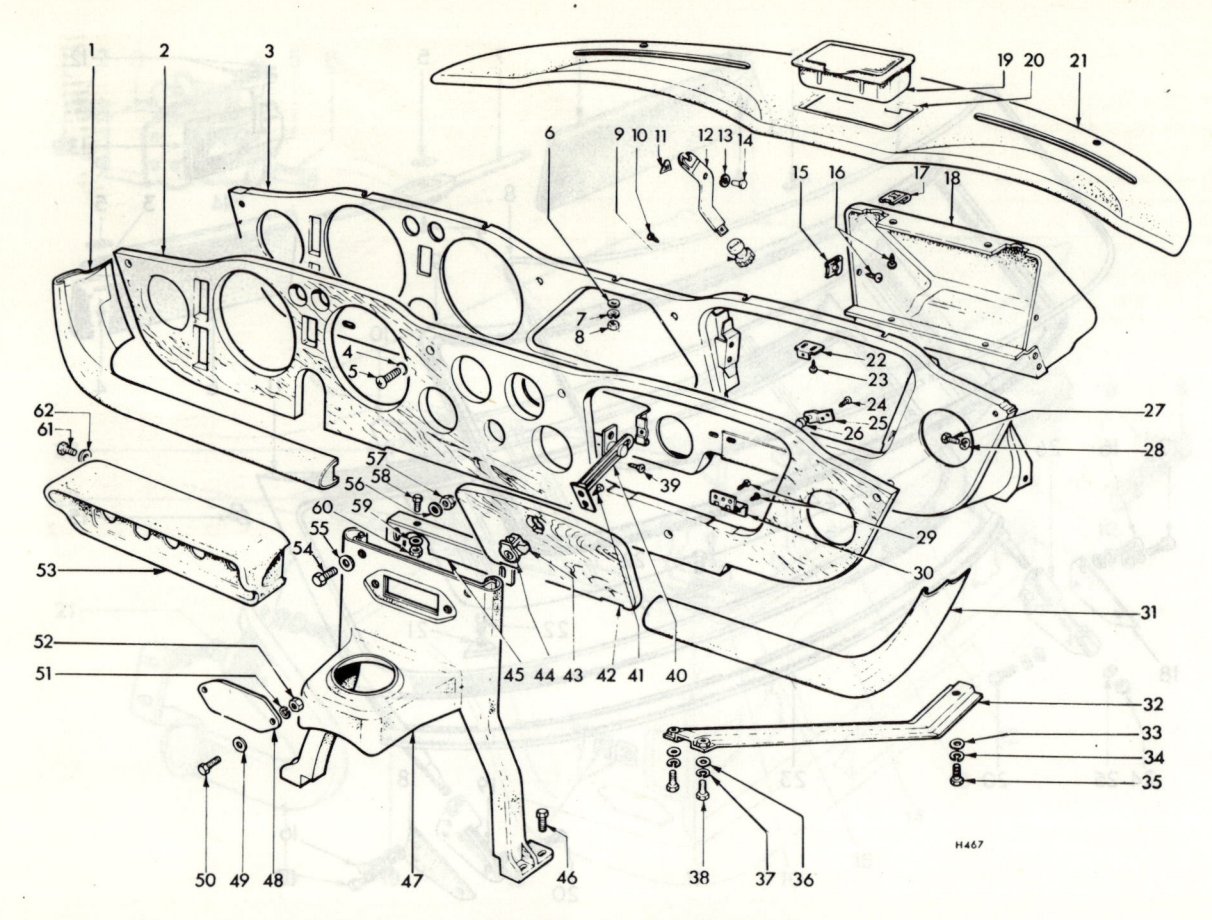

FIG 12:15 Facia panel details

Key to Figs 12:15, 12:16 and 12:17 1 Crash pad 2 Veneered facia panel 3 Metal facia panel 4 Cup washer (Veneered facia to metal facia) 5 Screw (Veneered facia to metal facia) 6 Washer (Complete facia to scuttle top panel) 7 Lockwasher (Complete facia to scuttle top panel) 8 Nut (Complete facia to scuttle top panel) 9 Vent lever-knob 10 Screw 11 Retainer 12 Vent lever 13 Lock washer 14 Rivet 15 Spire nut (Glove box to facia) 16 Screw (Glove box to facia) 17 Spire nut (Glove box to facia) 18 Glove box 19 Ash tray 20 Ash tray retainer 21 Scuttle top-crash pad 22 Striker bracket 23 Striker screw 24 Screw—buffer bracket 25 Buffer bracket 26 Buffer 27 Bolt (Complete facia to 'A' post) 28 Lock washer (Complete facia to 'A' post) 29 Screw—hinge 30 Hinge—glove box 31 Crash pad 32 Support channel—facia to dash 33 Washer (Support channel to dash) 34 Lock washer (Support channel to dash) 35 Setscrew (Support channel to dash) 36 Washer (Support channel to facia panel) 37 Lockwasher (Support channel to facia panel) 38 Setscrew (Support channel to facia panel) 39 Screw—check link 40 Check link—glove box lid 41 Screw—check link 42 Glove box lid 43 Clamp—glove box lock 44 Glove box lock 45 Bracket 46 Bolt—support bracket to floor 47 Support bracket—facia to floor 48 Coverplate—radio mounting 49 Washer (Coverplate to support bracket) 50 Setscrew (Coverplate to support bracket) 51 Lockwasher 52 Nut 53 Switch plinth 54 Bolt (Support bracket to fixing bracket) 55 Washer (Support bracket to fixing bracket) 56 Washer (Support bracket to fixing bracket) 57 Nyloc nut (Support bracket to fixing bracket) 58 Setscrew (Fixing bracket to facia) 59 Washer (Fixing bracket to facia) 60 Nut 61 Setscrew (Switch plinth to facia panel) 62 Washer (Switch plinth to facia panel)

the heat control knob 32 to within $\frac{1}{8}$ inch of its fully in position, threading the inner cable through the ferrule. Put the valve to the closed position (fully clockwise when viewed from above) and tighten the nut 49 to grip the cable.

Fresh air vents:

The clip for securing the facia air vent to the facia panel is shown in **FIG 12:20**. Slacken the clip and remove the hose from the vent. Slacken the knurled nuts 1 sufficiently to allow the body of the vent to rotate. Turn the vent until the retaining pins 4 line up with the slots in the retaining retaining clamp 3 and the vent can then be pulled out of the facia, catching the retaining clamp assembly as it falls free. The bottom fresh air vent is held to the bracket 17 by the clamp bolt 15 and nut 18.

Weak airflow through the vents can be caused either by a hose coming loose or chafing sufficiently to form a hole through which the air escapes. Check for either

130

defect at periodic intervals.

Removing the heater unit:

1 Remove the facia assembly as previously instructed. Drain the cooling system leaving the heater water valve open (knob 32 pulled out). Disconnect the control cable 34 from the heater.
2 Disconnect all four heater hoses 27 from the heater. Stand a bowl under the heater to catch the water and disconnect the water hoses 25 and 28 from the heater.
3 Remove the three bolts 41 and associated washers and spacers securing the heater to the scuttle top panel. Similarly remove the nut 38 and washers securing the heater unit to the dash front panel. Lift the heater out of the car. Either block the heater inlet and outlet pipes or take great care not to spill any residual water in the heater on the carpets or upholstery. The water in the bottom of the heater will contain dirt and rust, which will stain the upholstery.

The heater and facia assembly are replaced in the reverse order of dismantling. Push the distribution knob to within $\frac{1}{8}$ inch of its fully closed position and set the internal flap valve to direct the air to the windscreen before securing the inner cable 34 to the flap valve lever.

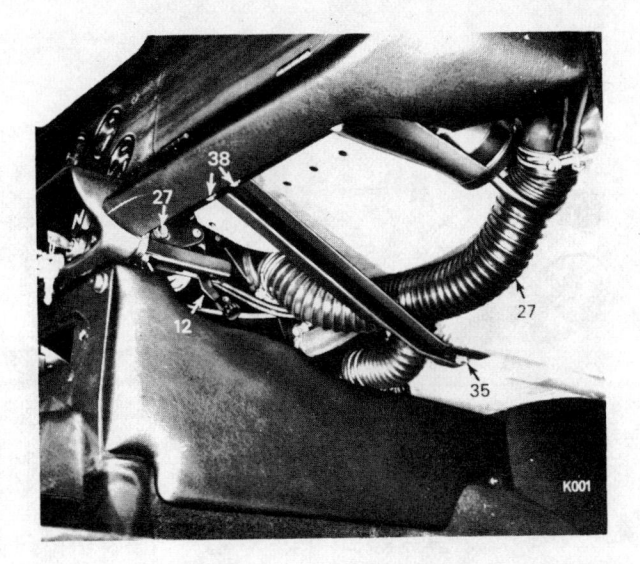

FIG 12:16 Underside view of facia

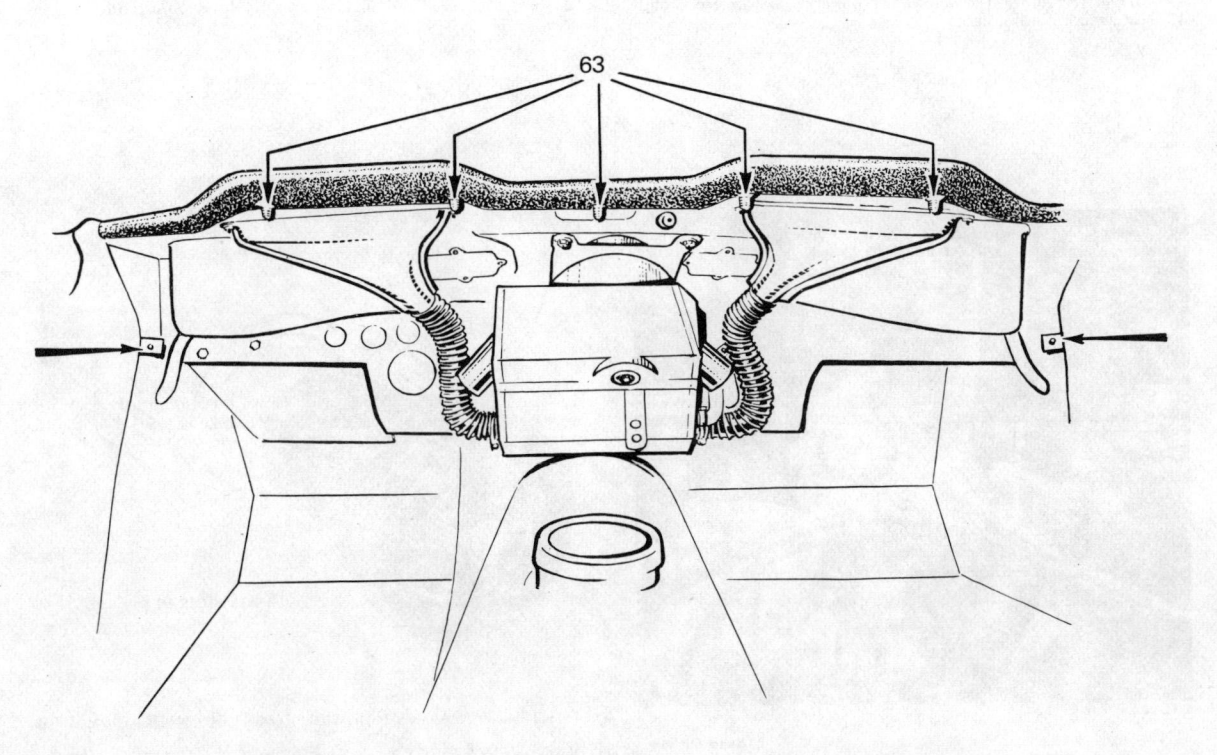

FIG 12:17 Facia support points, arrows indicate **A** frame mounting points

TR5/6

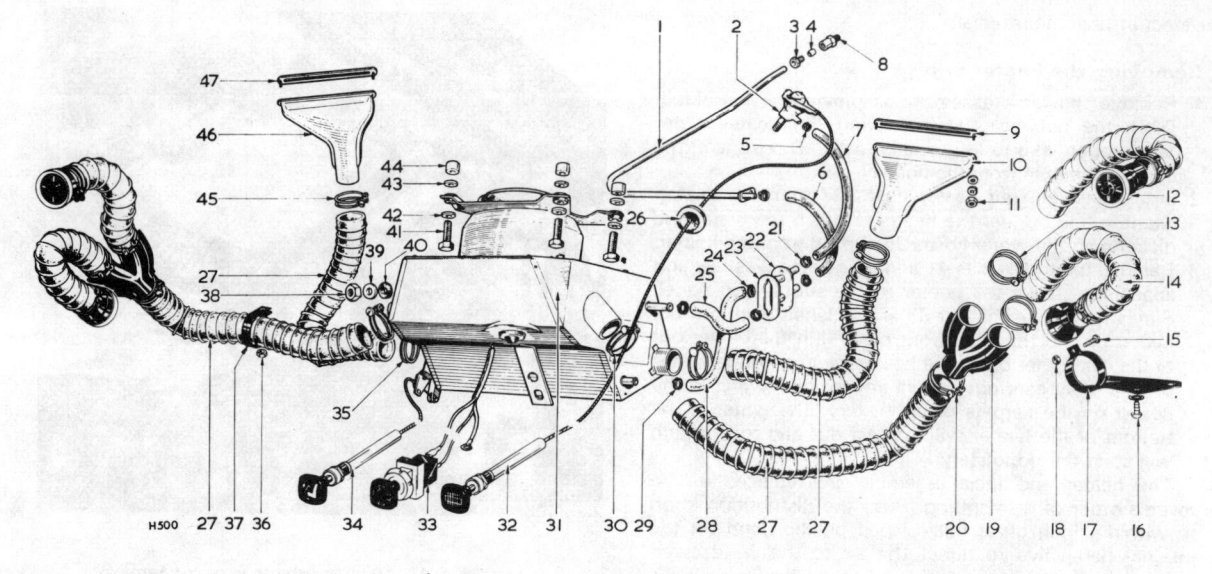

FIG 12:18 Heater details

Key to Figs 12:18 and 12:19 1 Water return pipe 2 Water control valve 3 Nut 4 Olive 5 Clip 6 Hose 7 Hose
8 Adaptor 9 Finisher 10 Air duct 11 Nut–duct attachment 12 Air vent 13 Hose clip 14 Ventilation hose
15 Setscrew–hose attachment 16 Screw–bracket attachment 17 Hose bracket 18 Nut–bracket attachment 19 Tube
'Y' piece 20 Hose clip 21 Hose clip 22 Bulkhead adaptor 23 Seal–adaptor 24 Hose clip 25 Water hose
26 Control cable grommet 27 Ventilation hose 28 Water hose 29 Hose clip 30 Hose clip 31 Heater unit 32 Heat
control 33 Blower switch 34 Air distribution control 35 Hose clip 36 Nut–hose 37 Hose support clip 38 Nut
(Heater unit to dash panel) 39 Washer (Heater unit to dash panel) 40 Washer (Heater unit to dash panel) 41 Bolt (Heater
unit to scuttle top panel) 42 Washer (Heater unit to scuttle top panel) 43 Washer (Heater unit to scuttle top panel)
44 Spacer (Heater unit to scuttle top panel) 45 Hose clip 46 Air duct 47 Finisher 48 Nut securing outer cable
49 Nut securing inner cable

FIG 12:19 Heater water valve

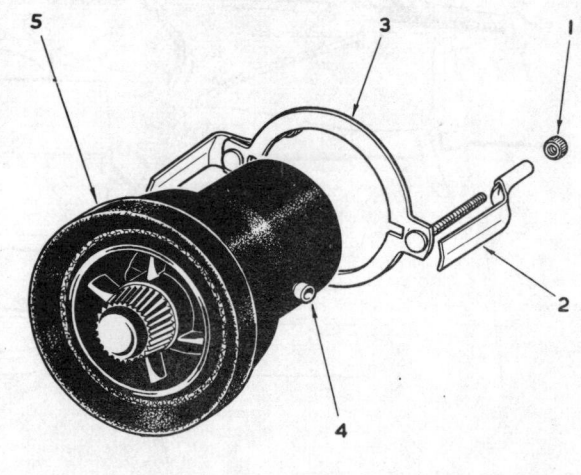

FIG 12:20 Facia mounted fresh air vent mounting

Key to Fig 12:20 1 Knurled nuts 2 Clamp supports
3 Retaining clamp 4 Retaining pin 5 Fresh air vent

132

APPENDIX

TECHNICAL DATA

        Engine   Cooling system   Fuel system   Ignition system
        Clutch   Gearbox and overdrive   Rear axle
        Steering   Front suspension   Rear suspension
        Dampers   Brakes   Electrical system   Capacities
        Wheels and tyres   Dimensions and weights   Road speed data
        Torque wrench settings   Special tools

WIRING DIAGRAMS

        FIG 13:1   Righthand drive TR5
        FIG 13:2   Lefthand drive TR5
        FIG 13:3   Facia connections TR5
        FIG 13:4   Righthand drive TR6
        FIG 13:5   TR250 and lefthand drive TR6
        FIG 13:6   Facia connections TR250 and lefthand drive TR6

RUNNING-IN

STANDARD MEASURE AND METRIC EQUIVALENTS

FRACTIONAL AND METRIC EQUIVALENTS

HINTS ON MAINTENANCE AND OVERHAUL

GLOSSARY OF TERMS

INDEX

TECHNICAL DATA

Dimensions are given in inches; figures in brackets are in millimetres

ENGINE

Type:	6 cylinder in-line, OHV, watercooled
Compression ratio:	9.5:1
TR250, TR6 (USA) to 1972	8.5:1, 1972 on 7.75:1
Cubic capacity:	2498cc, 152 cu in
Bore:	2.94 (74.7)
Stroke:	3.74 (95)
Firing order:	1.5.3.6.2.4

Crankshaft:

Type	4 main bearing, integral balance weights
End float	.006 to .008 (.1524 to .2032)
Thrust washers	.091 to .093 (2.31 to 2.36)
Journals:	
Diameter	2.311 to 2.3115 (58.6994 to 58.7121)
Undersize bearings	−.010, −.020, −.030 (−.254, −.508, −.762)
Crankpins:	
Diameter	1.875 to 1.8755 (47.625 to 47.638)
Undersize bearings	−.010, −.020, −.030 (−.254, −.508, −.762)

Connecting rods:

Type	Offset big-end allowing connecting rod to pass through cylinder bore
Maximum bend and twist	.0015 (.038) in length of gudgeon pin
Small-end bush internal diameter	.8128 to .8129 (20.64 to 20.648). Push fit by hand at room temperature

Camshaft:

End float	.004 to .008 (.102 to .20) controlled by thickness of keeper plate
Journal diameter	1.8402 to 1.8407 (46.7411 to 46.7538)

Cam followers:

Diameter	.799 to .80 (20.31 to 20.12)
Bore in cylinder block	.8002 to .8009 (20.325 to 20.343)

Pistons:

Number of rings	2 compression, 1 oil control
Removal	With connecting rods from top of cylinder block
Oversize pistons	+.020 (+.508)

Piston grades, standard bore:

Piston top diameter:

F	2.9363 to 2.9367 (74.582 to 74.592)
G	2.9367 to 2.9371 (74.592 to 74.602)
H	2.9371 to 2.9375 (74.602 to 74.612)

Piston bottom diameter:

F	2.9380 to 2.9384 (74.625 to 74.635)
G	2.9384 to 2.9388 (74.635 to 74.645)
H	2.9388 to 2.9392 (74.645 to 74.655)

Cylinder bore:

F	2.9405 to 2.9408 (74.689 to 74.696)
G	2.9409 to 2.9412 (74.699 to 74.705)
H	2.9413 to 2.9416 (74.709 to 74.717)

Piston rings:
  Height:
    Top compression ... ... .0615 to .0625 (1.562 to 1.588)
    2nd compression ... ... .0615 to .0625 (1.562 to 1.588)
  Gap when fitted:
    Top compression ring ... ... .012 to .017 (.305 to .432)
    2nd compression ring ... ... .008 to .013 (.203 to .33)
    Oil control scrapers ... ... .015 to .055 (.381 to 1.397)
    Oil control spacer ... ... Ring ends to butt
  Groove width in piston:
    Both compression rings ... ... .064 to .065 (1.625 to 1.650)
    Oil control ring ... ... .1265 to .1275 (3.213 to 3.238)
  Groove root diameter:
    Both compression rings ... ... 2.6535 to 2.6574 (67.4 to 67.5)
    Oil control ring ... ... 2.5826 to 2.5866 (65.6 to 65.7)
    Oversize piston rings ... ... +.010, +.020, +.030 (+.254, +.508, +.762)

Gudgeon pin:
  Type ... ... Fully floating secured by circlips
  Diameter ... ... .8123 to .8125 (20.632 to 20.645)
  Length ... ... 2.447 to 2.451 (62.153 to 62.274)

Valves
  Angle of seat:
    Valve ... ... 45 deg.
    Cylinder head ... ... 44½ deg.
  Head seat diameter not to exceed:
    Inlet seat 1.4285 (36.21)
    Exhaust seat 1.255 (31.13)
      (If these dimensions are exceeded it will be impossible to fit inserts)
  Head diameter:
    Inlet ... ... 1.441 to 1.445 (36.6 to 36.7)
    Exhaust ... ... 1.256 to 1.26 (31.9 to 32.0)
  Stem diameter:
    Inlet ... ... .3107 to .3112 (7.891 to 7.904)
    Exhaust ... ... .31 to .3105 (7.87 to 7.89)
  Length (both) ... ... 4.597 to 4.607 (116.764 to 117.018)

Valve guides:
  Length:
    Inlet 2.0625 (52.386), TR6 2.71 (68.834)
    Exhaust 2.25 (57.15), TR6 2.71 (68.834)
  Bore ... ... .312 to .313 (7.925 to 7.950)
  External diameter ... ... .501 to .502 (12.725 to 12.751)
  Protrusion above cylinder head (both) ... .63 (16.002), TR6 .75 (19.05)

Valve springs:
  Free length:
    Inner 1.56 (39.624)
    Outer 1.57 (39.878)
  Rate fitted:
    Inner ... ... 28.5 lb/in
    Outer ... ... 150 lb/in ± 3 per cent

Valve timing:
  Timing marks ... ... Scribed lines on sprockets and pop marks on camshaft and camshaft sprocket. TDC marks on flywheel and crankshaft pulley
  Inlet valve opens ... ... 35 deg. BTDC
  Inlet valve closes ... ... 65 deg. ABDC
  Exhaust valve opens ... ... 65 deg. BBDC
  Exhaust valve closes ... ... 35 deg. ATDC

Valve rockers:
  Bore ... .563 to .564 (14.3 to 14.33)
  Shaft diameter ... .5607 to .5612 (4.243 to 4.254)
  Clearance:
    Running ... .010 (.25) cold
    Timing only ... .040 (1.02)
    TR6 ... .015 (.381)

Flywheel:
  Maximum runout ... .003 (.0762) at 5 inch (127 mm) radius
  Balance ... Within 1 dram

Oil pump:
  Type ... Hobourn-Eaton eccentric rotor
  Clearance between rotor and body ... Not to exceed .010 (.254)
  Clearance between rotors ... .001 to .004 (.0254 to .102)
  Rotor end clearance ... Not to exceed .004 (.102)
  Oil pressure relief valve:
    Spring free length ... 1.55 (39.37)
    Spring fitted length ... 1.25 (31.75)
    Spring load, fitted ... 14.5 lb (6.58 kg)
  Oil capacity ... 8 Imperial pints (4.52 litres) 9.64 U.S.A. pints

COOLING SYSTEM

Thermostat:
  Type ... Wax filled
  Summer thermostat ... Starts opening at 82°C
  Winter thermostat ... Starts opening at 88°C

Filler cap release pressure: ... 4 lb/sq in (.28 kg/sq cm)
Antifreeze: ... BSI.3151 or 3152 specification
Capacity: ... 11 Imperial pints (13.2 U.S.A. pints) 6.2 litres

FUEL SYSTEM

Type: ... Lucas Mk II petrol injection
Fuel pump pressure: ... 106 to 110 lb/sq in (7.452 to 7.733 kg/sq cm)
Injectors open: ... 40 to 50 lb/sq in (2.812 to 3.515 kg/sq cm)
Air cleaner: ... Renewable paper element
Fuel filter: ... Renewable element (must be marked for use with petrol or gasolene)

Fuel pump:
  Running current ... 4 amps approximately
  Light running current ... 1.4 amps at 2200 rev/min on 13.5 volts
  Armature resistance ... .16 to .24 ohms at 15°C on adjacent commutator bars
  Armature end float ... .004 to .010 (.102 to .254)
  Brush length:
    New ... $\frac{3}{8}$ inch
    Renew ... If less than $\frac{3}{16}$ inch
  Brush spring pressure ... 5 to 7 oz when compressed to .158 inch
  Maximum delivery ... 16 galls/hr (Imperial)

TR250, TR6 (USA):
  Carburetters ... Twin Stromberg 175 CDSE
  Fuel pump ... AC Mechanical

Fuel tank capacity: ... 11$\frac{1}{4}$ Imperial galls (13.5 U.S.A. galls) 51 litres

IGNITION SYSTEM

Sparking plugs:
  Type ... Champion N-9Y
    TR250, TR6 (USA) ... UN-12Y
  Gap ... .025 (.63)

Ignition coil: ... Lucas HA12, later 15C6

Ignition timing: ... ... 11 deg. BTDC (static), late models 4.5 deg. BTDC
  TR250 ... ... 10 deg. BTDC (static)
Firing order: 1–5–3–6–2–4
Distributor:
  Type ... ... Lucas 22D6
  Rotation ... ... Anticlockwise viewed on rotor
  Contact breaker gap ... ... .014 to .016 (.35 to .41)
  Capacitor capacity ... ... .20 Microfarad
  Contact breaker spring tension ... ... 18 to 24 oz

Centrifugal advance:

Note that the distributor runs at half engine speed, so if the unit is tested out of the car, both the speed and degrees crankshaft advance should be halved to give readings related to distributor only. Run up to top speed and then check while decelerating.

Lucas part No. 41219 (fitted to earlier TR5s):

Crankshaft rev/min	Degrees crankshaft advance
Below 500	No advance to occur
800	0 to 4
1700	4 to 8
2600	8 to 12
4000	8 to 12

Lucas part No. 41219 B or D:

Crankshaft rev/min	Degrees crankshaft advance
Below 350	No advance to occur
900	0 to 4
1600	5 to 9
2600	12 to 16
4000	12 to 16

Distributor drive gear clearance ... ... .003 to .007 (.0762 to .1778)

Lucas part No. 41202 (TR250):

Crankshaft rev/min	Degrees crankshaft advance
Below 750	No advance to occur
900	0 to 2
1700	8 to 12
3000	12 to 16
5000	18 to 22
6000	18 to 22

Lucas part No. 41542:

Crankshaft rev/min	Degrees distributor advance
Below 400	None
500	0 to 1
700	2 to 4
900	5 to 7
1100	8 to 10

Retard unit (TR250):

Inches of mercury vacuum	Degrees distributor retard	Crankshaft retard
Below 1.5	No retard to occur	
2.5	0 to 1	0 to 2
4.0	0 to 3	0 to 6
8.0	5 to 8	10 to 16
15.0	7 to 9	14 to 18

CLUTCH

Type: ... ... 8½ (21.5 cm) diaphragm spring
Adjustment: ... ... Self-adjusting
Fluid: ... ... Castrol Girling Clutch and Brake fluid to SAE.70 R3 specification

Facings:		Ferodo RYZ
		Mintex HIB
Flywheel to spring tips:		1.465±.050 (37.21±172)
Clutch slave cylinder:		Lockheed 1 inch (25.4 mm) diameter bore

GEARBOX AND OVERDRIVE

Gearbox type:	Four forward gears, synchromesh on all four. One reverse gear
Overdrive type:	Laycock de Normanville, operating on top three speeds
Overdrive ratio:	.82:1, later .797:1 operating on top and third

Gearbox ratios:

Gear	Top	Third	Second	First	Reverse
Gearbox ratio	1.00	1.33	2.01	3.14	3.22
Overall ratio	3.45	4.59	6.94	10.83	11.11
TR250	3.70	4.92	7.44	11.62	11.9

Overall end float on bushes: .003 to .009; obtained by selective fitting of thrust washers

Thrust washers available:

Part number	Colour	Thickness
129941	Self-finish	.120 to .118 (3.048 to 2.997)
129942	Green	.123 to .121 (3.124 to 3.0734)
129943	Blue	.126 to .124 (3.200 to 3.1496)
129944	Orange	.129 to .127 (3.2766 to 3.2258)
134670	Yellow	.134 to .132 (.34036 to .3528)

End float of gears on bushes ... .004 to .006 (.1016 to .1524)

Axial release loads on selector shafts:

Top/third shaft	26 to 28 lb (11.793 to 12.701 Kgs)
First/second shaft	32 to 34 lb (14.515 to 15.422 Kgs)
Reverse shaft	26 to 28 lb (11.793 to 12.701 Kgs)

Capacities:

Gearbox only	2 Imperial pints (2.4 U.S.A. pints) 1.13 litres
Gearbox and overdrive	3½ Imperial pints (4.2 U.S.A. pints) 2.0 litres

REAR AXLE

Type:	IRS with semi-floating halfshafts and Hypoid bevel gear in differential
Ratio:	3.45:1
TR250	3.7:1
Capacity:	2½ Imperial pints (3.0 U.S.A. pints) 1.42 litres

STEERING

Type:	Rack and pinion
Turns from lock to lock:	3¼
Turning circle:	33 feet (10.1 metres)
Toe-in (front and rear):	0 to 1/16 (0 to 1.6)
*Front wheel camber:	
TR5, TR6	0 deg. ± ½ deg.
TR6 (USA) (and TR250)	¼ deg. negative ± ½ deg.
*Kingpin inclination:	
TR5, TR6	9 deg. ± ¾ deg.
TR6 (USA) (and TR250)	9¼ deg. ± ¾ deg.
*Castor angle:	2¾ deg. ± ½ deg.
Maximum back lock:	30 deg.
Maximum front lock:	31½ deg. (20 deg. front lock gives 19¾ deg. back lock)

* Set and checked with car statically laden with 150 lb (68 kg) in each front seat

FRONT SUSPENSION

TR5 Front springs:
  No. of coils ... 6
  Free length ... 10.28 inch
  Rate ... 312 lb/in (3.595 kg/m)

TR6 and TR250 front springs:
  No. of coils ... $5\frac{1}{4}$
  Free length ... 10.03 (261)
  Rate ... 312 lb/in

REAR SUSPENSION

*Toe-in (front and rear): 0 to $\frac{1}{16}$ (0 to 1.6)
*Rear wheel camber: 1 deg. negative $\pm \frac{1}{2}$ deg.

Rear road spring:
  TR5:
    Number of coils ... $6\frac{3}{4}$
    Free length ... 10.28 inch
  TR6 and TR250:
    Number of coils ... $6\frac{3}{4}$
    Free length ... 10.92 (261)
    Rate ... 349 lb in (4.01 kg/m)

* Set and checked with car statically laden

DAMPERS

Front: Non-adjustable sealed units
Fluid for rear dampers: Armstrong Shock Absorber Fluid

BRAKES

Type: Girling hydraulic, disc front drum rear
Master cylinder: Girling dual hydraulic tandem
Handbrake: Centrally mounted, operating rear wheels only through twin cables
Servo: Vacuum operated fitted as standard
Brake fluid: Castrol Girling Crimson Clutch and Brake Fluid to SAE.70 R3 specification
Maximum retardation: .98 G

Rear brakes:
  Type ... Drum 9 inch dia. x $1\frac{3}{4}$ inch (22.9 x 4.45)
  Lining area ... 60.5 sq in (419.3 sq cm)
  Swept area ... 99 sq in (638.7 sq cm)

Front brakes:
  Type ... Caliper disc $10\frac{7}{8}$ inch dia. (27.62)
  Lining area ... 20.7 sq in (174.2 sq cm)
  Swept area ... 233 sq in (1483.8 sq cm)

ELECTRICAL SYSTEM

Type: 12-volt, negative earth

Battery TR5:
  Type ... Lucas BT9A
  Capacity at 20 hrs rate ... 57 amp/hr
  Plates per cell ... 9
  Normal charge rate ... 5 amps

Battery TR6 and TR250:
  Type ... Lucas C9
  Capacity at 20 hrs rate ... 60 amp/hr
  Plates per cell ... 9
  Normal charge rate ... 5 amps

Starter motor:
- Type ... Lucas M418G or 2M100 pre-engage type
- Light running current ... 80 amp, 5500 to 8000 rev/min
- Torque at 1000 rev/min ... 7 lb ft using 280 amp at 9.0 volts
- Lock torque ... 15 lb ft using 465 amp at 7.0 volts
- Minimum brush length ... $\frac{5}{16}$ inch
- Brush spring tension ... 36 oz

Starter solenoid:
- Pull in winding resistance ... .13 to .15 ohm
- Hold in winding resistance ... .63 to .73 ohm

Alternator:
- TR5 type ... Lucas 15AC
- TR6 and TR250 type ... Lucas 15ACR, 16ACR, 17ACR
- Drive ratio engine rev/min: alt rev/min ... 11:23
- Polarity ... Negative earth only
- Brush length:
  - New ... .5 inch
  - Renew ... if less than .2 inch protrudes when free
- Brush spring pressure ... 7 to 10 oz when face flush with brushbox
- Field winding resistance ... 4.33 ± 5 per cent ohm at 20°C
- Maximum permissible speed ... 12,500 alternator rev/min
- Output (hot) ... 28 amp at 6000 alternator rev/min, 14-volt

Alternator control unit:
- Lucas 15ACR, 16ACR, 17ACR ... Integral in alternator
- Lucas 15AC ... Bulkhead mounted Lucas 4TR

Windscreen washer pump:
- Type ... Lucas Screenjet 5SJ
- Maximum running current ... 2 amps
- Minimum brush length ... $\frac{1}{16}$ (1.6)
- Minimum delivery ... 3.5 cc per second
- Minimum pressure ... 4.5 lb/sq in
- Container usable capacity ... 1 litre (1.1 litre total capacity)
- Antifreeze ... 1 part methylated spirits (denatured alcohol) to 2 parts of water

Windscreen wiper motor TR5:
- Type ... Lucas DR.3A shunt wound single speed
- Light running speed ... 44 to 48 cycles per minute
- Light running current ... 2.7 to 3.4 amps
- Stall current ... 13 to 15 amps
- Resistance of field winding ... 8.0 to 9.5 ohms at 20°C (68°F)
- Resistance of armature winding ... .29 to .352 ohms at 20°C
- Brush tension ... 125 to 140 grammes

Windscreen wiper motor TR6 and TR250:
- Type ... Lucas 14W two-speed
- Light running speed:
  - Normal speed ... 46 to 52 cycles per minute
  - High speed ... 60 to 70 cycles per minute
- Light running current:
  - Normal speed ... 1.5 amp
  - High speed ... 2.0 amp
- Minimum brush length:
  - Earth brush ... $\frac{3}{16}$ inch
  - Normal brush ... $\frac{3}{16}$ inch
  - High speed brush ... .280 inch
- Brush spring pressure ... 5 to 7 oz. (brush bottom aligned with brushbox end slot)

Maximum force to move rack: ... 6 lb with arms and blades removed

CAPACITIES

	Imp. pints	U.S. pints	Litres
Cooling system: (Including heater and overflow bottle)	11	13.2	6.2
Engine sump:	8	9.64	4.52
Fuel tank:	11¼ gall	13.5 gall	51
USA model	10¼	12.3	46.5
Gearbox from dry:	2	2.4	1.13
Gearbox and overdrive	3½	4.2	2.0
Rear axle	2½	3.0	1.42

WHEELS AND TYRES

Wheels:
- TR5 ... Steel disc type 4½J or centre locking wire wheels as optional extra
- TR6 and TR250 ... Steel disc type 5½J or centre locking 5½K wire wheels as optional extra

Tyres:
- TR5 type ... Dunlop SP.41, 165.HR–15 or Michelin 165.HR–15.XAS
- TR5, TR6 tyre pressure:
  - Front ... 22 lb/sq in (1.547 kg/sq cm)
  - Rear ... 26 lb/sq in (1.828 kg/sq cm)
- TR6 (USA) and TR250 type ... Goodyear G800 185 SR-15-15X (optional SR)
- TR6 (USA) and TR250 tyre pressure:
  - Front ... 20 lb/sq in (1.41 kg/sq cm)
  - Rear ... 24 lb/sq in (1.69 kg/sq cm)

DIMENSIONS AND WEIGHTS

Overall length:
- TR5 ... 12 ft 9⅝ in (3902 mm)
- TR6 and TR250 ... 12 ft 11 in (3937 mm)

Width:
- TR5 ... 4 ft 10 in (1470 mm)
- TR6 and TR250 ... 4 ft 10 in (1470 mm)

Height:
- Hood up (unladen) ... 4 ft 2 inch (1270 mm)
- Hood down (unladen) ... 3 ft 10 inch (1170 mm)

Weight:
- TR5 dry ... 19¼ cwt (938 kg)
- TR5 complete ... 20¼ cwt (1034 kg)
- TR5 maximum weight ... 24 cwt (1226 kg)
- TR6 dry ... 2324 lb (1053 kg)
- TR6 complete ... 2408 lb (1092 kg)
- TR6 maximum weight ... 2884 lb (1308 kg)
- TR250 dry ... 2280 lb (1034 kg)
- TR250 complete ... 2390 lb (1084 kg)
- TR250 maximum weight ... 2855 lb (1295 kg)

Ground clearance (laden): 6 inch (152 mm)

ROAD SPEED DATA

Engine speed at road speed of:

	Top	O/D Top	3rd	O/D 3rd	2nd	O/D 2nd	1st
10 miles/hour	386	471	514	626	777	947	1479
10 kilometres/hr	240	296	319	393	482	585	940

TR5/6

TORQUE WRENCH SETTINGS

Engine: lb ft   kg m
   Cylinder head nuts (cold) ... ... 65 to 70 (8.99 to 9.69)
   Big-end bolts ... ... 38 to 42 (5.25 to 5.81)
   Main bearing bolts ... ... 55 to 60 (7.60 to 8.29)
   Flywheel to crankshaft ... ... 55 to 60 (7.60 to 8.29)
   Rocker pedestal nuts ... ... 24 to 26 (3.32 to 3.60)
   Rocker cover ... ... $1\frac{1}{2}$ (.21)
   Manifold attachments ... ... 24 to 26 (3.32 to 3.60)
   Sump bolts ... ... 16 to 18 (2.21 to 2.49)
      (maintain minimum of 8 lb ft after settling)
   Camshaft sprocket ... ... 24 to 26 (3.32 to 3.56)
   Timing cover:
      $\frac{5}{16}$ UNF x 1.16 stud ... ... 12 to 14 (1.66 to 1.94)
      $\frac{7}{16}$ UNF x $\frac{7}{8}$ setscrew ... ... 16 to 18 (2.21 to 2.49)
      $\frac{5}{16}$ UNF x $\frac{3}{8}$ pan head ... 8 to 10 (1.11 to 1.38)
   Fan attachment ... ... 12 to 14 (1.66 to 1.94)
   Rear oil seal housing ... ... 16 to 18 (2.21 to 2.49)
   Clutch to flywheel 20 (2.77)
   Rear engine plate attachment ... 18 to 20 (2.49 to 2.77)
   Gearbox to engine ... ... 18 to 20 (2.49 to 2.77)
   Front engine plate and camshaft keeper
      plate ... ... 18 to 20 (2.49 to 2.77)
   Starter motor bolts ... ... 28 to 30 (3.87 to 4.15)
   Water pump pulley ... ... 14 to 16 (1.94 to 2.21)
   Water pump attachment ... ... 12 to 14 (1.66 to 1.94)
   Water pump to cylinder head ... 18 to 20 (2.49 to 2.77)
   Mounting rubber bracket to engine ... 26 to 28 (3.60 to 3.87)
   Mounting rubber to bracket ... ... 26 to 28 (3.60 to 3.87)
   Mounting rubber to frame ... ... 28 to 30 (3.87 to 4.15)

Petrol injection equipment:
   Pedestal attachment ... ... 12 to 14 (1.66 to 1.94)
   Distributor to pedestal ... ... 18 to 20 (2.49 to 2.77)
   Injector nozzle attachment ... ... 6 to 8 (.83 to 1.11)

Carburetter equipment:
   Fuel pump attachment ... ... 12 to 14
   Carburetter attachment ... ... 12 to 14
   Carburetter control rod assembly ... 4 to 6
   Carburetter control rod bellcrank ... 16 to 18
   Air cleaner attachment ... ... 6 to 8
   Manifold attachment nuts (outer 2) ... 12 to 14
   Manifold attachment nuts (inner) ... 16 to 18
   Manifold attachment bolts ... ... 18 to 20

Gearbox:
   Clutch slave cylinder attachment ... 18 to 20 (2.49 to 2.77)
   Countershaft end cover to gearbox ... 16 to 18 (2.21 to 2.49)
   Countershaft and reverse shaft ... 16 to 18 (2.21 to 2.49)
   Extension to gearbox ... ... 14 to 16 (1.94 to 2.21)
   Gear selectors and forks to shaft ... 8 to 10 (1.11 to 1.38)
   Mounting rubber to gearbox extension ... 50 to 55 (6.91 to 7.60)
   Mounting rubber to frame ... ... 35 to 40 (4.84 to 5.53)
   Overdrive adaptor plate ... ... 16 to 18 (2.21 to 2.49)
   Propshaft flange to mainshaft ... ... 80 to 120 (11.06 to 16.59)
   Propshaft attachment ... ... 24 to 26 (3.32 to 3.60)
   Top cover to gearbox ... ... 14 to 16 (1.94 to 2.21)
   Front cover to gearbox ... ... 16 to 18 (2.21 to 2.49)

Rear axle:
- Cover and rear mounting plate ... ... 26 to 28 (3.60 to 3.87)
- Inner driving flange to inner axle ... ... 100 to 110 (13.83 to 15.21)
- Nose plate to axle 35 (4.84)
- Oil seal housing to hypoid housing ... 16 to 18 (2.21 to 2.49)
- Prop shaft flange to pinion ... ... 90 to 100 (12.44 to 13.83)
- Rear mounting plate to frame ... ... 26 to 28 (3.60 to 3.87)

Front suspension:
- Brake disc attachment ... ... 32 to 35 (4.42 to 4.84)
- Brake caliper attachment ... ... 50 to 55 (6.91 to 7.60)
- Caliper mounting bracket and tie rod lever ... 26 to 28 (3.60 to 3.87)
- Damper to bottom mounting ... ... 55 to 60 (7.60 to 8.30)
- Lower wishbone bracket to frame ... 28 to 30 (3.87 to 4.15)
- Lower wishbone to bracket ... ... 45 to 50 (6.22 to 6.91)
- Lower wishbone to vertical link ... 45 to 60 (6.22 to 8.30)
- Lower wishbone to spring pan ... 28 to 30 (3.87 to 4.15)
- Lower damper mounting to spring pan ... 26 to 28 (3.60 to 3.87)
- Stub axle to vertical link ... ... 55 to 60 (7.60 to 8.30)
- Top ball joint to upper wishbone ... 26 to 28 (3.60 to 3.87)
- Top ball joint to vertical link ... 55 to 65 (7.60 to 8.99)
- Upper wishbone to fulcrum pin ... 26 to 40 (3.60 to 5.54)
- Upper wishbone fulcrum to frame ... 28 to 30 (3.87 to 4.15)

Rear suspension:
- Damper to mounting bracket ... ... 55 to 60 (7.60 to 8.30)
- Damper link ... ... 18 to 20 (2.49 to 2.77)
- Inner driven flange to outer axle ... 28 to 30 (3.87 to 4.15)
- Rear hub assembly ... ... 100 to 110 (13.83 to 15.21)
- Trailing arm to mounting bracket ... 45 to 50 (6.22 to 6.91)
- Trailing arm mounting brackets to frame ... 28 to 30 (3.87 to 4.15)

Miscellaneous:
- Wire wheel extension nuts 65 (8.99)
- Wheel attachment ... ... 55 to 60 (7.60 to 8.30)
- Safety harness pivot bolt ... ... 28 to 30 (3.87 to 4.15)
- Safety harness eye bolts ... ... 28 to 30 (3.87 to 4.15)
- Steering wheel nut ... ... 28 to 30 (3.87 to 4.15)

SPECIAL TOOLS

The part numbers of special tools required have been given in the relevant sections. Not all special tools are essential, and some can be made from scrap materials or modified out of other tools. For some special extractors a light press, with made up packing pieces, or even a large fitters' vice can be used. When attempting to do the task without the proper special tool, take great care not to damage the parts by haphazard hammering or levering. Use lead or wood packing to prevent parts being marked by the jaws of a vice.

All the special tools required for the models covered by this manual are available from:
Messrs. V. L. Churchill Ltd.,
London Road,
Daventry
Northants
Daventry 2276

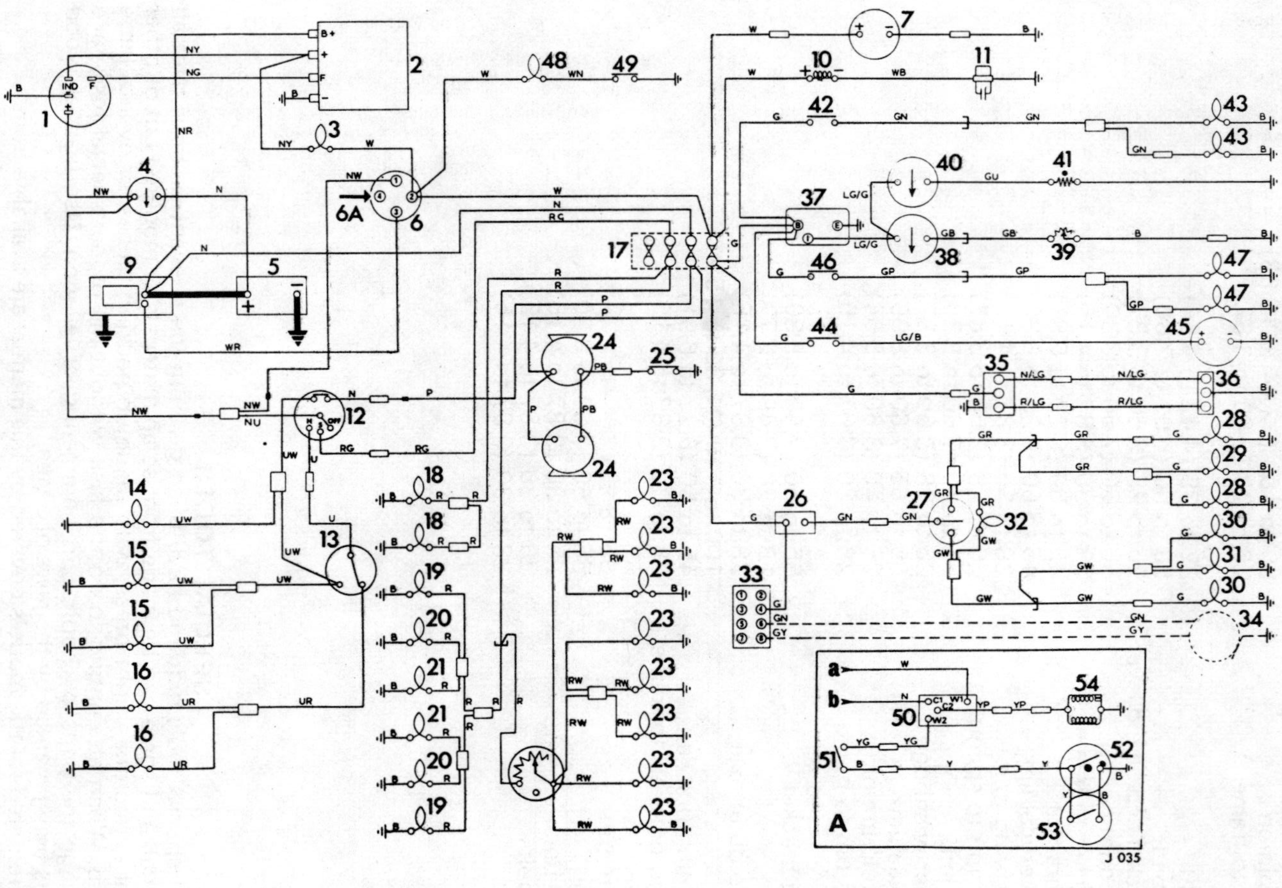

FIG 13:1 Wiring diagram, righthand drive TR5

Key to Fig 13:1 1 Alternator 2 Alternator control unit 3 Ignition warning light 4 Ammeter 5 Battery 6 Ignition/starter switch 6a Ignition/starter switch radio supply connector 7 Petrol pump 9 Starter motor 10 Ignition coil 11 Ignition distributor 12 Column light switch 13 Dip switch 14 Main beam warning light 15 Main beam 16 Dip beam 17 Fuse box 18 Front parking lamp 19 Rear marker lamp 20 Tail lamp 21 Plate illumination lamp 22 Panel rheostat 23 Instrument illumination 24 Horn 25 Horn push 26 Turn signal flasher unit 27 Turn signal flasher switch 28 Lefthand Flasher lamp 29 Lefthand Flasher repeater lamp 30 Righthand Flasher lamp 31 Righthand Flasher repeater lamp 32 Flasher warning light 33 Heater switch 34 Heater motor 35 Windscreen wiper motor 36 Windscreen wiper switch 37 Voltage stabilizer 38 Fuel indicator 39 Fuel tank unit 40 Temperature indicator 41 Temperature transmitter 42 Reverse lamp switch 43 Reverse lamp 44 Windscreen washer switch 45 Windscreen washer motor 46 Stop lamp switch 47 Stop lamp 48 Oil pressure warning light 49 Oil pressure switch 50 Overdrive relay 51 Overdrive column switch 52 Overdrive gearbox switch - 2nd gear ON 53 Overdrive gearbox switch - 3rd and 4th gear ON 54 Overdrive solenoid **A** Overdrive (optional extra) (a) From fuse box (b) From fuse box

Cable colour code: **N** Brown   **U** Blue   **P** Purple   **R** Red   **G** Green   **L/G** Light Green   **W** White   **Y** Yellow   **S** Slate   **B** Black

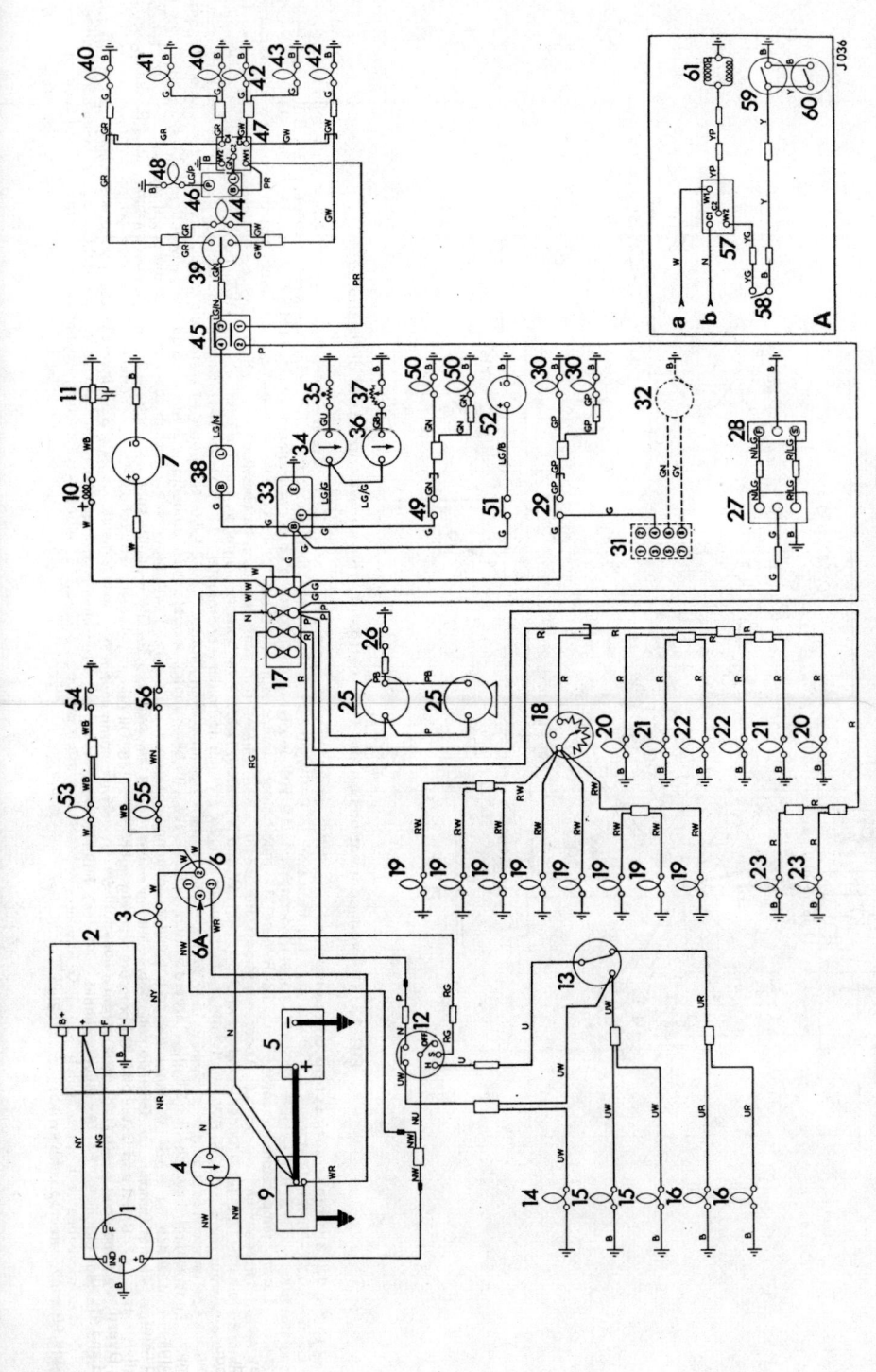

FIG 13:2 Wiring diagram, lefthand drive TR5

Key to Fig 13:2   1 Alternator   2 Alternator control unit   3 Ignition warning light   4 Ammeter   5 Battery   6 Ignition/starter switch   6a Ignition/starter switch—radio supply connector   7 Petrol pump   9 Starter motor   10 Ignition coil   11 Fuse box   12 Column light switch   13 Dip switch   14 Main beam warning light   15 Main beam   16 Dip beam   17 Fuse box   18 Panel rheostat   19 Instrument illumination   20 Rear marker lamp   21 Tail lamp   22 Plate illumination lamp   23 Front parking lamp   25 Horn   26 Horn push   27 Temperature transmitter   28 Windscreen wiper motor   29 Stop lamp switch   30 Stop lamp   31 Heater switch   32 Heater motor   33 Voltage stabilizer   34 Temperature indicator   35 Windscreen wiper switch   36 Fuel indicator   37 Fuel tank unit   38 Turn signal flasher unit   39 Turn signal flasher switch   40 Lefthand flasher lamp   41 Lefthand flasher repeater lamp   42 Righthand flasher lamp   43 Righthand flasher repeater lamp   44 Flasher warning light   45 Hazard switch   46 Hazard flasher unit   47 Hazard warning light   48 Hazard relay   49 Reverse lamp switch   50 Reverse lamp   51 Windscreen washer switch   52 Windscreen washer motor   53 Brake line failure warning light   54 Brake line failure switch   55 Oil pressure warning light   56 Oil pressure switch   57 Overdrive solenoid   58 From fuse box   59 Overdrive gearbox switch—2nd gear ON   60 Overdrive gearbox switch—3rd and 4th gear ON
A Overdrive (optional extra)   57 Overdrive relay   58 Overdrive column switch   (a) From fuse box   (b) From fuse box   61 Overdrive solenoid

Cable colour code   N Brown   U Blue   R Red   P Purple   G Green   L/G Light Green   W White   Y Yellow   S Slate   B Black

TR5/6   145

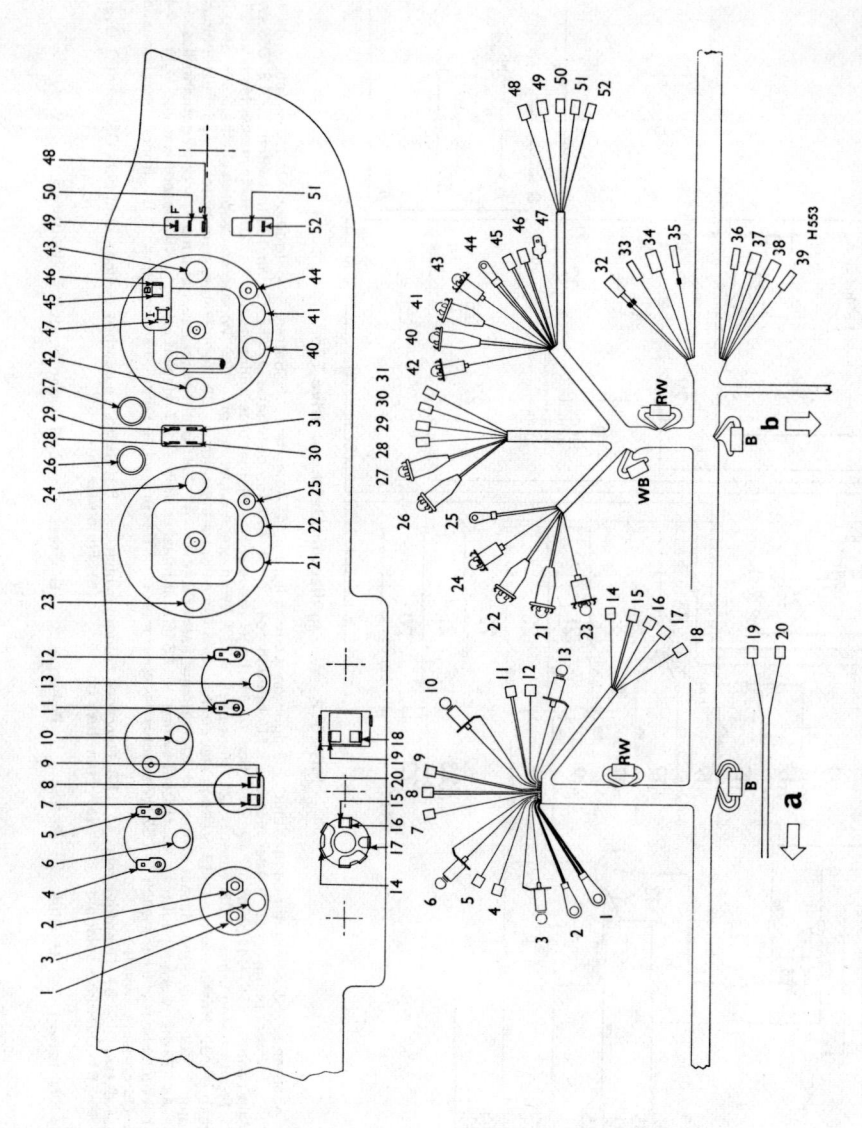

FIG 13:3 Facia connections on the TR5. Lefthand drive shown, righthand drive similar

Key to Fig 13:3 (Colour/connection/component) NW—eyelet—2 wire—ammeter 2 N—eyelet—ammeter 3 RW and B—bulb holder—ammeter 4 LG/G—Lucar—fuel indicator 5 GB—Lucar—fuel indicator 6 RW and B—bulb holder—fuel indicator 7 R—Lucar—panel rheostat 8 RW—Lucar—2 wire—panel rheostat 9 RW—Lucar—2 wire—panel rheostat 10 RW and B—bulb holder—oil pressure indicator 11 LG/G—Lucar—2 wire—temperature indicator 12 GU—Lucar—temperature indicator 13 RW and B—bulb holder—temperature indicator 14 NW—Lucar—ignition/starter switch 15 W—Lucar—2 wire—ignition/starter switch 16 W—Lucar—ignition/starter switch 17 WR—Lucar—ignition/starter switch 18 LG—Lucar—heater switch 19 GN—Lucar—heater switch 20 GY—Lucar—heater switch 21 W and NY—bulb holder—ignition warning light 22 WB and WN—bulb holder—oil pressure warning light 23 RW—bulb holder—tachometer 24 RW—Lucar—tachometer 25 B—eyelet—2 wire—tachometer 26 W and WB—bulb holder—tachometer 27 IG/P and B—bulb holder—hazard warning light 28 LG/N—Lucar—hazard warning switch 29 LG/N—Lucar—hazard warning switch 30 P—Lucar—hazard switch 31 PR—Lucar—hazard switch 32 NW with blue idents.—double snap connector—2 wire—column light switch 33 RG—snap connector—column light switch 34 U—double snap connector—column light switch 35 P with brown ident.—snap connector—column light switch 36 LG/N—snap connector—flasher switch 37 GR—double snap connector—2 wire—flasher switch 38 GW—double snap connector—flasher switch 39 PB—snap connector—flasher switch 40 GR and GW—bulb holder—speedometer—flasher warning light 41 UW—bulb holder—speedometer—main beam warning light 42 RW—bulb holder—speedometer 43 RW—Lucar—bulb holder—speedometer 44 B—eyelet—3 wire—speedometer 45 G—Lucar—2 wire—voltage stabilizer 46 RW—Lucar—voltage stabilizer 47 LG/G—Lucar blade—voltage stabilizer 48 R/LG—Lucar—windscreen wiper switch 49 N/LG—Lucar—windscreen wiper switch 50 B—Lucar—windscreen wiper switch 51 G—Lucar—windscreen washer switch 52 LG/B—Lucar—windscreen washer switch (a) GN and GY—to heater motor (b) G and GP—to stop lamp switch

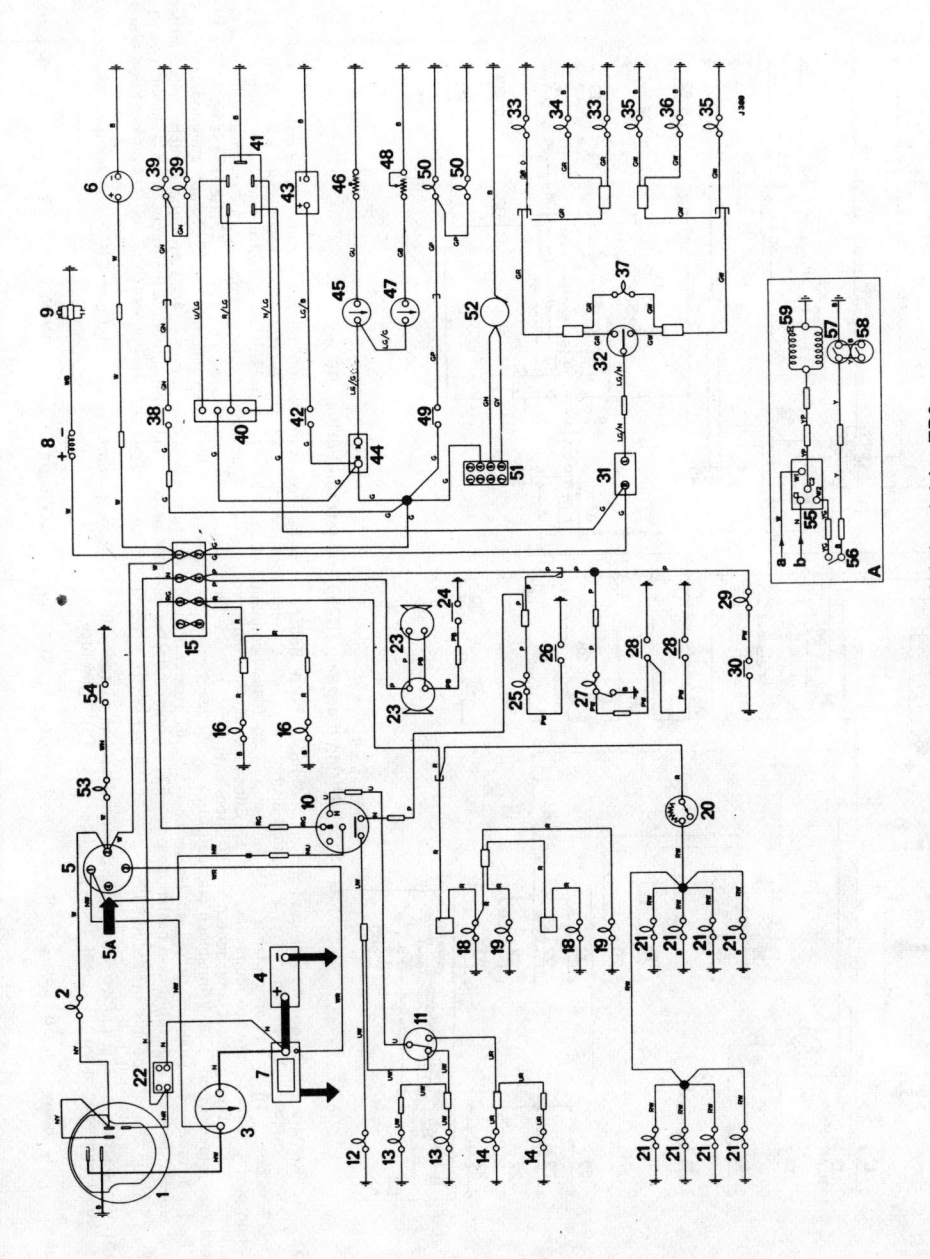

FIG 13:4 Wiring diagram, righthand drive TR6

Key to Fig 13:4 1 Alternator 2 Ignition warning light 3 Ammeter 4 Battery 5 Ignition/starter switch 5a Ignition/starter switch—radio supply connector
6 Petrol pump 7 Starter motor 8 Ignition coil 9 Ignition distributor 10 Column light switch 11 Dip switch 12 Main beam warning light 13 Main beam
14 Dip beam 15 Fuse box 16 Front parking lamp 18 Tail lamp 19 Plate illumination lamp 20 Panel rheostat 21 Instrument illumination 22 Connector block
23 Horn 24 Horn push 25 Cubby box illumination 26 Cubby box illumination switch 27 Transmission tunnel lamp 28 Transmission tunnel lamp door switch
29 Luggage boot lamp 30 Luggage boot lamp switch 31 Turn signal flasher unit 32 Turn signal switch 33 Lefthand flasher lamp 34 Lefthand flasher repeater
lamp 35 Righthand flasher lamp 36 Righthand flasher repeater lamp 37 Turn signal warning light 38 Reverse lamp switch 39 Reverse lamp 40 Windscreen
wiper switch 41 Windscreen wiper motor 42 Windscreen washer switch 43 Windscreen washer pump 44 Voltage stabilizer 45 Temperature indicator
46 Temperature transmitter 47 Oil pressure switch 48 Fuel indicator 49 Stop lamp switch 50 Stop lamp 51 Heater switch 52 Heater motor 53 Oil pressure
warning light 54 Oil pressure switch 55 Overdrive solenoid 56 Overdrive relay 57 Overdrive column switch 58 Overdrive gearbox switch—2nd gear ON
A Overdrive (optional extra) 59 Overdrive solenoid (a) From fuse box (b) From fuse box
3rd and 4th gear ON

Cable colour code: N Brown U Blue R Red P Purple G Green LG Light Green W White Y Yellow S Slate B Black

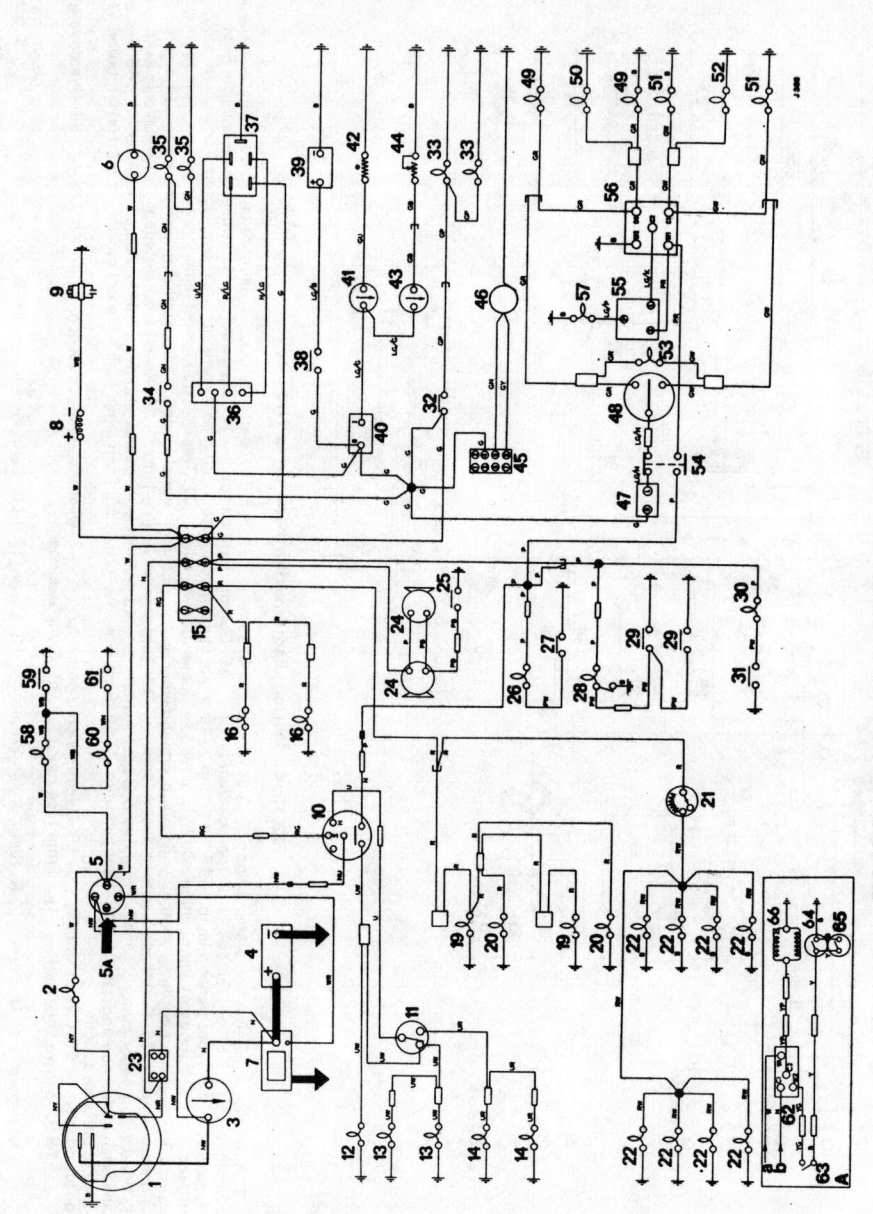

FIG 13:5 Wiring diagram, TR250 and lefthand drive TR6

Key to Fig 13:5   1 Alternator   2 Ignition warning light   3 Ammeter   4 Battery   5 Ignition/starter switch   5a Ignition/starter switch—radio supply connector
6 Petrol pump   7 Starter motor   8 Ignition coil   9 Ignition distributor   10 Column light switch   11 Dip switch   12 Main beam warning light   13 Main beam
14 Dip beam   15 Fuse box   16 Front parking lamp   19 Tail lamp   20 Plate illumination lamp   21 Panel rheostat   22 Instrument illumination   23 Connector block
24 Horn   25 Horn push   26 Cubby box illumination   27 Cubby box illumination switch   28 Transmission tunnel lamp   29 Transmission tunnel lamp door switch
30 Luggage boot lamp   31 Luggage boot lamp switch   32 Stop lamp switch   33 Stop lamp   34 Reverse lamp switch   35 Reverse lamp   36 Windscreen wiper
switch   37 Windscreen wiper motor   38 Windscreen washer switch   39 Windscreen washer pump   40 Voltage stabilizer   41 Temperature indicator   42 Temperature
transmitter   43 Fuel indicator   44 Fuel tank unit   45 Heater switch   46 Heater motor   47 Turn signal flasher unit   48 Turn signal switch   49 Lefthand flasher lamp
50 Lefthand flasher repeater lamp   51 Righthand flasher lamp   52 Righthand flasher repeater lamp   53 Turn signal warning light   54 Hazard switch   55 Hazard
flasher unit   56 Hazard relay   57 Hazard warning light   58 Brake line failure warning light   59 Brake line failure switch   60 Oil pressure warning light   61 Oil
pressure switch
A Overdrive (optional extra)   62 Overdrive relay   63 Overdrive column switch   64 Overdrive gearbox switch—2nd gear ON   65 Overdrive gearbox switch—3rd and
4th gear ON   66 Overdrive solenoid   (a) From fuse box   (b) From fuse box

Cable colour code: N Brown   U Blue   R Red   P Purple   G Green   LG Light Green   W White   Y Yellow   S Slate   B Black

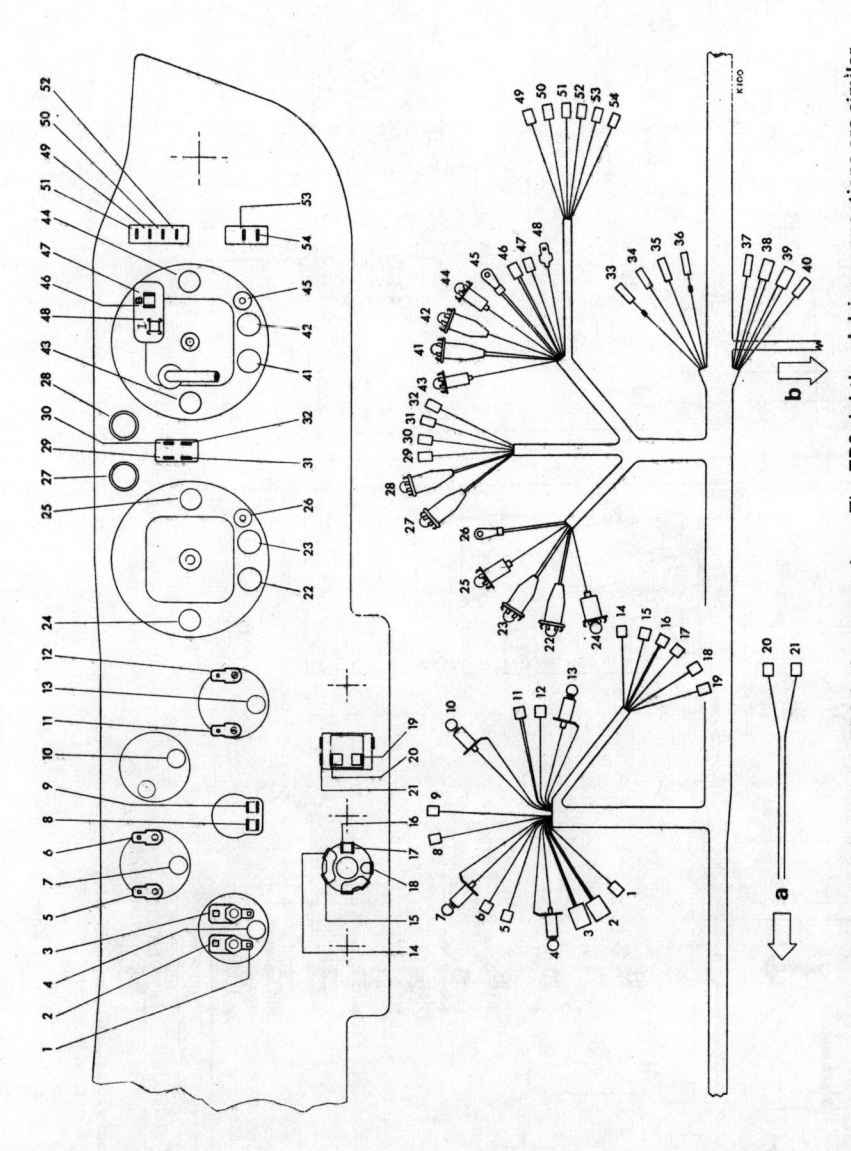

FIG 13:6 TR250 and lefthand drive TR6 facia connections. The TR6 righthand drive connections are similar

Key to Fig 13:6 (Colour/connection/component) 1 NW—Lucar—ammeter 2 NW—Lucar—ammeter 3 N—Lucar—ammeter 4 RW and B—bulb holder—ammeter 5 LG/G—Lucar—fuel indicator 6 GB—Lucar fuel indicator 7 RW and B—bulb holder—fuel indicator 8 R—Lucar—panel rheostat 9 RW—Lucar—panel rheostat 10 RW and B—bulb holder—temperature indicator 11 LG/G—Lucar—2 wire—temperature indicator 12 GU—Lucar—temperature indicator 13 RW and B—bulb holder—oil pressure indicator 14 NW—Lucar—ignition/starter switch 15 NW—Lucar—ignition/starter switch 16 W—Lucar—2 wire—ignition/starter switch 17 W—Lucar—ignition/starter switch 18 WR—Lucar—ignition/starter switch 19 G—Lucar—heater switch 20 GN—Lucar—heater switch 21 GY—Lucar—heater switch 22 W and NY—bulb holder—ignition warning light 23 WB and WN—bulb holder—tachometer 24 RW—bulb holder—tachometer 25 RW—bulb holder—tachometer 26 B—eyelet—2 wire—tachometer 27 W and WB—bulb holder—brake line failure warning light—lefthand steer only 28 LG/P and B—bulb holder—hazard warning light—lefthand steer only 29 LG/N—Lucar—hazard switch—lefthand steer only 30 LG/N—Lucar—hazard switch—lefthand steer only 31 P—Lucar—hazard switch—lefthand steer only 32 PR—Lucar—hazard switch—lefthand steer only 33 NW with blue blue ident.—snap connector—column light switch 34 RG—snap connector—column light switch 35 U—snap connector—column light switch 36 P with brown ident.—snap connector—column light switch 37 LG/N—snap connector—turn signal switch 38 GR—double snap connector—2 wire—turn signal switch 39 GW—double snap connector—2 wire—turn signal switch 40 PB—snap connector—horn push 41 GR and GW—bulb holder—speedometer—turn signal warning light 42 UW—bulb holder—speedometer—main beam warning light 43 RW—bulb holder—speedometer 44 RW—bulb holder—speedometer 45 B—eyelet—speedometer 46 G—Lucar—2 wire—voltage stabilizer 47 LG/LG—Lucar—voltage stabilizer 48 LG/G Lucar blade—voltage stabilizer 49 LG—Lucar—windscreen wiper switch 50 R/LG—Lucar—windscreen wiper switch 51 U/LG—Lucar—windscreen wiper switch 52 N/LG—Lucar—windscreen wiper switch 53 G—Lucar—windscreen washer switch 54 LG/B—Lucar—windscreen washer switch

(a) GN and GY—to heater motor (b) G and GP—to stop lamp switch

TR5/6

149

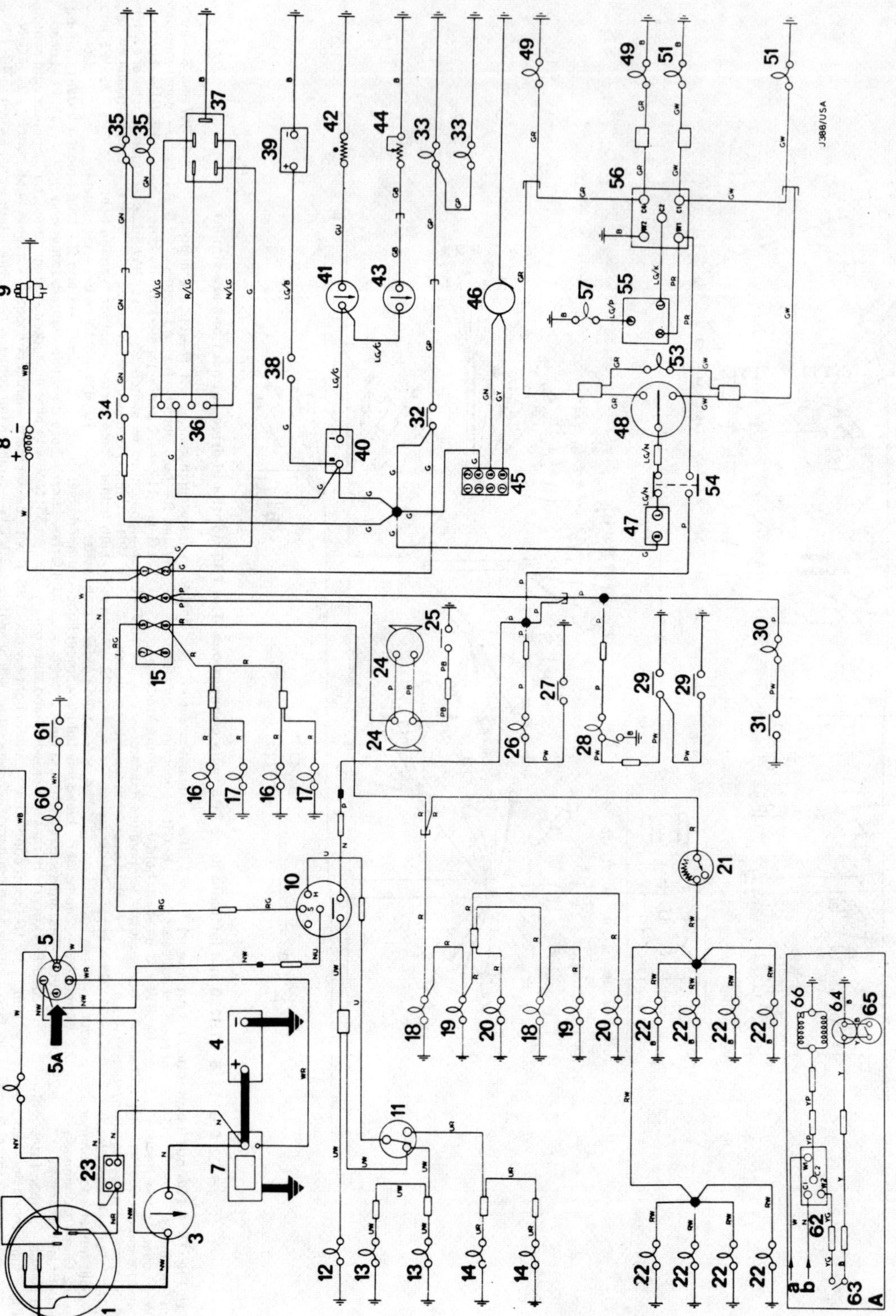
J388/USA

FIG 13:7   Wiring diagram TR6 (USA). To end of 1971 model

Key to Fig 13:7   1 Alternator   2 Ignition warning light   3 Ammeter   4 Battery   5 Ignition/starter switch   5A Ignition/starter switch—radio supply connector
7 Starter motor   8 Ignition coil   9 Ignition distributor   10 Column light switch   11 Dip switch   12 Main beam warning light   13 Main beam   14 Dip beam
15 Fuse box   16 Front parking lamp   17 Front marker lamp   18 Horn push   19 Tail lamp   20 Plate illumination lamp   21 Panel rheostat   22 Instrument illumination
23 Connector block   24 Horn   25 Rear marker lamp   26 Cubby box illumination   27 Cubby box illumination switch   28 Transmission tunnel lamp
29 Transmission tunnel lamp door switch   30 Luggage boot lamp   31 Luggage boot lamp switch   32 Stop lamp switch   33 Stop lamp   34 Reverse lamp switch
35 Reverse lamp   36 Windscreen wiper switch   37 Windscreen wiper motor   38 Windscreen washer switch   39 Windscreen washer pump   40 Voltage stabilizer
41 Temperature indicator   42 Temperature transmitter   43 Fuel indicator   44 Fuel tank unit   45 Heater switch   46 Heater motor   47 Turn signal flasher unit
48 Turn signal switch   49 Lefthand flasher lamp   51 Righthand flasher lamp   53 Turn signal warning light   54 Hazard switch   55 Hazard flasher unit   56 Hazard
relay   57 Hazard warning light   58 Brake line failure switch   59 Brake line failure warning light   60 Oil pressure warning light   61 Oil pressure switch
A Overdrive (optional extra)   62 Overdrive relay   63 Overdrive column switch   64 Overdrive gearbox switch—2nd gear ON   65 Overdrive gearbox switch—3rd
and 4th gear ON   66 Overdrive solenoid   (a) From fuse box   (b) From fuse box

Cable colour code: N Brown   U Blue   R Red   P Purple   G Green   LG Light Green   W White   Y Yellow   S Slate   B Black

152

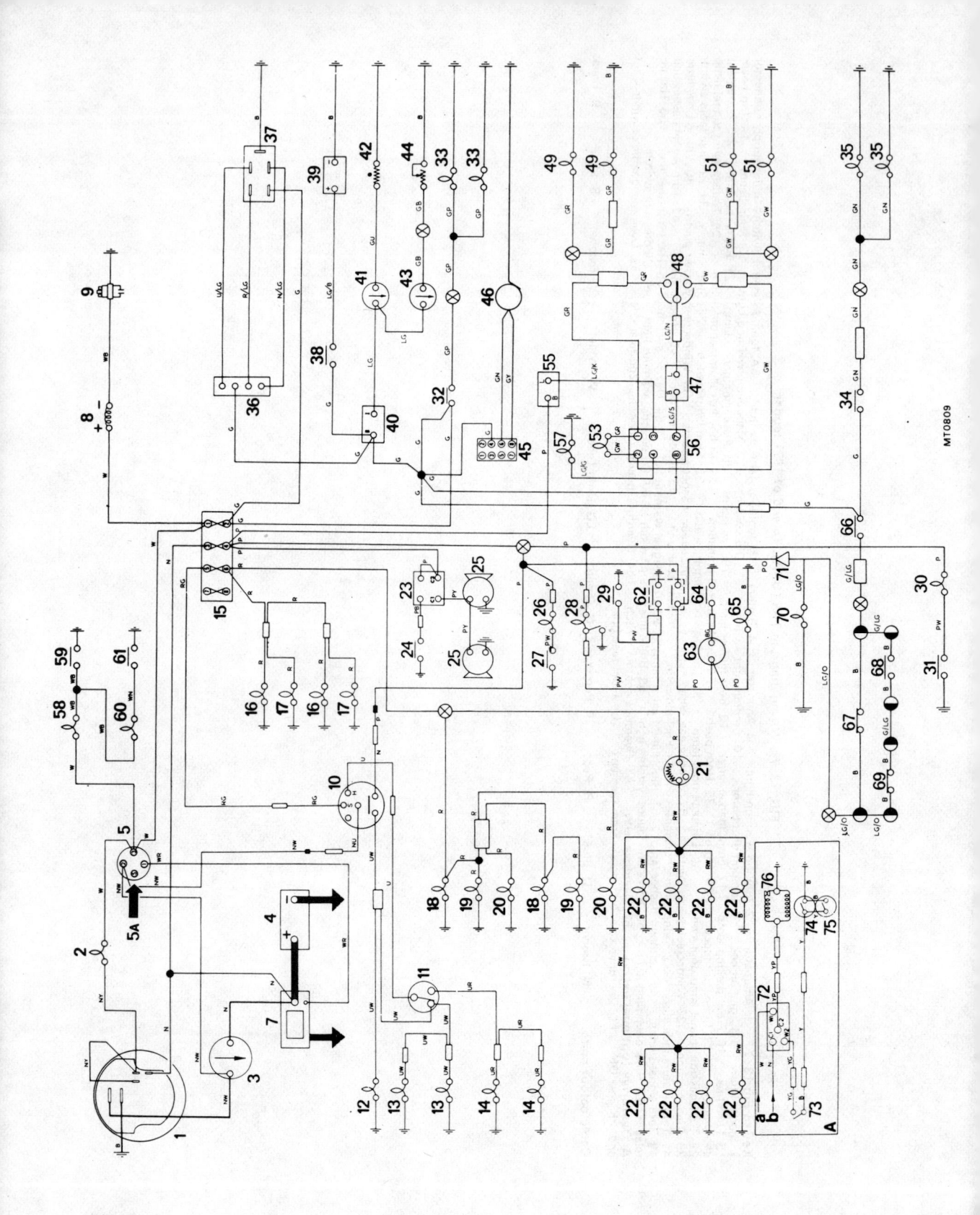

FIG 13:8 Wiring diagram TR6 (USA) 1972 model

Key to Fig 13:8 1 Alternator 2 Ignition warning light 3 Ammeter 4 Battery 5 Ignition/starter switch 5A Ignition/starter switch—radio supply connector 7 Starter motor 8 Ignition coil 9 Ignition distributor 10 Column light switch 11 Dip switch 12 Main beam warning light 13 Main beam 14 Dip beam 15 Fuse box 16 Front parking lamp 17 Rear marker lamp 18 Tail lamp 19 Tail lamp 20 Plate illumination lamp 21 Panel rheostat 22 Instrument illumination 23 Horn relay 24 Horn push 25 Horn 26 Cubby box illumination 27 Cubby box illumination switch 28 Transmission tunnel lamp 29 Transmission tunnel lamp door switch 30 Luggage boot lamp 31 Luggage boot lamp switch 32 Stop lamp switch 33 Stop lamp 34 Reverse lamp switch 35 Reverse lamp 36 Windscreen wiper switch 37 Windscreen wiper motor 38 Windscreen washer switch 39 Windscreen washer pump 40 Voltage stabilizer 41 Temperature indicator 42 Temperature transmitter 43 Fuel indicator 44 Fuel tank unit 45 Heater switch 46 Heater motor 47 Turn signal flasher unit 48 Turn signal switch 49 Lefthand flasher lamp 51 Righthand flasher lamp 53 Turn signal warning light 55 Hazard flasher unit 56 Lefthand door switch 57 Hazard warning light 58 Brake line failure warning light 59 Brake line failure switch 60 Oil pressure warning light 61 Oil pressure switch 62 Lefthand door switch 63 Buzzer 64 Key switch 65 Key light 66 Seat belt warning gearbox switch 67 Drivers belt switch 68 Passengers seat switch 69 Passengers belt switch 70 Seat belt warning light 71 Diode **A** Overdrive (optional extra) 72 Overdrive relay 73 Overdrive column switch 74 Overdrive gearbox switch—2nd gear ON 75 Overdrive gearbox switch—3rd and 4th gear ON 76 Overdrive solenoid (a) From fuse box (b) From fuse box

Cable colour code: **N** Brown   **U** Blue   **R** Red   **P** Purple   **G** Green   **LG** Light Green   **W** White   **Y** Yellow   **S** Slate   **B** Black

153

RUNNING-IN

However accurately new parts are made they are always microscopically rough. In use the parts are worn and polished until they exactly mate together and if one part is replaced by another new part then the whole process is repeated. This 'bedding-in' process takes time so for this reason the engine must be run in whenever new parts are fitted.

Power and performance will suffer, the working life of the engine will be shortened and it will always have a touch of 'roughness' about it if the running-in period is not complied with. Rebore cylinders and new pistons require full running-in. If only new piston rings or crankshaft bearings (including big-end bearings) have been fitted, the running-in period need not be as rigorous but the engine should still be treated with care for the first 1000 miles.

No specified speeds are recommended for running-in, but the engine should not be allowed to labour. Warm it at a fast-idle before driving away and use minimum excess fuel sufficient to prevent the engine from stalling. Avoid full throttle at slow speeds. The running-in period is progressive but for the first 500 miles full power should not be used. The engine may be allowed to 'rev' fairly fast provided it is not under load. It is better to change down a gear and let the engine 'rev' freely than to make it 'slog' in a higher gear at a lower engine speed. Full power may be used after the first 500 miles, but for short periods only. The amount of time at full power may be gradually extended as the engine becomes more responsive and the mileage reaches 1000 miles. Provided the car has been carefully run-in the engine parts may be considered to be fully bedded-in after 1000 miles.

STANDARD MEASURE AND METRIC EQUIVALENTS

English to Metric (linear)
1 inch = 2.54 centimetres
1 foot = 30.4799 centimetres
1 yard = .914399 metre
1 mile = 1.6093 kilometre

English to Metric (square)
1 sq inch = 6.4516 sq centimetres
1 sq foot = 9.203 sq decimetres
1 sq yard = .836126 sq metres

English to Metric (cubic)
1 cu inch = 16.387 cc
1 cu ft = 28.317 litres
1 gallon = 4.546 litres
(.1605 cu feet)

English to Metric (weight)
1 pound = .45359 kilo
1 cwt = 50.8 kilo
1 ton = 1016 kilo

Torque loading
1 lb ft = .1382 kg metre

Metric to English (linear)
1 centimetre = .3937 inch
1 metre = 39.3702 inches
       = 1.0936 yard
1 kilometre = .62137 mile

Metric to English (square)
1 sq centimetre = .1550 sq inch
1 sq metre = 1550.01 sq inch
          = 10.7639 sq feet
          = 1.196 sq yard

Metric to English (cubic)
1 cc = .61 cu inch
1 litre = .22 gallons
(1000 cc) = 1.7598 pints

Metric to English (weight)
1 kilogramme = 2.20462 pounds
100 kilo = 1.968 cwt
1000 kilo = .9842 tons

1 kg metre = 7.2350 lb ft

Inches	Decimals	Milli-metres	Inches to Millimetres Inches	Inches to Millimetres mm	Millimetres to Inches mm	Millimetres to Inches Inches
1/64	.015625	.3969	.001	.0254	.01	.00039
1/32	.03125	.7937	.002	.0508	.02	.00079
3/64	.046875	1.1906	.003	.0762	.03	.00118
1/16	.0625	1.5875	.004	.1016	.04	.00157
5/64	.078125	1.9844	.005	.1270	.05	.00197
3/32	.09375	2.3812	.006	.1524	.06	.00236
7/64	.109375	2.7781	.007	.1778	.07	.00276
1/8	.125	3.1750	.008	.2032	.08	.00315
9/64	.140625	3.5719	.009	.2286	.09	.00354
5/32	.15625	3.9687	.01	.254	.1	.00394
11/64	.171875	4.3656	.02	.508	.2	.00787
3/16	.1875	4.7625	.03	.762	.3	.01181
13/64	.203125	5.1594	.04	1.016	.4	.01575
7/32	.21875	5.5562	.05	1.270	.5	.01969
15/64	.234375	5.9531	.06	1.524	.6	.02362
1/4	.25	6.3500	.07	1.778	.7	.02756
17/64	.265625	6.7469	.08	2.032	.8	.03150
9/32	.28125	7.1437	.09	2.286	.9	.03543
19/64	.296875	7.5406	.1	2.54	1	.03937
5/16	.3125	7.9375	.2	5.08	2	.07874
21/64	.328125	8.3344	.3	7.62	3	.11811
11/32	.34375	8.7312	.4	10.16	4	.15748
23/64	.359375	9.1281	.5	12.70	5	.19685
3/8	.375	9.5250	.6	15.24	6	.23622
25/64	.390625	9.9219	.7	17.78	7	.27559
13/32	.40625	10.3187	.8	20.32	8	.31496
27/64	.421875	10.7156	.9	22.86	9	.35433
7/16	.4375	11.1125	1	25.4	10	.39370
29/64	.453125	11.5094	2	50.8	11	.43307
15/32	.46875	11.9062	3	76.2	12	.47244
31/64	.484375	12.3031	4	101.6	13	.51181
1/2	.5	12.7000	5	127.0	14	.55118
33/64	.515625	13.0969	6	152.4	15	.59055
17/32	.53125	13.4937	7	177.8	16	.62992
35/64	.546875	13.8906	8	203.2	17	.66929
9/16	.5625	14.2875	9	228.6	18	.70866
37/64	.578125	14.6844	10	254.0	19	.74803
19/32	.59375	15.0812	11	279.4	20	.78740
39/64	.609375	15.4781	12	304.8	21	.82677
5/8	.625	15.8750	13	330.2	22	.86614
41/64	.640625	16.2719	14	355.6	23	.90551
21/32	.65625	16.6687	15	381.0	24	.94488
43/64	.671875	17.0656	16	406.4	25	.98425
11/16	.6875	17.4625	17	431.8	26	1.02362
45/64	.703125	17.8594	18	457.2	27	1.06299
23/32	.71875	18.2562	19	482.6	28	1.10236
47/64	.734375	18.6531	20	508.0	29	1.14173
3/4	.75	19.0500	21	533.4	30	1.18110
49/64	.765625	19.4469	22	558.8	31	1.22047
25/32	.78125	19.8437	23	584.2	32	1.25984
51/64	.796875	20.2406	24	609.6	33	1.29921
13/16	.8125	20.6375	25	635.0	34	1.33858
53/64	.828125	21.0344	26	660.4	35	1.37795
27/32	.84375	21.4312	27	685.8	36	1.41732
55/64	.859375	21.8281	28	711.2	37	1.4567
7/8	.875	22.2250	29	736.6	38	1.4961
57/64	.890625	22.6219	30	762.0	39	1.5354
29/32	.90625	23.0187	31	787.4	40	1.5748
59/64	.921875	23.4156	32	812.8	41	1.6142
15/16	.9375	23.8125	33	838.2	42	1.6535
61/64	.953125	24.2094	34	863.6	43	1.6929
31/32	.96875	24.6062	35	889.0	44	1.7323
63/64	.984375	25.0031	36	914.4	45	1.7717

UNITS	Pints to Litres	Gallons to Litres	Litres to Pints	Litres to Gallons	Miles to Kilometres	Kilometres to Miles	Lbs. per sq. In. to Kg. per sq. Cm.	Kg. per sq. Cm. to Lbs. per sq. In.
1	.57	4.55	1.76	.22	1.61	.62	.07	14.22
2	1.14	9.09	3.52	.44	3.22	1.24	.14	28.50
3	1.70	13.64	5.28	.66	4.83	1.86	.21	42.67
4	2.27	18.18	7.04	.88	6.44	2.49	.28	56.89
5	2.84	22.73	8.80	1.10	8.05	3.11	.35	71.12
6	3.41	27.28	10.56	1.32	9.66	3.73	.42	85.34
7	3.98	31.82	12.32	1.54	11.27	4.35	.49	99.56
8	4.55	36.37	14.08	1.76	12.88	4.97	.56	113.79
9		40.91	15.84	1.98	14.48	5.59	.63	128.00
10		45.46	17.60	2.20	16.09	6.21	.70	142.23
20				4.40	32.19	12.43	1.41	284.47
30				6.60	48.28	18.64	2.11	426.70
40				8.80	64.37	24.85		
50					80.47	31.07		
60					96.56	37.28		
70					112.65	43.50		
80					128.75	49.71		
90					144.84	55.92		
100					160.93	62.14		

UNITS	Lb ft to kgm	Kgm to lb ft	UNITS	Lb ft to kgm	Kgm to lb ft
1	.138	7.233	7	.967	50.631
2	.276	14.466	8	1.106	57.864
3	.414	21.699	9	1.244	65.097
4	.553	28.932	10	1.382	72.330
5	.691	36.165	20	2.765	144.660
6	.829	43.398	30	4.147	216.990

TR5/6

NOTES

HINTS ON MAINTENANCE AND OVERHAUL

There are few things more rewarding than the restoration of a vehicle's original peak of efficiency and smooth performance.

The following notes are intended to help the owner to reach that state of perfection. Providing that he possesses the basic manual skills he should have no difficulty in performing most of the operations detailed in this manual. It must be stressed, however, that where recommended in the manual, highly-skilled operations ought to be entrusted to experts, who have the necessary equipment, to carry out the work satisfactorily.

Quality of workmanship:

The hazardous driving conditions on the roads to-day demand that vehicles should be as nearly perfect, mechanically, as possible. It is therefore most important that amateur work be carried out with care, bearing in mind the often inadequate working conditions, and also the inferior tools which may have to be used. It is easy to counsel perfection in all things, and we recognize that it may be setting an impossibly high standard. We do, however, suggest that every care should be taken to ensure that a vehicle is as safe to take on the road as it is humanly possible to make it.

Safe working conditions:

Even though a vehicle may be stationary, it is still potentially dangerous if certain sensible precautions are not taken when working on it while it is supported on jacks or blocks. It is indeed preferable not to use jacks alone, but to supplement them with carefully placed blocks, so that there will be plenty of support if the car rolls off the jacks during a strenuous manoeuvre. Axle stands are an excellent way of providing a rigid base which is not readily disturbed. Piles of bricks are a dangerous substitute. Be careful not to get under heavy loads on lifting tackle, the load could fall. It is preferable not to work alone when lifting an engine, or when working underneath a vehicle which is supported well off the ground. To be trapped, particularly under the vehicle, may have unpleasant results if help is not quickly forthcoming. Make some provision, however humble, to deal with fires. Always disconnect a battery if there is a likelihood of electrical shorts. These may start a fire if there is leaking fuel about. This applies particularly to leads which can carry a heavy current, like those in the starter circuit. While on the subject of electricity, we must also stress the danger of using equipment which is run off the mains and which has no earth or has faulty wiring or connections. So many workshops have damp floors, and electrical shocks are of such a nature that it is sometimes impossible to let go of a live lead or piece of equipment due to the muscular spasms which take place.

Work demanding special care:

This involves the servicing of braking, steering and suspension systems. On the road, failure of the braking system may be disastrous. Make quite sure that there can be no possibility of failure through the bursting of rusty brake pipes or rotten hoses, nor to a sudden loss of pressure due to defective seals or valves.

Problems:

The chief problems which may face an operator are:
1 External dirt.
2 Difficulty in undoing tight fixings
3 Dismantling unfamiliar mechanisms.
4 Deciding in what respect parts are defective.
5 Confusion about the correct order for reassembly.
6 Adjusting running clearances.
7 Road testing.
8 Final tuning.

Practical suggestion to solve the problems:

1 Preliminary cleaning of large parts—engines, transmissions, steering, suspensions, etc.,—should be carried out before removal from the car. Where road dirt and mud alone are present, wash clean with a high-pressure water jet, brushing to remove stubborn adhesions, and allow to drain and dry. Where oil or grease is also present, wash down with a proprietary compound (Gunk, Teepol etc.,) applying with a stiff brush—an old paint brush is suitable—into all crevices. Cover the distributor and ignition coils with a polythene bag and then apply a strong water jet to clear the loosened deposits. Allow to drain and dry. The assemblies will then be sufficiently clean to remove and transfer to the bench for the next stage.

On the bench, further cleaning can be carried out, first wiping the parts as free as possible from grease with old newspaper. Avoid using rag or cotton waste which can leave clogging fibres behind. Any remaining grease can be removed with a brush dipped in paraffin. If necessary, traces of paraffin can be removed by carbon tetrachloride. Avoid using paraffin or petrol in large quantities for cleaning in enclosed areas, such as garages, on account of the high fire risk.

When all exteriors have been cleaned, and not before, dismantling can be commenced. This ensures that dirt will not enter into interiors and orifices revealed by dismantling. In the next phases, where components have to be cleaned, use carbon tetrachloride in preference to petrol and keep the containers covered except when in use. After the components have been cleaned, plug small holes with tapered hard wood plugs cut to size and blank off larger orifices with greaseproof paper and masking tape. Do not use soft wood plugs or matchsticks as they may break.
2 It is not advisable to hammer on the end of a screw thread, but if it must be done, first screw on a nut to protect the thread, and use a lead hammer. This applies particularly to the removal of tapered cotters. Nuts and bolts seem to 'grow' together, especially in exhaust systems. If penetrating oil does not work, try the judicious application of heat, but be careful of starting a fire. Asbestos sheet or cloth is useful to isolate heat.

Tight bushes or pieces of tail-pipe rusted into a silencer can be removed by splitting them with an open-ended hacksaw. Tight screws can sometimes be started by a tap from a hammer on the end of a suitable screwdriver. Many tight fittings will yield to the judicious use of a hammer, but it must be a soft-faced hammer if damage is to be avoided, use a heavy block on the opposite side to absorb shock. Any parts of the steering system which have been damaged should be renewed, as attempts to repair them may lead to cracking and subsequent failure, and steering ball joints should be disconnected using a recommended tool to prevent damage.

3 If often happens that an owner is baffled when trying to dismantle an unfamiliar piece of equipment. So many modern devices are pressed together or assembled by spinning-over flanges, that they must be sawn apart. The intention is that the whole assembly must be renewed. However, parts which appear to be in one piece to the naked eye, may reveal close-fitting joint lines when inspected with a magnifying glass, and, this may provide the necessary clue to dismantling. Left-handed screw threads are used where rotational forces would tend to unscrew a right-handed screw thread.

Be very careful when dismantling mechanisms which may come apart suddenly. Work in an enclosed space where the parts will be contained, and drape a piece of cloth over the device if springs are likely to fly in all directions. Mark everything which might be reassembled in the wrong position, scratched symbols may be used on unstressed parts, or a sequence of tiny dots from a centre punch can be useful. Stressed parts should never be scratched or centre-popped as this may lead to cracking under working conditions. Store parts which look alike in the correct order for reassembly. Never rely upon memory to assist in the assembly of complicated mechanisms, especially when they will be dismantled for a long time, but make notes, and drawings to supplement the diagrams in the manual, and put labels on detached wires. Rust stains may indicate unlubricated wear. This can sometimes be seen round the outside edge of a bearing cup in a universal joint. Look for bright rubbing marks on parts which normally should not make heavy contact. These might prove that something is bent or running out of truth. For example, there might be bright marks on one side of a piston, at the top near the ring grooves, and others at the bottom of the skirt on the other side. This could well be the clue to a bent connecting rod. Suspected cracks can be proved by heating the component in a light oil to approximately 100°C, removing, drying off, and dusting with french chalk, if a crack is present the oil retained in the crack will stain the french chalk.

4 In determining wear, and the degree, against the permissible limits set in the manual, accurate measurement can only be achieved by the use of a micrometer. In many cases, the wear is given to the fourth place of decimals; that is in ten-thousandths of an inch. This can be read by the vernier scale on the barrel of a good micrometer. Bore diameters are more difficult to determine. If, however, the matching shaft is accurately measured, the degree of play in the bore can be felt as a guide to its suitability. In other cases, the shank of a twist drill of known diameter is a handy check.

Many methods have been devised for determining the clearance between bearing surfaces. To-day the best and simplest is by the use of Plastigage, obtainable from most garages. A thin plastic thread is laid between the two surfaces and the bearing is tightened, flattening the thread. On removal, the width of the thread is compared with a scale supplied with the thread and the clearance is read off directly. Sometimes joint faces leak persistently, even after gasket renewal. The fault will then be traceable to distortion, dirt or burrs. Studs which are screwed into soft metal frequently raise burrs at the point of entry. A quick cure for this is to chamfer the edge of the hole in the part which fits over the stud.

5 **Always check a replacement part with the original one before it is fitted.**

If parts are not marked, and the order for reassembly is not known, a little detective work will help. Look for marks which are due to wear to see if they can be mated. Joint faces may not be identical due to manufacturing errors, and parts which overlap may be stained, giving a clue to the correct position. Most fixings leave identifying marks especially if they were painted over on assembly. It is then easier to decide whether a nut, for instance, has a plain, a spring, or a shakeproof washer under it. All running surfaces become 'bedded' together after long spells of work and tiny imperfections on one part will be found to have left corresponding marks on the other. This is particularly true of shafts and bearings and even a score on a cylinder wall will show on the piston.

6 Checking end float or rocker clearances by feeler gauge may not always give accurate results because of wear. For instance, the rocker tip which bears on a valve stem may be deeply pitted, in which case the feeler will simply be bridging a depression. Thrust washers may also wear depressions in opposing faces to make accurate measurement difficult. End float is then easier to check by using a dial gauge. It is common practice to adjust end play in bearing assemblies. like front hubs with taper rollers, by doing up the axle nut until the hub becomes stiff to turn and then backing it off a little. Do not use this method with ballbearing hubs as the assembly is often preloaded by tightening the axle nut to its fullest extent. If the splitpin hole will not line up, file the base of the nut a little.

Steering assemblies often.wear in the straight-ahead position. If any part is adjusted, make sure that it remains free when moved from lock to lock. Do not be surprised if an assembly like a steering gearbox, which is known to be carefully adjusted outside the car, becomes stiff when it is bolted in place. This will be due to distortion of the case by the pull of the mounting bolts, particularly if the mounting points are not all touching together. This problem may be met in other equipment and is cured by careful attention to the alignment of mounting points.

When a spanner is stamped with a size and A/F it means that the dimension is the width between the jaws and has no connection with ANF, which is the designation for the American National Fine thread. Coarse threads like Whitworth are rarely used on cars to-day except for studs which screw into soft aluminium or cast iron. For this reason it might be found that the top end of a cylinder head stud has a fine thread and the lower end a coarse thread to screw into the cylinder block. If the car has mainly UNF threads then it is likely that any coarse threads will be UNC, which are not the same as Whitworth. Small sizes have the same number of threads in Whitworth and UNC, but in the $\frac{1}{2}$ inch size for example, there are twelve threads to the inch in the former and thirteen in the latter.

7 After a major overhaul, particularly if a great deal of work has been done on the braking, steering and suspension systems, it is advisable to approach the problem of testing with care. If the braking system has been overhauled, apply heavy pressure to the brake pedal and get a second operator to check every possible source of leakage. The brakes may work extremely well, but a leak could cause complete failure after a few miles.

Do not fit the hub caps until every wheel nut has been checked for tightness, and make sure the tyre pressures are correct. Check the levels of coolant, lubricants and hydraulic fluids. Being satisfied that all is well, take the car on the road and test the brakes at once. Check the steering and the action of the handbrake. Do all this at moderate speeds on quiet roads, and make sure there is no other vehicle behind you when you try a rapid stop.

Finally, remember that many parts settle down after a time, so check for tightness of all fixings after the car has been on the road for a hundred miles or so.

8 It is useless to tune an engine which has not reached its normal running temperature. In the same way, the tune of an engine which is stiff after a rebore will be different when the engine is again running free. Remember too, that rocker clearances on pushrod operated valve gear will change when the cylinder head nuts are tightened after an initial period of running with a new head gasket.

Trouble may not always be due to what seems the obvious cause. Ignition, carburation and mechanical condition are interdependent and spitting back through the carburetter, which might be attributed to a weak mixture, can be caused by a sticking inlet valve.

For one final hint on tuning, never adjust more than one thing at a time or it will be impossible to tell which adjustment produced the desired result.

GLOSSARY OF TERMS

Allen key	Cranked wrench of hexagonal section for use with socket head screws.
Alternator	Electrical generator producing alternating current. Rectified to direct current for battery charging.
Ambient temperature	Surrounding atmospheric temperature.
Annulus	Used in engineering to indicate the outer ring gear of an epicyclic gear train.
Armature	The shaft carrying the windings, which rotates in the magnetic field of a generator or starter motor. That part of a solenoid or relay which is activated by the magnetic field.
Axial	In line with, or pertaining to, an axis.
Backlash	Play in meshing gears.
Balance lever	A bar where force applied at the centre is equally divided between connections at the ends.
Banjo axle	Axle casing with large diameter housing for the crownwheel and differential.
Bendix pinion	A self-engaging and self-disengaging drive on a starter motor shaft.
Bevel pinion	A conical shaped gearwheel, designed to mesh with a similar gear with an axis usually at 90 deg. to its own.
bhp	Brake horse power, measured on a dynamometer.
bmep	Brake mean effective pressure. Average pressure on a piston during the working stroke.
Brake cylinder	Cylinder with hydraulically operated piston(s) acting on brake shoes or pad(s).
Brake regulator	Control valve fitted in hydraulic braking system which limits brake pressure to rear brakes during heavy braking to prevent rear wheel locking.
Camber	Angle at which a wheel is tilted from the vertical.
Capacitor	Modern term for an electrical condenser. Part of distributor assembly, connected across contact breaker points, acts as an interference suppressor.
Castellated	Top face of a nut, slotted across the flats, to take a locking splitpin.
Castor	Angle at which the kingpin or swivel pin is tilted when viewed from the side.
cc	Cubic centimetres. Engine capacity is arrived at by multiplying the area of the bore in sq cm by the stroke in cm by the number of cylinders.
Clevis	U-shaped forked connector used with a clevis pin, usually at handbrake connections.
Collet	A type of collar, usually split and located in a groove in a shaft, and held in place by a retainer. The arrangement used to retain the spring(s) on a valve stem in most cases.
Commutator	Rotating segmented current distributor between armature windings and brushes in generator or motor.
Compression ratio	The ratio, or quantitative relation, of the total volume (piston at bottom of stroke) to the unswept volume (piston at top of stroke) in an engine cylinder.
Condenser	See capacitor.
Core plug	Plug for blanking off a manufacturing hole in a casting.
Crownwheel	Large bevel gear in rear axle, driven by a bevel pinion attached to the propeller shaft. Sometimes called a 'ring gear'.
'C'-spanner	Like a 'C' with a handle. For use on screwed collars without flats, but with slots or holes.
Damper	Modern term for shock-absorber, used in vehicle suspension systems to damp out spring oscillations.
Depression	The lowering of atmospheric pressure as in the inlet manifold and carburetter.
Dowel	Close tolerance pin, peg, tube, or bolt, which accurately locates mating parts.
Drag link	Rod connecting steering box drop arm (pitman arm) to nearest front wheel steering arm in certain types of steering systems.
Dry liner	Thinwall tube pressed into cylinder bore
Dry sump	Lubrication system where all oil is scavenged from the sump, and returned to a separate tank.
Dynamo	See Generator.
Electrode	Terminal, part of an electrical component, such as the points or 'Electrodes' of a sparking plug.
Electrolyte	In lead-acid car batteries a solution of sulphuric acid and distilled water.
End float	The axial movement between associated parts, end play.
EP	Extreme pressure. In lubricants, special grades for heavily loaded bearing surfaces, such as gear teeth in a gearbox, or crownwheel and pinion in a rear axle.

Fade	Of brakes. Reduced efficiency due to overheating.	**Journals**	Those parts of a shaft that are in contact with the bearings.
Field coils	Windings on the polepieces of motors and generators.	**Kingpin**	The main vertical pin which carries the front wheel spindle, and permits steering movement. May be called 'steering pin' or 'swivel pin'.
Fillets	Narrow finishing strips usually applied to interior bodywork.		
First motion shaft	Input shaft from clutch to gearbox.	**Layshaft**	The shaft which carries the laygear in the gearbox. The laygear is driven by the first motion shaft and drives the third motion shaft according to the gear selected. Sometimes called the 'countershaft' or 'second motion shaft.'
Fullflow filter	Filters in which all the oil is pumped to the engine. If the element becomes clogged, a bypass valve operates to pass unfiltered oil to the engine.		
		lb ft	A measure of twist or torque. A pull of 10 lb at a radius of 1 ft is a torque of 10 lb ft.
FWD	Front wheel drive.		
Gear pump	Two meshing gears in a close fitting casing. Oil is carried from the inlet round the outside of both gears in the spaces between the gear teeth and casing to the outlet, the meshing gear teeth prevent oil passing back to the inlet, and the oil is forced through the outlet port.	**lb/sq in**	Pounds per square inch.
		Little-end	The small, or piston end of a connecting rod. Sometimes called the 'small-end'.
		LT	Low Tension. The current output from the battery.
		Mandrel	Accurately manufactured bar or rod used for test or centring purposes.
Generator	Modern term for 'Dynamo'. When rotated produces electrical current.	**Manifold**	A pipe, duct, or chamber, with several branches.
Grommet	A ring of protective or sealing material. Can be used to protect pipes or leads passing through bulkheads.	**Needle rollers**	Bearing rollers with a length many times their diameter.
Grubscrew	Fully threaded headless screw with screwdriver slot. Used for locking, or alignment purposes.	**Oil bath**	Reservoir which lubricates parts by immersion. In air filters, a separate oil supply for wetting a wire mesh element to hold the dust.
Gudgeon pin	Shaft which connects a piston to its connecting rod. Sometimes called 'wrist pin', or 'piston pin'.	**Oil wetted**	In air filters, a wire mesh element lightly oiled to trap and hold airborne dust.
Halfshaft	One of a pair transmitting drive from the differential.	**Overlap**	Period during which inlet and exhaust valves are open together.
Helical	In spiral form. The teeth of helical gears are cut at a spiral angle to the side faces of the gearwheel.	**Panhard rod**	Bar connected between fixed point on chassis and another on axle to control sideways movement.
Hot spot	Hot area that assists vapourisation of fuel on its way to cylinders. Often provided by close contact between inlet and exhaust manifolds.	**Pawl**	Pivoted catch which engages in the teeth of a ratchet to permit movement in one direction only.
		Peg spanner	Tool with pegs, or pins, to engage in holes or slots in the part to be turned.
HT	High Tension. Applied to electrical current produced by the ignition coil for the sparking plugs.	**Pendant pedals**	Pedals with levers that are pivoted at the top end.
Hydrometer	A device for checking specific gravity of liquids. Used to check specific gravity of electrolyte.	**Phillips screwdriver**	A cross-point screwdriver for use with the cross-slotted heads of Phillips screws.
Hypoid bevel gears	A form of bevel gear used in the rear axle drive gears. The bevel pinion meshes below the centre line of the crownwheel, giving a lower propeller shaft line.	**Pinion**	A small gear, usually in relation to another gear.
		Piston-type damper	Shock absorber in which damping is controlled by a piston working in a closed oil-filled cylinder.
Idler	A device for passing on movement. A free running gear between driving and driven gears. A lever transmitting track rod movement to a side rod in steering gear.	**Preloading**	Preset static pressure on ball or roller bearings not due to working loads.
		Radial	Radiating from a centre, like the spokes of a wheel.
Impeller	A centrifugal pumping element. Used in water pumps to stimulate flow.		

TR5/6

161

Radius rod	Pivoted arm confining movement of a part to an arc of fixed radius.
Ratchet	Toothed wheel or rack which can move in one direction only, movement in the other being prevented by a pawl.
Ring gear	A gear tooth ring attached to outer periphery of flywheel. Starter pinion engages with it during starting.
Runout	Amount by which rotating part is out of true.
Semi-floating axle	Outer end of rear axle halfshaft is carried on bearing inside axle casing. Wheel hub is secured to end of shaft.
Servo	A hydraulic or pneumatic system for assisting, or, augmenting a physical effort. See 'Vacuum Servo'.
Setscrew	One which is threaded for the full length of the shank.
Shackle	A coupling link, used in the form of two parallel pins connected by side plates to secure the end of the master suspension spring and absorb the effects of deflection.
Shell bearing	Thinwalled steel shell lined with anti-friction metal. Usually semi-circular and used in pairs for main and big-end bearings.
Shock absorber	See 'Damper'.
Silentbloc	Rubber bush bonded to inner and outer metal sleeves.
Socket-head screw	Screw with hexagonal socket for an Allen key.
Solenoid	A coil of wire creating a magnetic field when electric current passes through it. Used with a soft iron core to operate contacts or a mechanical device.
Spur gear	A gear with teeth cut axially across the periphery.
Stub axle	Short axle fixed at one end only.
Tachometer	An instrument for accurate measurement of rotating speed. Usually indicates in revolutions per minute.
TDC	Top Dead Centre. The highest point reached by a piston in a cylinder, with the crank and connecting rod in line.
Thermostat	Automatic device for regulating temperature. Used in vehicle coolant systems to open a valve which restricts circulation at low temperature.
Third motion shaft	Output shaft of gearbox.
Threequarter floating axle	Outer end of rear axle halfshaft flanged and bolted to wheel hub, which runs on bearing mounted on outside of axle casing. Vehicle weight is not carried by the axle shaft.
Thrust bearing or washer	Used to reduce friction in rotating parts subject to axial loads.
Torque	Turning or twisting effort. See 'lb ft'.
Track rod	The bar(s) across the vehicle which connect the steering arms and maintain the front wheels in their correct alignment.
UJ	Universal joint. A coupling between shafts which permits angular movement.
UNF	Unified National Fine screw thread.
Vacuum servo	Device used in brake system, using difference between atmospheric pressure and inlet manifold depression to operate a piston which acts to augment brake pressure as required. See 'Servo'.
Venturi	A restriction or 'choke' in a tube, as in a carburetter, used to increase velocity to obtain a reduction in pressure.
Vernier	A sliding scale for obtaining fractional readings of the graduations of an adjacent scale.
Welch plug	A domed thin metal disc which is partially flattened to lock in a recess. Used to plug core holes in castings.
Wet liner	Removable cylinder barrel, sealed against coolant leakage, where the coolant is in direct contact with the outer surface.
Wet sump	A reservoir attached to the crankcase to hold the lubricating oil.

INDEX

A
Air cleaner	40
Air filter, brake servo	102
Air valve (TR6)	30
Antifreeze	51
Anti-roll bar	83
Alternator brushgear	110
Alternator diodes	108
Alternator tests	108
Armature, starter	114

B
Ball joints, steering	88
Ball joints, suspension	82
Battery testing	106
Belt tension	50
Beam setting, headlamps	119
Bleeding brakes	100
Bleeding clutch	55
Brushes, alternator	110
Brushes, starter	113
Brushes, windscreen wiper	116, 117
Bonnet lock	125

C
Camshaft driving chain	15
Camshaft end float	15
Capacitor, distributor	45
Capacities	140
Carburetters, adjustment	38
Carburetters, description	38
Carburetters, maintenance	38
Carburetters, refitting	39
Carburetters, removal	39
Centrifugal advance	43
Choke (excess fuel)	32
Clutch master cylinder	54
Clutch linings	56
Clutch slave cylinder	55
Commutator, starter	113
Cooling system maintenance	49
Compression ratio	134
Contact breaker cleaning	43
Contact breaker setting	44
Controls, heater	128
Crankcase ventilation	10
Crankshaft wear	20
Crankshaft end float	21
Cylinder bore grading	134
Cylinder bore wear	19
Cylinder liners	19
Cylinder head nut sequence	13
Cylinder head distortion	13

D
Dampers (shock absorbers) front	81
Dampers (shock absorbers) rear	75
Damper, steering rack	87
Decarbonizing	13
Diaphragms, fuel metering	32
Diaphragm spring, clutch	53
Diaphragm plate, brake servo	102
Differential	74
Dimensions	141
Direction indicator switch	91
Disc brake pads	95
Distributor adjustment	43
Distributor drive shaft	16
Distributor maintenance	43
Distributor, TR250	47
Door glass	124
Door locks	123
Door removal	123
Door trim	123
Draining cooling system	50
Draining engine oil	17
Draining rear axle	72

E
Electrolyte, battery	106
Emission control valve	41
Engine description	9
Engine removal	10
Engine reassembly	22
Exhaust manifold	29
Exhaust system	23
Excess fuel setting	36
Excess fuel cable adjustment	30, 31

F
Field coil, alternator	107
Field coil, starter	115
Field coil, windscreen wiper	117
Filter, fuel	25
Filter, oil	18
Firing order	134
Flasher unit	118
Flywheel ring gear	17
Flywheel run-out	17
Friction linings, drum brakes	97
Friction linings, clutch	56
Friction pads, disc brakes	95
Front hubs, adjustment	81
Front hubs, lubrication	77
Front road springs	81
Front road spring data	138
Front suspension, description	77
Front suspension, lubrication	77
Front wheel alignment	90
Fuel control unit	31
Fuel gauge	119
Fuel pump tests	26
Fuel pump, TR250	40
Fuel pressure	36
Fuel system, description	25
Fuel system, precautions	28
Fuses	118

G
Gasket, cylinder head	12
Gearbox, lubrication	57
Gearbox removal	57
Gearbox replacement	58

TR5/6

Gear selector mechanism	63
Glossary of terms	157
Grinding-in valves	13
Gudgeon pins	19

H

Handbrake adjustment	102
Handbrake cables	102
Headlamp beam setting	119
Hazard warning system	118
Head removal	12
Head nut sequence	13
Heater cable adjustments	129, 131
Heater flushing	128
Heater settings	128
Hints on maintenance and overhaul	153
Hubs, rear	74
Hubs, front	81
Hydraulic operation, brakes	93
Hydraulic operation, clutch	54
Hydraulic Pressure Differential Warning Actuator (PDWA)	100
Hydraulic pipelines	94
Hydraulic fluid	95
Hydrometer tests for electrolyte	106

I

Idling adjustment, TR5	30
Idling adjustment, TR6	31
Ignition faults	44
Ignition retiming	47
Ignition leads	47
Ignition testing	48
Ignition timing, TR250	48
Impact clamp, steering	91
Impeller, water pump	51
Injector cleaning	30
Injector testing	29
Injector operation	25
Inlet throttles	30
Instruments	126
Inhibiting fuel system	28

J

Journal bearings	20
Journal bearing, undersize	134

L

Lighting circuit faults	119
Lock, bonnet	125
Lock, door	123
Lock, luggage locker	126
Low-tension circuit, ignition	45
Leads, high-tension ignition	47

M

Manifolds	29
Master cylinder, brakes	99
Master cylinder, clutch	54
Master cylinder mountings	99
Master cylinder, topping-up	53, 95
Metering unit operation	31
Metering unit servicing	34
Metering unit drive pedestal	32

O

Oil filter	18
Oil pressure relief valve	18
Oil seals, crankshaft	21
Oil seals, gearbox	61
Oil seals, differential	71
Oilways, crankshaft	21
Overdrive lubrication	66
Overdrive removal	66
Overdrive solenoid valve	67
Overdrive operating valve	67

P

Park position, windscreen wiper	115
Pedal mountings	99
Piston grades	134
Piston removal	18
Piston ring dimensions	135
Piston ring fitting	19
Pushrods	12
Propeller shaft checking	69
Propeller shaft sliding joint	27
Propeller shaft universal joints	69

R

Rack, steering, adjustment	88
Rack, steering, lubrication	85
Radiator flushing	50
Radiator removal	50
Rear axle	72
Rear axle shafts	72
Rear brake adjustment	95
Rear brake linings	97
Rear road spring removal	75
Rear road spring data	139
Rear suspension	75
Rear suspension geometry	75
Refilling cooling system	50
Regulator, window	124
Removing engine and gearbox	10
Remote control door lock	124
Rocker shaft assembly	13
Rocker clearance	22

S

Safety belts	123
Selector mechanism, gears	63
Servo, vacuum for brakes	102
Shock absorbers (see Dampers)	
Slave cylinder, clutch	55
Slow-running TR5	30
Slow-running TR6	31
Sparking plug condition	47
Sparking plug gap	47
Sparking plug test	47
Sparking plug type	136
Specific gravity, electrolyte	106
Springs, road, data	138, 139
Springs, valve, data	135
Springs, valve, examining	14
Starter motor armature	114
Starter motor brushgear	113
Starter motor commutator	113
Starter motor solenoid	113
Starter motor tests	111

Starter motor pinion movement	114
Steering column servicing	90
Steering rack removal and replacement	85
Steering rack servicing	87
Steering wheel removal	90
Sump removal	17
Synchronizing throttles TR5	30
Synchronizing throttles TR6	31

T

Tachometer drive	46
Tappets	15
Technical data	134
Thermostat testing	50
Temperature gauge	119
Timing chain sprocket alignment	15
Timing ignition	47
Timing valves	15
Track adjustment	90
Trim removal, door	123

U

Universal couplings, propeller shaft	69
Universal couplings, axle shafts	74
Universal couplings, steering column	91

V

Vacuum control, ignition	47
Valves, engine, servicing	13
Valve guides	13
Valve seat renovation	13
Valve clearance	22
Voltage stabilizer, instruments	119

W

Water circulation	49
Water drain taps	50
Water filler cap	49
Water pump	51
Water pump lubrication	49
Window glass, door	124
Window regulator, door	124
Windscreen	126
Wiper motor testing	116
Wiper motor data	140
Windscreen washer data	140
Wiring diagrams	143

NOTES

THE AUTOBOOK SERIES OF WORKSHOP MANUALS

Alfa Romeo Giulia 1600, 1750, 2000 1962 on
Aston Martin 1921-58
Auto Union Audi 70, 80, Super 90, 1966-72
Audi 100 1969 on
Austin, Morris etc. 1100 Mk. 1 1962-67
Austin, Morris etc. 1100 Mk. 2, 3, 1300 Mk. 1, 2, 3 America 1968 on
Austin A30, A35, A40 Farina 1951-67
Austin A55 Mk. 2, A60 1958-69
Austin A99, A110 1959-68
Austin J4 1960 on
Austin Allegro 1973 on
Austin Maxi 1969 on
Austin, Morris 1800 1964 on
Austin, Morris 2200 1972 on
Austin Kimberley, Tasman 1970 on
Austin, Morris 1300, 1500 Nomad 1969 on
BMC 3 (Austin A50, A55 Mk. 1, Morris Oxford 2, 3 1954-59)
Austin Healey 100/6, 3000 1956-68
Austin Healey, MG Sprite, Midget 1958 on
Bedford CA Mk. 2 1964-69
Bedford CF Vans 1969 on
Bedford Beagle HA Vans 1964 on
BMW 1600 1966 on
BMW 1800 1964-71
BMW 2000, 2002 1966 on
Chevrolet Corvair 1960-69
Chevrolet Corvette V8 1957-65
Chevrolet Corvette V8 1965 on
Chevrolet Vega 2300 1970 on
Chrysler Valiant V8 1965 on
Chrysler Valiant Straight Six 1963 on
Citroen DS 19, ID 19 1955-66
Citroen ID 19, DS 19, 20, 21 1966 on
Citroen Dyane Ami 1964 on
Daf 31, 32, 33, 44, 55 1961 on
Datsun Bluebird 610 series 1972 on
Datsun Cherry 100A, 120A 1971 on
Datsun 1000, 1200 1968 on
Datsun 1300, 1400, 1600 1968 on
Datsun 240C 1971 on

Datsun 240Z Sport 1970 on
Fiat 124 1966 on
Fiat 124 Sport 1966 on
Fiat 125 1967-72
Fiat 127 1971 on
Fiat 128 1969 on
Fiat 500 1957 on
Fiat 600, 600D 1955-69
Fiat 850 1964 on
Fiat 1100 1957-69
Fiat 1300, 1500 1961-67
Ford Anglia Prefect 100E 1953-62
Ford Anglia 105E, Prefect 107E 1959-67
Ford Capri 1300, 1600 OHV 1968 on
Ford Capri 1300, 1600, 2000 OHC 1972 on
Ford Capri 2000 V4, 3000 V6 1969 on
Ford Classic, Capri 1961-64
Ford Consul, Zephyr, Zodiac, 1, 2 1950-62
Ford Corsair Straight Four 1963-65
Ford Corsair V4 1965-68
Ford Corsair V4 2000 1969-70
Ford Cortina 1962-66
Ford Cortina 1967-68
Ford Cortina 1969-70
Ford Cortina Mk. 3 1970 on
Ford Escort 1967 on
Ford Falcon 6 1964-70
Ford Falcon XK, XL 1960-63
Ford Falcon 6 XR/XA 1966 on
Ford Falcon V8 (U.S.A.) 1965-71
Ford Falcon V8 (Aust.) 1966 on
Ford Pinto 1970 on
Ford Maverick 6 1969 on
Ford Maverick V8 1970 on
Ford Mustang 6 1964-72
Ford Mustang V8 1965 on
Ford Thames 10, 12, 15 cwt 1957-65
Ford Transit V4 1965 on
Ford Zephyr Zodiac Mk. 3 1962-66
Ford Zephyr Zodiac V4, V6, Mk. 4 1966-72
Ford Consul, Granada 1972 on
Hillman Avenger 1970 on
Hillman Hunter 1966 on
Hillman Imp 1963-68
Hillman Imp 1969 on
Hillman Minx 1 to 5 1956-65
Hillman Minx 1965-67

Hillman Minx 1966-70
Hillman Super Minx 1961-65
Jaguar XK120, 140, 150, Mk. 7, 8, 9 1948-61
Jaguar 2.4, 3.4, 3.8 Mk. 1, 2 1955-69
Jaguar 'E' Type 1961-72
Jaguar 'S' Type 420 1963-68
Jaguar XJ6 1968 on
Jowett Javelin Jupiter 1947-53
Landrover 1, 2 1948-61
Landrover 2, 2a, 3 1959 on
Mazda 616 1970 on
Mazda 808, 818 1972 on
Mazda 1200, 1300 1969 on
Mazda 1500, 1800 1967 on
Mazda RX-2 1971 on
Mazda R100, RX-3 1970 on
Mercedes-Benz 190b, 190c, 200 1959-68
Mercedes-Benz 220 1959-65
Mercedes-Benz 220/8 1968 on
Mercedes-Benz 230 1963-68
Mercedes-Benz 250 1965-67
Mercedes-Benz 250 1968 on
Mercedes-Benz 280 1968 on
MG TA to TF 1936-55
MGA MGB 1955-68
MGB 1969 on
Mini 1959 on
Mini Cooper 1961-72
Morgan Four 1936-72
Morris Marina 1971 on
Morris (Aust) Marina 1972 on
Morris Minor 2, 1000 1952-71
Morris Oxford 5, 6 1959-71
NSU 1000 1963-72
NSU Prinz 1 to 4 1957-72
Opel Ascona, Manta 1970 on
Opel GT 1900 1968 on
Opel Kadett, Olympia 993 cc 1078 cc 1962 on
Opel Kadett, Olympia 1492, 1698, 1897 cc 1967 on
Opel Rekord C 1966-72
Peugeot 204 1965 on
Peugeot 304 1970 on
Peugeot 404 1960 on
Peugeot 504 1968 on
Porsche 356A, B, C 1957-65
Porsche 911 1964 on
Porsche 912 1965-69
Porsche 914 S 1969 on
Reliant Regal 1952-73

Renault R4, R4L, 4 1961 on
Renault 5 1972 on
Renault 6 1968 on
Renault 8, 10, 1100 1962-71
Renault 12, 1969 on
Renault 15, 17 1971 on
Renault R16 1965 on
Renault Dauphine Floride 1957-67
Renault Caravelle 1962-68
Rover 60 to 110 1953-64
Rover 2000 1963-73
Rover 3 Litre 1958-67
Rover 3500, 3500S 1968 on
Saab 95, 96, Sport 1960-68
Saab 99 1969 on
Saab V4 1966 on
Simca 1000 1961 on
Simca 1100 1967 on
Simca 1300, 1301, 1500, 1501 1963 on
Skoda One (440, 445, 450) 1955-70
Sunbeam Rapier Alpine 1955-65
Toyota Carina, Celica 1971 on
Toyota Corolla 1100, 1200 1967 on
Toyota Corona 1500 Mk. 1 1965-70
Toyota Corona Mk. 2 1969 on
Triumph TR2, TR3, TR3A 1952-62
Triumph TR4, TR4A 1961-67
Triumph TR5, TR250, TR6 1967 on
Triumph 1300, 1500 1965-73
Triumph 2000 Mk. 1, 2.5 PI Mk. 1 1963-69
Triumph 2000 Mk. 2, 2.5 PI Mk. 2 1969 on
Triumph Dolomite 1972 on
Triumph Herald 1959-68
Triumph Herald 1969-71
Triumph Spitfire, Vitesse 1962-68
Triumph Spitfire Mk. 3, 4 1969 on
Triumph GT6, Vitesse 2 Litre 1969 on
Triumph Stag 1970 on
Triumph Toledo 1970 on
Vauxhall Velox, Cresta 1957-72
Vauxhall Victor 1, 2, FB 1957-64
Vauxhall Victor 101 1964-67
Vauxhall Victor FD 1600, 2000 1967-72

Continued on following page

TR5/6

167

THE AUTOBOOK SERIES OF WORKSHOP MANUALS

Vauxhall Victor 3300, Ventora 1968-72
Vauxhall Victor FE Ventora 1972 on
Vauxhall Viva HA 1963-66
Vauxhall Viva HB 1966-70

Vauxhall Viva, HC Firenza 1971 on
Volkswagen Beetle 1954-67
Volkswagen Beetle 1968 on
Volkswagen 1500 1961-66

Volkswagen 1600 Fastback 1965-73
Volkswagen Transporter 1954-67
Volkswagen Transporter 1968 on

Volkswagen 411 1968-72
Volvo 120 series 1961-70
Volvo 140 series 1966 on
Volvo 160 series 1968 on
Volvo 1800 1960-73